The
Public Face
of Modernism

The
Public Face
of Modernism

LITTLE MAGAZINES,
AUDIENCES, AND RECEPTION,
1905–1920

Mark S. Morrisson

The University of Wisconsin Press

The University of Wisconsin Press
2537 Daniels Street
Madison, Wisconsin 53718

3 Henrietta Street
London WC2E 8LU, England

Library of Congress Cataloging-in-Publication Data

Morrisson, Mark S.
The public face of modernism : little magazines, audiences,
and reception, 1905–1920 / Mark S. Morrisson.
294 pp.   cm.
Includes bibliographical references and index.
ISBN 0-299-16920-0 (cloth:alk. paper)
ISBN 0-299-16924-3 (pbk.:alk. paper)
1. English literature—20th century—History and criticism.   2. Modernism
(Literature)—Great Britain.   3. American literature—20th century—History and criticism.
4. Literature publishing—History—20th century.   5. Authors and
readers—History—20th century.   6. Books and reading—History—
20th century.   7. Little magazines—History—20th century.
8. Modernism (Literature)—United States.   I. Title.
PR478.M6M67   2001
820.9'112—dc21

00-008425

To Laura, Devin, Dad, Mom,
and Mary—for all their love

Contents

Illustrations

Acknowledgments

Many people have contributed to the shape of this book over the years, and I owe an enormous debt of gratitude to Bob von Hallberg and Lisa Ruddick, whose thoughtful discussions and commentary helped launch this work, and whose patient direction, careful scholarship, and warm friendship have helped me to understand the rewards and responsibilities of literary research; Kevin Dettmar and Robert Spoo, whose insightful readings of my manuscript helped sharpen my arguments, and whose support was instrumental in making this book possible; Janet Lyon for her perceptive comments on this work, and for her friendship; members of the Avant-Garde Studies Workshop at the University of Chicago, especially Jessica Burstein, Lee Garver, David Kadlec, Stephen Lewis, Paul Peppis, Andrew Rathmann, and David Thompson for their critical insights and sense of intellectual community; Paige Reynolds for her provocative work on modernism and advertising that helped turn me down this path, her generous readings of much of this work, and her unfailing friendship; David Nicholls and Angela Sorby for their friendship and intellectual support; the Modernism Workshop at the Pennsylvania State University, and especially those colleagues who have created the supportive and intellectually challenging environment that makes my research possible, including modernists Sanford Schwartz, Robin Schulze, Susan Squier, Michael Begnal, Jack Selzer, Deborah Clarke, Sandy Spanier, and Caren Irr, early modernist Garrett Sullivan, and premodernist Alice Sheppard. My special thanks go to Don Bialostosky for the long discussions and the essential encouragement and advice that helped me to complete this project. I am also grateful to Steve Salemson and David Bethea, whose faith in this project was instrumental in turning it into a book, and to Carole Schwager, whose careful editing and helpful suggestions were invaluable.

Acknowledgments

I would like to thank my parents, Clovis and Marilyn Morrisson, for the emotional, intellectual, and financial support and ready encouragement that have made both my education and this book possible. They have always been the best advocates I know for a life of the mind and of the heart, and in more ways than I can count, none of this would have been possible without them. I also thank my sister, Mary von Ahnen, for her constant faith in my work and her much-needed encouragement. And, finally, I thank my wife, Laura Reed-Morrisson, whose keen intellect, thoughtful suggestions, and incisive comments have marked every draft of every chapter in this book, even as our first child, Devin, entered the world. I can never thank her enough for her lasting love and support.

Early versions and sections of chapters 1, 2, and 3 of this book have previously appeared in *English Literary History, Modernism/Modernity,* and *Twentieth Century Literature,* and I thank those journals for permission to use portions of those articles. Grateful acknowledgment is made to the following for their generous permission to quote from published materials and unpublished letters and manuscripts: Catherine Aldington for poems and unpublished letters by Richard Aldington; John Taylor Caldwell for boldly placing the words of Guy Aldred in the public domain; Mathilda Hills for the unpublished letters of Margaret Anderson and materials related to the *Little Review;* the trustees of the Joseph Conrad Estate for an unpublished letter by Joseph Conrad; Yvette Eastman for an unpublished letter by Max Eastman; Oliver Flint for a poem by F. S. Flint; Janice Biala Brustlein, Theodora Zavin, and David Higham Associates for unpublished letters by Ford Madox Ford, with special thanks to Janice Biala Brustlein for her help and encouragement with Ford's letters; Jennifer Gosse for an unpublished letter by Edmund Gosse and for her kindness and generosity; Freda McGregor for unpublished letters and materials of Harold Monro; *Letters of Ezra Pound to Harold Monro,* copyright © 2000 by Mary de Rachewiltz and Omar S. Pound, used by permission of New Directions Publishing Corporation, and special thanks to Declan Spring for all his help over the years; the John Quinn Memorial Collection, Manuscripts and Archives Division, the New York Public Library, Astor, Lenox and Tilden Foundations for unpublished letters by John Quinn; David Cory for an unpublished letter by George Santayana, and special thanks to Kris Frost and Herman J. Saatkamp, Jr., for their help; Barbara von Bethmann-Hollweg for unpublished letters by Edward Wadsworth; Hester Hawkes for unpublished materials of Harriet Shaw Weaver, and for her generosity and warmth, and a special remembrance of the late Jane Lidderdale for her past generosity with the works of Harriet Shaw Weaver and her groundbreaking work on Weaver; the unpublished letters of Rebecca West are reprinted by permission of the Peters Fraser and Dunlop Group Limited on behalf of Rebecca West; *Two Poems, by Wil-*

Acknowledgments

liam Carlos Williams, copyright © 1917 by William Carlos Williams, used by permission of New Directions Publishing Corporation. My special thanks also goes to VAGA for permission to reproduce Stuart Davis's "Gee Mag, Think of Us Bein' on a Magazine Cover!" cover of the *Masses* (June 1913), copyright © Estate of Stuart Davis/Licensed by VAGA, New York, New York; for pages from *Blast,* Omar Pound, and the Estate of Mrs. G. A. Wyndham Lewis, by permission; and to Belinda Marcus and the Mary Ryan Gallery, New York, for their help with the work of Hugo Gellert. A good-faith effort has been made to locate the copyright holders for all materials used in this book, and I would appreciate hearing from anyone who has been overlooked.

Several libraries and collections have been instrumental to the research of this book, and I extend my warm thanks to the following libraries for their permission to use archival resources: the British Library with special thanks to Sally Brown for the Harriet Shaw Weaver Papers, MSS.57345–57365; the Division of Rare and Manuscript Collections, Cornell University Library, with special thanks to Katherine Reagan and C. J. Lance-Duboscq, for the Wyndham Lewis (4612) and Ford Madox Ford (4605) collections; the Harry Ransom Humanities Research Center, the University of Texas at Austin, with special thanks to John Kirkpatrick, for use of the letters of Ford Madox Ford; the McCormick Library of Special Collections, Northwestern University Library, Evanston, Illinois, for the James B. Pinker Papers, with special thanks to Russell Maylone for all his help; the Newberry Library in Chicago for the Floyd Dell Papers; the Lilly Library, Indiana University Bloomington, for the Max Eastman MSS, Claude McKay MSS, James Whitcomb Riley MSS III, and Upton Sinclair MSS, and with special thanks to Saundra Taylor and Lisa Browar for their help; the Manuscripts Division, Department of Rare Books and Special Collections, Princeton University Libraries, for the Dora Marsden Collection, with special thanks to Margaret M. Sherry for all her help; the Department of Special Collections, Charles E. Young Research Library, University of California, Los Angeles, for the Harold Monro Papers (745); Archives–Golda Meir Library, University of Wisconsin–Milwaukee for the *Little Review Records,* and the image of the advertising flier for the *Little Review,* and my special thanks to Tim Ericson and Leslie Heinrichs for their generous help; the University of Chicago Library for permission to use the image from the *Ladies' Home Journal,* and the Department of Special Collections, the University of Chicago Library, for the images from Stuart Davis, Hugo Gellerts, Frank Walts, Alice Beach Winter, and the Washington Shirt Company's *Progressive Chicago* pamphlet, and my special thanks to Alice Schreyer and Debra Levine for their frequent and generous help.

I would like to thank the Newberry Library for its hospitality and a

Acknowledgments

Newberry Library Fellowship, the Lilly Library for its assistance and for an Everett Helm Visiting Fellowship, the Institute for the Arts and Humanistic Studies at the Pennsylvania State University for a Faculty Research Fellowship, and the Research and Graduate Office at the Pennsylvania State University for a research grant. The financial assistance and support of these institutions made it possible for me to complete this book.

The
Public Face
of Modernism

Introduction

Mass Market Publicity—Modernism's
Crisis and Opportunity

Cheap paper, the rotary press, the Linotype machine—at the most mundane level, these inventions led to the explosion of mass market print publications and advertising at the end of the nineteenth century in Britain and America. Indeed, Gladstone's prediction that the cultural impact of inexpensive paper "will not be fully apparent until we of the nineteenth century are gone" (in R. Pound 12) demonstrated more prescience than he might have imagined. Even before this great prime minister of the nineteenth century died in 1898, both England and America had witnessed an unprecedented proliferation of mass market magazines and newspapers. In England, the publishing houses of Alfred Harmsworth (Lord Northcliffe), Sir George Newnes, and C. Arthur Pearson were flourishing by the mid-1890s with mass market papers like the *Daily Mail,* and magazines like the *Strand, Tit-Bits,* and *Pearson's Weekly;* across the Atlantic, Cyrus Curtis, William Randolph Hearst, Frank Munsey, and S. S. McClure were building their empires with publications like *Ladies' Home Journal, Cosmopolitan, Munsey's,* and *McClure's.* Morcover, this burgeoning of cheap mass market periodicals of a truly modern variety was accompanied by a rapid expansion in the publication of mass market fiction in both countries (as Keating has demonstrated). The sheer volume of printed material staggered the Victorian imagination.

3

Introduction

Although advances in technology and inexpensive paper made mass market publication successful, it was the advertisement and the mass market periodical that in many ways made commercial culture possible. In the United States and Britain, serious economic turmoil in the late nineteenth century—the depression in Britain from 1873 to around the middle of the 1890s, the massive corporate failures in late-nineteenth-century America, problems of overproduction and underconsumption, and the price fixing and cutthroat competition of liberal capitalism on both sides of the ocean—led to the need for a new kind of industrial organization. Highly capitalized industrial combines instituted systems to control the market from production to consumption, using advertising to craft market niches and foster consumer demand for the products they produced.[1] As cultural historians from Raymond Williams to Richard Ohmann argued, the links between advertising and the mass market press were deeply implicated in the creation of the twentieth-century culture of consumption.

Not surprisingly, mass market periodicals occupied a central position in this cultural and economic shift, as sites for advertising and as beneficiaries themselves of the new systems. Advertising revenues quickly surpassed subscription revenues as publishers realized the secret to mass market publication—lowering the price of the issue, even below its printing cost (thereby vastly increasing circulation), and then reaping fantastic profits from advertisers. The birth of the modern advertising agency and national brand name advertising campaigns in both Britain and America coincided with this rise of mass market periodicals, and these magazines became the focal point of the new world of commodity consumption, as the most successful agencies explicitly urged their clients to pursue magazine advertising as their primary strategy (Ohmann 104–105).

What Ohmann calls the "magazine revolution" in the United States (which was clearly paralleled in Britain) created a new kind of cultural production that helped to steer its audiences toward defining themselves in terms of commodities (Ohmann 340). Advertising and commodity consumption became an organizing social and cultural principle, and not just a method of keeping the economic fires lit. In America and Britain, commodity advertising grew, as Jennifer Wicke notes, into "a center of knowledge production, a determining economic site, as well as a representational system comprising a vastly heterogenous set of individual artifacts" (Wicke 1)—a mobilizer of desire that has been the center of twentieth-century consumer culture.

But as the new century approached those "of the nineteenth century" who recognized these massive cultural shifts voiced dismay about the decay of public deliberation and public reason, emphasizing the villainous role of the commercialized press. Victorian concerns, like Carlyle's in *Past and Present* about the "all-deafening blast of puffery" or Arnold's about

4

the mass press, were augmented at the end of the century, as institutions like the Society for the Checking of Abuses in Public Advertising (SCAPA, formed in 1893) lobbied Parliament for legislation controlling advertising and expressed concern about the contamination of public areas by promotional activities (Turner 112–115). Similarly, the Associated Advertising Clubs of the World were pressured to adopt the slogan "Truth in Advertising" to reassure a concerned American public (Turner 168).

This sense of a crisis of publicity bears witness to the momentous cultural work of magazines and advertising from roughly the mid-1890s to the 1920s, the formative period that produced not only twentieth-century consumer culture but also, and not coincidentally, the modernist magazines this book addresses: the *English Review, Poetry and Drama,* the *Egoist, Blast,* the *Little Review,* and the *Masses.* A similar sense of crisis pervaded much modernist rhetoric about the masses and the mass market as well; this has led to the commonplace that modernists turned their backs on mass audiences, publishing for coteries in little magazines and participating in what Richard Poirier calls a "snob's game."[2] Many of the writers and editors I will discuss, such as Ford Madox Ford, Ezra Pound, Dora Marsden, Margaret Anderson, and Max Eastman, expressed what has become a familiar set of concerns: culture controlled by corporations; public debate constricted by advertisers' prejudices; profit and "the bottom line" sacrificing the original, the creative, to the tried and true, to the "lowest common denominator"; copy that requires little thought and panders to readers' taste for the sensational, uncritical, and merely entertaining. Mass market journals, and the impact they had on the intellectual press, helped set the stage for modernism's understanding of the public sphere in the twentieth century.

In turn, this particular reaction of modernists to the mass press has shaped critical understandings of modernism today. For example, scholars like Andreas Huyssen—who characterizes modernist authors' relation to mass culture as "an anxiety of contamination" (vii)—uphold the idea of modernism and mass culture as polar opposites. Some modernists certainly did fear "contamination" by mass culture, as Huyssen argues, and viewed their work as "high" art. However, much scholarship since Huyssen's seminal *After the Great Divide* has explored the relationships of modernism to mass culture in greater detail, challenging the commonplace of modernism's inveterate antagonism to mass culture and portraying modernists as more savvy about self-promotion and audiences than had previously been understood.[3] I wish to contribute to this "re-visioning" of modernism by exploring its complex and fascinating interdependence with the mass market press.

Contrary to the "contamination anxiety" theory, I argue that modernists' engagements with the commercial mass market were rich and diverse.

The publicity and mass publication techniques that made wealthy men of publishers like Harmsworth, Pearson, and Newnes in England and Curtis, Hearst, Munsey, and McClure in America were quickly adapted, in varying degrees, by suffragist, socialist, and anarchist groups for their own purposes. These radical groups influenced modernist authors and editors to adapt commercial culture to the needs of modernist literature, thus complicating the polarization of modernism and mass culture. Many modernists found the energies of promotional culture too attractive to ignore, especially when it came to advertising and publication techniques. This is not to say that they all wholeheartedly approved of mass culture. But— as I discuss in the book's later chapters—the institutional adaptation of promotional culture by young modernists suggests an early optimism about the power of mass market technologies and institutions to transform and rejuvenate contemporary culture.

Indeed, the intricate relationship between modernist production and the mass market involved not only the dissemination and reception of works, but also the actual form and content of works in the magazines I explore. Participating in the popular verse-recitation movement of the day, poems in *Poetry and Drama* were written to emphasize aural and recitative qualities; poems like Allen Upward's in the *Egoist* even took the form of advertisements, and Wyndham Lewis's *Enemy of the Stars* and the manifestoes in *Blast* adopt the language, typographical forms, and visual images of promotional culture; the "Nausicaa" chapter from *Ulysses* that got the *Little Review* into trouble with New York postal censors used the language, slogans, and images of commercialized youth culture; the poems and cartoons in the *Masses* by Amy Lowell, William Carlos Williams, John Sloan, and others, drew upon and modified the dialect and racial representations of the commercial magazines; and the modernist covers of late issues of the *Masses* drew upon and enlivened the popular "cover girl" strategy that caught readers' eyes. Clearly, modernism not only did not disdain mass culture, but it actually drew positive lessons from Alfred Harmsworth, Gordon Selfridge, and Cyrus Curtis.

Perhaps the one aspect common to all of the magazines I examine that draws them into contact with mass market practices is the bedrock assumption that art must have a public function. Whether this involved the look backward to an oral culture and communal reception by the verse-recitation movement and *Poetry and Drama,* a vision of cultural cohesion in Enlightenment France in the *English Review,* the bringing into alignment of aesthetic radicalism and proletarian revolution in the *Masses,* or the assertion of art's ability to remake and renew society in the *Egoist, Blast,* and *Little Review,* modernists in these magazines tended to see the social role of art as an issue related to the nature of public discourse. They regretted what had come to seem the increasingly private character of art.

Indeed, Peter Bürger notes that the bourgeois aesthetic reception of this period was marked by a tendency toward private reception and public incommunicability along with a distance from life praxis evident in the "solitary absorption in the work"—all traits of "aesthetic autonomy" (the status of the aesthetic as a pure and self-contained realm, distinct from other kinds of social and cultural experiences) that, for him, defines the bourgeois institution of Art (*Theory* 48). He notes that this trend culminates in aestheticism, which "necessarily entails a shrinkage of the attainable public to a small circle of connoisseurs so that the fact that works change nothing whatever in the real world becomes the very criterion of their value" ("Institution of 'Art'" 30).

However, most British and American modernists of this early period did not pursue the radical attacks on aesthetic autonomy and aura that characterize the dada and surrealist practices Bürger considers avant-garde.[4] Rather, they lamented art's loss of its public sociocultural function—by losing communal oral reception (as art moved into the private realm of the study), losing contact with other realms of experience, or, simply, losing its ability to transform life—and wished to forge a more significant public function for it. In other words, they still saw their work as something distinctly "aesthetic" but challenged aesthetic autonomy's tendency to isolate this experience and strip it of social significance.[5] As British and American modernists tried to find ways to use the new institutions of culture of the period to create a prominent public role for their art and literature, they felt that the mass market was the key to restoring the central cultural position of aesthetic experiment. Economist Tyler Cowen has recently argued that a commercial market economy best supports the arts. Modernists may not have had Cowen's faith that a commercial market society always ends up supporting its deserving artists, but at the birth of the century, they shared some of his optimism about markets, and they certainly did not believe that commercial culture is a monolithic and totalizing phenomenon that cannot be turned to vital cultural use.

Such sweeping cultural changes as those ushered in with the rise of modern commercial culture entailed changes in the public sphere during this period, and, as I have suggested, British and American modernists felt it vital for the arts to intervene in the public culture of the early twentieth century. But whether the tools of publicity offered by the mass market represented a crisis of publicity or a new opportunity for the arts to participate in the public sphere was a key question for the authors and editors who launched modernism's early phase in Britain and America between roughly 1905 and 1920.

The crisis view finds its contemporary voice in the work of Jürgen Habermas, who espouses modernity's promise of critical reason but, beginning in his *Structural Transformation of the Public Sphere,* laments what he perceives as a qualitative decline of publicity, publicness, and public discourse—all aspects of what Habermas refers to as *Öffentlichkeit,* or the "public sphere." The constellation of issues surrounding the categories "public" and "private" in civil society were crucial for the culture of modernity during these turbulent years, and Habermas's pessimistic narrative of the birth and transformation of the bourgeois public sphere can serve as a starting point from which to examine modernists' conception of the nature of public discourse, since the view that the commercial mass market and its publication industries represented a decline in public culture was held in varying degrees by Ford Madox Ford, T. S. Eliot, Ezra Pound, and many of the authors involved in Harold Monro's Poetry Bookshop in London.

Habermas traces what he sees as the disintegration of an ideal moment of public deliberative reason into the contemporary pseudo public sphere, in which "publicity" and consensus are manufactured by private interests which manipulate "public opinion" rather than foster meaningful rational public discourse. He summarizes this shift as one from a "culture-debating" to a "culture-consuming" society. To describe it, he chronicles the emergence of a bourgeois public sphere during the seventeenth and eighteenth centuries, which, while supported by the private sphere of the market and the intimate sphere of the bourgeois family, mediated between the private sphere and the state apparatus. This bourgeois public sphere was a public discursive space (maintained by forums like coffee houses and clubs, along with the newly prolific print media of newspapers and journals) in which private citizens—that is, property-owning men—came together as a "public," with access theoretically open to everyone, to deliberate disinterestedly about the public good and forge consensus. Moreover, the power of the newly formed sense of "public opinion" challenged the absolutist state's control of commerce and liberties.

Habermas's diagnosis of the disintegration of such public deliberation and the decline of the public sphere involves a complicated etiology, including the expansion of education and the franchise, changes in the political system, and, most important, the commercialization of the press—the chief institution of the bourgeois public sphere. This commercialization, of course, increases exponentially in Britain and the United States between 1905 and 1920. In Habermas's view, the entrance of the working classes into the public sphere broke down the homogeneity and cohesion of "the public" and necessitated compromises based on pressure and threat rather than on a public consensus (that had, in fact, always excluded the working classes from the discussion). Later in the nineteenth century, the rise of the party apparatus gave private interests greater control of partisan discourse, and, by the early twentieth century, the birth of the modern welfare state blurred the distinctions between public and private.

Many recent historians, economists, and political theorists, even those whose work has been informed by Habermas, have come to challenge and revise aspects of his theory—especially its idealization of the eighteenth-century bourgeois public sphere. They argue that such a "disinterested" use of public reason was predicated from the start on exclusions, for example, of the working classes and of women (who were drawn even further into the intimate sphere of the bourgeois patriarchal family).[6] Geoff Eley has explored the pervasive prohibitions upon which the public sphere was constructed by bourgeois men who began to see themselves as "universal," and Mary Ryan argues that women, excluded from the male public sphere, constructed alternative routes to public politics. These essays and other recent works point out the problem of uncritically accepting the principle of open access to the bourgeois public sphere (and at some level Habermas admits this, at least acknowledging the problem of making "citizen" equivalent to "property-owning male"), but they also show that the bourgeois public sphere was not *the* public sphere; there were alternative public spheres even during the eighteenth century.

This vision of an open and vital public sphere of the past, which Habermas accepts too quickly as historical rather than mythic, very much parallels the mythologizing of the Enlightenment and of contemporary French culture by Ford Madox Ford, and of an even more historically distant oral public culture by Harold Monro and others. These early modernists, though espousing a myth of a public sphere in decline that has not stood up to historical scrutiny, saw the wide dissemination of vital new literature as a way of rejuvenating the public sphere. I would argue, too, that this myth of decline gave them a useful rhetorical enemy (the new commercial mass-market publications) against which to position their work—in effect, to *promote,* to *market* their own efforts to use modernist literature and art to reshape public culture. Yet even these efforts involved other lucrative segments of commercial publishing, like the review journals, and the elocution and verse-recitation industry.

However, if the mass market magazines seemed to some modernists to represent a degeneration of the public sphere, to other modernists and political and intellectual radicals during this period of flux they seemed to open up the possibility of oppositional space, even of counterpublicity and counterpublics. The relatively low cost of producing a small-scale magazine—to return to those technological advances in paper making, printing, and typesetting—and the fantastic successes new advertising techniques and print venues were having with vast audiences presented the seductive possibility of intervening in public discourse. An early and influential set of modernist authors and editors, including Dora Marsden, Wyndham Lewis, James Joyce, Margaret Anderson, Jane Heap, Ezra Pound (at times), William Carlos Williams, and even socialist experimenters like Floyd Dell and Max Eastman, did not promote a myth of decline about the early twentieth-century public sphere, and, indeed, saw the new commercial magazine genres and the advertising that supported them as providing opportunities for modernism.[7]

I, then, argue for an understanding of early modernism as engaged with the public sphere and with the commercial culture of the early twentieth century: modernists in this period searched for ways of rejuvenating the public sphere (as those who promoted the myth of decline saw their mission) or simply making their voices and their art prominent in the vibrant and exciting new print venues of the public sphere that the commercial culture had helped to create and sustain (as those who saw a more positive potential for the commercial mass market imagined *their* mission). Neither group wished to retreat into the private and elite confines of coterie publication. To make such a claim, I must chart a different course than those taken by some recent scholars who have largely offered intellectual histories of modernism.[8] Instead, I chronicle modernists' engagements with social institutions and material practices. This approach reconnects the birth of literary modernism with the sociocultural contexts from which it emerged, especially those of the institutions of publication and publicity, and thus sheds new light on the social and cultural history of modernity. I draw upon archival holdings to provide a nuanced account of the discourses and institutions that played important roles in modernism's self-fashioning, its reception, and its understanding of the public sphere—including advertising practices; discourses on youth, education, and the purity of language in oral performance; the tactics of suffragist, anarchist, and socialist political movements; understandings of ethnic and racial difference in America; and the institutions of the publishing industry. These contexts illuminate the tensions of the rapidly changing cultures that produced literary modernism and also the responsiveness and adaptability of modernism itself to the larger cultural arena.

In focusing on the field of cultural production and its public character, I organize this book not around individual authors, but rather around magazines: in London, the *English Review, Poetry and Drama,* the *Egoist,* and *Blast;* in Chicago, the *Little Review;* and in New York, the *Masses.* Though these periodicals have been mined for years for source material related to individual authors, few studies have been written since the 1960s on particular modernist magazines.[9] Beyond the initial attempt in the 1940s by Hoffman, Allen, and Ulrich to analyze the little magazine as a genre, almost no scholarship has explored the material practices and genre markers of the modernist magazines themselves as a field of study.

Introduction

Unlike individual literary works, magazines are public forums—frequently including lively correspondence pages for public discussion. They highlight the engagement of literary production with nonliterary discourse, and they often mediate the initial reception of an author's work. This was especially true in the case of prewar modernists, since changes in the institutions of book publication paradoxically both made cheap books more widely available to the reading public and ensured that a new or experimental author, especially a poet, could not make a living or reach wide audiences through book publication alone.[10] The cheaper printing and paper costs that made the mass market press possible also made small-scale magazine publication affordable.

In these new contexts, then, all of the early modernists I examine— whether espousing a mythic vision of public discourse fallen from some earlier state of perfection or affirming the energies of the new world of advertising and mass publication—shared an optimism about redirecting the public function of the press, an optimism that helps to explain Ford's attempt to reform the dominant public sphere from within and to illuminate the interest of modernists like Ford and Pound in the Enlightenment and in French periodicals, like the *Mercure de France,* that they saw as the contemporary embodiment of an enlightened and cohesive society. It also elucidates Harold Monro's and other writers' hopes that *Poetry and Drama* could popularize the verse-recitation movement and verse drama and use them to rejuvenate the public sphere by returning it to an oral, communal basis. It sheds light on attempts by modernist authors and editors involved in the *Freewoman, New Freewoman,* and *Egoist* to foster public deliberation of controversial social, political, and aesthetic issues, both in the correspondence columns of the magazine and in open discussion circles, and the attempts by Wyndham Lewis and *Blast* to forge a modernist aesthetic based on modern advertising. And it highlights the efforts by the authors and editors of the *Little Review* and even the anti-capitalist *Masses* in America to make their magazines lively public forums based on successful commercial models.

Although making the arts crucial to the public sphere was a shared motive, the differences in understanding of the role of commercial culture in the public sphere led to a new emphasis by many modernists on counterpublic spheres. After the early attempts by Ford's *English Review* and Harold Monro's magazines to reshape the institutions of the dominant public sphere, the optimism that I find in modernist little magazines like the *Egoist, Little Review,* and the *Masses* responds to the possibility of appropriating some of the institutions of the newly emerging mass publishing world to create counterpublicity, counterpublic spheres whose ultimate aim was to influence the dominant public sphere. In articulating the useful concept of counterpublic spheres—of alternative institutions and varieties of publicity—social theorists like Oskar Negt, Alexander Kluge, and Rita Felski remain indebted to Habermas's arguments but, like Nancy Fraser, Geoff Eley, and Mary Ryan, revise his vision of disintegration. They have analyzed counterpublic spheres that have sprung up in the twentieth century to challenge the dominant public sphere's control of public discourse. Negt and Kluge critique Habermas's tendency to describe the public sphere in singular terms, preferring instead to emphasize the multiplicity of types of publicity or public life and the existence and critical potential of counterpublic spheres. Applying such a concept to the American feminist movement, Felski notes that "the category of a feminist counter-public sphere provides a useful means to theorizing the existence of an oppositional discursive space within contemporary society grounded in gender politics, making it possible to examine the mechanisms by which this collectivity is constituted, its political implications and effects, as well as its potential limitations" (155). These conceptions of "oppositional discursive spaces" and their political consequences help illuminate the variety of strategies and tactics employed by modernists hoping to intervene in the public discussion.

Drawing on the work of Habermas and his critics, I explore modernist authors' and editors' attempts to ally literary experimentation with radical social and political counterpublic spheres before and during World War I. Like the later phases in feminist movements in the West that Felski analyzes, the suffrage movement created its own institutions of publicity— papers, meetings, book shops, publishers, street-selling, spectacles, and parades. Anarchists and socialists created alternative presses and forms of publicity as well. Although early British and American modernists were concerned about the nature of public culture, they felt that new forms of publicity adopted by radical political groups and cultural institutions offered them the opportunity to help reshape the social function of literature. Moreover, these radical movements and their magazines reveal the surprising imbrication of counterpublic spheres and commercial mass market culture, and this understanding challenges a vision like Habermas's that sees commercial mass market print culture as presenting no possibility other than the degeneration of public deliberation. Cowen criticizes Habermas for seeing "the market as hindering rather than aiding critical communication" (11), and, indeed, these counterpublic spheres, as I will show, were supported by the contemporary institutions and modes of cultural transmission of the commercial market.

This book, then, uncovers a distinctive sense of optimism that British and American modernists felt before the war about the public nature of art as well as an active engagement of modernists with the ever-transforming institutions of culture. Rather than fostering the rejection of commercial culture, which has long been attributed to modernism, the birth of British and American modernism sparked an explosion of publication and self-promotion and several serious attempts to address the institutions of the dominant culture. While different contexts give a rich variety to these local engagements, the following chapters suggest that the alienation and isolation from the dominant culture that have often been ascribed to modernism cannot be seen as originating with the emergence of modernism. Rather, a more careful examination of this cultural moment reveals a surprisingly consistent desire to renew or engage the public sphere and to strive for a critical heterogeneity in public discourse.

Chapter 1 focuses on the *English Review* (the magazine that first published fiction by Lewis and Lawrence and early work by Pound) to illustrate an impulse in early British modernism to "make new" the public sphere. I turn to letters from archives at Cornell, the University of Texas at Austin, and Northwestern, as well as to Edwardian magazine and newspaper articles and Ford's own fiction and nonfiction writings, to suggest that Ford attempted to create an institution that would embody his own conceptions of heterodoxy and disinterestedness. Like Habermas, Ford created a vision of a mythic ideal public sphere now in decline in England, but he also constructed a vision of contemporary French literature and culture as a living expression of his Enlightenment ideal, and this idealized distortion of French culture underscores an important motivation for Ford and other modernists (e.g., Pound and Eliot): the desire for social and cultural cohesion based neither on what they saw as middle-class philistinism nor on mass market taste. I question current understandings of Ford as skeptical of generalized cultural authority by demonstrating that, in the context of the momentary illusion of consensus fostered by the liberal landslide of 1906, Ford tried to reproduce in England a journal like the *Mercure de France*—one that could simultaneously publish avant-garde literature *and* enjoy a central position of cultural authority, attract a large readership, and cover a wide range of fields as a "general intelligencer," as Pound put it.

Chapter 2 examines oral performance—another important medium through which modernist poets sought out publics—in the context of class anxieties that gave surprising significance to the speaking voice. I analyze the verse-recitation movement in late Victorian and Edwardian England and the attempt by Harold Monro and contributors to the *Poetry Review* and *Poetry and Drama* to support it. This movement, which was both a product of liberal education reform and a response to middle-class tensions that reform may have partially caused, privileged oral performance over visual spectacle (which had become associated with the artifice of working-class entertainment). Following Bourdieu's account of the "pure gaze" in *Distinction,* I suggest that the culturally legitimating marker of distinction in middle- and upper-class London was the "pure voice." Harold Monro's *Poetry Review* and *Poetry and Drama* and his Poetry Bookshop (a site for public poetry readings), as well as elocution and recitation manuals and correspondence in the Harold Monro Papers at the University of California, Los Angeles, suggest a sociological interpretation of the speech orientation of modernist poetry. Ideas prevalent in elocution and verse-recitation manuals that reached a pinnacle of popularity around 1914—the year of the popular English debut of Shaw's *Pygmalion*—worked their way into modernist circles through the *Poetry Review/Poetry and Drama*. These discourses about the purity of speech, impersonality, and verse drama were appropriated and transformed by experimental poets, who used them to reach new audiences through public readings. They also point to a class context for modernist aesthetic imperatives, especially those in T. S. Eliot's early criticism.

Chapter 3 explores the influence of the rapidly expanding commodity culture on one of the most important of the British little magazines, the *Egoist,* and its predecessors, the *Freewoman* and the *New Freewoman*. Although the editors, Dora Marsden and Harriet Shaw Weaver, and modernist contributors like Pound, Richard Aldington, F. S. Flint, and Allen Upward, tended rhetorically to uphold an ideal of high culture against mass cultural "contamination" (as Huyssen describes it), I argue that they were nevertheless strongly attracted to the proliferating types of publicity in an energetic advertising industry. I examine editorial correspondence and records from Princeton, the British Library, and the Public Records Office, and I explore mass market advertisements as well as radical political papers from the period, to suggest that modernists followed the lead of suffragettes and anarchists in borrowing mass publicity strategies to seek out large audiences within the prewar London masses. The transformation of the public sphere contributed to new strategies for inclusion in public discourse by marginalized groups and to the creation of "counterpublics." Suffragists and other radical groups borrowed from commercial culture to create their own mass publishing enterprises in opposition to the dominant Edwardian newspaper and periodical presses. The writers and editors of Marsden's magazines displayed a surprising optimism about creating an inclusive public forum for audiences in opposition to bourgeois social norms, liberal and statist politics, and—above all for modernist authors—conventional literary taste. The ideal of open public discourse was realized in the lively and expansive correspondence section of these magazines and in the public discussion circles that they generated.

This chapter also explores the short-lived but fascinating avant-garde magazine *Blast,* which Wyndham Lewis edited in 1914 and 1915. Though it had a greater emphasis on visual art, *Blast* published many writers who contributed to the *Egoist,* in which *Blast* was advertised and discussed, and it emerged from the same context of counter public spheres sustained by mass publicity. However, I will argue that *Blast* and Lewis's enigmatic play, *Enemy of the Stars*, offer the most extreme version of modernism's espousal of promotional culture in prewar London, and that Lewis refigures the egoist artist from a figure of self-assertion to one of self-promotion.

Chapter 4 turns to the *Egoist*'s transatlantic counterpart, the *Little Review*, to suggest that Margaret Anderson's quintessential little magazine borrowed directly from mass market publications and advertising rhetorics to style a popular periodical that would, however, eschew mass appeal as the basis of its editorial decisions. I argue that the *Little Review* fashioned modernism as a youth movement, and I explore the significance of this move by discussing two crucial contexts from American commercial culture: the development of the marketing potential of the relatively new concept of adolescence, and the youth columns in popular magazines. By turning not only to the *Little Review* and its archives at the University of Wisconsin–Milwaukee, but also to mass market periodicals (like *Ladies' Home Journal* and *Good Housekeeping*) that targeted youth with special columns, I uncover a tension in America over youth's place in the expanding commercial culture. While mass market institutions crafted positive images of youth, characterized by abandon and consumerism, they also attempted to regulate youth's relationship to commercial culture by carefully constructing "open" forums to discuss issues important to youth. The *Little Review*, however, actually dared to create an open public institution—and attracted young, even adolescent, readers. These contexts illuminate one of the best-known episodes in the *Little Review*'s history—its head-on collision with the law and the Society for the Suppression of Vice—and give a new context for understanding the American reception of Joyce's "Nausicaa" chapter, the *Ulysses* chapter for which the *Little Review* was prosecuted and censored.

Chapter 5 explores the attempt by the Greenwich Village socialist magazine, the *Masses,* and the many modernist writers and artists who contributed to it, to imagine and foster a pluralistic counter public sphere. Drawing many illustrators and writers from the commercial press, the *Masses* tried to create a popular illustrated socialist monthly that could compete with the mass market monthlies and comic magazines on their own grounds, while engaging with a wide variety of social and political issues of its day. The frequent use of dialect writing and ethnic cartoons, I argue, expresses modernist and radical anxieties about the nature of the public sphere. Like the British *Egoist,* the *Masses* tried to foster a broadly based oppositional counter public sphere that could bring together a modern aesthetic, socialism, sex radicalism, suffragism, and other concerns. But even following the leads of highly successful mass market magazines, the *Masses* was unable to prevent the fragmentation of such a public discursive space. This examination of the *Masses* and *Liberator* and the archives of Max Eastman, Claude McKay, and Floyd Dell at the Lilly and Newberry Libraries shows that, in an American context, the magazine's pluralistic configuration of identity around ethnic and racial and class divisions, and the need to bridge differences within audiences, complicated and ultimately undermined the *Masses'* attempt to be a free discursive space for the discussion of aesthetic and social revolt and an instrument of proletarian revolution all at the same time.

Many of these projects did not achieve the grand goals that modernist authors and editors had set for them, and this book may be considered a study of unrealized hopes. Despite attempts to reach broad audiences, because of problems of reception and finances, and the logic of the mass market, ultimately these modernist magazines found only small readerships and led brief lives. Yet, these magazines created a lively, even exhilarating, awareness of opposition and of the possibilities that the new century provided for an alternative art to become part of the public sphere. The very publication and advertising institutions that provoked a sense of crisis in some—and an expectation of opportunity in others—held out to all the modernists I examine the promise that inexpensive mass distribution magazines and new promotional techniques could foster counter public spheres based on heterogeneity, critical public discourse, and a rejuvenating public function for the arts. Their efforts to bring modernist literary experiments into broader public discourse provide us new insight into a pivotal historical moment, during which the social, political, and cultural turmoil of the prewar period and the birth of mass market culture gave young writers feelings of both urgency and optimism about the public face of modernism.

I

The Myth of the Whole and Ford's *English Review*

Edwardian Monthlies, the *Mercure de France,* and Early British Modernism

The birth of modernism in Britain evokes visions of stridently opposi-tional little magazines like Wyndham Lewis's *Blast* (1914–1915) and small-press radical journals like the *Egoist* (1914–1919) or stories of the Egoist Press's struggle to bring Joyce's *Ulysses* to a hesitant English public. Yet modernist authors often saw their earliest publications in Alfred Orage's weekly *New Age* (founded 1907), Ford Madox Ford's monthly *English Re-view* (founded 1908), and other magazines that seemed much more recog-nizably like the established Edwardian journals, and it is with this field of journals that we begin our exploration of the public face of modernism. Ford's *English Review* was the first journal to bring together the most bril-liant of the Edwardian lights—Conrad, Wells, Bennett, Galsworthy, and Hudson—with the new talent of young modernist writers such as Pound, Lewis, and Lawrence; it illustrates the important impulse in early British modernism to enter into what we now call the public sphere, rather than to create magazines to cater to a small elite (a vision of modernism that this study challenges).

Although Ford intended to engage the public sphere through the popular journal genres and major publishing houses of the Edwardian period, modernists like him (and, following him, Pound and Eliot) adopted a vision of the public sphere in decline like the one elaborated through Habermas and created what I will call the "myth of the whole." As modernist literature emerged in prewar London, modernists like Ford lamented that the public sphere seemed no longer to be a realm of disinterested critical reason. But alluding to a lost vital and cohesive public culture served an oppositional rhetoric that could help promote modernism as crucial to the Edwardian public sphere. Although his vision, in some ways, makes Ford sound mid-Victorian, Ford's fledgling *English Review* used this ideal of "disinterestedness" as a means to bring modernist aesthetics to bear upon Edwardian public culture, and it was strategically important to the emergence of modernism in England.

In his first *English Review* editorial, "The Function of the Arts in the Republic: I. Literature" (1908), Ford proclaimed that the *English Review* would be "impersonal" (158), and he emphasized that "The English Review sets boldly upon its front the words 'No party bias.' This means to say that we are here not to cry out 'Go in this direction,' but simply to point out where we stand" (159). The imaginative artist benefits the republic by expressing "his view of life as it is, not as he would like it to be" (160). The tone and rhetoric of this editorial—or "antimanifesto," as one might call it—contrasts sharply with the militant advocacy of the magazines discussed in later chapters, like the *Egoist, Blast,* the *Little Review,* and the *Masses,* but Ford was employing a different strategy. This editorial set the tone of disinterestedness that Ford wished the *English Review* to embody—one essentially of precise expression of the state of the republic rather than advocacy for a predetermined set of ideas or interests. And Ford fashioned this attempt to create a discursive space for disinterested critical deliberation as grounded in Enlightenment thinking. Ford tried to bring modernism before the English public, not by proclaiming it the "new thing," but rather by trying to make literary experiment seem crucial to the restoration of an imagined older conception of the public sphere.

But to understand Ford's vision of the public sphere and of "disinterestedness," we must sort out the genealogy and implications of such concepts. Indeed, disinterestedness had its roots in the emerging bourgeoisie of the eighteenth century, as Habermas points out. Although Habermas sees the eighteenth-century liberal public sphere as disinterested in that private citizens left behind private interests to deliberate on the "public good," submerged in his argument is the fact that the liberal public sphere was always "interested" in that it explicitly protected the rights of the bourgeoisie against the power of the government and the aristocracy. The homogeneity of interests of the white male bourgeoisie allowed it to create a space for itself as "the public" that deceptively appeared to transcend individual private interests. But even the concepts of political or aesthetic disinterestedness that emerged among the eighteenth-century bourgeoisie were based on a social cohesion predicated on bourgeois hegemony in the political and aesthetic realms and on a tendency to universalize bourgeois taste and sensibilities.[1] Both concepts—aesthetic disinterestedness and a liberal public sphere—rely on a high degree of cultural cohesion or homogeneity, a cohesion that seemed possible to eighteenth-century bourgeois white men but seemed much more problematic by the twentieth century.

Even by the mid-Victorian period, Matthew Arnold had set the terms by which middle-class Edwardians would understand the "decline" of social cohesion. The increasingly organized and rebellious working classes at midcentury not only created a sense of social fragmentation, but also put a liberal thinker like Arnold in a position analogous to that of the aristocracy a century earlier which used discussion of "public good" and "disinterestedness" to mask hierarchical domination.[2] *Culture and Anarchy*'s every page exudes the fear of rebellion and social fragmentation— the kind of lack of social cohesion that would continue to be an important factor for the Victorian and Edwardian ages—as Arnold vehemently lambasts middle-class philistinism and vulgarity, along with lower-class rioters at Hyde Park Gate.

Habermas, analyzing the working classes' entrance into the public sphere through the early nineteenth-century press, describes the resulting loss of social cohesion as a degeneration of public reason: "Because of the diffusion of press and propaganda, the public body expanded beyond the bounds of the bourgeoisie. The public body lost not only its social exclusivity; it lost in addition the *coherence* created by bourgeois social institutions and a relatively high standard of education. Conflicts hitherto restricted to the private sphere now intrude into the public sphere. . . . Laws which obviously have come about under the 'pressure of the street' can scarcely still be understood as arising from the consensus of private individuals engaged in public discussion. They correspond in a more or less unconcealed manner to the compromise of conflicting private interests" ("Public Sphere" 54; emphasis mine). (One might ask if the sacrifice of coherence in the public sphere was not a price worth paying for the inclusion of the largest portion of the population in the political process.) And Habermas further blames the rise of the national political party apparatus for the decline of the liberal public sphere. Such an alteration in the nature of the political public sphere saw its culmination in mid-Victorian England with Gladstone's introduction of the caucus system, a system which augmented the power of professional politicians and led to the eclipse of the local committees by central direction of the party and propagandizing.[3]

Ford's proclamation of "No party bias" in the *English Review* arises from a similar hope for a coherent public sphere—one stabilized not by strong party structures, but by an imaginative and cohesive culture—but also locates him in (and in opposition to) the political climate of the Edwardian period. It is clear that the increasingly organized class-based activity of workers, whether it constituted socialism, trade unions, or the push for reform legislation, confronted many of the seemingly stable assumptions and foundations of British class and power relations in Victorian England. With labor agitation, the suffrage movement, the increasing push for Irish Home Rule, and the Constitutional Crisis of 1910 and 1911, the late Victorian and the entire Edwardian periods were an enormous challenge for Liberalism to adapt itself to changing conditions—a challenge that the Liberal party ultimately failed to meet (see Dangerfield).

However, the years leading up to the founding of the *English Review* made consensus and genuine "progress" seem more possible than ever before, but at the same time more insidiously problematic. The Liberals at the turn of the century wanted to be a centrist party, a party of consensus. As George L. Bernstein puts it, "The view that labour had definable interests that were opposed to those of capital, and thus needed promotion in Parliament, challenged the Liberal belief that Parliament should promote the interests of society as a whole rather than those of any section" (66). The Liberals disapproved of a class-based party and particularly disliked Labour candidates tied to trade unions, who seemed to represent only particular interest groups and not the constituencies they were elected to serve. The Liberal party felt that "even socialists should work with Liberals to secure agreed measures of practical reform rather than promote unattainable policies which were in advance of public opinion" (Bernstein 66). At the turn of the century, Herbert Gladstone, the chief Liberal whip, urged the party to be more receptive to and work with the independent labor candidates, in order to avoid three-cornered races in which the Unionist candidate often prevailed (Bernstein 67–75). Finally, the "progressive alliance" was momentarily a reality, and the Liberals won the 1906 elections with the greatest landslide in British history (Bernstein 67–77). Although the progressive alliance and the Liberal triumph in 1906 seemed to indicate a consensus for social reform, just below the surface, the conflicts were great: not only between the Independent Labour party and the Liberal party, but also between the workers and the large Nonconformist faction of the Liberal party, and between the imperialist and nonimperialist wings of the Liberal party, and between the free-trade Conservatives of the Balfour stamp and the protectionist Unionists, many of whom had broken ranks with the Liberals after Gladstone's 1886 push for Home Rule (Bernstein 77–78). Countless rifts not only ensured that there was no consensus, but also guaranteed that the Liberal party could not retain power for long. At the same time that consensus and disinterestedness seemed to be affirmed by the elections of 1906, the kind of partisanship and party infighting that Ford wished the *English Review* to eschew even led some to see the aristocratic House of Lords, who generally were viewed as Tory partisans for their veto of Liberal legislation, as the only truly disinterested participants in the government (coming full circle back to the nemesis of Enlightenment Republicans) (see Barrie 341).

The coincidence of the political atmosphere of the Edwardian period and the birth of twentieth-century commercial culture made Ford's understanding of a fragmenting public sphere both possible and strategically useful in the publishing world. Ford's goal for the *English Review* was to cleanse the dominant public sphere of two phenomena that Habermas later identified as partly responsible for the fragmentation and transformation of the bourgeois public sphere during the nineteenth century—commercialism's undermining of a critical press and the increasing public power of competing private interests.[4] Both Ford and Habermas located an idealized vision of "disinterested" critical thinking in the Enlightenment past. But, as recent revisionist critiques of Habermas's notion of the liberal public sphere have amply demonstrated, such a vision is deeply problematic. Critics like Fraser and Eley, for example, argue that the bourgeois public sphere used the rhetoric of rational disinterested discussion of the public good to elide the concerns of the excluded lower classes and women; moreover, Stephen Holmes argues that Enlightenment political theorists, in fact, held claims of disinterestedness in great suspicion, and thinkers from Smith and Hume to Voltaire, Diderot, and Pascal advocated *self-interest* instead. The principle of universal self-interest was held up by republican theorists as egalitarian and democratic in the face of self-serving aristocratic rhetorics of glory and "disinterested" control of society.[5]

Like Habermas, Ford imagined such a disinterested culture to have existed in the eighteenth century; unlike Habermas, he also felt that contemporary French culture carried on the Enlightenment tradition. Just as Habermas values what revisionist historiography has shown to be the *myth* of the liberal public sphere, Ford looked to his own myth of the French public and French culture. This construction of the French allowed Ford to promote modernism and his new journal in the commercially viable field of Edwardian "high-culture" review magazines. Ford attempted to create a discursive space in the *English Review* that would embody his conception of "disinterestedness," and this effort evolved into a larger issue both for Ford and for British modernism: the desire for a social and cultural cohesion based neither on perceived middle-class philistinism nor on mass market taste. Hence the commercial culture that greatly expanded the modern press, in spite of Ford's and Habermas's negative assessments, also provided a rhetorical opponent against which modernists could position themselves to declare the public value of their work. Moreover, though Ford criticized the publicity-building stunts and the content of many mass market papers and magazines, the field of publication—the review journals—through which Ford chose to launch modernism in England was itself commercially successful, read by large audiences, and seen as greatly significant for public culture.

Michael Levenson's insightful chapter on Ford in *A Genealogy of Modernism* portrays Ford as profoundly skeptical of the possibility of cultural authority exemplified by, for instance, the *Saturday Review* of the 1860s: "Arnold . . . never doubts that there is indeed a 'scale of value,' however obscured beneath the prevailing cultural chaos. He depends still on the authority of the *Saturday Review*. Ford, on the other hand, has no confidence in such persisting values. Where Arnold's point is that right reason must be redeemed from vulgarity, Ford suggests that right reason has lapsed altogether, leaving the modern world in a state of 'social agnosticism'" (53). Levenson shows us a Ford who witnessed the death of the Victorian "great figure"—the destruction of the potential for a generalized cultural authority in the face of the mass market press, the complexity and heterogeneity of modern life, and the mediocrity he saw embodied in the newly literate reading masses. He suggests that Ford turned this profound social and cultural skepticism not only into personal escapism but also into an opportunity for pure literature to jettison the moral and social weight of the Victorian age.

Levenson helps illuminate the anxieties and strains of modernity that Ford felt, but in this early period Ford did not simply retreat into skepticism at the passing of the Victorian "great figure." It is significant, I think, that Levenson mentions the *English Review* only once in his chapter on Ford; by instead examining Ford's career as the editor of the *English Review* (and not primarily as the author of *The Good Soldier*, as he is now mainly known) and by exploring the material practices and institutional contexts of the production and advertising of the *English Review*, we can to see that the *English Review* began as a deeply optimistic enterprise. And this optimism about entering the public sphere is characteristic of early modernism.

Ford and the Mass Market

If one were looking for signs of a broad cultural cohesion in Edwardian England, one place to start might be in the flourishing of commercial culture. In the years leading up to his launching of the *English Review*, Ford, like all the modernists I will examine, became increasingly drawn into the world of early twentieth-century mass market print culture. This was, of course, unavoidable for an author, whether one was awed by the money-making potential and the possibility of reaching staggeringly large audiences or concerned that the quality of the nation's literature and media—whether newspapers, magazines, reviews, or even advertisements—was in jeopardy. Habermas, of course, blames the commercialization of the press as a profitable business concern in the nineteenth century as a major factor in what he sees as the shift "from a culture-debating to a culture-consuming public" (*Structural* 159). But in the middle of the Edwardian expansion of the press, such an assessment was by no means the only way of interpreting the commercial press. Ford had to address the phenomena of mass market literature and the mass market press, because they raised questions for him about the possibility for an organ such as the *English Review* to be a critical and a centrist or consensus-based cultural institution simultaneously. Two of the elements that Habermas suggests had undermined the liberal public sphere—the commercialization of the press and the intrusion into the public sphere of the working classes—were foundations of the mass market itself. Modernity raised for Ford a troubling question: if disinterested criticism seems to necessitate a degree of cultural cohesion, is there any critical potential in the mass market literature and "organs of opinion" that reach the largest portion of society—the middle and the working classes? Modernism, born in this time of the expansion of the press, was indelibly marked by the sense that print culture was about to surge into a new cultural prominence.

During the few years leading up to the birth of the *English Review* in December 1908, Ford became closely involved with the world of mass market publication in London. On March 14, 1906, he published *The Fifth Queen.* Though it hardly rivaled a best-seller like Marie Corelli's *Sorrows of Satan,* it sold steadily and helped seal Ford's position as an established writer.[6] The next month, Alfred Harmsworth, the king of mass market publications and newspapers (soon to be Lord Northcliffe and the owner of the *Times*), approached Ford with a proposition: he would purchase the *Academy,* a London weekly founded in 1869, and install Ford as its new editor (see Mizener 120–121). Ford was then asked to contribute regularly to the new Books Supplement of Harmsworth's *Daily Mail,* one of the largest circulation newspapers in the country, and one of the first major dailies to circulate widely among the working classes (Altick 355). From January 19 to July 20, 1907, Ford supplied to the Books Supplement two poems and a series of fourteen "Literary Portraits."[7] The subjects of his portraits ranged from Hardy, Shaw, and Wells to the successful *Strand* humorist, W. W. Jacobs, and the most popular of the popular fiction writers, Marie Corelli.[8] Though Ford had published in a wide variety of journals and papers, these sketches were his largest foray yet into mass market periodical publication. His choice of subjects suggests an early attempt to imagine a literary public sphere that encompassed a broad range of tastes (in a popular newspaper read by both the working and middle classes)—a consensus analogous to the ideal of the progressive alliance in the political arena. While the intriguing prospect of Ford Madox Ford as the editor of a Harmsworth magazine never materialized, his experiences with Harmsworth marked his thinking about the English reading public, and it eventually influenced his decisions about the *English Review*—not just about its relationship to mass audiences, but also about how it would incorporate or reject the strategies and goals of mass market publication.

During this period, I believe Ford not only was exploring the mass market with his sketches but also was self-consciously trying to write "popular" fiction. While still working on his "Literary Portraits," he completed a new novel, *The "Half Moon."* The *Fifth Queen* trilogy had marked him as a writer in a popular Edwardian genre, the historical romance, and he continued in this vein with his new novel, a novel about Hudson's voyage to America (the first of a planned trilogy that would next have turned to the *Mayflower*). He explained to his agent, James Pinker, "I send you herewith a first installment of the *Half Moon*. I've put in exciting situations for the benefit of the serial market which it's much my desire to capture."[9] Ford, not generally a writer of "exciting situations," clearly meant this concession to popular taste as an overt attempt to attract a wide audience.[10]

Ford continued to flirt with topics of mass market interest even while editing the *English Review*. On March 24, 1909, he wrote to Pinker: "By the bye, some devil, or some angel has filled me with a wild desire to write a series of articles on Music Hall Stars,—for some of whom I have a great admiration—and on the Music Hall Stage as a factor in popular life. . . . What I want to do is, in my own matchless way, to visualize, say Victoria Monks, and then point out why she is applauded and what light the applause casts on the circumstances and ideals of the lower middle class. The articles would be both beautiful and instructive" (*Letters* 38–39). This project would have been in line with very popular sections on celebrities in Harmsworth's *Daily Mail,* which tried to glamorize the lives of stars. It also evokes the *Strand*'s popular features like "Portraits of Celebrities" and "Illustrated Interviews."[11] Ford himself, like T. S. Eliot, was a fan of the music hall—especially of Victoria Monks—and he even made the Shepherd's Bush Empire, a popular music-hall venue, the scene of his usual evening's editorial decisions for the *English Review* (see Goldring, *South Lodge,* 32).

However, Ford's proposal for this series of music-hall portraits, which seems never to have come to fruition, betrays a difference in attitude between Ford and someone like Harmsworth at the *Daily Mail* or George Newnes at the *Strand.* For Ford, the project would be of a critical nature, exploring a class of people to which Ford clearly does not belong and to which, presumably, his readers either do not belong or would not be allowed unreflectively to belong. Ford shared the taste of the lower middle class for music hall. But the difference between Ford's proposed articles on music-hall stars and the features in mass market publications is not so much in subject as in attitude toward the subject.

While Ford was conceiving the idea of running his own literary magazine, he was clearly intrigued by mass market publication like the *Daily Mail,* attempting to reach mass audiences with his own novels, and interested in the subjects of mass market journal publications like music-hall stars. However, Ford also began to have reservations about what he saw as the uncritical project of mass market publications. Although (as I will argue) he wanted not a tiny elite but a wide audience for the *English Review,* he eventually rejected mass market publication strategies and their goal of unreflective entertainment in favor of the commercially viable but less widely circulated monthly reviews.

Mr. Apollo and the *English Review*

The conflict between Ford's aspiration to engage a wide reading audience and his desire for a critical, even educational basis for writing can nowhere be better observed than in *Mr. Apollo* (published on Aug. 20, 1908), the last of his novels to appear before the birth of the *English Review* in December 1908. *Mr. Apollo,* like *The "Half Moon,"* was intended to be a popular novel, and, I suggest, to imitate mass market novels like Marie Corelli's *Sorrows of Satan* in order to reach a large audience that would cut across class and educational categories. In *Mr. Apollo* Ford explored the possibility of writing a popular novel that would be thoughtful and critical, and not merely entertaining, as he judged Corelli's novels. Fittingly, it was in this novel that he also explored the relationship of a journal of opinion to mass audiences. Ford, I believe, was working out for himself the role that mass market publication tactics might play in the *English Review*'s intention to reach large audiences, but the novel ultimately was unable to resolve his ambivalent stance toward commercialism or imagine how a journal might reach mass audiences without compromising its critical function. *Mr. Apollo* represents a reluctant closing of the door on the Harmsworth-style mass market periodical as a model for the *English Review.*

The plot of *Mr. Apollo,* one of Ford's most bizarre and least studied novels, is simple: the god Apollo comes to London to study modern life. Mizener suggests that H. G. Wells's *Wonderful Visit* (1895) or *Sea Lady* (1902) may have been the inspiration for this new type of novel by Ford. This seems plausible, but I propose another context, Marie Corelli's *Sorrows of Satan* (1895), with which Ford (as well as the young James Joyce) was familiar. The striking similarities between *Mr. Apollo* and *The Sorrows of Satan* suggest that Ford attempted to incorporate features of the popular novel in his own writing. Both novels play on the reader's knowledge that the strange personage is, in fact, a divinity. Not only the humor but also the moral focus of each novel is based upon the characters' inability to recognize what the reader so clearly perceives, and on the characters' reactions when the truth is revealed to them. In both novels, the divine personage is generally assumed to be a "prince" of some mysterious country in the East.

Certain scenes in *Mr. Apollo* echo scenes in *The Sorrows of Satan.* Early in Ford's novel, the Reverend Mr. Todd and his family listen to Apollo play the piano. Without his fingers even touching the keys, he produces an unsettling music that grips them all with powerful emotion. The "miracle" of the popular pianola, which was advertised as a marker of middle-class attainment, is superseded by a *real* miracle.[12] The Todd family's pianola plays the "Turkish Tinkle Waltz," a melody whose title combines a safe sense of the exotic East (from which the "prince" is thought to have come) and the insipid connotations of "tinkle," in order to signify the middle-class philistinism of Reverend Todd. But this tune turns to something mysterious and gripping under Apollo's influence: "They listened with their heads, each in unison, a little on one side. Sound came from the piano in rhythm, in masses, in huge and triumphal chords; they died low; they swelled out again" (62). This moment turns Todd's daughter and her fiancé, who were otherwise good skeptical socialists, toward the recognition of Apollo's divinity (64–66). Similarly, in Corelli's *The Sorrows of Satan,* Geoffrey Tempest (for whose soul Satan vies) accompanies his fiendish friend to an evening at the house of Tempest's beloved Lady Sybil. "The Prince" plays the piano for the family and a few friends. As in *Mr. Apollo,* the music sounds miraculous: "The music swelled into passionate cadence,—melodies crossed and re-crossed each other like rays of light glittering among green leaves,—voices of birds and streams and tossing waterfalls chimed in with songs of love and playful merriment;—anon came wilder strains of grief and angry clamour; cries of despair were heard echoing through the thunderous noise of some relentless storm" (150). As in *Mr. Apollo,* the audience responds with amazement and emotion, even terror: "No one spoke,—our hearts were yet beating too wildly with the pulsations roused by that wondrous lyric storm" (150–151), and, as in *Mr. Apollo,* they ponder the pianist's miraculous compositions.

It is also during this scene in *The Sorrows of Satan* that the old countess, Lady Elton, shrieks in horror as she realizes that "the Prince" is in fact the Devil (157). In a similar though less sinister scene in *Mr. Apollo,* as "the Prince" causes the rays of the sun to illuminate the night sky and makes audible the music of the spheres, Margery Snyde shrieks: "It was wicked. . . . It is the work of devils" (137). It is suggestive that Margery like the countess in Corelli's novel, leaves sobbing and believes that "the Prince" (Apollo) is Satan (141), and that Corelli had even written of her "Prince" (Satan): "He smiled,—a musing, dreamy smile that transfigured his countenance and made him look like a fine Apollo absorbed in the thought of some new and glorious song" (168). Ford's witnesses to Apollo's miracle "approached the manifestations with a certain timidity; if they had occurred at a music-hall they would have laughed at them" (138).[13] Ford, with his familiarity with the Shepherd's Bush Empire, knew that melodramatic scenes like this were the staple not only of mass market novels, but also of the music hall; thus he tried, self-consciously, to work them into his romance.

It would be difficult to overestimate Corelli's popularity with many classes of readers during this period. Though the *Dictionary of National Biography* suggests her popularity began to wane around the beginning of the war, from the mid-1890s through 1908, the year Ford published *Mr. Apollo,* she wrote several best-sellers that sold hundreds of thousands of copies each (fourteen of them were listed in the Methuen catalogue at the back of *Mr. Apollo*). While writers such as Wells, Galsworthy, and Bennett were popular with certain sectors of the reading public, Corelli's readership crossed class and educational lines.[14] Whether or not *The Sorrows of Satan* inspired *Mr. Apollo,* Ford attempted to reproduce tried and true features of the popular novel in order to cut across class barriers and find a wide audience.[15]

It is not surprising, then, that it is in this novel that Ford—as he began to discuss plans for the *English Review* with Conrad, Arthur Marwood, and others—addressed explicitly another institution that was reaching wide audiences, the mass market daily. Toward the end of the novel, Alfred Milne, a teacher in the newly expanded mass education system and the protagonist of *Mr. Apollo,* brings Apollo to the offices of the *Daily Outlook.* Ford uses Milne's experience of Fleet Street and his conversation with Apollo about the paper to explore not only the significance of the mass market daily press, but also the relationship of class and educational positions to critical thinking and to the mass market.

In spite of the narrator's tone of self-assured maturity in his jibes at the daily press, *Mr. Apollo* evokes an uncertainty about the proper relationship between journals and the public that Ford would try to resolve with the publication of his own *English Review.* Milne's vision of Fleet Street brings Gissing's *New Grub Street* into the twentieth century and highlights the peculiarly modern excitement of the machinery of the newspaper press and its atmosphere of global importance: "To be in small alleys descried from Fleet Street, when the newspaper presses were at work, was already somewhat of a romance for Alfred Milne; when they passed basements of a steep ravine between houses of an obscure and suspect air, there came the vast roar of the presses at work; huge carts laden with rolls, like the cylinders of mangles, each roll labeled '500 miles of paper for the *Daily*–'; hurrying carters, chains and ropes, obscured the alley, lit up with flaring lights that gave to faces vivid tints, and turned green the sickly crescent of an unearthly and remote moon. Men without hats or men with them, hurried with tablets from building to building, wearing aspects of pensiveness, of irritation, or of jocularity; leonine, well got up, merely imbecile or unshaven" (212). Ford combines an ominous underworld atmosphere with an enticing vision of the modern vitality of the roaring presses, the transports carrying huge cylinders of paper, and the scurrying couriers that might have interested a Marinetti;[16] but the romance of Fleet Street falters. Milne is an interesting hybrid of educational and class positions, having fallen with his family's fortunes from the elite confines of Cambridge into the new mass education system. Likewise, the disintegration of his romantic conception of Fleet Street is figured as a tumble down the class ladder:

To the romantic side of Alfred Milne's mind these gentlemen represented Editors, Leaders of Opinion, or at least the powerful authors of leading articles. It pleased him to imagine this; and why, indeed, should he not indulge these imaginings? Subconsciously he was aware that the Great Ones would hardly be found in the streets without hats or bearing note-books; and, when he desired to be more precise, he set them down as descriptive reporters, readers for the press, sporting journalists, or the mere reviewers of books. But, to be sure, he could not be certain that even these lesser lights would be found at night in the courts and alleys of a black and devious neighborhood. Nevertheless, he was fairly certain that what was spun out of brains here, and reverberated into papers that night, would be all over England—all over the Empire and the world—on the morrow, and the lot of these men, with contented, assured, or even merely hungry aspects, appeared to him supremely desirable. For it seemed to him as if they must wield power. (212–213)

His vision of the inhabitants of Fleet Street degenerates from editors and opinion-molding writers to sports reporters (important especially to the lower and lower middle classes) and lowly reviewers, and finally to something slumlike and criminal in the "courts and alleys of a black and devious neighborhood."

Milne teaches in and was educated by the Board School system, the mass education that leads to mass mediocrity in Levenson's portrait of Ford (50). However, by granting Milne the cultural capital of his birth to country gentry and of his year at Cambridge Ford can more easily envision the possibility of "taste" and intelligence even in the product of the Board Schools. Milne's circle of socialists and advanced thinkers, in spite of their sometimes comical character, is composed of lower-middle-class products of the Board Schools and is a positive and critical group of thinkers in comparison to Reverend Todd's philistine middle-class circle. Ford posits the possibility of a lower- or lower-middle-class intelligentsia, but he does not explore its implications.

While Ford raises here the possibility that the reforms of the progressive alliance might create a broad-based reasoning society, the shady power of the vapid *Daily Outlook* seems far more important. Ford imagines the fragmentation of the public sphere to be less problematic, since education and reform might be able to supply the needed cohesion. However, he finds no ready solution to what he sees as the commercial press's debasement of critical thinking. Milne buttresses himself against the deflation of his romantic vision of Fleet Street by attributing power not to the unsavory people he sees in the street but to the newspaper itself. However, Ford undercuts this strategy immediately by adding, "It must be remembered that he was still young and inexperienced" (213). Ford's narrator positions himself as experienced, knowledgeable, mature, and able to see through the daily press. Indeed, childishness will become the central characteristic of mass audiences in the remainder of the novel. As they descend into the "crown of daily thought itself," Milne skeptically proclaims Lord Aldington's *Daily Outlook* to be "the organ of the greatest vulgarity in the world," by which he means the organ that appeals "to the commonest in the sense that they have the worst appetites—the appetites for the most evil fare" (213–214). Milne is at once excited by the vision of a powerful organ of public opinion and skeptical—it vulgarizes knowledge by pandering to vulgar taste, and clearly, in *Mr. Apollo,* vulgar taste is not merely a product of mass education or class position. Ford raises the possibility that the wider, Board School–educated reading public might be capable of critical thinking if it were offered a different type of journalism, but he cannot ignore the fact that to attract a readership in the millions, the press must pander to the most "vulgar" of tastes.

Ford uses *Mr. Apollo* to criticize the hypocrisy of the mass market press's pretensions to cultural improvement. Milne and Apollo visit Lord Aldington, a thinly veiled version of Harmsworth.[17] Aldington, often referred to satirically by the narrator as "the great man," proclaims that the paper is "a great duty; a great responsibility. We haven't only to appeal: we have to be an influence: we've got to educate" (255). But the novel portrays him as an opportunistic sensationalist, more interested in séances and mind readers than critical thinking. He is too childish to assume the role of educator. Milne and Apollo leave the office: "The visit over, most of the romance that beforehand had attached itself in [Milne's] mind to visiting the office of an Organ of Opinion had vanished . . . [Aldington] simply stood for the paper and the paper stood for him. They were a bi-une affair, you could not tell which led. . . . They would not ever lead the public, they were merely extraordinarily sympathetic to the Public breath" (286). Milne angrily feels that by "giving children straws to be amused with, [the paper] betrays its trust and is a danger. For it and its proprietor ought surely to regard themselves as schoolmaster and school; they ought to direct the public play with a view to a development of tastes and morality" (288).

The novel, however, complicates this stance, which would seem to be that of Ford and many others who railed against the irresponsibility and vacuousness of the popular press: Apollo *disagrees* with Milne's condemnation. To him, Aldington and in fact modern man seem (from his perspective as a god) to have the brain and heart of a child anyway. He adds that Milne has already proclaimed that it takes all sorts to make a republic, and that England is a great republic (a challenge that Ford would try to meet in his first *English Review* editorials, "The Function of the Arts in the Republic"). Milne cannot reconcile himself to this position, but the novel ends shortly thereafter with Milne and his wife devoting themselves to Apollo as his priest and priestess—in a sense endorsing his god's-eye view of humanity and his divine wisdom. This seems to have been as close as Ford could come in 1908 to recognizing that the mass circulation papers and the newly educated lower- to lower-middle-class readers who bought them represented an expansion of the print-driven public sphere to new, unheard-of dimensions that could have positive effects.

Mr. Apollo, with all its ambiguity and inability to resolve the issue of the proper relationship between journals and the public, marks an impasse in Ford's thinking about audiences and his role as a future editor of a journal of opinion. On the one hand, journals should foster a critical faculty in their readership; a true "Organ of Opinion" should be a part of a public sphere in which enlightened debate occurs without the corruption of commercialization; on the other hand, to reach a large enough sector of the population to be of national significance, papers and magazines must move toward the merely entertaining and unreflective—and this just suits mankind in the long run, Apollo would affirm. Although the mass audiences of the Harmsworth, Newnes, and Pearson papers made them enticing to Ford, he ultimately felt that he had to reject the methods and goals of the mass market papers as he began the *English Review,* and he makes this decision explicit in the prospectus (or manifesto) he circulated stating its goals and policies. Again, using metaphors of childhood and games, Ford attacks what he sees as the main characteristic of the popular press: "What will be avoided will be superficiality of the specially modern kind, which is the inevitable consequence when nothing but brevity of statement is aimed at. *The English Review* will treat its readers, not as spoiled children who must be amused by a variety of games, but with the respectful consideration due to grown-up minds whose leisure can be interested by something else than the crispness and glitter of a popular statement" (*English Review* Prospectus, repr. in Goldring, *South Lodge,* 24). In a diatribe that sounds remarkably like that against the "sound bite" of our own television age, but that has been repeated in each generation since at least the mid-Victorian age, Ford reduces the modern popular press to the fun and games and features that were so popular in the Edwardian period: the *Strand,* whose advertising filled an average of one hundred pages a month (R. Pound 79), ran for many years a feature called "Curiosities," which showcased freaks and aberrations of nature, such as "queer-shaped potatoes" (R. Pound 54), and *Tit-Bits,* the paper that made Newnes a millionaire, ran a contest in which it buried five hundred gold sovereigns in the countryside and hid clues to their whereabouts in a serial by Arthur Morrison (R. Pound 39). The half-penny *Daily Mail,* which advertised a "daily circulation *five times* as large as that of any penny London journal," also ran contests wherein readers could win up to one hundred guineas for answering riddles and questions. These games and the attitude toward intellectual inquiry and literature in these journals were, for Ford, the kind of child's play that the *English Review* would avoid.

Within a few years, Ford rounded off his swipe at Harmsworth and those who publish merely what they believe will be most entertaining to the widest audience. In the Twain-like *Ladies Whose Bright Eyes* (first published in July 1911), a modern man finds himself back in the Middle Ages. Ford chose for his modern man Mr. Sorrell, "a publisher and at the top of the tree" (7): "He was, too, proud of his profession. In the old days a publisher had to consider what was Literature. It had been uncommercial. Publishers had worked in a kid-glove sort of way, trying to establish friendly relations with authors. Now it was just a business. You found out what the public had to have and gave it them. And Mr. Sorrell held up his head with pride" (11). Of course, by the end of the novel, Mr. Sorrell is ready to abandon his modern life and live happily in fourteenth-century England. As he began to conceive the idea for this novel, Ford was trying to return a consideration of "what was literature" to publishing. But, stepping outside Ford's nostalgic longing for some golden age in which the press had been serious and enlightened, Keating's *Haunted Study* shows us that the expanded press and print culture of the period, in fact, provided *more* opportunities than ever for publishing fiction, and that the readership was wider than ever. While other modernist magazines turned to some aspects of the new mass marketing to promote themselves, as I shall discuss in chapters 3, 4, and 5, Ford turned to a different sector of

Edwardian mass publication—the venerable and commercially successful review journals—and to France for a model for his intervention into public life.

Ford and the *Mercure de France*

In an undated letter, probably from late 1908 or early 1909, Ford proclaimed to Arnold Bennett, then living in France, "I should like to exchange advertisements with the Mercure de France."[18] In another letter of December 2, 1908, shortly before the first issue of the *English Review* appeared, he eagerly discussed such an advertisement with a certain "Monsieur et cher Confrère": "I am asking the Assistant Editor to communicate at once with M. Vallette," the editor of the *Mercure de France*.[19] In this letter Ford also announced his desire to have French "diplomatic contributions" to the *English Review*, and to make them "as far as possible official." Ford hoped to bring to English audiences not only French literature, but also French political opinion. Moreover, Ford, who was notoriously inept at handling advertising and business affairs,[20] set aside editorial concerns to pursue an advertising exchange with the *Mercure de France* in particular. His effort underscores the crucial importance of the *Mercure* to Ford's thinking about what type of journal the *English Review* should be.

Although Ford decided not to pursue the forms and strategies of mass market periodicals like the *Daily Mail* and the *Strand*, I want to challenge any assumption that Ford wanted the *English Review* to cater to the exquisite tastes of a coterie. Between these two extremes, there was room in Edwardian London for other types of periodicals that took their literary and intellectual responsibilities seriously while also attempting to cultivate large readerships. Contrary to Habermas's concern about the public sphere and to Ford's own rhetoric, the expansion of the commercial press did not occur at the expense of serious intellectual journals, even if Ford wished to change the nature of these journals. Ford turned to the *Mercure de France* as his inspiration for a journal that could critically cover a wider range of materials and appeal to a broader audience than the dominant English reviews did. In the *Mercure*, the journal that also influenced Ezra Pound and Richard Aldington,[21] he saw an embodiment of the spirit of the Enlightenment, an age during which, Ford felt, rationality and order were spread throughout the populace. The use of an evenhanded and centrist tone to incorporate a wide range of common experience, from the orthodox to the heterodox, allowed the *Mercure* to create a sense not only of public space, but also of a cohesive French culture—an achievement that Ford wished to emulate in England.

To understand Ford's interest in the *Mercure de France* as a model for the *English Review,* one must understand that Ford perceived France as a culture of rationality, of broad-ranging inquiry, of responsibility to the all-important exactitudes of language; a culture resilient (and in its own way conservative), with a bedrock of ordering traditions and centralizing institutions like the French Academy. In short, France for Ford was the Enlightenment. The critical project of the *English Review*—espousing a spirit of disinterested inquiry inherited from Matthew Arnold in an English cultural context—found fertile ground in Ford's vision of French culture.

In "The Function of the Arts in the Republic: IV. The Plastic Arts," a 1909 *English Review* editorial with Arnoldian resonances, Ford laments that English writers and artists are too individualistic and that they subordinate their art to social aspirations: they try to become "men of action." Because they envision their art instrumentally, as a means to an end, and not terminally, as aesthetic disinterestedness would require, they pay no attention to craft, and this lack has disastrous consequences: "The actual practice of his craft thus loses its cohesive force, so that it is almost impossible to find in England what is found in almost every other European capital—a society of men eagerly discussing their Art, sinking personal jealousies in the thirst for mutual sharpening of the wits, in the divine curiosity to discover how things are done. The English man of letters of any distinction lives apart, dotted over the face of the country, each one isolated, as it were, upon a little hill." The English writer suffers from the lack of central institutions and critical forums: "He has no Academy like that of the Immortal Forty; he belongs to no movement and in consequence the Art of Letters in England has practically no social weight and practically no contact with the life of the people. It is with the attempt to form some such meeting-place that The English Review has set out upon its career." It is neither a coincidence, nor entirely due to Arnold, that Ford turns to the *French* Academy in this passage. Ford felt that France had a vital culture characterized by public discussion—by public institutions like the Academy and by artists disinterestedly "sinking personal jealousies" for "mutual sharpening of wits." Thus disinterestedness implies intellectual and artistic community. In contrast, Ford felt that England had no cultural consensus and inspired only isolated artistic endeavor. While Ford ultimately rejected publishing mass market "popular" fiction as a means to bring literature into "contact with the life of the people," he also anathematized high-brow artistic isolation and cultural fragmentation just as vehemently. If literature were to rejuvenate the republic, it would have to have centralizing cultural institutions at its disposal, and Ford wanted the *English Review* to play such a role.

Ford also turned to France to support his vision of a rejuvenated English poetry. He felt that poetry should be a "record of events, assimilated by the human mind today" ("The Function of the Arts in the Republic: I.

33

Literature," 159). In his famous preface to the *Collected Poems of Ford Madox Hueffer* (1914), a preface that probably had more impact on modernist poetry of the period than did the poems themselves, Ford remembered the importance of French literary traditions to the founding of the *English Review* (24–25), and he called for modern poets to write not of "love," "country lanes," or "the singing of birds," but of urban mass events like music hall and public exhibitions: "I think pathos and poetry are to be found beneath those lights and in those sounds."[22] Ford's point in this guarded affirmation of the crowd and of mass culture in his preface is that poetry ought to document contemporaneity with precision and depth, and that mass culture is a vital part of modern urban life. But this preface is not a call for poems like the occasional verse printed in mass market periodicals, which almost always employed self-consciously "poetic" diction, inversion, and archaism and were usually either humorous or sappily sentimental. Rather, Ford imagines a "mass," even "vulgar," poetry of the contemporary. Because it had restricted its subjects and language to those fashionable in poetry half a century before, Ford argued, English poetry artificially perpetuated cultural fragmentation and marginalized itself. To facilitate cultural cohesion, and yet not to descend to the level of mass market poetics, Ford saw the possibility of a distinction between "public" and "popular," which, I believe, was inflected by his vision of French literature. But this poetry would involve not only a shift of subjects, but also of language, and Ford projects onto France his desire for a populace whose language is vital and to whom the arts are still relevant: France becomes the imaginary culture that Ford desired for England, a myth of the whole through which Ford could promote the literature he admired.

Ford suggested that the lack of a large audience for poetry in England was due to the artificiality and irrelevance of English poetry to modern life, particularly in poets' avoidance of contemporary language.[23] He emphasized the need for English poetry to break from self-consciously "poetic" diction and themes, and from the archaisms and superfluities of Tennyson that had stultified it, to something more like the prose line of Flaubert. For Ford there is something particularly French about this precise and marvelously productive language of the everyday: "It is something a matter of diction. In France, upon the whole, a poet—and even a quite literary poet—can write in a language that, roughly speaking, any hatter can use" (*Collected Poems* 14). France cannot (or so it seems to Ford) be culturally fragmented along class or high–low culture lines if the language of the poet is also that of the hatter.

For Ford, the French language exemplifies France's vital everyday cultural cohesion, but the French people's precision with their language also takes part in *creating* that cultural cohesion. In 1915, in the second of his war propaganda books, Ford writes, "In the end, the relative values of civilizations come down always to being matters of scrupulosity of language" (*Between St. Dennis and St. George,* hereafter cited as *BSD* 67).[24] He notes that "France is always exactly right according to her aspirations as she is true in her phraseology" (69), and that "it is only by the careful and strained attention to the fine shades of language in common use that comprehension of language can be reached" (205). French writers, as he laboriously shows by attempting the intricacies of translating the first sentence of Flaubert's *Un Coeur Simple,* command the precision and potential of their language in a way that English writers often do not. As early as the turn of the century he had written to Edward Garnett about starting a "popular library of literature . . . conceived on the broad general idea of making manifest, to the most unintelligent, how great writers *get their effects*" (*Letters* 15). Ford frequently figures the proper artist as a scientist, and he hoped to discover in England "any trace of a sober, sincere, conscientious and scientific body of artists, crystallising, as it were, modern life in its several aspects" (*Critical Attitude* 29). Good art is imagined, as it would be by T. E. Hulme and by imagists and vorticists in a few years, as hard, precise, ascetic—attributes which for Ford also characterize French language and culture.

But what is at stake for Ford is not just the issue of poetic craft, but a larger cultural vision. The French peasants' age-old adages reinforce or even create a stability that Ford felt might save Europe from ruin, and, he warns, it is by "the madness of inexact and aspiring phrase-making of the industrial system, of materialism, of false Napolconism and the rest of the paraphernalia of life as we live it to-day, Europe, if it be lost, will have been lost" (*BSD* 68).[25] French rationality as reflected in common language gives the French the resilience to survive under many different types of government (*BSD* 197).

Ford imagined that this strength was best reflected in the eighteenth-century preindustrial France of the Enlightenment, and he often explicitly linked contemporary France with the eighteenth century. In the novel *Some Do Not* (1924), he writes of the protagonist Christopher Tietjens (who is based in many ways on Marwood and on Ford himself), "The French he admired: for their tremendous efficiency, for their frugality of life, for the logic of their minds, for their admirable achievements in the arts, for their neglect of the industrial system, for their devotion, above all, to the eighteenth century" (*Parade's End* 187). Valentine Wannop, a suffragette, sees Tietjens himself as increasingly out of place in the twentieth century: "*He* was eighteenth-century all right. . . . But then the eighteenth century never went mad. The only century that never went mad" (*Parade's End* 647). In this novel of the war, England and Germany epitomize the twentieth century and France the eighteenth: "But [the English] coming in [to the war] had changed the aspect at once. It was one part of the twentieth century using the eighteenth as a catspaw to bash the other half of the twentieth" (*Parade's End* 236).

Yet Ford is not a reactionary calling for a return to the politics of preindustrial France or, as his preface to the *Collected Poems* makes clear, to earlier literary conventions. Rather, he imagined the spirit of the French Enlightenment and of current French culture to be based on a vital sense of contemporaneity. Moreover, as it had for Arnold, the Enlightenment provided Ford with an ideal of rational deliberation, or Hellenism; and both the Enlightenment and the chivalric code supplied a vision of cultural order and cohesion that he felt modern England lacked.[26] Ford and Arnold saw French order and rationality embodied in France's institutions and traditions, but, above all, in its prose, and they both looked back to the eighteenth-century Enlightenment as the origin of a prose of critical reason.[27] Ford traces a genealogy of this type of writing from Richardson to Diderot and the Encyclopedists, to Chateaubriand, to Flaubert, Maupassant, Turgenev and the Goncourts, and finally to James and Conrad (*Critical Attitude* 93). The sequence both begins and ends in England, but it ends with two nonnative modern writers who were both deeply steeped in French literature: James and Conrad embody Ford's vision of a rejuvenated English culture.

With this Enlightenment vision of French culture in mind, we may now begin to answer the question, why did the *Mercure de France* in particular appeal to Ford as he assembled the *English Review*? The *Mercure de France* represented everything Ford hoped his magazine would bring to English culture. It ranged broadly in its inquiry, adopted a centrist position and what could be called a disinterested tone, incorporated the heterodox (including much of the best avant-garde work of several countries), enjoyed cultural prestige and authority in France, created an inclusive sense of a public, and had a venerable history as an Enlightenment periodical.

The *Mercure de France* in its modern form was founded in December 1889 by a group of important young writers led by Alfred Vallette and including Rémy de Gourmont, the novelist Rachilde (Vallette's wife), and Laurent Tailhade.[28] Though the editors had tried to avoid being only "un recueil symboliste," the early issues of the *Mercure* were almost entirely devoted to literature, the theater, and art, taking a great interest in symbolism, van Gogh, and aesthetic theories.[29] But as it began to increase in size, it also gradually expanded its scope to include more essays, reviews, and subjects other than art and literature. Most of the French little magazines of the 1880s and 1890s died quickly, and even some of the larger ones collapsed early in the new century.[30] Michel Décaudin suggests that Vallette saved the *Mercure* in 1896 by realizing "l'union du journal et du recueil" (15)—what, in an English literary framework, might be the result of joining a small serious journal of pure literature and art, like the *Yellow Book,* with a broad-ranging review like the *Fortnightly* or the *Contemporary.* This combination allowed the *Mercure* to maintain a wide readership while still publishing experimental literature. By the addition in April 1896 of a section entitled "Revue du Mois," the *Mercure* had ceased entirely to be a "recueil symboliste" and became one of the leading French periodicals, a position it still held at the time of the founding of the *English Review* (see Bussard).

The "Revue du Mois," I would argue, appealed to Ford because it created a sense of a public and of common experience. It regularly reviewed publications on many facets of French life. It provided the intellectual "glue" to hold seemingly every element of a culture together, to give the public a sense of the cohesion of a wide range of experiences and beliefs. In the first issue, Vallette had expressed his wish for the *Mercure* to be able to publish "ouvres purement artistiques et . . . conceptions assez hétérodoxes pour n'être point accueillies des feuilles qui compétent avec la clientèle" ("Mercure" 4). The *Mercure* maintained a very high quality of literature and intellectual articles without falling prey to overt partisanship or elitist disdain for the quotidian or the public. It followed symbolism, Sorel, Joyce, Yeats, Pound, and new developments in art, published articles by Severini, and ran a regular section by Apollinaire. It published reviews of foreign literature,[31] and soon added sections on history, moral and religious questions, foreign countries, politics, archaeology, psychology, concerts, art galleries, the circus, theater, the cabaret, and the colonies—to name a few—and numerous current debates. The *Mercure* even began to print readers' responses to its articles, thus acknowledging and including its audience and furthering a sense of public space.[32] The expansion of the magazine's scope and its disinterested tone allowed it to include the heterodox safely alongside the most conservative views.

The *Mercure de France* had quickly emerged as an authoritative and centrist review that put comprehensiveness at a premium.[33] Its brief reviews of just about every imaginable topic projected an even tone, not the heated, doctrinaire attacks we associate with avant-gardism and little magazines. It passed judgment, but in a polite and respectful way. Ford was able to believe that French periodicals, like the *Mercure* and the *Revue des Deux Mondes* (a similarly centrist journal), were able to speak for the nation in a way that English periodicals could not.[34] Though French *revue* magazines were polarized by such conflicts as the Dreyfus Affair, and no single periodical could really speak for such a divided culture (see Tuchman 206), set against the partisan tone of the English journals, Ford's construction of the French magazines allowed him to position his magazine as a new kind of literary product.

Since Ford imagined the Enlightenment as the historical embodiment of disinterested criticism and centrist cultural institutions, the *Mercure de France* was the perfect model for his *English Review.* When the *Mercure* reappeared in 1890, it already had a venerable history (see Deville). The small group of *jeunes* who forsook the *Pléiade* to form their journal chose to resurrect one of the oldest and longest running of all French journals. On the title page the *Mercure* boasted that it was "fondé en 1672," and that this was the "serie moderne." It even employed the symbol of the old *Mercure de France,* the winged Mercury traveling across the clouds, bringing the knowledge and wisdom of the entire world to its French readers. Like its modern counterpart, the original *Mercure* had catered to a broad scope of interests; it had represented enlightened inquiry and the support of serious literature and even enjoyed a court audience and the patronage of the king.[35] In invoking this venerable journal, Vallette and his young cutting-edge writers positioned themselves not as an avant-garde opposition to any establishment or institution, but rather as a new incarnation of an Enlightenment institution, from a long tradition of cultural centrality—a move that no doubt increased Ford's attraction to the journal.

Using the *Mercure de France* as his model, Ford began each number of the *English Review* with the nonmainstream literature of James, Conrad, Lewis, Pound, and others, while including more popular writers like Vernon Lee and Maurice Hewlett. He ended the issue with his own version of the "Revue du Mois": "The Month" was a section in which he, like Remy de Gourmont, would begin with an editorial that would be followed by a series of articles and reviews of wider interest.[36] Ford explains in the first issue of the *English Review* (in his section of "The Month") that "the topics of the month are the production of a well-flavoured book, the commencement of a historic series, the production of a play not too shallow, the chronicling of a symphony, the opening of a gallery containing fine etchings" (Dec. 1908, 158). "The Month" occasionally included sections like "Spectacle and the Drama" (May 1909), which reviewed current productions at five London theaters. Though it never attained the close interaction with the everyday cultural life of London that the *Mercure* did with Paris, this involvement seems to have been Ford's goal.

Like the "Revue de la Quinzaine" (which the "Revue du Mois" had become after the *Mercure* became a fortnightly in 1905), "The Month" included articles on politics, world affairs, and economics, and it featured reviews by established and respected writers, such as Conrad's review of Anatole France's *L'Ile des Pingouins,* and just as the *Mercure* did not eschew members of the French Academy or established university academics, the *English Review* was not interested only in the marginalized avant-gardist. Like the *Mercure's* sections of reviews of foreign literature, "The Month" included articles like Camille Mauclair's "Le Roman Français Contemporaire," and Doctor Levin Schücking's "Some Notes on Present-

Day German Literature." It had taken the *Mercure* a number of years to expand the "Revue du Mois" section into the ambitious and comprehensive organ that it became, and Ford was forced out of the magazine too early to have had the chance to equal this achievement. But the tentative and small-scale experiment of "The Month" gestures in the direction of the *Mercure de France*'s example.

Ford, then, tried to create for England a magazine that had not only the disinterestedness and wide range of inquiry of the *Mercure,* but also its ability to publish nonmainstream and even avant-garde literature while maintaining a central position of cultural authority and a large reading audience. Such a position would allow Ford to make literary modernism key to his intervention in public culture. No single magazine in the English periodical scene embodied all of these features. The *Mercure de France* resonated with Ford's "myth of the whole" about French culture and served as a model for his literary aspirations in the *English Review.* However, the *Mercure* could not be directly transplanted to English soil.

The Edwardian Reviews: The *English Review* and the *Fortnightly Review*

To understand the form in which the *English Review* entered the Edwardian public sphere as well as the way in which this very form contributed to a reception that undermined Ford's intentions to create a discursive space of disinterested critical reason and cultural revitalization, we now turn to the institutions of Edwardian periodical publication. The concept of genre is key to understanding the reception of the *English Review:* as Hans Robert Jauss argues, the literary work "predisposes its audience to a very specific kind of reception by announcements, overt and covert signals, familiar characteristics, or implicit allusions" (23).[37] A literary magazine is a text whose reception and creation are based on genre conventions established by other periodicals. Moreover, a magazine is not just a collection of individual literary works, each of which also has its own reception; it is something more than the sum of its parts. Material markers of genre, such as price, page size, types of advertising, and frequency of publication, all contribute to a reader's horizon of expectations for a magazine. The combination of types of literary activity that regularly make up a successful literary journal reflects a literary culture in a way that any particular piece in it cannot. In Ford's attempt to promote the *English Review* as a disinterested centrist forum that could accommodate a wide range of heterodoxy, he tried to redraw the boundaries of the genre by which it was interpreted. Ford's successes and failures with the *English Review* enhance our understanding both of the literary culture of Edwardian London in which early British modernism struggled to take hold and of that struggle itself.

Jauss explores the changing meanings of literary texts over time, positing the "initial horizon" as a crucial element in the understanding of a work of literature. It is this initial horizon that I wish to uncover for the *English Review*. In 1908, as Ford conceived his magazine, there were several prominent genres of Edwardian periodicals that published or discussed literature. There were ½d. or 1d. daily papers, like the *Daily News,* the *Daily Mail,* or the *Pall Mall Gazette,* some of which ran fiction serials in brief installments (generally sentimental or love stories) and often included a literary supplement (like the one for which Ford wrote in the *Daily Mail*). The daily newspapers leaned in partisan directions but were devoted as well to reporting sports, the weather, crime cases, and the like. The weeklies, in contrast, typically ran to about thirty multicolumn, folio-sized pages; they moved far beyond the reporting and short editorials of the dailies into the realm of political and cultural debate, running longer analyses and polemics. They tended to cost from 3d. (the *Athenæum* and the *Academy*) to 6d. (the *Spectator* and the *Saturday Review*) per issue, and they often were unabashedly partisan in their politics, even including this affiliation in advertising directories like *Willings* or the *Newspaper Press Directory.* Generally, the weeklies did not publish literature (only an occasional poem, often of a political nature) and consisted of editorials on politics and reviews of current art and literature. Their weekly status allowed them to follow current events and political and literary developments in a timely fashion. The quarterlies (increasingly rare in the Edwardian period), such as the *Edinburgh* and the *Quarterly,* used the smaller page size of the monthlies, with single columns, but were enormous—often exceeding three hundred pages in length. They cost 6s. (the cost of a new novel). Like the weeklies, they were often partisan and did not publish literature. They reviewed political affairs, literature, and cultural events but were able to print longer essays than the weeklies could. Monthlies could be mass market entertainment venues like the 6d. illustrated *Strand,* with its circulation of more than half a million readers. Or they could be almost purely literary magazines like the *Cornhill* at 1s., whose material included conventional popular fiction serials, works by established authors such as Hewlett, Housman, and Mrs. Humphry Ward, some poetry, and articles on literature by academics.

The most prominent class of monthly, however, was the great monthly review—the mainstay of "serious" Edwardian intellectual, political, and literary culture and the genre by which English audiences interpreted the *English Review.* Beginning with magazines like the *Fortnightly Review* (1865), the Victorian era produced a new magazine genre that aspired to represent multiple conflicting political and social points of view. While Habermas sees the political press as instrumental to the creation of the liberal public sphere, the newspapers and magazines that created this discursive public space each represented a single point of view: they were often even written by a single person (*Structural* 183–184). The diversity of these voices created a sense of public space. However, the mid-Victorian reviews for a time tried to create a public space for rational deliberation *within* each magazine—an impulse important to the *English Review.* Founded by G. H. Lewes and Anthony Trollope in 1865, the *Fortnightly* (which only briefly remained a fortnightly) quickly became one of the major monthly reviews of the later Victorian period and maintained its enviable position of authority and respectability through the Edwardian period. The *Fortnightly* brought a new genre of Victorian review to the educated reading public. Like Ford, Lewes and Trollope had turned to a French journal for inspiration and explicitly cited the Parisian *Revue des Deux Mondes* as its model in a prospectus in the *Saturday Review* of March 25, 1865. The *Fortnightly* combined two previously popular Victorian journal genres: the monthly miscellany magazine, with its patchwork of literature and articles on a variety of topics of interest, and the review (like the *Spectator, Edinburgh,* and the *Quarterly*) that discussed literature and politics but did not publish fiction or poetry itself. Perhaps most important and controversial, the *Fortnightly* broke from the longstanding review convention of anonymity and popularized the signed article.

The *Fortnightly Review* aimed (not always successfully) to avoid the overt partisanship of the old reviews by publishing a wide range of opinion. Adopting this strategy from the *Revue des Deux Mondes* and employing a strong Arnoldian tone (Arnold himself was a contributor), the *Fortnightly*'s prospectus claimed that the journal would reach out to readers of all classes with articles by the best writers in several fields, and it would avoid the kind of partisan or editorial consistency that in other journals "hamper[ed] the full and free expression of opinion." With the rising power of central party organizations, disinterestedness at midcentury had very emphatically come to mean avoidance of party affiliation. As I have noted, the party apparatus had helped to transform political debate into the public relations work of the central party. While the nineteenth century saw the rise of the practice of partisan sponsorship and creation of newspapers,[38] the mid-Victorian monthlies tried to answer Arnold's call for a disinterested criticism aloof from daily parliamentary politics. John Mason notes that "Even journals like the *Nineteenth Century* and *National Review,* which stood close to the Liberal and Conservative party establishments, rarely spoke with sympathy for the parliamentary viewpoint. Indeed, one of the distinguishing characteristics of the reviews was their undisguised scorn for the compromise of party politics" (292). From Arnold's time to Ford's, free expression, even if consistent with party ideology, seemed to entail the ability to proclaim oneself "above" the mechanics of the party.

The early *Fortnightly* also attempted to confront the entrance of the working classes into the public sphere by opening itself up to the interests and concerns of all classes. The strictures of partisanship seemed to foreclose debate and imply fragmentation into private interests, whereas creating a single organ to encompass all classes gestured toward cultural cohesion and, again, the transcendence of private interest in the name of the disinterested free play of thought. The differing positions held by each magazine or newspaper in the liberal public sphere had largely remained within the range of interests of the bourgeoisie, because "the public" did not include the lower classes. The *Fortnightly* itself tried to *become* a discursive space that could expand the dimensions of "the public."

However, in reality there was very little in the *Fortnightly* that would have appealed to a wide working-class audience, and even its attempts to avoid the strictures of partisanship did not wholly succeed. Trollope complained that whereas liberals and radicals would willingly publish alongside conservatives, the Tories generally avoided sharing pages with liberals, so the *Fortnightly* displayed a liberal or radical tendency. The *Fortnightly*'s Arnoldian vision of disinterested thought was predicated on a level of social cohesion that did not exist in mid-Victorian England and perhaps never could exist.

Moreover, Mason argues that magazines in the 1860s and 1870s had attacked the established order, but "the combination of the socialist attack on property and Gladstone's attempt to pass the Irish Home Rule Bill in 1886 pushed a majority of the liberal intelligentsia closer to the conservative party in defense of the existing economic and social system" (293). I suggest that this trend further undermines Habermas's historical notions that the liberal public sphere was ever an arena of rational deliberation about the public good and that commercialism was a key cause of the "decline." Rather, the retrenchment of the liberal press that Mason discusses shows that within a certain safe homogeneity and cohesion, heterodoxy can be tolerated as disinterested criticism—and thus the mid-Victorian monthlies could accommodate a certain range of opinion. But when the stability of the system is radically challenged by a voice previously excluded from the "public," disinterestedness is revealed as private interests—in this case, of property owners and those who benefited most from imperial control of Ireland.

The *Fortnightly*'s format, however, was a commercial success and spawned other prosperous imitators, such as the *Contemporary* (1866) and the *Nineteenth Century* (1877) (see Everett; and Graham 256–270). And, in spite of their inability to live up to their early goals, these journals rose to cultural prominence in the Victorian period and continued to be venues for those with authority to speak on political, social, and literary affairs. Members of Parliament and professors, presidents of major institutions, cabinet members, eminent scientists, men of letters, novelists, poets, and playwrights all wrote substantial articles and contributed literature to these monthly organs of opinion. In 1908, the major reviews were the *Fortnightly, Contemporary, Nineteenth Century and After,* and *National,* with *Blackwood's* and the *Westminster* following closely behind. They averaged from around 150 to 200 pages in length, typically on 9 ½-by-6-inch paper with single columns, and in 1908, they each cost 2s. 6d. per issue (five times the cost of the popular *Strand*). The weeklies and dailies almost always kept up with the major articles coming out in the monthlies, and, collectively, they encapsulated much of the intellectual and political culture of the Edwardian period.

Ford's attempt to rejuvenate the public sphere had turned to French models, as had the mid-Victorian *Fortnightly Review.* In many ways, the earlier effort serves as a precursor to the *English Review,* but the *Fortnightly,* one of the most important journals of the Edwardian period, was not entirely what Ford had in mind for the *English Review.* During the Edwardian period, the *Fortnightly* was edited by W. L. Courtney, a director and one-time chairman of Chapman and Hall Publishers and a leader writer for the *Daily Telegraph.* Courtney edited the review from 1895 until his death in 1928, and, abandoning the more radical political frays of the Victorian journal and its hopes to embody a truly inclusive ideal of publicity,[39] he achieved a solid, respectable, and authoritative cultural position for it while continuing to publish "high-quality" literature. The daring experiment of Lewes's *Fortnightly* changed the field of reviews and was, in turn, changed by them—it yielded to more commercial and political concerns, and it flourished. Though this safer *Fortnightly* was not Ford's ideal, he certainly must have admired the magazine's success.

Under Courtney, the *Fortnightly* was one of the privileged few monthlies to be reviewed every month in W. T. Stead's successful and internationally distributed experiment in brief summary, the *Review of Reviews,* as well as in the *Spectator*'s "The Magazines" section. Diverse periodicals regularly followed the *Fortnightly,* and, in general, when a daily or weekly reviewed the monthly reviews, it always discussed the *Fortnightly*—often in more detail than it granted the other monthlies.

The *Fortnightly* possessed the intellectual prestige and cultural authority that Ford wished the *English Review* to acquire. It featured the top names in a wide variety of fields. It published academic literary critics like Professors Maurice Gerothwohl and John Churton Collins—the crusader for English literature in the universities—and it frequently included Edmund Gosse, John Galsworthy, and William Archer (the apostle for Ibsen and modern drama). It published political articles by Wells, Belloc, Arthur Griffiths, *New Age* regular J. M. Kennedy, and Ramsay MacDonald, and it kept readers apprised of world events and domestic issues like the suffrage movement. The *Fortnightly* occasionally ran articles on art, such as those by Walter Sickert and Roger Fry, and it gave space to emerging fields like anthropology, with essays by Sir James Frazer and Jane Harrison. It covered science, and it even devoted regular space to sports. It nodded to the original spirit of the review by occasionally publishing some Conservative and Unionist articles, but it tended toward Liberal and even socialist pieces. Indeed, as heirs to the genre that the *Fortnightly Review* had created, Edwardian monthly reviews officially tried to avoid the overt party affiliation of the weeklies, sometimes publishing opposing points of view, but they nevertheless had discernible partisan tendencies; thus Ford's claim that the *English Review* would have "no party bias" was especially significant.

Finally, the *Fortnightly* dedicated a large portion of each issue—up to one-third—to literary articles, fiction, and poetry. Its frequent prominent contributors included Hardy, Maeterlinck, Tolstoy, Hewlett, Eden Philpotts, and Vernon Lee, and it published such important figures of the day as Wells, Meredith, Ford, Binyon, and Housman, as well as occasional lesser-knowns like May Sinclair and Ezra Pound. So, Courtney's *Fortnightly Review* featured a wide variety of articles and literature. It had a major publisher, steady readership, and strong intellectual content; it mixed the general with the more specific article, and it rarely slipped into pedantry or unpopular esoteric studies. Before the founding of Orage's *New Age* in 1907 and Ford's *English Review* in December 1908, the *Fortnightly* was *the* place to publish modern and even mildly controversial literature. James Pinker, the pioneering literary agent of hundreds of authors from Bennett, Ford, Hunt, and even, briefly, James Joyce, to the most mass market writers, and the man who probably knew the ins and outs of London literary publication better than any other man of his day, counseled Violet Hunt about a group of unconventional stories she was trying to publish. In a letter of February 28, 1908, he wrote: "'The Coach of Death,' indeed, seems to me first class, but it is only likely to appeal to something like the *Fortnightly;* and the others, though in a less degree, would also be unacceptable to most editors," and he added, "It becomes increasingly difficult to place stories of this calibre, as most of the magazines exact something more or less conventional in plot and treatment."[40]

This was the state of affairs in 1908 when the *English Review* began publication. The monthly reviews enjoyed the sort of cultural authority that Levenson suggests Ford was forced to reject. But it is precisely this niche of the Edwardian periodical world that Ford attempted to enter with his *English Review.* Ford adapted his vision of an English *Mercure de France* to meet the requirements of the Edwardian scene and thus made his *English Review* a monthly, not a fortnightly like the *Mercure* or *Revue des Deux Mondes* (there were no prominent fortnightly journals in Edwardian England). The *English Review's* material character—its length and page size—was comparable to the Edwardian monthly reviews, and Ford gave it a title that certainly would steer its reception in this direction. He also priced it at 2s. 6d., the price of all the major monthly reviews, and advertised it in the same way that they advertised—for a while, running advertisements in the dailies, but always publishing in the weeklies advertisements that listed the contents of the upcoming issue. Like the *Fortnightly,* the *English Review* advertised in the *Spectator* and the *Saturday Review* (even advertising *twice* monthly in the *Saturday Review,* once at the end of the month and again as the new issue came out), as well as in more liberal weeklies such as the *Nation.* Thus it tried to acquire its audience from readers with a wide range of political affiliations.

Emphasizing its affinity with the reviews, rather than with the almost purely literary *Cornhill,* the *English Review's* advertisements always mentioned some of the political articles in addition to the literary content.[41] Like the other monthly reviews, the *English Review* eschewed such eye-catching advertising gimmicks of mass market papers and products as illustrations, hyperbolic catchphrases, extreme variance in print type or size, and contests or prizes for subscribers. By the end of 1909, like the *Fortnightly,* the *English Review* had gained the advantage of frequent reviews in Stead's *Review of Reviews* and in the *Spectator.* It was discussed regularly by the *Saturday Review, Academy, Athenæum,* and the *Pall Mall Gazette* alongside the *Fortnightly.*

The links between the *Fortnightly* and the *English Review* are highlighted by the aftermath of a squabble between the *Spectator* and the *English Review* provoked by Frank Harris (an old *Fortnightly* editor who eventually earned the distinction of being "blessed" by Lewis in *Blast*). The *English Review* published an article on morality by Harris that seemed so scandalous to the ever-conservative John St. Loe Strachey, editor of the *Spectator,* that in the June 10, 1911, issue, in "The Great Adult Review," the *Spectator* announced its refusal to review the magazine again in its columns. This, of course, provoked angry letters written to the *Spectator* as well as a reply in the *English Review.* The response, merely entitled "*The Spectator:* A Reply," was a list of ninety-six famous and respectable contributors to the *English Review,* from Hardy, Shaw, Conrad, James, and Wells, to Gosse, Belloc, Swinburne, and Yeats, to the soon-to-be poet laureate Robert Bridges, to such worthies as the Duchess of Sutherland, Lady Margaret Sackville, and several members of Parliament—Ramsay MacDonald and Sir Gilbert Parker among them. They lent their reputations to attest to the absurdity of the *Spectator's* charges that the *English Review* was an immoral publication.

The list reads like a Who's Who of Edwardian literature, criticism, and politics, but most important for my purposes, it also reads like a table of contents for the *Fortnightly Review* during the same period. Of the ninety-six signatories, more than half contributed to the *Fortnightly Review* from 1905 to the end of the war years. Most published multiple pieces in it, and nine of them appeared frequently or regularly in the *Fortnightly Review*.[42] So the *English Review* and the *Fortnightly Review* not only occupied a similar cultural niche in the Edwardian journal-reading world, but also shared many of their regular contributors. These respected authors were largely responsible for the success of the *English Review*. After Ford was ousted as editor and the publisher, Duckworth, abandoned the magazine, fittingly, the *Fortnightly*'s publisher, Chapman and Hall, took over the *English Review*. Of all the magazines to move in more radical literary directions, the *English Review* was not only the most like the *Fortnightly* but also the most successful in the long run. The *New Age* ran only into the early 1920s, and, of the more avant-garde magazines, *Poetry and Drama* lasted two years, *Blast* two issues, and the *Egoist,* even with Harriet Shaw Weaver's patronage, only five years. The *Fortnightly* ran from 1865 to 1954 and the *English Review* from 1908 to 1937.

So, while Ford's *English Review* has been widely lauded as the great literary magazine of its day, and a major supporter of literary modernism in both poetry and fiction, its cultural position and reception must be understood against the background of the genre of journal whose founder and greatest surviving member was the *Fortnightly*.[43] However, though Ford was looking to the *Mercure de France* of the present, he was following the *Fortnightly Review* of the past. He aimed at broad-ranging nonpartisan critical inquiry,[44] and, as has been widely documented, he attempted to foster a critical sense that would improve not only the writing, but also the reception of modern literature in England.[45] Ford and Conrad, who helped him conceive the review, attempted to steer it clear of factionalism in both politics and literature.[46] Fostering a "school of literature," for the *English Review,* meant providing a public space to gather the best of the writers whom Ford felt were modern and important, rather than insisting on conformity to a certain style of writing, or furthering the careers of a handful of writers regardless of the merit of their latest work. As I have suggested, from the mid-Victorian era through Ford's time party politics seemed to represent "interestedness" and underscored the fragmentation of English culture and society. Ford's vision of France, and the rational, cohesive, ordered culture of the Enlightenment, led him to view the ability to entertain multiple perspectives within a single institution as the mark of disinterestedness.

As important as the *Fortnightly* was to Edwardian literary and intellectual culture, though, it was not adequate to the needs of the younger generation of the modernists: despite the similarities between the *English Review* and the *Fortnightly,* there were important differences that highlight what I see as modernist about Ford's magazine. The *English Review,* like the *Mercure de France,* included the heterodox alongside its more orthodox contributions; like the *Fortnightly,* it published such noncommercial writers as Hardy and Maeterlinck, but it welcomed the work eschewed by the *Fortnightly.* For instance, in a story so often repeated that it barely needs rehearsing here, Ford even claimed (with typical embellishment) to have launched the *English Review* solely to publish Hardy's "Sunday Morning Tragedy," a poem about premarital sex and a botched abortion that no other journal would accept. Remaining faithful to the established talents that it shared with the *Fortnightly,* like Hewlett, Cunninghame Graham, Vernon Lee, and James, the *English Review* also took more risks with new and more radical writers. Not only did the *English Review* publish more literature per volume than the *Fortnightly,* confusing the reading public who wanted to view it either as a literary magazine or a monthly review, but it also featured more young, unknown talent. D. H. Lawrence's long allegiance to the *English Review,* even after he felt that it had declined under Austin Harrison, derives from the excitement he felt reading it as a young man—and from the fact that this was where his work first appeared under his own name. Wyndham Lewis's first published work also ran in the *English Review,* as did early work by Ezra Pound.

But the *English Review* is a modernist magazine not merely because it published modernist authors: it is the cultural vision guiding the collection of contributions to the *English Review* that I consider a departure from Victorian and Edwardian magazine conventions. Though the *English Review* did not adopt a deliberately combative tone such as Lewis would use a few years later in *Blast,* Ford saw heterodox experimentation as vital to both literary and cultural renewal. Not only did he wish to expand the horizon of material publishable in commercial publications, but, like Vallette in the *Mercure de France,* he also considered essential the challenge that heterodox ideas and art posed to the audience and to the public sphere. But this material had to be brought to bear upon the broader culture to stay consistent with Ford's vision. And this is where the *English Review* departed from Victorian precedents, which established that wildly unorthodox material could be published, but primarily in small, purely literary and artistic coterie publications (like the Pre-Raphaelite *Germ*) or in radical political magazines (like the anarchist *Torch*). Ironically, this very departure from Victorian and Edwardian precedents is very much in line with the unrealized mid-Victorian liberal ideal of the *Fortnightly*'s founders. But the firing of Frank Harris as editor of the *Fortnightly* by the publisher Chapman and Hall in 1894 for publishing "Some Anarchist Portraits" by Charles Malato, an avowed anarchist, marked the limits that could be challenged within this field of publication.

The *English Review* wanted to forge a relationship between its most unorthodox literature (such as Lewis's stories[47]) and not only its other literary pieces, but also the nonliterary contributions (such as letters to the editor regarding farming issues). Like other modernist literary enterprises soon to emerge, the *English Review* was an attempt to shore up what Ford saw as the fragments of a culture by turning to a semimythologized vision of cultural cohesion. While such a quest would lead Pound to Provence, ancient China, Renaissance Italy, Jeffersonian America, and finally to fascist Italy, in 1908 it led Ford to Enlightenment and contemporary France.

His quest did not, however, lead Ford to commercial success. The *English Review* fell victim to its audience's horizon of expectations for a monthly review in a fragmented public sphere. Ford saw the elements of his disinterested critical review as connected to each other; his audiences did not. The *English Review* under Harrison inevitably became more commercially viable and politically partisan, and it conformed more to generic expectations.

The Reception of the *English Review*

Although Ford had successfully launched the *English Review* into the ranks of the established reviews, its press reception illustrates the way in which conventions and genres of periodical publication affected and constrained the magazine's potential for cultural influence of the kind Ford desired. The first issue of Ford's new magazine was reviewed by numerous journals, ranging from the London and provincial daily newspapers to the monthlies, for whom its launching created something of a stir. As is the case with the reception of most new journals, the reviewers attempted to understand it in relationship to current journal genres. At first, confusion arose around the placement of the *English Review* in the field of periodical publication. In their reviews of the first issue, the dailies envisioned the *English Review* as a purely literary magazine, and one that succeeded in collecting the most important "serious" Edwardian authors, but most felt that it was in some way not quite like other literary magazines.[48] These dailies—whether the Liberal *Daily News,* the Unionist *Pall Mall Gazette,* the mass market *Daily Mail,* or other London papers (the *Times,* the *Sunday Times,* the *Financial Times*), provincial papers like the *Yorkshire Post,* or even the American *Chicago Evening Post*—all responded positively to the first issue of the *English Review* but mostly restricted their comment to its literary content. Whether deriving from a hesitancy to commit themselves to sorting out the patchwork of its political writings or from the star-studded quality of the literary figures in the first issue, the dailies saw it as a new type of literary magazine. But they primarily responded only to its debut rather than closely following its progress.

Major monthly reviews generally did not review other monthlies and so did not notice the *English Review*. However, the most prominent monthly to follow the *English Review* regularly was Stead's *Review of Reviews*, which, beginning with the September 1909 issue, firmly linked it with the major monthly reviews, not with purely literary magazines. Not only did the *Review of Reviews* place the *English Review* physically among the other prominent monthly reviews in its columns, but, as with the other reviews, it largely commented on its political and social articles rather than its literature. For instance, in its December 1909 issue (Australasian ed. 276–277), it shruggingly dismissed the literary side ("The *English Review* for September opens with some weird 'modern poetry'") and quickly moved on to the more important issues at hand, the caricature of Lloyd George and the essays on Spain and South Africa. It occasionally noted new serials, but it was clearly more interested in the articles. The *Review of Reviews*, with a circulation of more than 200,000 around the world, served roughly the same function for the politically or culturally interested Edwardian that *Tit-Bits* served for less intellectual audiences. It kept up with the major publication events of each month and condensed them into an easily digestible format. Having a wide experience of the Edwardian periodical milieu and the position of an arbiter of importance, it aligned the *English Review* with the monthly political and literary reviews, and this also would become the response from the weeklies—the most frequent and regular reviewers of the *English Review*.

The weeklies regularly discussed the monthly reviews and provided perspectives on the *English Review* that probably reflected the interest of their readership in such a journal. The *Academy,* the *Spectator* and the *Saturday Review* (on the Conservative or Unionist side), the *Athenæum, Country Life, T. P.'s Weekly,* and *Vanity Fair,* the Liberal *Nation,* and the Socialist *New Age*—all scanned the early issues of the *English Review*. Not only the politics, but also the stances toward modernist literature, varied widely in these journals: naturally, their reception of the *English Review* covered a broad spectrum of opinions. But the interest of such a diverse group of weeklies suggests that Ford's attempt at disinterestedness succeeded at least in this limited way.

However, though much of the literature by established authors was well-received (most of the weeklies praised Wells's *Tono-Bungay*), the more experimental writing was frequently either ignored or attacked. In spite of Lord Alfred Douglas's monotonous denigration of the *English Review* as a dangerous socialist magazine, his reviews in the *Academy* do underscore common elements in its reception.[49] What the *Review of Reviews* had called "weird modern poetry," Douglas and many of the weekly reviews also dismissed or glossed over. Referring to Ezra Pound's *English Review* poems, Douglas writes, "His verses have all the appearance of having been

written by Melchizidick Hundredweight" (June 5, 1909, 172), and, like the
Spectator, he found Hardy's leadoff "Sunday Morning Tragedy" "not fit
for a verse or a magazine" (Nov. 28, 1908, 514). The *Spectator,* as did and
the *Academy* (Mar. 5, 1910, 220), preferred, for instance, William Watson's
poetry to what St. Loe Strachey dismissed as "much of the modern verse
we are accustomed to find in this review" (Mar. 5, 1910, 386). Naturally,
there were also charges of factionalism, in spite of Ford's efforts to avoid
this.[50] However, when the weeklies bothered to discuss the *English Review*'s
literature, they generally agreed that, except for the experimental work of
the younger writers—the modernists—it was high quality. In an obvious
comparison to a magazine like the *Strand,* Arnold Bennett wrote in the
New Age (Dec. 16, 1909, 159): "The gulf that divides the mentality of
'The English Review' from that of a popular sixpenny with coloured
photographs is so vast that the latter cannot even see across it to the other
side." And the *Saturday Review* quoted a newspaper proclaiming that the
English Review is "a magazine that has printed more *real* literature in
eighteen months than all the others have printed in three years" (Dec. 3,
1910, 728).

Some magazines, like *Country Life,* focused on the literary quality of
the *English Review,* praising it as a "magazine of a kind which is practically
new to this country. Although called a review, it is in reality a high-class
magazine; that is to say, its main function does not appear to be the study
of the questions of the day by the greatest authorities of the day . . . but
the provision of a month's reading mostly in the shape of imaginative
work" (Dec. 5, 1908, 768). But Ford was trying to establish neither a
purely literary magazine nor a primarily political journal: rather, Ford
wanted his review to be a place in which the great minds of the day study
"the questions of the day," and one in which imaginative literature would
be emphasized.[51] Ford saw such an ideal in the *Mercure* and in the old
Victorian aspirations for the monthly review. He had a vision of the *English Review* as a public space—a meeting of minds of an international
scope with direct cultural benefit to England, bringing in the "most valuable thought," recalling Arnold's "best that has been thought or said"—
not just the rambling following of current political and social thought that
the weeklies (and frequently the monthlies) pursued. He wrote in an *English Review* advertisement in the *Saturday Review:* "Forming, as it does,
a speaking place for the best imaginative writers of Europe, the *English
Review* gives its readers not the chronicles and dissertations upon current
political facts that will be found in its contemporaries, but the more intimate thoughts or brilliant imaginations of English and foreign writers of
excelling ability. Critical deliberation and imagination would transcend
the fray of private interests" (Mar. 27, 1909, 413).

However, the content of the majority of the weekly reviews of the *En-

glish Review highlights a quandary that Ford faced in his critical project: can a literary magazine maintain a critical impact upon a culture without conforming to the generic expectations of either a literary magazine or a monthly review with a politically partisan agenda? The answer during the Edwardian period seems to have been no. During these politically charged years in which England was slouching toward the Constitutional Crisis, the destabilizing of the empire, greater confrontations with suffragettes, Irish liberation movements, and labor unrest, the *English Review* was mainly interpreted as another one of the political monthlies. Whether the weeklies saw it as "dangerous, in the sense that it is tainted with Social-ism" (*Academy,* Mar. 6, 1909, 844) or insightful, or, in Ford's editorials, "impartial" only by being "frankly pessimistic" (*Saturday Review,* Jan. 8, 1910, 54), they tracked carefully only the political articles in the *English Review.*[52]

At this time, in Edwardian London the consumption of periodical fiction was perhaps greater than ever before and the interest in political and cultural articles by the thinkers of the day was avid, yet the reception of the *English Review* shows that Ford was unable to form a meaningful link in the public mind between the "purely" literary and the political and cultural article. Although Ford was clearly trying to reach a mass audience, and to create an important public institution in his *English Review,* in the world of the reviews, literature was often seen only as entertaining or, in the case of an author like Wells, didactic. Ford's vision of an Enlightenment ideal of disinterested inquiry, one that emphasized an attention to the detail and precise functioning of language, had difficulty flourishing in that field of publication.

Although the *English Review* after Austin Harrison became editor in 1910 has largely been ignored or treated as a pathetic footnote to Ford's promising start, much of the credit for the commercial success of the *English Review* should go to Harrison. During Ford's tenure the magazine was not able to keep up its original print run of five thousand copies, and the circulation rarely exceeded one thousand copies per month (Bradbury; MacShane 319). While Harrison was justifiably proud of continuing to publish such authors as Conrad, Tolstoy, Wells, and other "big names,"[53] and while he officially adopted Ford's editorial goals, including his desire to sustain a *Mercure de France* in England,[54] the very changes that established the financial solvency and success of Harrison's *English Review* recapitulated the historical fragmentation and transformation of the liberal public sphere as Ford (and later Habermas) had mythologized it. Both the party machinery and the commercialization that Ford had tried so hard to avoid became the tools Harrison used to make the *English Review* conform to Edwardian horizons of expectation.

Harrison gradually excluded the heterodox from the magazine and made much safer commercial choices about its literature. The literary figures about whom Harrison boasts were all well-established and popular writers before the founding of the *English Review;* it would be in the area of finding and publishing good new authors that Harrison failed to live up to Ford's editorial example. Under Harrison, the magazine emphasized literature by the likes of Maurice Hewlett and Eden Philpotts, both mainstream Edwardian authors. Georgian poems by Harold Monro, John Masefield, or Walter De la Mare were about as challenging as Harrison felt he could risk, and the poetry more frequently came from such forgotten names as William Watson, Mary Webb, or Gilbert Waterhouse. In 1912 he lowered the price of the *English Review* from 2s. 6d. to 1s., comfortably undercutting the half-crown price of the monthly reviews and the 6s. quarterlies and making a bold move for a larger audience, and he more actively sought to accommodate wider audience tastes than Ford had.[55]

In addition, the Liberal party's political agenda took greater precedence in the journal during Harrison's tenure. While Ford had failed to create a politically disinterested magazine in that his *English Review* was composed primarily of liberal and socialist articles,[56] it had avoided the overt partisan connections desired by the new owner, Sir Alfred Mond, a Liberal member of Parliament who fired Ford over political disagreements and replaced him with Harrison. Harrison quickly either left out "The Month" or used it simply as a forum for his political editorials.[57] In it he attacked the House of Lords (a hot topic in the year or so preceding the Constitutional Crisis), Balfour, protectionism, and any number of other Conservative or Unionist targets, and his diatribe would often be followed by a related liberal article.[58] Party concerns began to dictate the contents of the review in a way that they had not under Ford: it became a magazine with an explicitly partisan agenda.

Ironically, at the same time that many English modernists (such as Pound, Lawrence, and Ford) felt that the *English Review* was sliding downhill under Harrison, the *Mercure de France,* which had enjoyed the respect of modernist circles, seemed to feel that it was precisely Harrison who made the *English Review* great. The *Mercure* always admired Ford's *English Review,* but it was Harrison's safer version that drew its greatest praise. Though he followed modernist writers in London, reviewing books by Pound, Monro, West, Yeats, and others, Henry Davray, who wrote the *Mercure*'s "Lettres Anglaises" section, seems to have approached the *English Review* with a similar horizon of expectations about English monthly reviews as the English reading audiences had.[59] While Ford had clearly wanted a wide audience like the *Mercure de France* had, Davray seems to have felt that Harrison could deliver that, without compromising quality.

Thus Ford's attempt to graft the *Mercure de France* onto an English monthly review had ended in a little over a year. Inheriting Ford's oppositional rhetoric of the cohesiveness and vitality of French culture and society, and his exaltation of the *Mercure,* Ford's subeditor Douglas Goldring lamented: "Whereas in France culture is so widely diffused that a literary periodical like the *Mercure de France* can find readers in remote country towns and among all classes of society, such has never been the case in England. . . . in 1909 the *English Review,* unfortunately for Ford, was several decades in advance of its time" (Goldring, *Trained,* 151). The impulse to enter the dominant public sphere through the established institutions of periodical publication was based on Ford's desire to create a culturally authoritative critical forum that would be both disinterested and capable of accommodating a wide range of heterodox thought. This ideal in early British modernism arose at the moment that the progressive alliance raised hopes for consensus, and it found inspiration in a mythic vision of the cohesiveness and rationality of French culture. However, the *English Review* had joined the journalistic field represented by the *Fortnightly Review,* with its large educated audience. Because it worked from within the Edwardian literary establishment—rather than mounting an attack on it from without as more avant-garde magazines soon would—the *English Review* managed to set literary modernism on the drawing-room tables of middle-and upper-class London.

2

Performing the Pure Voice

Poetry and Drama,
Elocution, Verse Recitation,
and Modernist Poetry in Prewar London

While Ford's *English Review* attempted to institutionalize a critical and heterodox public sphere within the print medium, Harold Monro and exponents of the verse recitation movement in prewar London used print to try to imagine a public rejuvenated by a return to preprint ideals of oral community and oral performance. This vision attributed an important public function to poetry—one that affirmed modernist aesthetics but also implicated them in the unspoken class agenda of the verse-recitation movement. Even while he reshaped the discourse of what I will call "the pure voice" with allusions to prebourgeois communal performance, Monro retained many of the ideals of the liberal public sphere for which Ford had fought—disinterestedness and free critical deliberation—but, unlike Ford, he applied these ideals only to poetry and the public dimension of aesthetics. Like Ford, Monro and his followers, then, invoked a myth of the decline of the public sphere in order to popularize modern poetry, but they imagined the decline primarily to have involved the loss of an oral community in which poetry played a key role. They then adapted this vision to the modern mass market print age in which the mass production of inexpensive books of poetry and the profitable voice-instruction publishing industry could be used to assert the public importance of live readings of modernist poetry.

British and American modernist poets shared a preoccupation with the importance of speech to poetry—and, conversely, of poetry to speech. As T. S. Eliot put it in "Little Gidding": "our concern was speech, and speech impelled us / To purify the dialect of the tribe" (204). He approximates Dante's terza rima in the *Divine Comedy* to describe an encounter with the shade of a past master—perhaps Yeats, or Dante himself—who underscores this ideal of the poet's relationship to the spoken language. For Eliot, then, the poet expands the expressive capacity of common speech; like Dante in the *Divine Comedy,* he writes in the "middle style" to purify the "vernacular" of the day (see Gaskell; Schmidt). In his first prose work, *The Spirit of Romance* (1910), Ezra Pound paid careful attention to Dante's *De Vulgari Eloquentia,* in which Dante affirms poetry written in the common speech. As Pound would later attempt in the *Cantos,* Dante imagines poets creating an ideal version of the vernacular, borrowing elements from different regional dialects to create a precise and concise language.[1] Yeats, in the decades preceding both Pound's and Eliot's migrations to London, had similarly sought to rid poetic language of abstraction and rhetoric in favor of the clarity and naturalness of "living speech"—through experiments with Anglo-Irish dialect. He tried not to write dialect verse, but instead a poetry that sounded as natural as the spoken word (Meir 83–84). And, across the ocean, William Carlos Williams pursued a poetry free of "poetic" language and European traditions—an American poetry based on the American spoken word: "It is in the newness of a live speech that the new line exists undiscovered" (in Ferry 144).

This chapter gives a social context to the speech orientation of modernist poetry, with its emphasis on the oral, as opposed to the visual.[2] I will examine the important social role of elocution teaching and the verse-recitation movement in late Victorian and Edwardian England in terms of the sociology of culture. Following Pierre Bourdieu, who characterizes the aesthetic disposition of the contemporary French cultural elite (those who affirm the autonomy of the aesthetic) as that of the "pure gaze" (*Distinction* 31), I suggest that the culturally legitimating marker of distinction in middle- and upper-class London before the war was, indeed, the "pure voice." This context helps to elucidate modernist critical and aesthetic categories like those that preoccupied Eliot in his early criticism—the purity of language, impersonality, and verse drama—and historicizes their role in the public emergence of modernist poetry.

Bourdieu suggests that "art and cultural consumption are predisposed, consciously and deliberately or not, to fulfil a social function of legitimating social differences" (*Distinction* 6–7). I believe that Victorian elocution and recitation practices, which served the clergy, barristers, members of Parliament, and other male members of the privileged classes who envisioned a career involving public speaking, evolved into a much more elaborate and widespread vehicle of cultural reproduction, legitimation, and distinction for the male *and* female upper *and* middle classes. The new elocution, with its emphasis on verse-recitation, had its own institutions of consecration and professionalization, the support of a profitable corner of the publishing industry, and a growing presence in official pedagogy. The verse recitation movement, which was both part of liberal education reform trends and a response to class anxieties that were partially caused by those same reforms, privileged oral cultural production over visual spectacle, which it associated with artifice, theatricality, and, especially, working-class music hall.

To expand this notion of pure voice and its role in modernist aesthetics, I examine the nexus of modernist poetry and prewar class anxieties through a strange dual text—the copublication (as a single magazine) of Harold Monro's *Poetry Review* (1912), an important organ for the aesthetic innovations of both Georgian and modernist poets,[3] and the *Poetical Gazette,* the journal of the aesthetically moribund and conservative Poetry Society. With this magazine and its successor, *Poetry and Drama* (1913–1914), Harold Monro published and disseminated the work of poets ranging from John Masefield to Ezra Pound and F. T. Marinetti. The Poetry Society, as an institution of the verse-recitation movement, both influenced young modernist poets and provided an opportunity for them to use public performance to seek wider audiences and help popularize experimental verse. Ideas of purity of diction, impersonality, and verse drama that were discussed in the magazine became important modernist aesthetic imperatives, but each of these issues at this early period was involved in creating a public dimension for modernist poetry. Modernist poets challenged the power of the conservative Poetry Society to consecrate its own poetic taste, and thus used the cultural legitimacy of the pure voice to produce the value and cultural meaning of aesthetic experiments.

Adopting and modifying contemporary verse-recitation practices and commonplaces, Monro created the Poetry Bookshop as a center for the oral performance of poetry by poets ranging from the most conservative to the most avant-garde.[4] This precursor of the immensely popular public readings later in the century—by Dylan Thomas, transatlantic visitors like Allen Ginsberg, and even young working-class poets at British poetry festivals of the 1960s and 1970s (see Johnson)—adapted class-based verse-recitation paradigms to emphasize the power of oral recitation to convey an understanding of formal experimentation. Above all, the Poetry Bookshop brought poetry readings out of the Victorian parlor and in front of

56

the public. Monro and others attempted to restore to poetry through oral performance the stature they imagined it had attained in prebourgeois, preprint societies.

Elocution and Verse Recitation

Around the turn of the century, the speaking voice assumed increasing social and cultural importance in British culture. Elocution and recitation manuals proliferated, targeting ever-broader audiences, and speech training became a profession with an expanded role in the education system. New discourses about proper diction and verse recitation attested to the role of a newly emphasized "pure voice" in bourgeois self-legitimation and cultural reproduction.

Victorian elocution manuals and public speaking primers, even as late as the 1870s and 1880s, were frequently written by clergy holding university positions and were aimed at the university-educated upper- and upper-middle-class males who would be pursuing careers involving public speaking.[5] For instance, a manual published in 1874 by the Reverend J. J. Halcombe, M.A., Rector of Balsham, Cambridge, and W. H. Stone, M.A., M.D., of Balliol, was explicitly aimed at "the younger members of the Universities, in the confident hope that the subjects of which they treat will soon be recognised in their full importance by every man who is looking forward to serve in the Christian ministry" (v). Halcombe suggested readings for discussion—Junius, Cicero, Demosthenes—while foregrounding the role of a classical education in precise verbal understanding.[6] The manual provided exercises for the young scholars who had not yet developed such proficiency in the classics, but it was obviously aimed at the university-bound upper classes.

Dr. Stone's contribution to the manual typified mid-Victorian elocution books: he looked to an emerging physiological science of the throat, lungs, and mouth to provide helpful speaking aids. But even Dr. Stone admitted that "speech is by no means a 'natural' function in the usual sense of the word. It is a complex and difficult acquirement, perfected through many centuries in the course of progressive civilisation," which the "intellectual community of the ages . . . must pass on" (153). Such manuals did not naturalize the attainments of public speaking; they instead clearly viewed their educated elite male audiences as bearers of a cultural heritage preserved from the ancient Greeks. Demosthenes was the model, and the future leaders of England were the audience.

However, by the later Victorian and Edwardian periods a change was occurring in the publication of elocution and recitation manuals. They began to aim at a far broader audience than had the technical tomes of high Victorian elocutionary technique. Herbert Jennings's *Voice and Its*

Natural Development (1911) began, "The present volume is compiled expressly for the busy man and woman who have little leisure time to bestow in rudimentary and arduous study" (ix); he intended to "deal in a practical manner with vocal development" (xi). Elocution was now not just for the leisured class, but also for the busy and less-educated middle class. In *The Speaking Voice: Principles of Training Simplified and Condensed* (1908), Katherine Jewell Everts likewise noted that "there are volumes of recognized authority, considerable in length and exhaustive in detail, which one who intends to use his voice professionally should master, if possible, but which it is almost impossible for the college, society, or business man or woman to study and follow, from sheer lack of time" (iii–iv). The appeal of elocution, or vocal training, was broadening beyond the male elite confines of Oxbridge to include larger numbers of both men and women of the non–university-bound bourgeoisie.

Furthermore, these later elocution and recitation manuals began to employ new discourses that suggest middle-class anxieties about cultural reproduction and legitimacy. They reveal an attempt to naturalize "proper" speaking, to elide the explicit class basis of the earlier manuals. Canon Fleming's *The Art of Reading and Speaking* (1896) asserted that "It is an art which, with all its refinement, belongs to no particular class to the exclusion of others" (205), and he urged his readers to "Speak so naturally that your words may go from the heart to the heart, and that people may forget the messenger while they listen to the message" (5).[7] Fleming also brought up a theme that was to be a rallying cry for many elocution books: he attacked the "artificiality" of elocution rules, preferring a practice that is "to make none artificial or stilted, but to help all to be natural and real" (3–4). These manuals rejected the rules and gestures prescribed by earlier elocution systems, but they also implied that the speech of the educated middle and upper classes was "natural," thus clearly reinforcing distinctions at a pedagogical level that accent and dialect had preserved between the classes in England for centuries. The expanding bourgeoisie was universalizing its language in a strategy of self-legitimation.

Modernist hopes to "purify the dialect of the tribe" thus emerged in England against the backdrop of a class-based sociocultural movement. Middle-class strategies of legitimation could involve an appeal to a linguistic nationalism, but within a "classless" paradigm gesturing at pedagogical reforms. Jennings wrote, "Purity of diction is the birthright of every English man and woman, and it is largely due to the indifference shown in educational administration at home and at school that our mother-tongue has been robbed of its grandeur and beauty of tone. If only justice were done to the English language, it would not only hold its own in sweetness and musical distinction, but, if we accept the verdict of a celebrated German philologist, it also possesses 'a veritable power of expression and comprehension unsurpassed by any language on earth—whether ancient or modern'" (xiii). The grandeur of the nation depended on vigilance against impurity, which, of course, implied the dialects of the working classes. The attainment of pure voice was not just a social grace or a career requirement for the upper classes, as the Victorian manuals had emphasized, but rather a broader marker of cultural legitimacy and distinction for the middle classes.

This heightened concern with the purity of English speech arose as the English school system expanded and reached out to more working-class children (Halsey et al.). In 1870 the Forster Act had made government responsible for education when voluntary efforts were insufficient, thus continuing earlier trends toward broad literacy (Altick 171–172). In a move applauded by Matthew Arnold himself, educational reformers also introduced "English literature" into the curriculum for the first time in 1871 and called for the memorization of lines of poetry (Altick 161). The Board Schools opened educational opportunities that helped many climb up the class ladder, but I suggest that the expansion of the educational system, which dramatically increased during the Edwardian period, helped fuel class anxieties that metamorphosed into an emphasis on speech training in the school system, on reading the "proper" set of English literary works, and on the professionalization of elocution.

The class anxieties lying hidden beneath school reforms, and especially the English literature curriculum, were stated explicitly by Henry Newbolt, a vice president of the Poetry Society, a prominent literary critic, and an occasional reader at the Poetry Bookshop. Appearing soon after the war, the famous "Newbolt Report," *The Teaching of English in England* . . . (1921), resulted from the lobbying efforts of the English Association, which Brian Doyle characterizes as "a class-based mobilisation which drew in not only most professors of English Language and Literature, but also like-minded politicians, administrators, and men-of-letters" (103; see also P. Scott 92–97). Compiled for the government by Newbolt and a committee of other primarily upper-middle-class public school–educated men, *The Teaching of English in England.* . . noted: "Literature, in fact, seems to be classed by a large number of thinking working men with antimacassars, fish-knives and other unintelligible and futile trivialities of 'middle class' culture, and, as a subject of instruction, is suspect as an attempt to 'sidetrack the working-class movement.' . . . We were told . . . working men felt any attempt to teach them literature or art was an attempt to impose on them the culture of another class" (253–254). The report revealed a fear of the utilitarian uses to which the working classes might put their education: "They see education mainly as something to equip them to fight their capitalistic enemies" (254). It also cautioned that if the working classes remained alienated from the dominant culture, England might soon encounter "the hostility toward capitalism now prevalent in Bolshevist Russia" (254). Against the threat to the middle class posed by an educated working class, the report urged public schools to emphasize an agenda of enculturation through education "based upon the English language and literature" (21).

Among factors the report saw as dividing the classes was "a marked difference in their modes of speech" (22). It argued that "pride in the national language would be a bond of union between classes, and would beget the right kind of national pride. Even more certainly should pride and joy in the national literature serve as such a bond" (22). The rhetoric raised the specter of international communism that, of course, would have inspired fear in the middle and upper classes. However, Newbolt and the committee proposed a national and class unity that affirmed, naturalized, and institutionalized middle-class markers of distinction: speech and literary taste. The Newbolt Report was only a systematic statement of attitudes that had been developing since the late Victorian period.

The focus of anxiety about the Board Schools was not just on the students' critical abilities, but also on their speech and the role of reading aloud in the schools (the subject of a set of Education Department circulars published in 1898). One circular lamented the poor job elementary schools were doing in teaching expressive reading and articulation. It complained that "there are too few signs in reading aloud of the individuality of expression which we call 'intelligence'" (in Burrell 155–156). Another circular sent to the training colleges and pupil-teacher centres complained of the lack of progress in teaching pupils to read aloud, partially because the pupil-teachers themselves were generally not taught sufficiently (Burrell 156–157). In other words, the faults in diction and pronunciation of the lower- or lower-middle-class participants in the pupil-teacher centres were reproduced in the "unintelligent" dialects of their students.[8] One prominent member of the English Association in 1909 cautioned against the influence of the "debased dialect of the Cockney . . . which is spreading from our schools and training-colleges all over the country. In ten years' time the English language will not be worth speaking" (in Doyle 108). The Newbolt Report recommended training in voice and diction in the teacher training colleges and called for oral examinations to judge the results (178–179).

Pygmalion and "the Language of Shakespear and Milton and the Bible"

These anxieties about the voice, and the voice-instruction industry that sprang up around them, crystallized in literary form in the London debut of Shaw's wildly popular *Pygmalion* in the spring of 1914 at His Majesty's

Theatre.[9] *Pygmalion*—which is probably best known to current American audiences in its 1950s incarnation as *My Fair Lady*—involves a wager. The gentlemanly Colonel Pickering bets Professor of Phonetics Henry Higgins that Higgins cannot use his phonetics magic to change the dreaded Cockney drawl of the flower girl Eliza Doolittle so utterly that she could pass as a duchess at a high society party—a bet that Higgins, of course, wins. The fantastic success of *Pygmalion* can be seen as a measure of the centrality of the "pure voice" and the professionalization of speech instruction (in this case, through the new "science" of phonetics) to the public perception of class in 1914.

In his preface to *Pygmalion,* Shaw noted that some of Henry Higgins's traits were based on those of his old friend Henry Sweet (1845–1912), the phonetician who in 1901 convinced Oxford to create a Readership in Phonetics especially for him (Shaw, *Autobiography,* 273). Shaw glorifies the scientific basis of phonetics, and, in keeping with the professionalization of voice instruction we have seen in elocution and voice manuals (and the scientific trappings that accompanied them), he emphasizes the necessity of professionalized knowledge of the voice: "Ambitious flower-girls who read this play must not imagine that they can pass themselves off as fine ladies by untutored imitation" (Shaw, *Pygmalion,* 331). And this specialist knowledge makes the "energetic phonetic enthusiast," as Shaw puts it, "the reformer we need most today" (327), because he offers a means of transforming society: "For the encouragement of people troubled with accents that cut them off from all high employment, I may add that the change wrought by Professor Higgins in the flower-girl is neither impossible nor uncommon," Shaw proclaims, noting that there are "many thousands of men and women who have sloughed off their native dialects and acquired a new tongue" (331). And indeed, Shaw's proclamations of the reforming, democratizing effects of speech instruction—of the attainment of the "pure voice"—were clearly consonant with the rhetoric of voice manuals like Hardress O'Grady's *Reading Aloud and Literary Appreciation* (1914), which notes, with idealistic hyperbole, that through "the vital embodiment of *speech,* man's gift of communication with his fellows, we shall be admitted presently to that great republic wherein all men are equal, all men are free, and all men converse together" (9).

Because of *Pygmalion*'s challenge to notions of essential class inequalities, Lynda Mugglestone has compellingly read the play as a "socialist parable" of "the inherent superficiality of those symbols commonly used to determine social acceptability" (381). But reading *Pygmalion*'s popularity in the context of the institutionalization of the pure voice in school reforms and the voice-instruction industry allows us to complicate the "socialist parable" interpretation. Although a critique of the superficiality and manipulability of the symbolic markers of class is clearly Shaw's intention in the play, no one in the play actually challenges the idea that the exquisite pronunciation, the voice that Henry Higgins gives Eliza, is, in fact, the way to bring Eliza into equality with the middle classes. Though it does, of course, take changes in cleanliness, dress, and manners to make the transformation believable,[10] Shaw, in his call for "the regeneration of the human race thought the most difficult science in the world" (in Mugglestone 382), leaves in place the middle-class ideal of the pure voice as a means of class leveling. To put it bluntly, why not democratize society by teaching everyone Cockney pronunciation?[11]

Pygmalion, in its comic opening, in fact presents a London with a rich variety of accents and idioms. Merely by listening carefully to their voices, Higgins has the remarkable ability to divine the neighborhood of origin of complete strangers, and not just the working-class bystanders from Selsey or Lisson Grove, but even Pickering, whose educational institutions and career have marked his voice: "Cheltenham, Harrow, Cambridge, and India" (339). But rather than celebrating the rich plurality of English tongues that can serve as precise markers of identity and, by extension, the diversity of identities in British society, Shaw, in fact, affirms a twofold value of the pure voice: first, as providing opportunities to those whose accents keep them impoverished, and second, as *significant in its own right.* As Higgins says of Eliza's Cockney accent, "A woman who utters such depressing and disgusting sounds has no right to be anywhere—no right to live. Remember that you are a human being with a soul and the divine gift of articulate speech: that your native language is the language of Shakespear and Milton and The Bible; and don't sit there crooning like a bilious pigeon" (341). As do the voice handbooks I have discussed, Higgins naturalizes an abstracted ideal of middle-class diction as "the divine gift of articulate speech"—the pure voice, and thereby portrays lower-class dialects as a sort of blight on the language. Jennings's assertion that "the purity of diction is the birthright of every English man and woman" (xiii) might without alteration have been inserted into Henry Higgins's dialogue. Theatergoers, even of the rising lower middle classes, who had bought Jennings's *Voice and Its Natural Development* or Everts's *The Speaking Voice: Principles of Training Simplified and Condensed* might, in fact, have felt inspired to follow Eliza Doolittle's upward linguistic mobility, thus legitimizing the hegemony of the middle-class voice after all.

But Shaw also had something beyond phonetics and elocution instruction in mind as he conceived Eliza's transformation. In a letter explaining Cockney pronunciation to Dorothy Dix, who played Eliza in some of the 1914 performances of *Pygmalion,* Shaw cautioned: "You will find the third act the hardest technically; for the effect is bad, even if there is a good deal of laughing, if Liza produces the effect of giving herself airs by imitating a lady badly. She is not imitating at all: she is pronouncing as Higgins has taught her; and his Miltonic taste must be assumed to be first rate. . . . *Play it as if you were reciting Shakespear for a prize in fine diction*" (*Collected Letters,* 248, emphasis mine). In 1912 when Shaw wrote *Pygmalion* and in 1914 when it was first produced in England, the concern about the state of the nation's voice led to many attempts to reform the school system around ideals of the pure voice, and at the center of these reforms were methods privileging verse recitation. Shaw's vision of Eliza's transformation from "crooning like a bilious pigeon" (*Pygmalion,* 341) to "speaking with pedantic correctness of pronunciation and great beauty of tone," as Shaw puts it in the stage direction (380), seems based upon the ideal voice striven after in the popular verse-recitation competitions in the newly reformed school system.

The class-based anxieties about the voice, not coincidentally, gathered momentum during the Edwardian expansion of the school system. Liberal reforms in 1907 created free secondary schooling and linked primary and secondary education by requiring 25 percent of the free places in secondary education to be reserved for pupils recruited from the public elementary schools (Halsey 153). Almost immediately, though, the 1908 Board of Education Report strongly criticized the standards of the teaching of English in secondary schools (Keating 452). New schools and programs emerged to deal with the problems of literary appreciation and, simply, of speech; the Central School of Speech Training and Dramatic Art, which taught speech and drama teachers, for example, was founded in 1906 by Elsie Fogerty, who attached great importance to verse recitation in her program.[12] The University of London and other adult educational institutions also offered courses to remedy "improper" speaking. The development of the pure voice was not simply a matter of public speaking but, rather part of a larger defensive strategy of cultural legitimation (exemplified by the Newbolt Report); thus it led to an emphasis on verse recitation and linked speech training to the teaching of English literature. By the late Victorian period, elocution had moved from the practical concerns of creating polished orators for the pulpit and Parliament, to become a "fine art" connected to the experience of literature (Haberman 392), and thus it shifted the means by which elocution served as a marker of social attainment.[13]

New ideas about reading verse aloud that were to be crucial to early modernist poets drew the notion of the pure voice into the discourse about the interpretation and appreciation of poetry and about the role of impersonality in recitation. Alison Byerly suggests that the Victorians distrusted the theater. Acting and the visual trappings of theatricality—dressing up as another character and assuming its persona—were associated with deception or duplicity (Byerly 125–126). This apprehension was circumvented by reading drama aloud with the entire family at home, safe from the shadowy and disreputable theaters themselves (see also Collins, *Reading Aloud,* 20–22). The problem of losing oneself (and especially one's moral responsibility) in a role was overcome by the overriding presence and personality of the dramatic reader who read multiple parts (Byerly, 127). However, the logic of the pure voice, as it related to verse recitation in the 1890s and the Edwardian period, led readers to almost the opposite extreme.

The prevalent critique of the artificiality of gesture and vocalization of Victorian elocution in favor of something more "natural" developed, in manuals specifically aimed at verse recitation, into the understanding that reading aloud helped to elucidate the true meaning of the poem, allowing a "surrender" to the personality of the poet or even to the poem itself. Against the "extravagance in speech and gesture, studied poses, artificial exaggeration of simple emotions, wooden and vulgar presentation of what is sweetest, noblest, and most delicate in our literature: inferior imitation of the third rate stage" (Burrell 88), Arthur Burrell, senior master at the Bradford Grammar School, proclaimed that "Intelligent expression may be taken to mean such modulation of the voice as correctly interprets the meanings of a writer for a hearer" (151). Bertha Skeat, Ph.D., lecturer at Newnham College and Cambridge Teacher's College and a mistress at the County Girl's School, Llandover, emphasized the presence of the author during oral performance: "In trying to express aloud the best thoughts of others in the best way, we enter almost unconsciously into their spirit" (1). Hardress O'Grady put it more explicitly, calling reading aloud "a road to the personality of the writer" (1). He explained: "What we read silently cannot possess the same value as that which we read aloud. The music and the rhythm are obscured, they are heard as in a dream darkly . . . but if, when we are making the acquaintance of new work, we use the instrument that Nature has given us, the whole beauty of prose or verse shall spring alive. By a magic within the reach of any of us we shall see the writer's self face to face" (3); and he added, "We put ourselves in direct communication with the inner mind of the writer" (119). Everts proclaimed that reading verses aloud allowed the reader to "catch the spirit of the creator of them" (114).

The Poetry Society

In the previous section we saw that the practices of elocution and verse recitation in middle-class culture positioned oral performance as a component of literary appreciation. In their development of an ideal of authorial presence mediated by the reciter, they were paving the way for the modernist poets to take the leap into the phenomenon of public poetry readings, given by the poets themselves. Perhaps the culmination of the trends in verse recitation that I have been discussing, and their direct link to modernist poets, was the Poetry Recital Society (founded in 1909 in London). The Poetry Society, as it came to be called, attempted to institutionalize and professionalize the discourses of elocution and recitation, to attain the power to consecrate taste and "culture," and to influence the London school system's efforts at verse recitation. In short, the Poetry Society helped to enhance the legitimation of the pure voice that so many manuals had been approaching as a marker of cultural and, hence, social distinction. And, most important for my purposes, though it was a culturally conservative foe of emerging modernist poets, the Poetry Society also helped to provide a unique opportunity for them to bring their work before the public.

Lady Margaret Sackville's inaugural address, "The Art of Speaking Verse," in the *Poetical Gazette,* epitomized the Poetry Society's goals for recitation. She continued the recent attacks on the artificiality and visual spectacle of elocution: "I believe as little gesture should be used as possible, and that, as a rule, the voice alone, provided it is flexible enough, is sufficiently effective. The speaking of verse is not acting" (455). Sackville also adhered to the (now common) explanation that the relationship between the reader's personality and the poem or even the poet distinguished bad elocution from the proper speaking of verse: "There should be no striving from outside to produce a definite effect—the soul of the interpreter should be so possessed by the poem that it follows it instinctively in every modulation and inflection as easily as water flows between winding banks" (454).[14]

This inaugural address enunciated not only the philosophy and goals of the Poetry Society, but also a system of cultural production that allowed the speaker with the proper "temperament" (456) and cultural capital to accrue symbolic value through the act of oral performance: "To my mind the proper rendering of a poem requires an attitude of surrender on the part of the speaker, and he must certainly possess a power of emotion equal to that contained in the poem itself" (455). This cultural capital consisted of the pure voice—gained through class privilege and the professional training and credentials meted out by the Poetry Society—and an education in the culturally consecrated poetic taste of the middle and upper middle classes. Sackville ascribes to the reciter the emotional power and cultural prestige of the author. Significantly, the marker of distinction was always the voice, the one thing that would be almost impossible for a working-class reciter to emulate. In a popular lecture entitled "The Reading of Poetry" given at many of the Poetry Society centers, Sturge Moore even argued that poetry only existed when audible and that a "curtain to hide the speaker and reduce him as nearly as possible to a voice" would facilitate the proper reception of a poetry reading.[15]

The Poetry Society buttressed its legitimacy with a number of different exclusionary tactics and markers of distinction. It used the prestige of the dominant classes to advertise itself, printing in almost every issue of the *Poetical Gazette* its list of important titled and degreed personages who were its numerous vice presidents, patrons, and honorary members. These included nobility, professors, doctors, clergy, elocutionists, and literary luminaries of the Edwardian period: Theodore Watts-Dunton, W. M. Rossetti, Edmund Gosse, Maurice Hewlett, G. K. Chesterton, John Galsworthy, Arnold Bennett, Sturge Moore, Newbolt, and others. The society banked with Barclay's, and, to display its respect for sound financial acumen, it even had its own honorary auditor. The list was regularly headed with the caption "Founded as the Poetry Recital Society to promote a more general recognition and appreciation of Poetry by encouraging the public and private reading of it and developing the art of speaking verse." However, the public dimension of the Poetry Society was in fact a restricted one, especially when compared to the Penny Reading movement of the mid-Victorian period.[16] Membership in the Poetry Society would have been fairly expensive to the working or lower middle class.[17] Most of the events were free or inexpensive to members, but nonmembers had to pay extra charges of at least 1s. to attend.

Like the Penny Reading movement, the Poetry Society assembled an organization to train readers and arrange events, but a key difference was that the Penny Reading organizers chose material that would be the most entertaining to their diverse audiences. At Penny Readings, poetry was only infrequently read, and humorous or entertaining prose anecdotes were the usual fare (Sivier, "Penny Readings," 227). The Poetry Society meetings, of course, centered around poetry, and, important for modernists, they also valued verse drama, even forming a Poetic Drama Society, whose activities were regularly covered in the *Poetical Gazette*'s pages. The poetry that the society recited and discussed was almost always that of the consecrated Victorian greats—Tennyson, Browning, Arnold, Rossetti—and frequently also Longfellow, Shakespeare, and the Elizabethans. The taste it enforced was "high-brow," but of the bourgeois sort, not necessarily that of the university-educated elite. For instance, many of the members were women, who usually lacked a classical education. Almost all of the authors read were English, rather than Greek or Roman, and when the Poetry Society tackled a classical project, like its much-touted production of *Hippolytus,* they used Gilbert Murray's translation, looked to his advice for understanding the text, and organized meetings in local centers to discuss it; most members, it seems, were not familiar with the text and had to read it in translation. Another major omission from their recitations, was contemporary poetry. A few nods were made to anachronisms like William Watson and Stephen Phillips, but generally the local centers showed little interest in contemporary verse, and none in anything experimental.

The exclusionary principles of price and taste had the consequence of a distinctly middle- and upper-middle-class makeup to the Poetry Society's chapters. The organization had a central headquarters, but its activities took place primarily at local chapters in London and other cities across Great Britain and even Australia. The London branches were almost all in the western and northwestern parts of the city—the middle- and upper-middle-class neighborhoods and suburbs. Continuing the tradition of Victorian salon readings, the meetings were usually held in the homes of local members and were not in any meaningful way "public."

Anticipating the recommendations of the Newbolt Report, the Poetry Society directed its efforts at an important means of cultural reproduction—the education system. The society intended to stimulate an interest in poetry, and it deemed the training of the voice with recently updated elocution techniques essential to this task. The society positioned itself as a legitimating body, professionalized and authoritative in granting cultural credentials. It drew on the prestige of the newly professionalized field of elocution and speech training and noted on its monthly list of officers a Dr. H. H. Hulbert, "Hon. Technical Adviser (Elocution) and Professional Examiner."[18] Hulbert not only trained society members to develop the pure voice, he also examined and certified them. In its "Important Examination Notices," the *Poetical Gazette* announced the examinations and regularly kept readers abreast of them: "A comprehensive and authoritative examination scheme has been drawn up. Recognition is being obtained for this test, which will give it a high professional value. Primarily it is intended to apply to teachers who wish to work in association with the Society or to have the Society's definite recognition and endorsement of their qualifications, but private members will derive great benefit from it, and are urged to enter for each section" (189). The test consisted of a "cultural" section with "testing of general knowledge and appreciation of poetry," a section on "theory and practice of teaching" conducted by Dr. Hulbert, and a "practical speaking test" administered by the president of the Poetry Society during which the examinee had to read aloud, answer some questions, and recite Matthew Arnold's "Shakespeare."[19] Although the examination was open to members of the society, nonmember professional candidates had to pay one guinea for the exam and up to five guineas for subsequent exams. Nonprofessional nonmembers paid 2s. 6d. per section, and professional reciters who were not teachers paid 15s. Again, cost would have discouraged anyone below the solidly middle class.

But beyond positioning the society as the arbiter of cultural competence and oral prowess, these examinations were part of a larger move to influence the educational system in London. In a time of school expansion and reform, the Poetry Society saw the importance of primary and secondary school literary and speech training programs to the reproduction of urban middle-class culture. It kept abreast of professional activities in the field of speech education, and it considered schemes "for developing its work among schools and colleges" ("A Junior Order" 53). The Poetry Society thus founded a "Junior Order" designed to "introduc[e] the work of the Society into public and private secondary schools." These organizations held regular meetings to read and discuss poetry sanctioned by the society. The society stipulated that "At least one teacher in each school adopting this Junior Order must be an ordinary member of the Society, he or she (or another member of the staff who is also a member of the Society) to be president of the school branch" ("A Junior Order" 45). These Junior Orders were established both in London and in other cities, and they were regularly reported on in the *Poetical Gazette.* Moreover, the Poetry Society enjoyed a close relationship with activities in the London elementary schools, for example, arranging recitations. The Poetry Society also received recognition by professional magazines, like *School World.* [20] School inspectors had noted in turn-of-the-century Board of Education reports that many Board School teachers themselves scarcely knew their English literature and spoke with "impure" dialects. The Poetry Society imposed a solution to these problems by effectively institutionalizing their own tastes and class paradigms within the schools.

Again anticipating the concerns of the Newbolt Report, the Poetry Society responded to class anxieties by organizing contests for judging the purity of schoolchildren's speech. A September 17, 1912, article from the *Star* reported that "Not only Dr. Hulbert, but various other authorities on speech, have noticed that everybody in the metropolis is becoming Cockney in speech, a tendency that can best be overcome by little local gatherings for the study and contemplation of the best poetry and the general practice of the art of speaking verse. And what is better still, it can be done quickly" (in *Poetical Gazette,* Oct. 1912, 489–490). The contest included high school and college contestants, but also for the first time "a contingent from the London County Council children, and the examination consisted mainly in speaking verse they had studied and in reading at sight unknown pieces. . . . They were not picked children, and their own readings gave no trace of the Cockney accent" (490). Clearly the accents of the dominant classes had become normalized as the language of culture.

The attempts by the Poetry Society to influence pedagogy and the public's literary taste can be seen as part of the reforming spirit of the Edwardian age. But the educational reforms and the Poetry Society's attempts to influence them clearly served a class agenda and addressed anxieties that the reforms themselves may have helped to produce. As Bourdieu notes, the educational system helps to "form a general, transposable disposition towards legitimate culture" (*Distinction* 23) and "channels pupils towards prestigious or devalued positions implying or excluding legitimate practice" (25). Education helps to justify markers of distinction even to those who cannot share in them: "The official differences produced by academic classifications tend to produce (or reinforce) real differences by including in the classified individuals a collectively recognized and supported belief in the differences, thus producing behaviors that are intended to bring real being into line with official being" (25). The pure voice that the school system and the Poetry Society encouraged served to sanction middle-class accents even to lower-class pupils, and the literary taste consecrated by the Poetry Society and their school programs served the same function. Working-class children could not lose strong Cockney accents during a few weeks of preparation for a contest; the institutionalization of the pure voice in poetry recitation meant that children whose families had instilled middle-class accents and literary tastes in them were the most likely to receive rewards and official affirmation of their tastes and accents through the educational system. Furthermore, the working-class children's belief in their own inferiority would be reinforced. The unacknowledged power dynamic of this pedagogy preserved the cultural privilege of the middle classes. Not surprisingly, the higher one was in the class system, the more one was likely to succeed in the school system (Halsey et. al.,161).

Modernism, Verse Recitation, and Public Performance

The Poetry Society and the larger educational and elocutionary communities rallied around the pure voice and the oral performance of poetry, whether as well-intentioned reform, class paranoia, or simply public displays of legitimacy. However, though educational reforms and the verse-recitation movement may seem unlikely contexts for emerging modernist poetry, these discourses opened an opportunity for modernist poets. Harold Monro—and the modernist and Georgian poets associated with his magazines and the successful *Georgian Poetry* anthologies—attempted to tap into the popular practice of verse recitation and the performance of the pure voice to bring modernist poetry before the public.

Monro and many of his readers envisioned even purely literary little magazines like the *Poetry Review* and *Poetry and Drama* not as elitist coterie organs, but as exactly the opposite—organs for the popularization of poetry. Monro shared with other early modernist writers an optimism about reaching new audiences within the urban masses. His first editorial in the *Poetry Review* asserted, "Poetry is said to be unpopular—generally by those who dislike it themselves. Good poetry is as much read now as at any time since the invention of printing, and bad poetry is certainly read a great deal too much" ("Preface" 3–4). And in an article entitled "Poetry and the Public," he proclaimed: "A majority of intelligent people still argues that poetry is unpopular: it is one of the objects of POETRY AND DRAMA to dispel this illusion" (126). His readers also assumed that the magazine was not to be a coterie affair.[21] Monro wanted not to inspire mass market verse, but rather to popularize Georgian and modernist challenges to Victorian orthodoxies.[22] As a step toward this goal, he accepted the editorship of the *Poetry Review* (offered by the Poetry Recital Society), which would be published with the society's regular monthly *Poetical Gazette*.[23]

What ensued from this odd pairing of experimental modernist poets and the proponents of Tennyson and William Watson was a battle over the power to consecrate poetry.[24] The taste for the long-accepted Victorian greats that helped provide legitimacy to Edwardian middle-class culture was challenged by the more restricted field of cultural production—the network of young poets and dramatists, avant-garde theaters, little magazines, and small presses. This network attempted to legitimate, even in the eyes (or ears) of middle-class audiences, contemporary poetry, which was largely ignored by the verse-recitation industry and the educational system as well as by the Poetry Society. Much energy was devoted in the early issues of the *Poetry Review* to defining critical practices and their role in elucidating the new verse experiments.[25] But the verse-recitation movement and the Poetry Society had given Monro and other modernist poets the opportunity to fight this battle not only within the magazines but, above all, in the public oral performances, lectures, and discussions that were the inspiration for the Poetry Bookshop, which even the conservative Edmund Gosse called "one of the most interesting experiments of our time."[26]

In Monro's magazines and at the Poetry Bookshop, much of the discussion about new poetry and verse drama was positioned in the larger field of cultural discourse I have charted that privileged the oral over the visual, the pure voice over the "artificiality" of music-hall spectacle and poetry written "for the page." The *Poetry Review* was strewn with advertisements for elocutionists seeking pupils; it advertised and reviewed recitation anthologies and even planned a special issue on verse recitation. The widespread affirmations by the verse recitationists of oral performance as a facilitator of literary appreciation, and their paired emphases on impersonality and authorial presence, were mainstays of the discussion of the "poetry renaissance" and of modernists' prewar aesthetic assumptions. Adopting the prevalent class-based discourses of the day, Monro noted of a recent poetry recital: "Miss Irwin's attempt to excite the senses of the audience was hopeless from the start . . . all her ringing of gongs and tricks with hideous limelight fell flat—as they should. . . . Poetry is not, and never will be, a music-hall art" ("The Nineties" 250).

Monro found that these bourgeois principles could accommodate avant-garde poetic practices as well. His excitement about F. T. Marinetti largely derived from the futurist's abilities not only as a modern verse innovator, but also as a public reader. Excitedly writing about Marinetti's "wonderful reading," Monro explained that "[Futurist] poetry is composed recklessly for immediate and wide circulation and declamation in large assemblies, frequently for purposes of propaganda. It is verse rather for the ear than for any close and studious scrutiny by the eye" ("Futurist Poetry,"). In his "Wireless Imagination and Words at Liberty" manifesto published in *Poetry and Drama,* Marinetti himself noted proudly that "the number of futurist reciters is steadily increasing" (326). But the English privileging of the ear over the eye was established long before the futurist invasion, whose reception it helped to shape.[27]

Even foreign works chosen for publication in *Poetry and Drama* affirm this oral emphasis. F. S. Flint, who regularly penned the "French Chronicle" for the magazine, translated the "Introductory Speech Delivered at the First Poetry Matinee of the Theatre du Vieux Colombier," in which Henri Ghéon praised the new practice of verse recitation preceding a play. Ghéon attacked those who felt that poetry should be left to the pages of a book: "There is not one of the words composing [a poem] that does not vibrate physically in our mind. . . . it may be said that they recite to us within. . . . Who knows but that the poem, by its enforced seclusion, runs the risk of losing, little by little, that authentic life which it owes to human speech, and which it will always find therein so long as speech is not divorced from poetry. We read too much with our eyes" (43). He explores a crucial element of the modernist appropriation of prewar recitation tenets: "These readings will provide a useful test of the new poetry, which, by its many innovations in sonority and rhythm, demands of the reader a personal effort that, either on account of indolence or habit, he is not always willing to make. He must be made to hear this music that as yet he does not hear alone" (44). Ghéon suggests that public readings aid the appreciation of formal experiment—an idea that Monro and his compatriots would underscore.

Monro and the contributors to his magazines appropriated contemporary discourse about verse recitation in order to put it to use for the popularization of new experimental poetry. In "Poetry and Sermons," Monro asserted that "It is abundantly proved that good poetry, well read, will interest the practical average man as well as the practical average woman," and that the lack of ability to recite verse skillfully was "responsible for the so-called 'unpopularity' of poetry." In the effort to create a discerning audience for the new verse, Monro founded the Poetry Bookshop, where one could not only buy new poetry (a rarity in London), but also hear it read. The Poetry Bookshop opened in January 1913 in an eighteenth-century house in Bloomsbury near the British Museum. It featured both new and old poetry for sale, rooms to lodge visiting young poets, and a room for verse readings. It was here, as much as in Monro's magazines and publications, that modernist poets attempted to challenge dominant bourgeois tastes by using the cultural practice that had emerged as a primary reinforcer of those tastes—the verse recitation.

As a space for oral performance, the Poetry Bookshop was central to Monro's hopes for a poetic revolution. He noted: "We make a regular practice of reading poetry aloud, and any one who wishes to stroll in and listen may do so. . . . We are absolutely certain that the proper values of poetry can only be conveyed through its vocal interpretation by a sympathetic and qualified reader. Indeed so obvious does this appear that we regard the books on sale in the shop merely as printed scores for the convenience of refreshing the memory in hours of study or indolence" ("The Bookshop," Dec. 1913). He proposed the Poetry Bookshop as an antidote to an increasingly visual society: "Every year humanity continues to use its ears less and to trust more to its eyes. At present there can be scarcely a hundred first-class readers of poetry in England, the demand for them having almost ceased. But we are on the way to altering this. We hope that Poetry Bookshops will eventually be established in all the principal towns of England" (Dec. 1913).[28] Monro explained that a customer could "hear the poetry he wishes to buy read aloud by someone who loves and understands it. Or he can come to our Poetry Recitals which will be held twice a week, to which all interested will be welcome."[29]

A dichotomy later familiar to readers of the vorticist diatribes in the periodical *Blast* emerged with the *Poetry Review*'s rhetorical privileging of the voice over the eye.[30] In "The Book of the Month," in the March 1912 *Poetry Review,* Pound had criticized some of the poems in Ford's *High Germany:* "[Ford's] flaw is the flaw of impressionism, impressionism, that is, carried out of its due medium. Impressionism belongs in paint, it is of the eye. The cinematograph records, for instance, the 'impression' of any given action or place, far more exactly than the finest writing, it transmits the impression to its 'audiences' with less work on their part. A ball of gold and a gilded ball give the same 'impression' to the painter. Poetry is in some odd way concerned with the specific gravity of things, with their nature" (133). Though Pound and Wyndham Lewis would blast impressionism far more forcefully a few years later, Pound's point is not just that Ford mistakenly tries to appropriate a practice that belongs properly in the visual realm, but also that impressionism, like the mass cultural cinematograph, merely records surface detail, which can be deceptive. Poetry, remaining in the verbal realm, grasps essences, and not just faithful visual reproductions of surface, which can more successfully be accomplished by a new machine.

Many articles in Monro's magazines made much the same case in calling for a popular verse drama. Several Georgian poets were involved in writing verse plays, as Yeats had been for years, and the argument was frequently made that the realist aesthetics of the current theater merely reproduced the superficial, whereas verse drama achieved a more profound sense of character and ideal. In "The Function of Poetry in the Drama," Lascelles Abercrombie argued that "the great difference between prose drama and poetry drama is that the first concentrates its imitation on the outermost reality, the second on the innermost" (112); further, characters in verse drama had "a greater precision and definiteness of design," which resulted from the "exaggeration in the *shape* of the speech they utter" (108). Emphasizing voice over spectacle, other *Poetry Review* authors made similar arguments for a "purer" theater, based on the "alive speech" of verse drama.[31]

Yeats, who read at the Poetry Bookshop, and whose oral performances and verse dramas were frequently discussed in the magazine, had developed an interest in verse drama in the 1890s as a means of reaching a wider public. His emphasis was strongly on "alive speech," rather than on spectacle. To convey the rhythms of his poetic line, he had even asked a company working up one of his plays "to let [him] rehearse them in barrels that they might forget gesture and have their minds free to think of speech for a while" (in Jeffares 119). Again, this privileging of the oral performance over the visual staging in experimental theater (whether by Georgians or by modernists like Yeats and, later, Eliot) was supported by larger cultural institutions. While the Poetry Society and its offspring, the Verse Drama Society, tried to revive interest in verse drama, educators began to explore the uses of verse drama and choral speaking in the classroom.[32]

This movement toward verse drama among speech instructors, the Poetry Society, and writers for *Poetry and Drama* found its modernist incarnation in the early criticism of a newcomer on the London scene—T. S. Eliot. In "The Possibility of a Poetic Drama," Eliot frequently imagines resurrecting the verse drama in England, claiming that "The essential thing is to get upon the stage this precise statement of life which is at the same time a point of view, a world—a world which the author's mind has subjected to a complete process of simplification" (*Sacred Wood* 68). Eliot, like Yeats, saw great opportunity to reach a broad audience for poetry through the verse drama. He claimed that "a large number of poets hanker for the stage; and . . . a not negligible public appears to want verse plays" (60). He explains that "The Elizabethan drama was aimed at a public which wanted *entertainment* of a crude sort, but would *stand* a good deal of poetry; our problem should be to take a form of entertainment, and subject it to the process which would leave it a form of art" (70). Eliot, himself a fan of the music hall, even cautiously raised the possibility that music-hall comedy might be the most appropriate form. He chose, however, to create verse drama, rather than working-class music-hall pieces.[33] Given that the context of discussion of verse drama and poetic performance was implicated in a normative middle-class movement emphasizing purity of diction and pronunciation, his decision, and the modernist movement toward verse drama, had a class aspect that was inescapable.

In addition to turning bourgeois discourse about verse recitation and literary appreciation to the advantage of modern poetry, Monro and fellow writers also picked up the call for the impersonality of the verse reciter that had been a mainstay of the attack on earlier elocution styles by the verse-recitation movement. In an article entitled "Readings of Poetry," Monro wrote of a reading by Alexander Watson: "Certainly his enunciation is clear, his elocution excellent, and his voice splendidly controlled; yet it was not 'The Everlasting Mercy' he gave us, but rather a demonstration of his own powers, using 'The Everlasting Mercy' as a medium. In the same way, Miss Nora Clarke at the Steinway Hall made herself throughout the sole element of importance in her recital. While fully realizing the difficulties of self-repression, particularly in the situation of sole occupant of a public platform, we cannot but think that the whole training of the actor or reciter is adapted to impede rather than to promote the enjoyable reading or recitation of good poetry." As in contemporaneous recitation manuals, bad reciters—often equated with actors and elocutionists—are faulted for imposing their personalities onto poems, and for not having the faculty of "self-repression," the sort of impersonality that allows the presence of the author to speak through the reciter and thus to convey the proper meaning of the poem.

For an example of the ideal reciter, Monro turns to Florence Farr, who had helped Yeats produce verse dramas in London and accompanied his lectures on verse-speaking with recitations of his poems. Her book *The Music of Speech* (1909) championed Yeats's methods of verse reading.[34] Monro praises her "clarity" and the "melodiousness of her voice," but what earns her the status of "artist," and not just elocutionist, is precisely her ability to surrender to the poem and to convey its formal qualities in live performance. He hoped other reciters would "have sufficient restraint and self-surrender to submit themselves, after her manner, to the cadence and rhythms of poetry, becoming, for the time being, a sensitive medium for their conveyance to the audience, rhapsodist rather than exponent, instrument rather than representative" ("Notes and Comments," June 1912, 424).[35]

During this prewar period, discourses about the impersonal performance of the pure voice worked their way into modernist literary circles via Monro's magazines and the Poetry Bookshop, and, by the end of the war, they had been picked up by Eliot.[36] Much of Eliot's first collection of criticism, *The Sacred Wood,* reads like a synthesis of the interests and ideals of the verse-recitation movement. Eliot, too, was adamant about the value of verse drama, and he shared in "The Possibility of a Poetic Drama" the concern about the personality of the performer overriding the emotion of the poetry: "The interest of a performer is almost certain to be centered in himself. . . . The performer is interested not in form but in opportunities for virtuosity or in the communication of his 'personality'" (*Sacred Wood* 69). He also addressed the murky imprecision about whether the proper reciter surrendered his or her personality to the poem or to the poet. In "Tradition and the Individual Talent," he explained that aesthetically "*significant* emotion" is "emotion which has its life in the poem and not in the history of the poet. The emotion of art is impersonal. And the poet cannot reach this impersonality without surrendering himself wholly to the work to be done" (*Sacred Wood* 59). Authors of verse-recitation and elocution manuals, as well as the president of the Poetry Society, had emphasized the distinction conferred on the impersonal reader who surrendered to the poem read; Eliot transformed this for modernist poetics by adding that the poet also must abdicate his or her own personality and emotions to those of the poem.

These interrelated notions of presence and impersonality also influenced the critical practice that emerged in later issues of *Poetry and Drama.* In laying out changes that would occur in the second volume of the magazine, Monro tried to reshape its critical practices around a notion of impersonality: "In spite of the admirable work of our staff of critics in the past, we have for some time doubted the efficacy of the orthodox methods of criticism in their application to current poetry, and it was only our failure to discover or invent some more compatible method which obliged us to continue along the orthodox lines. We have decided, however, with certain exceptions, to represent the volumes which come before us in 1914 solely by quotation, without comment. Thus the twenty or thirty pages at present usually devoted to reviews will be occupied instead by extracts from current volumes" ("Notes and Announcements," Dec. 1913, 391–392).

Monro preceded the quotations with a "Chronicle" to keep up with new poetry, and he noted, "By this combination between a Chronicle and a series of extracts, we hope to afford our readers a better opportunity of keeping in touch with modern poetry and deciding its qualities for themselves than they can possibly obtain by drawing their conclusions through the personal criticism of some individual reviewer, however competent and impartial" (392). As in much modernist poetry, the reader was asked to take a more active role, to confront the poetry directly rather than through any mediation beyond the selection process used to assemble the extracts. Juxtaposition of admired work with "ridiculous productions of bad poets" was to allow the reader to come to an understanding of modernist poetry beyond that which a discursive text might convey.

Readers seemed to approve of this procedure and equated it with an esteemed impersonality, as Dixon Scott wrote to Monro after the first issue to adopt the practice: "I admired your chronicle tremendously. It is most excellently designed—the massing of the quotations works splendidly; and your judgments have a beautiful sanity, strictness, and dignity. I envy you your power of *impersonality:* if I were you I'd make the impersonal my mark: *you've* no need to ask your I's to assert your individuality."[37] Monro's critical practice of "the massing of the quotations" was an extension of verse-performance commonplaces, but it will also look somewhat familiar to readers of *The Waste Land* or Pound's *Cantos*. The cantos are impersonal in that there is no single lyric voice at the center of each poem, but they nonetheless rely upon the "presence" of past voices in the form of letters, remembered conversations, engravings on stone pillars, and so forth, all organized by principles of juxtaposition. The aesthetics of presence—created by importing directly both poetic and nonliterary writing—became a far more sophisticated poetic practice than Monro might have envisioned, but it achieves its poetic power in much the same way.

Modernist and Georgian poets associated with the Poetry Bookshop turned the discourse of the pure voice and authorial presence into a call for the poets themselves to read their work publicly. As much as Monro and others praised the good reciter, Monro also had some quiet doubts about the sufficiency of verse reciters to his aims of popularizing modern poetry. In notes for a lecture on modern poetry, he wrote, "Today we have schools of speech training and also verse speaking competitions all over the country, and I wonder whether those who"; he then crossed this out and rephrased the thought: "Today the speaking of poetry has been divorced from the creation of poetry, just as the singing of song has been from the composition of song."[38] Monro saw the oral presence of the poet himself or herself, not just readings by elocutionists, as necessary to the public reception of modernist poetry. Though the verse-recitation movement had prepared the way for an emphasis on authorial presence through the impersonality of the reader, Monro used the Poetry Bookshop as a space for the performance of true authorial presence.

The readings at the Poetry Bookshop, which were the natural extension of a widespread public interest in verse recitation, represent a fundamental historical shift in the relationship of English poets to their public. Major Victorian poets like Tennyson, Browning, and Arnold enjoyed great public prestige (witness the late Victorian Browning Societies and the godlike public reputation of Tennyson), but it was not part of their understanding of the role of the poet in Victorian society to read publicly.[39] Whereas public verse reading by a poet was more common in America than in England, by the mid-twentieth century this cultural norm had dramatically reversed, with poetry reading nearly as popular in England as in America. The Poetry Bookshop was a major proponent of this shift.

The public space for discussion and reception of poetry that Monro wished to create involved poets reading their works twice a week at the bookshop. These readings, or "poetry squashes," as many called them, cost only 3d. (and each issue of *Poetry and Drama* contained a free ticket to a reading) (Ross 76). They were much more in line with the widely public goals of the Victorian Penny Reading movement than the largely private and expensive Poetry Society readings. Monro worked hard to convince poets of the importance of readings, twisting the arms of reluctant public performers like Rupert Brooke, who did the first "squash" in January 1913 (Ross 75), and he corresponded prodigiously with poets to arrange readings.

In addition to fostering audience appreciation of new poetry, these public readings helped the poets and underscored the centrality of the spoken word to modernist aesthetics. Francis Macnamara, who had just read his poems at the bookshop, wrote that "If [poets] will only give every word its natural stress, the rhythm would declare itself. This should be so, of course, in all poetry: it is the only way to mend the trouble of actors turning verse into prose. . . . I am sure that you are doing more for poetry by getting people to read aloud their own things than has been done in England for many a day . . . it is the only way for poets to learn."[40] In spite of his ridicule of what he saw as the audience's sympathies for Georgian poets like John Drinkwater, Lasecelles Abercrombie, and Wilfrid Gibson, Pound noted the value of these readings at the bookshop to his modernist ascetic impulse: "I should rather like to read again sometime if the audience will stand it. I find pouring stuff at that stolid mass of Drinkwaterian-Abercrombogibsonian stodge, I will not say exactly enjoyable, but instructive. I have already got rid of half a like of superfluous matter from one poem, and might with benefit continue the process. Shd. make another programme of entirely different items, 'going on from where I left off on Thursday.'"[41] Giving voice to his own poems helped Pound—who by this time had already penned his first cantos—revise them into leaner, more focused works.

Poetry and an Oral Public Sphere

The dominant practice of early modernist and Georgian poets and their readers of holding the pure voice over the artificiality of acting, elocution, and music hall histrionics managed class anxieties and preserved middle-class cultural dominance over the working classes. The same forces contrasted public verse recitation to a number of institutions and practices that were involved in building middle-class culture, and their nostalgia for the important social role poetry played in prebourgeois courtly cultures reflects middle-class anxieties about their cultural legitimacy in relation to the aristocracy. Their polemics targeted bourgeois cultural practices and institutions as well as their foundation—the printing press—including the newspaper (perhaps the strongest component in the creation of the bourgeois public sphere in Habermas's account),[42] poetry printed for the eye alone, and, perhaps above all, poetry printed for consumption in the study, in the domestic sphere of the bourgeois household. Monro and others essentially appropriated the bourgeois practice of verse recitation, using its own discourses, to affirm prebourgeois oral public literary production, but, importantly, one that was to embody some of the properties of the classic bourgeois liberal public sphere—public discussion and disinterestedness.

Much of the discussion of verse recitation and the mission of the Poetry Bookshop was couched in allusions to an idealized prebourgeois communal and courtly life and its tradition of oral performances. Harold Monro's preface to the first issue of the *Poetry Review* claimed that "There have been periods when labour was joyful and beautiful, and the poet sang because the community required his song: he expressed the keen and natural emotions of life" (3). He adds, "And in the future, when [poetry] has become natural and keen, there will be *improvisatori* again, who will lavish us their poems carelessly, like a plant its flowers. Then life will have become greater than literature, and days than verses" ("The Future of Poetry" 13). Later, he excitedly reported that "Masefield's narrative poems have been read aloud with startling success at village gatherings" ("Current English Poetry" 204). Monro used medieval metaphors to explain that the Poetry Bookshop would house poets and offer lectures and readings: "In short, we propose to establish an informal Guild" ("The Bookshop," Nov. 1912, 499). In a set of lecture notes, he even aligned his vision with Homeric Greece: "Before books public declamation was the only chance of a popular hearing—Public Religious Declamations and after-dinner (Homeric) were then as books."[43] He imagined a prebourgeois communal life in which the poet's oral performance played an integral role.

The constant insistence by almost all authors in the *Poetry Review* and *Poetry and Drama* that poetry be restored to some relationship with life—

78

apparently meaning a communal aesthetic experience—was encapsulated in the ideal of a pre-print society. Although Monro and other authors did not entirely condemn print (Monro was, after all, a publisher and magazine editor), they saw connections among the development of print, the move of poetry out of the community and into the bourgeois study, and the writing of verse for the printed page (relying on typographical manipulation, eye rhymes, illustration, and so forth). The public readings at the Poetry Bookshop were meant to counter this movement of poetry into the private sphere. Though the Poetry Society's recitation practices fostered many oral performances of poetry and helped provide the impetus for the Poetry Bookshop, the Poetry Society recitations still largely took place in the parlors of the middle and upper middle classes and were not in any meaningful way public.

It was this historical vision of the movement of poetry from oral public reception to print-based private reception and aesthetic autonomy that led many writers of the period to see oral performance as reinvesting poetry with contemporary social significance. Basil Watt, in an essay entitled "The Poet Articulate," called "the dominion of the printed word" "one of the saddest effects of a modern tyranny":

Print has become a pernicious vice, a shocking bully. From the age when George Herbert wrote those things of his in which the printed lines were so arranged as to represent pictorially such pretty devices as altars and church-doors, until Lewis Carroll worried his proof-reader with the typographical ingenuity of his "Mouse's Tale," print has developed its diabolical hold upon the visual centres of man. And now man has almost entirely capitulated. Words are no longer audible phenomena. They are things seen. The verb "to read" no longer implies the translation of hieroglyphs into uttered sounds for the benefit of those to whom hieroglyph are hieroglyphic. Reading is now a state of silent stupor, in which the mind absorbs meaning only in a visual way: the speech centres are dormant, the spoken word is dead. (502)

As in so many other articles in the magazine, Watt called for better poetry readers, for reforming the education system to include more poetry recitation. He added wryly, "If, to return to principles of book-incendiarism, it might be established that poetry should be invented and declaimed, but never written, the poets themselves would doubtless soon see to it that the practice of genuine recital should survive, and the art of poetry become articulate" (503). Glib as Watt's article may sound, his historical assignment of the problem, epitomized by Herbert's visual poetry, coincides with the seventeenth-century rise of a middle-class reading public, and the expansion of the print industry, through newspapers and even early protonovels.

The newspaper itself, whose seventeenth- and eighteenth-century antecedents were crucial to the creation of the bourgeois public sphere, came to epitomize the print-driven movement of the communal understanding of the social world into the domestic sphere—the private visual consumption of print as the mediator of experience. Monro wrote, "We desire to see a public created that may read verse as it now reads its newspapers; nor can we believe that our hope errs in any excess of optimism. The transplantation of poetry into the study is a modern development surely not to be tolerated" ("Broadsides and Chap-Books"). Monro wished not just that as many people would read poetry as read the mass market newspapers, which by now in some cases reached more than a million readers daily, but also that poetry might regain a lost function that had tied it to the life of the community before it became merely a matter for private aesthetic enjoyment: "It is illuminating to reflect that so recently as the seventeenth and eighteenth centuries the people still preferred its news and its romance in verse. The minstrel and the ballad-monger then represented our modern Northcliffe; Broadside and Chap-book, the modern newspaper" ("Broadsides and Chap-Books"). Oral performance not only involved a public communal reception, but it also tied aesthetics to the non-aesthetic aspects of everyday life. If news and public sentiment about current events could be given in verse, then poetry was not removed into an autonomous aesthetic realm. But, Monro added, "Let us not be accused of undue affection for the past"; he was not trying to revive the broadside as a rival for the modern newspaper, but instead wanted modern poetry to borrow newspaper industry methods of cheap production and broad distribution: "Such publications require to be accessible, portable, unconfusing, and, above all, inexpensive. They are meant to be sold anywhere and everywhere, carried in the pocket, read at any spare moment, left in the train, or committed to the memory and passed on. They should be put up for sale in large quantities" ("Broadsides and Chap-Books"). Even the inexpensive throwaway nature of the modern commodity presented opportunities to bring modern poetry out of the study. Monro did in fact publish chapbooks and broadsides for wide distribution as one print-medium attempt to complement the verse recitation he espoused.

At the Poetry Bookshop, the public space of oral performance, in spite of its prebourgeois trappings, mirrored the ideal of the liberal public sphere that Ford had tried to resurrect in the *English Review,* and Ezra Pound and Richard Aldington urged Monro to model *Poetry and Drama* on the *Mercure de France* or even to incorporate the *Mercure* directly into it.[44] In his preface to the January 1912 *Poetry Review* enunciating the aims of the magazine, Monro had complained, "Our weekly and monthly papers are nearly all tainted with party-politics, and treat literature as a form of mental athletics. Thought is difficult: it is wonderful when an Englishman achieves it. But poetry is far more native to the national genius. We have a strong capacity for enthusiasm; we have a calm obstinate persistence, and there is no one so inflexible as an Englishman who has finally set his eyes toward beauty" (5). Like Ford in the *English Review,* Monro rehearses the common Arnoldian notion that the English are predisposed toward the enthusiasms of Hebraism over the intellection of Hellenism. Like Ford, he also complains about the political partisanship of most of the weeklies and monthlies. Ford had attempted to import from France an ideal of, as Pound put it, a "general intelligencer" like the *Mercure de France* that would disinterestedly cover not only literature but also politics and other fields of modern discussion. However, Monro affirmed such an ideal of disinterestedness and discussion but restricted this vision to aesthetics, both in oral discussion and performance in the public space created by the Poetry Bookshop: "We believe that out of indefatigable discussion, unending fearless experiment, the great poet emerges" ("Notes and Comments," Aug. 1912, 354). He even included the Poetry Society in this public, putting up a special notice-board to announce its events ("The Bookshop," Nov. 1912, 499). Emphasizing contemporary poetry, he asserted: "Our purpose is to draw this public together and bring it into touch, through the Bookshop, with poetry as a living art, and as represented in the work of living poets" (498).[45]

While Monro's goal was clearly to publicize and gain an audience for Georgian and modernist verse, he also attempted to maintain an ideal of disinterestedness that seemed concomitant to his public role even in the poetry readings. As he wrote to John Drinkwater: "Personally, I have always endeavoured in my capacity of Proprietor of the Poetry Bookshop to represent it as a public institution independent of my private views and judgments." He continued: "As organiser of the Readings here, I am an intermediary between the poet and his public. Many people, with whom I am not entirely in sympathy, have given readings and lectures here. . . . If, in issuing invitations to read, I allowed my own private judgments to influence me, I should be doing an injustice to the Shop, to the audiences, and to the poets."[46] The poets Monro mentions range from the conservative formalist Gosse, the poet laureate Bridges, the sentimental Noyes, the Georgians Abercombie, Davies, De la Mare, and even Squire, the modernist Yeats and impressionist Ford, to the extreme avant-gardist Marinetti. So, for Monro, the idealized disinterestedness of the liberal public sphere was to be transposed to the realm of literary taste and preserved in public oral performance. The ideal, however, was not bloodless aestheticism, but rather a poetry reinvigorated by closer contact with life.

In his *Theory of the Avant-Garde,* Peter Bürger traces a history of bourgeois art similar to that elaborated in the pages of the *Poetry Review* and

Poetry and Drama. He describes the development of the bourgeois category of Art as one of increasing aesthetic autonomy—a distancing from life praxis evident even in the solitary absorption in the work of art that characterized aesthetic reception (48). Monro and other early British modernists envisioned this historical transformation of the institution of art during the print age as one of poetry abandoning the communal realm of oral performance and social significance, entering the private, stale realm of the bourgeois study. Though this critique anticipates the attacks on aesthetic autonomy by movements that Bürger considers avant-garde—dada, futurism, surrealism, and the Russian avant-garde—his understanding of avant-garde practices aimed at reintegrating art and praxis would not describe an activity that took place entirely within a discrete aesthetic realm.

Admitting the failures of the historic avant-garde, Bürger himself wonders if maintaining some distinction between art and praxis might not be necessary to "that free space within which alternatives to what exists become conceivable" (*Theory* 54). This was closer to Monro's and his compatriots' understanding of the social potential for art, but I suggest that the appropriation of the cultural practice of verse recitation, and its transformation of an indirect emphasis on authorial presence into a direct call for authors to read their own works in public, was in fact an attempt both to reach new audiences and foster literary appreciation of modernist poetry and to narrow the gap between art and life. The resuscitation in the *Poetry Review* and *Poetry and Drama* of prebourgeois terms of oral community—village readings, balladeers as newspapers, *improvisatori,* Homeric public declamations, the Poetry Bookshop as a "guild," and so forth—were part of a strategic attempt to envision a reinvigorated oral culture that would escape the privatized aesthetic reception and visual orientation of bourgeois culture. Although such projects were utopian, Monro's magazines and his Poetry Bookshop were able to appropriate the logic of the pure voice as a marker of distinction in order to change the field of production and reception of literary culture, and thus helped effect a transformation of the relationship of poet to public.

The class anxieties that brought the voice and the oral performance of poetry as well as verse drama into vogue also helped form and justify the speech orientation of modernist poetry in Britain. The popularity of verse drama in the 1940s and 1950s centered around Eliot's success at bringing it before West End middle-class audiences; after World War I, prominent speech-education pioneers like Elsie Fogerty and Marjorie Gullan helped to institutionalize in the British school curriculum tenets of verse speaking that they validated by talking to poets like Monro (Sivier, "English Poets," 283–298). Though these practices involved reciters who were not themselves poets, they helped prepare a generation to enjoy public poetry readings. After World War II, and following successes like Dylan Thomas, the 1960s and 1970s witnessed a poetry performance movement in Britain that built on the possibilities opened up by the Poetry Bookshop for poets to use public readings to gain an audience for their work. The widespread readings of the period, and such centers of the poetry performance movement as Morden Tower in Newcastle, owed much to Harold Monro's vision.[47] As Basil Bunting, a link between the modernists and this new generation, and the mentor of the young Newcastle poets, told them: "Poetry lies dead on the page, until some voice brings it to life" (in J. A. Johnson 304).

3

Marketing British Modernism

The *Freewoman,*
the *Egoist,*
and Counterpublic Spheres

In prewar London, mass circulation publications like Alfred Harmsworth's *Comic Cuts* and *Illustrated Chips* and best-selling novels like Marie
Corelli's *The Sorrows of Satan* epitomized an emerging commercial. As
consumer products, became increasingly available, the advertising industry expanded to create markets for the new goods. Ford and Monro and
their circles had embraced a vision of the public sphere in decline in order
to promote modernist literature as a means to rejuvenate it. Both groups
eschewed the Harmsworth-style mass market publication strategies and
intervened elsewhere in the commercial press—Ford though reviews,
Monro through the elocution and verse-recitation industry. But the other
modernist magazines I discuss in this book did not embrace such visions
of a public sphere in decline, instead engaging much more directly with
the world of commercial advertising and mass market publication to attempt, as Ford and Monro had, to bring modernism to bear upon public
culture.

84

As Andreas Huyssen suggests, some early modernists responded to aspects of this expanding commodity culture with "an anxiety of contamination" (Huyssen vi). Indeed, the *Egoist,* and its predecessors the *Freewoman* and *New Freewoman,* might seem to exemplify the type of coterie publication that turned its back on mass audiences and published either for posterity or for what Ezra Pound would call the "party of intelligence." These little magazines were arenas for radical political and economic theories, the "egoistic" philosophy affirmed by Dora Marsden, and the early work of modernist authors like Ezra Pound, Richard Aldington, H.D., F. S. Flint, and T. S. Eliot—all of whom generally appear to affirm the high-culture side of Huyssen's "great divide."[1] But Huyssen's argument overlooks an important phase of early modernism—one that blurs the separation of modernists from avant-gardists by their stances toward mass culture. In this chapter, I explore the close contact between modern commodity-advertising tactics and modernists, concluding that the fascination and opportunities offered by the brave new world of commercial culture—especially its new advertising techniques—outweighed the "anxiety of contamination" so often ascribed to modernism.

Many Edwardian oppositional groups discovered ways to deploy some of the same tactics that made Harmsworth a millionaire in order to unite large publics and support widespread social and political change. Suffragists and radical political groups created discursive spaces outside of the dominant public sphere—what I call counterpublic spheres—but the burgeoning commercial mass culture made these counterpublic spheres viable.[2] Commodity advertisers funded suffrage papers; public spectacles and popular advertising campaigns helped package, publicize, and sell causes like "the vote" to thousands of women. Anarchists, syndicalists, and socialists also turned to mass publication strategies to create an alternative press and to reach new followers.

The counterpublic spheres that I discuss—those of suffragism and of anticapitalist and antistatist political movements—showed these modernists how to adapt mass advertising tactics to further political, social, and cultural, rather than explicitly economic, goals. I argue that the writers and editors for the *Freewoman/New Freewoman/Egoist* were attracted to the proliferating types of publicity of an energetic advertising industry, and that they also attempted to adopt mass advertising tactics—not always directly from the commercial enterprises of the mass market magazines, but rather from the suffrage and anarchist movements—in order to seek out large audiences within the prewar London masses. Moreover, *Blast,* a short-lived companion magazine to the *Egoist,* even directly embraced modern commercial advertising and characterized the modernist artist as a figure of self-promotion. These efforts mark a surprising optimism about the possibility of using ideas from commercial culture to form a broad-based counterpublic sphere in opposition to bourgeois social norms, liberal and statist politics, and, above all for modernist authors, bourgeois literary taste.

Commodity Culture and Suffrage Publicity

Prewar oppositional groups, like women's suffrage organizations and socialist, anarchist, and syndicalist political movements, were intricately related to mass advertising and mass publication techniques, which were enjoying unprecedented success. Emerging counterpublic spheres greatly benefited from the confluence of several mutually augmenting trends that had begun in the late Victorian period: increasing literacy and education across many sectors of the population, an unprecedented proliferation of reading materials, the rise in availability of consumer commodities, and the use of advertising to create a demand for them.[3] Moreover, the turn of the century witnessed the rise of mass market periodicals (always with a price of 6d. or lower and filled with amusing light fiction, articles, and illustrations), cheap 6s. single-volume novels, and even cheaper "yellow back" paper reprints sold at railroad stalls (see Altick 317; Keating). Bestsellers broke all records, selling hundreds of thousands of copies. New mass market newspapers like Harmsworth's *Daily Mail* (one of the first dailies to reach out to the working and lower middle classes and specifically to women) began to hit truly astronomical six- and even seven-figure circulations through circulation-boosting stunts, sensational crime and sports reporting, and entertaining copy that required little concentration or education.[4]

But mass market publishing was partially made possible by the new and more affordable consumer products and sophisticated commodity advertisements that flooded late-Victorian and Edwardian markets. During most of the Victorian period, only the middle and upper classes could purchase these items, and Victorian merchandisers discovered that ever more spectacular advertising campaigns in middle-class periodicals created a demand for their new products (Richards 7). By the end of the century, however, an increase in working-class and middle-class expendable income and the reduction of the work week created millions of new consumers ((Altrick 365; Nevett 70,). Early twentieth-century commodity advertising became more sophisticated in order to take advantage of expanding consumer markets. Manufacturers of national brand-name products launched enormous advertising campaigns and gave increasingly active roles to advertising agencies in crafting them (see Leiss et al. 130–140; Richards 12). Perhaps most significant, the advertisements themselves were gradually evolving: at first they had merely announced the product, but they then moved to informing and educating the new consumers about

86

the need for and uses of their wares (what Leiss et al. call the "product-oriented approach"). Though product-oriented advertisements were dominant in prewar England, a different type of persuasion was emerging—one that convinced the consumer by suggestion to desire a commodity (what Leiss et al. call the "product symbols approach"). Advertisements began to focus less on the promised performance of the merchandise and more on the suggestion of a life-style, or some attribute of the consumer, that the product would affirm—glamour, intelligence, well-being, and so forth (Leiss et al. 153–155).

The mass market periodicals not only helped dramatically to expand the size of the audience that could be reached by these new commodity advertisements, but they also benefited from this wave of commercialism. As new print technologies and graphic capabilities dramatically increased the possibilities for advertising design (Leiss et al. 98–101; R. Pound 79–80), the Harmsworth and Newnes periodicals inaugurated the important shift in the basis of profitability from subscription income to advertising revenues.[5] Even with the cheaper raw materials and lower manufacturing costs of the late Victorian period, the Harmsworth and Newnes papers were sold for ¹⁄₂d., often less than they cost to produce, because the increased circulation brought in increased advertising revenues. By the end of the nineteenth century, advertising had become the largest generator of revenue for the print media (Leiss et al. 59, 95), both for daily papers like the *Daily Mail* and for magazines like the monthly *Strand,* in which advertisements from an average of 250 advertisers usually comprised around a hundred pages per issue (R. Pound 79).

Women were often the beneficiaries of late Victorian educational opportunities, the readers of new mass market publications, and the targets of the proliferating new commodity advertising campaigns, and they proved adroit at adapting institutions and tactics of the commercial mass market to support a feminist counterpublic sphere. The suffrage papers, often with large circulations of their own, were voices in this vast counterpublic sphere—a discursive space outside of the institutions of the dominant public sphere in which the vote and other women's issues were publicly discussed. These periodicals advertised in each other's pages, and public speaking engagements and rallies conducted by prominent members of one group, say the Pankhursts of the Women's Social and Political Union (WSPU), were often advertised in the organs of other groups, the National Union of Women's Suffrage Societies (NUWSS), or the Women's Freedom League, for instance. In spite of their differences on certain issues, especially that of militancy, these organizations and their papers united around a single goal, the vote.

Facing perpetual boycotting by distributors, suffrage organizations had to find other means of distributing their propaganda papers and attracting new members. They eschewed the advertising tactics of the established political weeklies—advertising in other weeklies of the dominant public sphere and the daily newspapers. Instead they turned to the highly visible advertising tactics of the commodity culture and mass market periodicals, and they circumvented printing and distribution boycotts by organizing their own distributing apparatuses and forming their own printing and publishing companies (like the Minerva Publishing Company or the Feminist Publishers, who worked out of the International Suffrage Shop, a bookstore selling feminist and suffrage literature and organizing lecture series).

Like the Harmsworth publications, suffrage papers were designed for mass sale, priced generally at 1d. weekly, and printed on large-sized paper. The principal means of advertising them were bold intrusions into public space: the spectacles documented by Lisa Tickner, scandals created by window-smashing and hunger-striking militancy, and such tactics as plastering train and tube stations and hoardings with catchy, colored posters that often hung alongside those advertising the *Daily Mail* (Ferris 81).[6] But, as *Votes for Women* put it, "The most effectively shown poster of VOTES FOR WOMEN will, however, always remain the one that is seen at the street corner, hung from the shoulders of the VOTES FOR WOMEN paper-sellers!" (June 28, 1912, 637).

The sandwich board was a popular advertising medium for consumer products (firing Joyce's imagination in *Ulysses*), and its sheer obtrusiveness made it the preferred public advertisement for the suffrage magazines. Posters and leaflets were of great importance to both commercial product and suffrage advertisements, but the scandalous physical presence in public of the middle-class woman was considered the most effective means of reaching the urban masses. Violet Hunt recalled the pain of sacrificing for the cause, as she and May Sinclair were drafted to collect money and advertise the vote in their High Street: "May and I flashed our boxes out. Much has been said of our heroism in 'standing outside to beg,' and I fancy she felt as I did—as if we had suddenly been stripped naked, with a cross-sensation of being drowned in a tank and gasping for breath" (Hunt 51). The public gaze made her feel exposed and violated, and the act of asking for money publicly rubbed against her class sensibilities, but many middle-class suffragettes sacrificed their bourgeois pride and privacy to advertise the cause.

Rebecca West's fictionalized account in *The Judge* of Ellen Melville selling *Votes for Women* in the streets with "a purple, white and green poster hung from her waist" speaks to both the sense of public mission and the sexual and class humiliation felt by many middle-class suffragettes: "This street-selling had always been a martyrdom to her proud spirit, for it was one of the least of her demands upon the universe that she should be well thought of eternally and by everyone; but she had hitherto been sustained by the reflection that while there were women in jail, as there were always in those days, it ill became her to mind because Lady Cumnock . . . laughed down her long nose as she went by. But now Ellen had lost all her moral stiffening, and as that had always been her speciality she was distressed by the lack; she felt like a dress-shirt that a careless washerwoman had forgotten to starch" (50). These advertisers publicly wore the mark of their cause on their bodies and paraded it around streets, selling magazines as they went. Sometimes public contestation and even sandwich board wars occurred between suffragettes and antisuffrage agitators wearing their own sandwich boards.[7] While suffragette planners attuned to the eye-catching used everything from wagons to elephants to display posters advertising suffrage magazines and events, street-selling was the most visible and successful tactic.

Perhaps most important to the modernists who would adopt tactics from the suffrage papers, the kind of mass advertising techniques these feminist journals used did in fact reach large audiences of women in London and around the country. Not only did the papers have significant circulations (*Votes for Women* had a circulation of more than 20,000 [J. Lyon 102]), but they were also able to raise enormous sums of money for the cause. *Votes for Women* ran a successful £250,000 fund-raising drive, and other papers raised thousands of pounds as well. Names of newly recruited subscribers and of contributors to the funds were published in the papers, increasing the sense of solidarity of masses of women "out there" involved in the institutions of a thriving counterpublic sphere.

Beyond learning from publication practices and advertising tactics of mass market newspapers, the suffrage groups also benefited from the evolution of commodity advertising. As new and cheaper consumer products emerged, and as the newspapers earned large revenues from advertising campaigns, one sign of this interlocking of interests was the marketing by a popular Harmsworth paper, *Answers,* of *Answers* consumer products: the *Answers* pen, *Answers* watch, tea, coffee, and cigarettes. The *Answers* toothache cure even capitalized on the popularity of patent medicines (Ferris 48). Using the rising power of the brand name both to advertise a noncommercial product (the cause) and to raise money by selling commodities, many suffrage magazines featured their own brand-name products. *Votes for Women* advertised *Votes for Women* cigarettes, *Votes for Women* tea, and even WSPU Suffragette Crackers, while *Common Cause* advertised a *Common Cause* Fountain Pen.

Consumer blocks embodied another crucial connection between the commercial realm and the suffrage movement. Although rigorous market research would not occur until the 1920s and 1930s, Harmsworth had early perceived the value to advertisers of creating new popular journals aimed at particular audiences.[8] Likewise, the suffrage journals with their large middle-class female readerships were a gold mine for advertising aimed at this group of consumers. A vast array of consumer items were advertised in the suffrage papers, from clothing, books, magazines, and patent medicines for "female" or childhood ailments, to national brand-name items (Coleman's Mustard, Flako Soap, and the like). Above all, enormous revenues were generated for the suffrage cause by advertisements for London's department stores. Major department stores had emerged in the 1870s, and by the early twentieth century they had even developed advertising departments and sophisticated advertising campaigns (Leiss et al. 83). Prominent London stores like Debenham and Freebody, Peter Robinson's, and Selfridges occupied a large portion of the advertising space in the suffrage magazines, and, as Kaplan and Stowell document, the suffragettes greatly influenced the fashions marketed by these stores.[9]

Sensing their own value as a ready-made consumer block, these magazines promoted themselves to businesses. In a notice entitled "How to Make Money for the Cause," the *Suffragette* wrote:

The advertisement manager urges all readers to remember the invaluable help they can give to the SUFFRAGETTE. We must all buy food and clothes and other commodities somewhere. Why not buy exclusively from our advertisers? This is most important. You may not be able to secure advertisements, but you can *keep* them by patronising the advertisers. Tell them—or better still, write on your bills—that your purchase is the outcome of advertising in the SUFFRAGETTE. Our advertisers comprise most of the best houses in all trades. ALL of us can swell the revenue for the cause by purchasing from advertisers—and tell them WHY YOU PATRONISE THEM. (July 3, 1914, 206)

Similarly, the *Vote* carried the frequent reminder to "Support those advertisers who support us." It ran an ad proclaiming that "THE VOTE IS A GOOD ADVERTISING MEDIUM. We know that our readers support THE VOTE. If you are an Advertiser, we want YOU to know it too," and printed testimonials from satisfied advertisers (Feb. 4, 1911). Like a product, the suffrage cause lent itself well to the packaging of astute advertisers, and it also organized a buying public that appealed to advertisers of other commercial products. This symbiosis sold countless consumer items for department stores and swelled the coffers of the suffrage journals with advertising revenues beyond the wildest dreams of many small literary magazines of the period.[10]

The *Freewoman* and Counterpublic Spheres

For many modernist authors, the *Freewoman* presented an important vision of a counterpublic sphere sustained by mass publicity. Dora Marsden and Mary Gawthorpe started the *Freewoman* in 1911 in an attempt to shift the discussion and basis of feminism away from a myopic insistence on the vote as the sole issue (the position of many suffrage associations, especially the WSPU), and to leave behind what had come to seem the all-too-costly militancy of the WSPU and the dictatorship of the Pankhursts. Their efforts were shaped by suffrage papers and modes of publicity. As another feminist weekly (though costing 3d. rather than 1d. because of its small beginnings), advertisers saw in the *Freewoman* the same market potential that led them to advertise in the major suffrage papers. Large London department stores like Debenham and Freebody and the fashionable A L'Ideal Cie advertised the latest styles in women's clothing to what they assumed was the female middle-class audience of the suffrage papers.[11] Advertisements for new national brand-name products, like "Douglafrocs," Horrocks's "flanalette," and the "Lady" combined knife and scissor sharpener appeared alongside advertisements for women's patent medicines and advertising gimmicks like Adori soap's "manly names competition."

But, as in the suffrage journals, advertisments for commercial products in the *Freewoman* were fellow travelers with advertisements for the institutions of a counterpublic sphere. Not surprisingly, the *Freewoman* carried notices for bookstores like the International Suffrage Shop and for radical publishers, including Stephen Swift,[12] which took a full-page at the back of every issue boasting of banned books like Reginald Wright Kauffman's *Daughters of Ishmael* and Rémy de Gourmont's *A Night in the Luxembourg.* Advertisements aimed at the new liberated woman, like those for Farrow's Bank for Women, "jujustsu" classes for women, and an agency specializing in patents for inventions by women, ran alongside those for literary magazines like the *Poetry Review* and the *Onlooker.*

What is most significant about the numerous consumer product advertisements in the *Freewoman* is that, in spite of its shaky beginning with only around 300 subscribers, the *Freewoman*—like the *Daily Mail*—actually made more money from advertising revenue than it did from subscriptions.[13] It had subscribers abroad, especially in the thriving feminist communities in New York and Chicago, but its readers were predominantly British. Not surprisingly for a magazine seen as part of the suffrage press, women subscribers outnumbered men almost four to one, and the largest single category of subscribers was that of unmarried women living in London, followed closely by married women.[14] In spite of Dora Marsden's harsh attacks on the WSPU, the *Freewoman* was still carried by the International Suffrage Shop and bought by suffrage organizations like the WSPU, the Women's Freedom League, the International Women's Franchise Club, and the National American Suffrage Association of New York, and it was perceived by both advertisers and other suffrage organizations as another suffrage paper.

However, counterpublic spheres have their own dynamics and structures, and that of the feminists/suffragettes favored institutional organization and legitimation. Unlike the major suffrage journals, the *Freewoman* did not have the backing of any particular suffrage organization, and this independence made it difficult to survive in the feminist/suffrage counterpublic sphere. The *Freewoman* struggled to build a subscription base—despite the advertisers' misguided assumption that they would secure the large readership of the major suffrage weeklies. By February 1912, after three months of existence, the paper called for readers to increase its circulation by bringing in two new subscribers each (Marsden, "An Appeal"). This faith in the direct appeal was based on the idea that there was a large enough public to support the magazine, and, following the lead of other suffrage papers, Marsden turned to the institutions of the commercial mass market to try to reach that audience. Beginning in the same month, she turned to an important new force in the world of commodity advertising and engaged an advertising agent, Mr. H. Winterton of the Gough Press agency, to help promote the paper.[15] Winterton corresponded with Willing and Co. about placing *Freewoman* advertisements around London, and they offered him positions in tube stations.[16] He advised the *Freewoman* staff on schemes to place notices in the "Cooperative Housekeeping or domestic papers," and, like many of the newer generation of advertising agents, he offered suggestions to increase the paper's marketability as a product.[17]

But the *Freewoman* was not simply part of the discursive space of the suffrage/feminist counterpublic sphere. A large measure of its importance to modernist authors came from its attempt to form a broader and more generally antibourgeois oppositional public sphere that would involve not just public discussion of suffrage but would include topics that the bourgeois suffrage magazines would consider "improper," like homosexuality, radical monetary reforms, experimental or radical art and literature, and antistatist politics. Few socialists of the "Great State" Fabian variety wrote for the *Freewoman,* and it became home to important syndicalists like Guy Bowman (editor of the *Syndicalist* and frequent contributor), followers of the radical individual "egoism" of the German philosopher Max Stirner like Steven T. Byington (the translator of the English edition of Stirner's *The Ego and His Own*), and anarchists like Guy Aldred and Benjamin Tucker, who wrote a regular column from Paris for the *New Freewoman.* Radical political groups had their own journals and alternative methods of advertising and distribution to get around boycotts similar to those against the suffrage journals. The *Freewoman* became part of this alternative public sphere that relied heavily upon public lectures and meetings and cheap mass publication processes.

During the period from 1890 to the beginning of the war, socialists and anarchists observed the huge expansion of the commercial press and believed that there was a connection between the increasing activity of the Liberal and Conservative parties and the general growth of the press. Just as suffragettes created their own mass press to rival the dominant public sphere's control of political discourse, the socialists and anarchists felt a need for their own press to counter that of the capitalists (Hopkin 295). Socialist individuals launched journals, like Robert Blatchford's *Clarion,* and groups like the Independent Labour party financed papers (the ILP created sixty-eight papers from 1893 to 1910). Syndicalists and anarchists also turned to the press, producing at least twenty-five anarchist papers from 1890 to 1910 (Hopkin 297). To help overcome the problems of boycott by printers who were wary of prosecution for sedition, the Metropolitan Co-operative Printing Works was formed to print all the major anarchist papers (Hopkin 301). The radical political milieu to which the *Freewoman* belonged shared suffragism's sense of militancy and of optimism that the commercial press did not hold a monopoly on mobilizing mass opinion.

Radical political movements helped to provide for the *Freewoman* an emphasis on public meetings and lectures both as mass advertising and as institutions of a counterpublic sphere that now included discussion of both feminist and radical political agendas. Guy Aldred, the anarchist editor and publisher of the *Herald of Revolt* and later the *Spur,* began to publish articles in the *Freewoman* and to publicize it in his own anarchist journal. He corresponded with Marsden and brought to the *Freewoman* another type of mass advertising, the public lecture. Because of its controversial nature, the *Freewoman* was boycotted by W. H. Smith and Sons, whose virtual monopoly on rail station book stalls helped make it one of the largest distributors of journals in England. In January 1912, to counter this crippling of the magazine's ability to sell on newsstands, Aldred offered to help organize lectures, and volunteered to keep a standing notice of the *Freewoman* in his paper.[18] Later in the year he wrote Marsden, volunteering to adopt a scheme used by another anarchist paper, the *Worker's Friend:* fundraising lectures at the South Place Institute. He would give a lecture on "The Necessity for Sex Radicalism" gratis if he could sell his *Herald of Revolt* alongside the *Freewoman,* and he would provide Marsden with people who would push the bills announcing the meeting; as he wrote, "You see you have to make yourself felt against boycott; and public meeting is the only way of doing it." Using a term from the commercial entertainment industry, Aldred added, "Among Anarchists, Freethinkers, and Socialists my name will 'draw.'"[19]

Although the *Freewoman* was never widely read by the working classes—Aldred had noted that its 3d. weekly price would put it out of reach of most of his readers[20]—it became an important point of contact between the women's movement and anti-statist sentiments, thus suggesting to modernist authors a vision of a broadly based oppositional public sphere. Articles on anarchism and syndicalism were regularly published in the *Freewoman,* and women's issues discussed in the *Freewoman* worked their way into the anarchist and syndicalist magazines like Aldred's penny monthly *Herald of Revolt* and Guy Bowman's *Syndicalist,* with which the *Freewoman* exchanged subscriptions.[21] In addition to sharing writers, like Aldred himself and the anarchist Selwyn Weston, the *Herald of Revolt* and the *Freewoman* also shared some subscribers, perhaps indicating the success of Aldred's efforts on behalf of the *Freewoman.*[22]

The *Freewoman* founded an important new forum of publicity in this more broadly envisioned counterpublic sphere—the Freewoman Discussion Circles. This hunger for public discussion of controversial issues, much like the coffeehouse debates on newspaper articles in the eighteenth century, had arisen from both the meetings of radical political groups and practices of the suffragettes. The suffragettes had their "At Homes" to discuss issues, and such institutions of the feminist counterpublic sphere as the International Suffrage Shop hosted series of public lectures, some of which Dora Marsden attended. The Discussion Circles ultimately would facilitate the rebirth of the *Freewoman* as the *New Freewoman* in 1913. Marsden wrote: "It has been pointed out to us by friendly critics that THE FREEWOMAN contains each week matter so highly debatable, and of such serious human import, that it is difficult to digest all that it contains, and to find one's bearings, in view of the many articles which express opposing points of view. It has been suggested, therefore, that FREEWOMAN clubs, or informal gatherings of men and women, should be started for discussions, of which the weekly FREEWOMAN would form the basis. Of this suggestion, coming from several readers, we highly approve, and pass it on to other readers for their consideration" ("'Freewoman' Clubs"). In the ensuing Freewoman Discussion Circles, which met every other week, the participants listened to a lecture, which usually would be published in the magazine, and then spent the rest of the evening in open discussion of the topic. The *Freewoman's* twenty-page weekly issue had become increasingly dominated by its correspondence section, which had grown to take up from eight to ten pages during particularly heated discussions. This sense of a discursive space for a public interested in progressive or even revolutionary issues, created by the paper itself and the other journals with which it was in dialogue, was furthered by the open forum of the Discussion Circle. The first Discussion Circle meeting, on April 25, 1912, was attended by one hundred people, setting a precedent for an active ongoing public institution.[23]

As the *Freewoman* tried to create a public space for a wide range of oppositional movements, its writers even began to manifest the conjunction of different revolutionary political discourses and ideas.[24] In a *Freewoman* editorial entitled "The New Prostitution," C. H. Norman adopted discourses about the ills of prostitution and the "diseased" state of society propagated by some writers in the *Freewoman* and by suffragists, especially Christabel Pankhurst in *The Great Scourge and How to End It*. Norman attacked the commercial press as "the new prostitution," spreading a "mental syphilis" through the populace. As an antidote to the misrepresentations of the press, in this case of the miners organizing in 1912, he upheld alternative forms of mass propaganda and praised the miners' manifesto (probably referring to the antistatist pamphlet *The Miner's Next Step*): "The miners struck a fatal blow at the new prostitution in their manifesto on the Press. The Iagos of the Press were surprised in their assassin work." Still using metaphors of social health and purity, Norman optimistically asserted that "a vast body of the public is untouched by the mental syphilis circulated by the new prostitution," and he adopted the syndicalist call for a general strike to destroy the tyranny of the commercial press: "The middle classes are ceasing to trust newspapers which cannot warn them of gigantic social upheavals. . . . A society must be very healthy which will soon spew out this poison. . . . A general strike, in which the daily papers could not be published, would bring the whole edifice toppling round the ears of the Harmsworth-Levi-Cadbury-Pearson gang. That is a comforting reflection, because the day of such a strike is approaching rapidly. When it is come, and gone, there will be a good many unemployed journalists, and a purified England, as a result" (402). The *Freewoman* created a public forum drawing together a wide range of oppositional stances, synthesizing the rhetorics of such politically distant sources as syndicalism and Christabel Pankhurst.

Up against the economic realities represented by the "Harmsworth-Levi-Cadbury-Pearson gang,"[25] the *Freewoman* collapsed in October 1912. However, it had shown young modernist authors in search of an audience an alternative path to publication. Marsden's resurrection of her journal as the *New Freewoman* in June 1913 provided an important vehicle for modernist and avant-garde literary and artistic activity. Through magazines like the *New Freewoman* and *New Age,* read by audiences interested in political and social radicalism, young British modernists experimented with stepping outside the normal Edwardian institutions of literary publication.

Imagism, Advertising, and the *Egoist*

Because this engagement by modernist authors with alternative publication networks brought them into contact with the institutions of commercial culture, it necessarily forced to a crisis their understanding of the modern poet's relationship to urban mass culture. These authors had a vexed relationship to what Huyssen characterizes as the "great divide." They conceived of their art as "high art" and sometimes attacked what they saw as debased commercial mass culture driven by profits and losses. When they turned from Hellenic themes to address contemporary London, some of the English imagist poets publishing in the *Egoist* connected commercialized mass culture with the loss of the integrity and vitality of the self, which these poets saw as essential to poetry. The "egoism" of the nonliterary contributors manifested itself in the poets as a sense of alienation and even animosity toward the London masses, characterized as debased, unindividuated, and intrusively antagonistic, not as hysterical women, as Huyssen might suggest. I believe that this fear or animosity was born of a sense of the power and success of the institutions of the mass market—a power that, in the field of advertising, was to become too attractive to ignore.

In the May 1915 special "Imagist Number" of the *Egoist,* F. S. Flint's work was represented by a poem entitled "Easter." Flint imagines walking through a beautiful park with an intimate friend, but he notices the people on the other side of the wall: "Are they not aliens? / You and I for a moment see them / shabby of limb and soul, / patched up to make shift." The park becomes more desolate as the poet shrinks from confrontation with the working classes, and he expresses the anxiety of losing identity in the multitude: "Is not the whole park made for them, / and the bushes and plants and trees and grasses, / have they not grown to their standard? / The paths are worn to the grave, with their feet; . . . and you and I must strive to remain two / and not to merge in the multitude." The death of beauty ("the paths are worn to the grave"), lowering of standards, loss of identity, loss of the special bond he has with his friend—these are the threats of the urban masses, even for Flint, a poet who, in his best mode, was more of a city poet than most of the other imagists. The poem ends as the two escape between hedges:

> beyond is a pool flanked with sedge,
> and a swan among the water-lilies.
> But here too is a group
> of men and women and children;
> and the swan has forgotten its pride;
> and thrusts its white neck among them,
> and gobbles at nothing;
> then tires of the cheat and sails off;
> but its breast urges before it
> a sheet of sodden newspaper
> that, drifting away,

> reveals beneath the immaculate white splendour
> of its neck and wings
> a breast black with scum.
>
> Friend, we are beaten.

What might simply be a poem in which lovers desire solitude away from the trivialized world outside of their relationship ends with something much more hostile, even sinister. The people in the park taunt and pretend to offer food to a swan, a stock poetic and artistic image for beauty, but also for the poet himself, in the French symbolist tradition that Flint authoritatively chronicled for British magazines.[26] Two of the most famous of these swan poems—Baudelaire's "Le Cygne" in *Les Fleurs du Mal* and Mallarmé's sonnet "Le vierge, le vivace et le bel aujourd'hui"—figure the poet as a swan attempting to escape sterility or degradation. "Le Cygne" was occasioned by Paris's "urban renewal" of 1852 (Hampton 446), and Baudelaire's nostalgia for the old city—"Old Paris is no more (a town, alas, / Changes more quickly than man's heart may change)"—is figured in the futile escape of a swan from a menagerie:

> A swan who had escaped his cage, and walked
> On the dry pavement with his webby feet,
> And trailed his spotless plumage on the ground.
> And near a waterless stream the piteous swan
> Opened his beak, and bathing in the dust
> His nervous wings, he cried (his heart the while
> Filled with a vision of his own fair lake):
> "Oh water, when then wilt thou come in rain?
> Lightning, when wilt thou glitter?

The poet's alienation in the new modern cityscape is mirrored by the swan's yearning for his "own fair lake." Echoing Baudelaire's "Le Cygne," Mallarmé's famous sonnet likewise figures the poet, or the creation of poetry, as a swan trying to escape "his useless exile," frozen in the ice "when sterile winter's ennui has shone forth."[27]

In "Easter," the swan attempts to eat the bread proffered to it by the masses, suggesting Flint's attempt as a poet of the city to bring the urban life of the masses into his aesthetic experience. But what most jarringly debases the swan, what summarizes the degradation and contamination of beauty and of poets before the lowered standards of the urban masses, is the sodden newspaper that stains its breast—not with its own blood (presaging its dying "swan song" in a tragic fairy-tale image), but rather with something that flows far thinner than blood—the cheap newsprint of the tabloid. As the masses are cheated by lack of intellectual or aesthetic nourishment provided by the commercial culture symbolized by the newspaper, they cheat the swan and starve beauty. They both attract the poet and ultimately reject him. As Baudelaire's escaping swan represents the problematic status of the poet in the new city, and Mallarmé's the poet's attempt to fly above the icy sterility of everyday life, Flint's swan poem suggests that the modern poet cannot survive unstained by urban mass market culture. There is a sense of inevitability to the ending of the poem: the modernist poet can turn away from the masses—the swan wearies of their game and swims away—but he cannot simply ignore the powerful commercial press and the changing culture of the city. Like Haussmann's Paris, they cannot be wished away. Likewise, the lovers can escape through the hedge but cannot escape the degradation of beauty represented by the swan's stained breast: they realize they are "beaten."

"In the Tube" is Richard Aldington's, contribution to "Imagist Number." Aldington, the chief English imagist and the assistant editor of the *Egoist*, evokes an even greater anxiety about the "masses" in an age of mass transit and mass advertisements:

> The electric car jerks:
> I stumble on the slats of the floor,
> Fall into a leather seat
> And look up.
>
> A row of advertisements,
> A row of windows.
> Set in brown woodwork pitted with brass nails,
> A row of hard faces,
> Immobile.
> In the swaying train.
> Rush across the flickering background of fluted dingy tunnel;
> A row of eyes.
> Eyes of greed, of pitiful blankness, of plethoric complacency,
> Immobile.
> Gaze, stare at one point,
> At my eyes.
>
> Antagonism,
> Disgust,
> Immediate antipathy,
> Cut my brain, as a sharp dry reed
> Cuts a finger.
>
> I surprise the same thought
> In the brasslike eyes:
>
> *"What right have you to live?"*

The paranoid antagonism and alienation the poet feels among the crowds riding the tube is figured in the poem by the sheer repetition that aligns "a row of advertisements" with "a row of windows," "a row of hard faces," and later "a row of eyes." The poet is unable even to stand, falling before the images of a commercial mass culture. The advertisements put up by firms like Willings on the tube cars, and the standardized mechanical alignment of the rows of windows, are echoed in the faces of those whose culture is poetically figured by posters and tube cars. The poem ends with the poet hating and being hated by men whose eyes are like the brass tacks holding the tube car together.

When Aldington's *Egoist* poems grappled with his life in London, they tended to be rather cruelly disdainful of the masses about him and of mass culture. In "Cinema Exit," for instance, he writes of "the banal sentimentality of the films / The hushed concentration of the people, / The tinkling piano" and ends watching "Millions of human vermin / Swarm sweating / Along the night-arched cavernous roads. / (Happily rapid chemical processes / Will disintegrate them all.)" These are not among the best poems even of the young Aldington, but they share an understanding like Flint's that commercial mass culture was not just inconsequentially banal and insipid, but also active and powerful. And this power could be seductive when it was that of the advertising industry.

However, some poets more optimistically affirmed the alluring vitality of modern advertising. A strange text by Allen Upward appeared at the end of the June 1, 1914, issue of the *Egoist* (see fig. 1). Upward, an important but largely forgotten figure in early British modernism who helped originate imagism and influenced Pound's *Cantos*.[28] Here he finds himself transported by the magic of advertising from the public hustle and bustle of Trafalgar Square to a realm of poetic imagination and creation. Upward uses images from an advertising poster as the substance of an imagistic poem. However, as if overcome by the orientalism and exotic fantasy of the advertisement, he permits himself the very excesses of symbolism or Coleridgean romanticism that the austere and ascetic doctrines of imagism intended to excise. Aware of the seductiveness of the vast array of new advertising images crowding the hoardings around Trafalgar Square, Upward adds his envoy: "_____ & Sons. / There is more poetry in your advertisement / Than many numbers of our best Reviews." Upward is much more sanguine than other imagists about the power and even aesthetics of advertising. (As Timothy Materer recently suggested, the manipulation and juxtaposition of images and the move to replace the discursive text with the evocative image in commodity advertising does suggestively parallel some aspects of the emerging imagist poetic ["Making It Sell" 27–28].)

But this text is more than a work of "high art" influenced by advertising aesthetics. Its status is ambiguous. It seems to be an advertisement, perhaps for a new book by Upward: it is boxed off by lines of print and ends with that ubiquitous marker of the growing commodity culture: "all

> # THE
> # Magic Carpet.
> ## ALLEN UPWARD.
>
> ———
>
> *This painted poster*
> *Has snatched me from Trafalgar Square.*
> *To camels fording Asia streams,*
> *Laden with woven dreams.*
> *The soul of Persia dyes the wool:*
> *The heart of the sad old Astronomer*
> *Bleeds once again beneath the maiden's*
> *foot.*
>
> ———
>
> ### ENVOY:
> ——————— **& Sons.**
> **There is more poetry in your adver-**
> **tisement**
> **Than many numbers of our best**
> **Reviews.**
> [ALL RIGHTS RESERVED.]

Figure 1. Allen Upward destabilizes the high–low divide in "The Magic Carpet"—poem, commodity advertisement, self-promotion, or all three? (*Egoist* 1 [June 1, 1914]: 220)

rights reserved." However, unlike all other book advertisements in the *Egoist,* it lists no publisher, no price, no address for inquiry. It plays on the audience's need to categorize it as either poem or advertisement—in order, simultaneously, to be both. Upward, who frequently traveled internationally, wrote to Harold Monro, the editor of *Poetry and Drama:* "My personal circle is too miscellaneous to be called a group, and I know no way of reaching it but by advertising." He suggested that "a poetical and mysterious announcement in the *Morning Post* . . . (where the cabaret advertises) would bring interviewers to inquire."[29] Upward's text in the *Egoist* may well have been both poem and just such a "poetical and mysterious announcement" designed to catch the eye of followers and new readers alike. In his enthusiasm for the power of commodity advertising, Upward attempted to destabilize the high–low opposition.

As Huyssen would affirm, most modernists publishing in the *New Freewoman/Egoist* largely saw their art as "high" culture and criticized what they perceived as the debased and homogenized result of commercial mass culture, yet they too were seduced by the power of mass publicity. But I believe that their optimistic attempts to appropriate mass advertising techniques were mediated by the suffragette and radical political roots of the *Freewoman*. The particular mass publicity tactics the *New Freewoman* and *Egoist* used were precisely those successfully employed by radical political and suffrage organizations and presses trying to present an alternative to the capitalist or Liberal press—not only advertising through the alternative network of radical publications and using public meetings and lectures, but also such commodity advertising devices as sandwich men, posters, fliers, advertising consultants, slogans, and the logic of the name brand. The power of the advertising industry of a burgeoning consumer mass culture not only threatened "high" art, but also offered new and effective ways of reaching large audiences; counterpublic spheres had shown the way for modernist authors to try their hands at the power of proliferating mass publicity techniques.

In this prewar period, Marsden felt that the revived *Freewoman,* now the *New Freewoman,* would easily be able to sustain itself on a base of 2,000 subscribers, and she was optimistic, given the support shown in both England and America in her Thousand Club drives, that 2,000 subscribers could easily be achieved.[30] After all, the *Clarion,* a socialist cycling magazine, had 60,000 subscribers throughout England, and the suffrage papers, with their £250,000 funds, could often add a thousand new subscribers in a few weeks' time. Before the war began, the audiences for revolutionary movements seemed to have been "out there," and the anarchist and suffrage magazines provided clues as to how to reach them.

The *New Freewoman* was clearly one of the alternative institutions of the counterpublic spheres. The Discussion Circle was started again to carry on the public meetings popularized by anarchist and suffrage groups, and advertisements and notices were placed in magazines or papers that were part of the press institutions of the counterpublic sphere—largely antiliberal and antibourgeois papers of many different types. Rebecca West suggested advertising in the *Citizen,* the *Daily Herald,* the *New Age, Daily News,* and the *Clarion,* and for good measure sent notices to some more mainstream venues as well—the *Times, Chronicle, Athenæum, Manchester Guardian,* and *Evening News.*[31] In addition to these, the directors decided to send announcements and advertisements to the *English Review, Occult Review, New Witness, New Statesman, Nation, Common Cause, Suffragette, Vote, Poetry Review,* and *Votes for Women.*[32] Despite the antisuffrage (because antiparliamentarian) and the antisocialist (because anticollectivist) attacks frequently appearing in the *Freewoman* and now in the *New Freewoman/Egoist,* many suffragettes and socialists still read the journal. Moreover, these lists of advertising possibilities included the major organs of suffragist feminism, the socialist dailies and weeklies, and several magazines of the socialist and liberal intelligentsia, like the *New Statesman,* with its strong Bloomsbury contingent—as well as literary magazines like the *Poetry Review* and the *English Review,* with an occult/theosophical journal thrown in for good measure (Marsden also promoted the *New Freewoman* in a lecture to a gathering of theosophists).[33] Marsden had even tried to solicit the members of the Fabian Society to help restart the *Freewoman.*[34] Both the International Suffrage Shop and Henderson's Bookstore—"Specialists in Socialist Literature"—carried the *Freewoman* and now the *New Freewoman/Egoist.*

The magazine also adopted the commercial mass publicity techniques that these counterpublic spheres had deployed. In December 1913, Richard Aldington, who was becoming the assistant editor of the *New Freewoman/Egoist,* wrote a letter to Dora Marsden: "I propose that on Jan. 1st and after we have two sandwichmen to advertise and sell the Egoist. We should print two bills. One containing in large letters the strange device: 'The Egoist, An Individualist Review, Price 6d.' The other with the same device in smaller letters and a list of the contents. These can be hung on the two men who will be given twenty copies of the N. F. and told to sell them *if* they can. They can return to Oakley house for more copies in the extremely unlikely event of their selling out. We will pay them so much per day and a percentage of what they sell. You can do the same thing in Southport if it would be any good."[35] That the same poet who wished "happily rapid" disintegration upon the crowds at the cinema would propose this mass advertising tactic might seem unusual. But the alluring power of mass publicity was great, and I suggest that the example of sandwich board–carrying suffragettes advertising their cause like a product—a tactic which helped to bring hundreds of thousands of women (and men) into contact with suffrage magazines—impressed Aldington as a viable use of mass publicity to attract a larger audience to what he felt was an equally important revolution, a poetic one. Of course, unlike Rebecca West, Violet Hunt, or May Sinclair, Aldington did not himself make the sacrifice to the imagist movement of his own body carrying sandwich boards through the streets and selling the *Egoist.* However, his letter, while cautiously skeptical, was not a jest, and, beginning with the hiring of two "street men" for four weeks in May 1914, the *Egoist* continued to hire street sellers regularly all the way through 1918.[36]

Like the suffragettes, but also like the Harmsworths, and many commodity advertisers, the *New Freewoman/Egoist* utilized an important medium for publicity: circulars, fliers, and posters.[37] They printed thousands of circulars about the new magazine (5,000 were initially printed for the *New Freewoman,* but more were made later) and generally printed 50 to 100 posters (occasionally as many as 200) for each issue, sometimes using multiple varieties (seen in the account book). The *New Freewoman* appealed to anyone who could arrange to have a poster shown, and it listed names of agents who stocked the magazine in other cities, like Manchester and Leeds in the north, where there was interest. To help maximize these efforts, the advertising agent, Mr. Winterton, was brought back to help promote the paper in January 1914, the first month it was published as the *Egoist*.[38]

The growing commodity culture also manifested itself in the magazine in other ways. As their advertising agent would doubtless have told them, the packaging of a commodity is all-important to its sale, and the name, *New Freewoman,* soon seemed inappropriate both to Dora Marsden and to the male authors of a letter protesting it (Allen Upward, Ezra Pound, Huntly Carter, Reginald Wright Kauffmann, and Richard Aldington). This letter adopted Marsden's polemics against representational democracy and against suffragism's preoccupation with the vote, which Marsden saw as an abstraction that obscured the more vital issues of freedom facing men and women alike. The signatories complained that "the present title of the paper causes it to be confounded with organs devoted solely to the advocates of an unimportant reform in an obsolete political institution [i.e., the suffragettes]" (Marsden, "Views and Comments," Dec. 15, 1913, 244). Marsden counseled changing the name to the *Egoist* and presented the situation in terms of commodity advertising: "We offer a commodity for sale under a description which is not only calculated to attract a section of the public for which in itself it can have no attraction, but which would be an active deterrent to those who should compose its natural audience" (244). Commodities were packaged to target specific audiences, and this commodity, Marsden felt, was packaged incorrectly as a suffrage magazine.

Having repackaged the magazine as the *Egoist,* Marsden and her authors turned next to an advertising strategy that used imagism like a brand name. Of course, Pound had invented the tag "imagiste" to help H.D. publish her poems, and the term helped to create group identity that otherwise would hardly have existed (Marinetti had even written the first futurist manifesto before there were any other "futurists"). However, the *Egoist* tried to make imagism carry an advertising value for the magazine. In April 1915, as its literary side came more and more to dominate, the *Egoist* advertised in large dark letters with arresting double-underlining: "Special Imagist Number / May 1915."

The following issue contained poems by the major imagists, both American and British (except for Pound, who had forsaken "Amygism" for the more voluble vorticism), as well as histories of imagism and essays on individual imagist poets, generally written by other imagist poets. Utilizing a phrase recalling the new trend in brand-name commodity advertising, the preface to *Some Imagist Poets* (1915), which Monro quotes in his review, proclaims that imagism "has already become a household word" ("The Imagists Discussed"). Monro notes the exaggeration of this claim, but also explains that the imagists "took every possible opportunity of preparing themselves a public" (78). The *Egoist,* under Aldington as assistant editor, had bet upon the advertising panache of "imagism," placing a huge "notice" at the back of the special issue: "Future numbers of the *Egoist* will contain contributions from all the authors represented in this number" (May 1915, 83). The print run of the *Egoist* had fallen from its initial 2,000 (as the *New Freewoman*) almost immediately to 1,500, then 1,000, and by 1915, was holding steady around 750. As a one-time gamble, Marsden and Marian Shaw Weaver, who was financing the *Egoist* and eventually took over as its main editor, printed 1,250 copies of the May 1915 "Imagist" number.

However, in spite of the *Freewoman's* role in prewar counterpublic spheres, when the *Egoist* increasingly became a literary magazine and began to slip out of that discursive arena, its strength as a vehicle for commodity advertising waned, sparking a crisis in its attempts to market itself. As the initial surge of interest in restarting the *Freewoman* had subsided, not only did the subscription base dwindle, but the magazine also lost any chance of bringing in significant advertising revenue. Though many of the faithful continued to respond regularly to Marsden's editorials and "Views and Comments," by 1915 the *Egoist* had become almost entirely a literary magazine. The length of each issue shortened and the magazine became a monthly at the beginning of 1915, with the correspondence section, the heart of the old *Freewoman,* scaled back to a few manageable pages. As a result of this shift, neither the *New Freewoman* nor the *Egoist,* at any period of its existence, ever brought in the large numbers of commodity advertisements that had laced the pages of the *Freewoman* and swelled its revenues.

Not surprisingly, the early issues of the *New Freewoman* had attracted advertisements for books on syndicalism, Stirner's *The Ego and His Own,* Floyd Dell's *Women as World Builders,* and other concerns seeking an audience of anarchists and feminists. However, by early 1914 the advertisements were almost entirely for American little magazines: *Poetry,* the *Drama, Little Review, Phoenix,* and *Poetry Journal* regularly filled the entire back page. Beyond these were advertisements for other American little magazines like *Greenwich Village* and *Bruno's Weekly* and for Aldington's American publisher, the Four Seas Publishing Company of Boston. Other than a regular advertisement from London's Peasant Pottery Shop, a few for *Blast* and the Poetry Bookshop's chapbooks, and a growing list of the publications of the Egoist Press, the advertisements were all for the American magazines that shared the *Egoist's* authors and many of its literary interests. To make matters worse for the *Egoist,* these American advertisements brought in no revenue: they were almost all exchanges.

To avoid subjecting the magazine's content to advertisers' concerns, Dora Marsden refused to follow the most important innovations of the Harmsworth empire—that a magazine can vastly increase its circulation, and thus bring in handsome advertising revenues, by lowering its price even below its cost of production. In the circular advertising the *New Freewoman* Thousand Club Membership Establishment Fund, Marsden noted that the *Freewoman* had cost more to produce than it had brought in through sales: "We believe that no more than in the case of any other commodity, should a paper be offered to the public at a figure less than cost price." Although she had come to think of the production of her "non-commercial" journal in commodity terms, she did not follow the logic of new mass market strategies: "The fact that practically all papers *are* sold below cost is the reason why the English Press has to be subsidized by advertiser or capitalist, and in consequence are laid open to corruption."[39] Harmsworth himself had expressed a similar fear in 1896 as he started the *Daily Mail* (Nevett 83), even though the heavy reliance on advertising revenues had been firmly established by his own papers. Marsden rejected this strategy, which she had connected entirely to commercial papers—not trying to emulate the success of the 1d. suffrage weeklies or of Robert Blatchford's socialist *Clarion* at 1d. with 60,000 subscribers and numerous commodity advertisements. During this period, the upper and middle classes and their dependents, even reaching as far down as shop assistants and the lowest paid clerks, accounted for only one-quarter of the population of Britain. The other three-quarters were manual laborers and their dependents (Stevenson 37). Not only the Harmsworths but also the socialists like Blatchford recognized this, and, though motivated by widely different goals, produced cheap and widely circulated papers. Aldred had noted that the 3d. price of the *Freewoman* placed it out of reach of his working-class readers: the 6d. *New Freewoman,* of course, had no chance in that market.

To respond to this marketing crisis, the more literature-oriented *Egoist* tried to take advantage of a new shift in commodity advertising to expand its readership. Just as commodity advertising was moving from a "product-oriented" approach to the modern "product-symbols" orientation, the *Egoist* advertisements combined traditional content—the contents, contributors, and interests of the magazine—with catchy product-oriented phrases, like "Recognises no taboos" (*Blast* 1, 1914 160), or the ubiquitous subtitle "An Individualist Review" on most of the advertisements. Most of these advertisements described the magazine in relation to dominant magazine forms: "This journal is not a chatty literary review: its mission is not to divert and amuse" (*Little Review,* June 1918, inside cover), or

"The Egoist has no point d'appui whatsoever with any other English journal. It is unique" (*Drama,* May 1914, back pages). They touted its philosophical individualism (Marsden's articles) and its ties to imagism, as well as upcoming serials (by Joyce, Lewis, and others).

However, these advertisement also employed the newer type of product-symbol persuasion in their attempts to create a reading audience for modernism, associating the reader with a select group marked by its intelligence. As an early advertisment in *Blast* claimed, the *Egoist* was "the only fortnightly in England that an intelligent man can read for three months running" (*Blast* 1, 1914, 160); an advertisement in the *Drama* (May 1914, back pages) proclaimed "although THE EGOIST is intended for the intelligent, it is read by most of the well-known people in London" (humorously capitalizing on readers' understanding of themselves as secretly more intelligent than the "well-known people," but also borrowing the prestige of social glamour). A later advertisement in the *Little Review* explained that the aim of the magazine was "to secure a fit audience, and to render available to that audience contemporary literary work bearing the stamp of originality and permanence: to present in the making those contemporary literary efforts which ultimately will constitute 20th century literature" (not a vain boast). And it continued, asserting, in italics, *"Obviously a journal of interest to virile readers only. Such should write, enclosing subscription, to"* followed by the address (June 1918, inside cover). These phrases, appearing intermixed with the content description and catchphrases about the magazine, were attempting to lure the potential reader by affirming his or her own "intelligence" and to align the "virile" reader against the feminized mass culture that Huyssen identifies in the period.

However, Huyssen's high–low and virility–femininity divides are complicated by the fact that this advertising strategy for a modernist magazine also drew on a convention of many commodity advertisement aimed at mass audiences. Advertisers often appealed to virility, as an advertisement for Eno's Fruit Salt that ran in several issues of the *Illustrated London News,* for instance, claimed in bold caps: "Men of powerful personality recognise the value of Health" (Jan. 22, 1916, 123). Advertisements of the period mostly used the text for product-oriented explanations of the value of the product. However, they also used the product-symbols tactic in the visual component of the advertisement, displaying images of masculinity, femininity, or well-being. De Reszke cigarettes, "the Aristocrat of Cigarettes," for example, ran a campaign using slogans like "You can judge a man by the brand of cigarettes he smokes. And you can judge a brand of cigarettes by the men who smoke them," implying the quality not just of the product, but, by implication, of the smoker. But at the heart of these advertisements were visual images, like that of a young, well-dressed man, surrounded by an adoring and beautiful wife in a low-cut dress, a faithful dog, and the comforts of the study (*Illustrated London News*, hereafter cited as *ILN*, Dec. 20, 1913, 4), or that of a man dancing with a fashionable woman who lights her cigarette against his in a sexually provocative pose (*ILN*, Feb. 7, 1914, 4). One advertisement even featured the highly erotized image of a young woman smoking, holding a box of cigarettes, saying, "Follow me," under the caption, "To you—an invitation" (*ILN*, Mar. 7, 1914, 4). These images exceeded the ability of slogans to suggest the virility of the potential smoker, but they were clearly part of the same product-symbols strategy.

Likewise, the *Egoist* projected a vision of an exclusive, intelligent reading audience, too virile to be interested in the (feminine) "chatty literary review," and then drew the subscriber with the covert suggestion that by subscribing to the magazine, he or she would be affirmed as one of the "party of intelligence." Although magazines had not yet made the leap that other commodity products were making to using visual symbols to increase the buyer's desire to be identified with the myth of well-being that the product implied, these *Egoist* advertisements adopted mass advertising tactics not normally associated with the intellectual reviews to create a wide audience based on what might at face value be taken as an exclusionary tactic, even an arrogant contempt. New audiences "out there" were more educated and perhaps susceptible to this type of seduction. It would have been almost unheard of in previous generations for someone like Dora Marsden—essentially a lower-middle-class, almost working-class, woman—not only to have been college educated, but also to dare to identify herself as a philosopher.

The audiences attracted by the promotional tactics of this oppositional little magazine illuminate the cultural position of modernist authors following this alternative path to mass readership. The *New Freewoman/Egoist*'s advertising reached an educated and middle-class readership. Subscribers included doctors, many of whom were women, some clergymen, including a canon, and even a few lawyers, but, more interesting, many of the women had college degrees (and advertised the fact). Women like Dora Marsden benefited from the increased educational opportunities available to women, both in universities and in teacher-training colleges, and many of these were readers of the *Freewoman/New Freewoman*.[40]

While the wealthy and titled floated in and out of the subscription lists of the *Freewoman* when it still bore a more direct relationship to suffrage groups, only a few nobles briefly subscribed to the *Egoist*.[41] However, many of the commodity advertising tactics of the period that the *Egoist* and oppositional groups had emulated were aimed at the lower middle and even the working classes, and most of the London readers of *The New Freewoman/Egoist* seem to have been of the lower-middle class or lower end of the solidly middle class.[42] Neither living in bohemian poverty, as one might imagine the devotees of revolutionary philosophies, politics, and aesthetics to do, nor living in the splendid grandeur of the aristocratic patrons the avant-gardists would like to have attracted, the London readers of this avant-garde magazine tended to live in the maisonettes, terrace houses, or semi-detached houses of the lower middle classes, while some took advantage of the great expansion in relatively inexpensive new housing in the suburbs.[43] Though most of the London subscribers to the *Freewoman* and the *Egoist* lived in the west (Kensington, Chelsea, and Holland Park, for example) and the northwest suburbs, by and large, they were living on the lower end of middle-class rents.

The *New Freewoman/Egoist,* and the aesthetic revolution it promoted, attracted a readership that was educated, but not so thoroughly a part of the "respectable" middle and upper middle classes that conservative bourgeois tastes would have been an important part of their class sensibilities. As Bourdieu proposes, aesthetic tastes "are very closely linked to the different possible positions in social space and, consequently, bound up with the systems of dispositions (habitus) characteristic of the different classes and class fractions" (*Distinction* 6). I suggest that the readership for modernist little magazines like the *Egoist* represents a rising middle-class fraction—one that was highly educated but not endowed with the social prestige and financial capital of the established middle and upper middle classes. But this fraction was much smaller than the large groups of workers interested in socialism or trade union movements, or of women supporting suffragism, and this presented a problem to the *Egoist.*

The sex of the readership changed markedly, not only from the *Freewoman* days but also from the first few years of the *New Freewoman* and the *Egoist,* and this significantly affected the magazine's ability to attract advertising revenue. As mentioned previously, unmarried women in London were the single largest group of readers of the *Freewoman,* with married women following closely. Men were outnumbered almost four to one. Of the English subscribers to the *New Freewoman* in 1913, unmarried women were still the largest group, though men now accounted for more than a third of the subscribers, and a strong showing from America brought the total subscribers up to 356, more than the *Freewoman* had. However, most of these initial readers of the *New Freewoman* never renewed their subscriptions. The number of subscribers hovered around eighty to a hundred until 1919, when it fell to only forty-five (ironically, a loss not attributable to the war). Furthermore, many of the unmarried women readers, as well as the married ones, dropped quickly out of the list, so that women subscribers maintained only a slight majority until the paper's demise (though given the masculinist strain of many of the major writers for the *Egoist*—Pound, Lewis, Aldington, Eliot, and others—it is significant that more than half of a modernist little magazine's subscribers would be women). But the proven ability of the major suffrage magazines to provide a consumer block of middle-class women had brought in large advertising revenues from department stores. The farther the *Egoist* moved from such a readership, the more impossible it became to secure such advertisers. Not only had the composition of the audience changed, but its size had dwindled alarmingly. Despite slight upsurges in 1916 and 1917, none of the attempts to increase circulation through advertising had materially succeeded. While subscription was not the only way of purchasing a copy of the magazine (several bookstores in London, New York, and Chicago carried it, and individual copies were sold out of the *Egoist* office), the print run dropped steeply and quickly so that the initial 2,000 copy run of the *New Freewoman* had fallen to 400 copies by the end of the war.[44]

Counterpublic Spheres and the Problem of Cohesion

What I have been describing is the attempt by a modernist little magazine to become part of a counterpublic sphere in opposition to the Edwardian establishment at political, social, and aesthetic levels. Many oppositional groups—socialist, anarchist, suffragist, or, more generally, feminist—saw the importance of the burgeoning periodical press to the establishment they opposed, and they created their own press, modes of printing and distribution, and modes of mass advertising, largely borrowed in various forms from the advertising of mercantile commodities. However, these movements never formed a united front joining in a single oppositional public sphere, even though the many periodicals speaking for them often advertised in and acknowledged articles from each other. Many suffragettes were staunchly and even conservatively middle class and procapitalist, and they certainly would have been sickened by the fiery speeches of the anarchists, or even the cycling and glee clubs of the *Clarion* socialists. Fabians were pro-statist, as opposed to Guy Bowman's syndicalists, and, even within anarchist and "egoist" camps, there was widespread disagreement (these debates frequently littered the pages of the *Freewoman* and *New Freewoman* correspondence sections). So, not only was there no united opposition to the Liberal and Conservative hegemony, but, as successful and widely circulated as many of the periodicals of the groups just mentioned were, the *New Freewoman/Egoist* ultimately was unable to achieve much of a position within any oppositional movement.

The failure of the *New Freewoman/Egoist* to attract and maintain a large audience reveals much about the plight of most modernist literary magazines of the period. Of course the war brought increasing taxes, rationing of paper, and rising printing costs.[45] There was also the general abeyance of oppositional movements: suffrage militancy was generally put on hold during the war (Tickner 229), and the revolutionary energies of many radical political labor movements, like syndicalism, were dissipated by the conflict. However, the *Egoist* was in trouble even before the war killed most nonestablishment literary activity. Given that it had attempted to graft revolutionary aesthetics onto revolutionary philosophical and political practices, the magazine began to founder when it lost the audiences that the *Freewoman* had reached.

The *Freewoman*'s attacks on the WSPU and on the single-minded pursuit of the vote had early on lost it many suffragette readers (see Garner), but it had maintained a feminist consciousness broader than that of the usual suffrage propaganda. However, ultimately two main issues seem to have hurt the *New Freewoman/Egoist.* The first was Dora Marsden's attack on causes: "*The New Freewoman* has *no* Cause. . . . The nearest approach to a Cause it desires to attain is to destroy Causes" ("Views and Comments," July 1, 1913, 25). While many of the articles and published letters to the *New Freewoman* dealt with the relation between individualism and movements or social collectivity (also an important issue to the dynamics of avant-garde movements and self-representation), the full weight of Dora Marsden's linguistic philosophy came to bear on ideas like the vote, duty, liberty, and anarchism, which Marsden considered empty abstractions in the face of her individualist will to freedom of thought and action. This insistent polemic finally alienated many of the oppositional readers who had supported the resurrection of the *Freewoman* in the first place.

The *New Freewoman/Egoist* seemed to drift into incoherence, and even staunchly supportive anarchists like Benjamin Tucker ceased contributing to the magazine (Parker 149–157). Tucker, who wrote a regular column in the *New Freewoman,* "Lego et Penso," clashed with Marsden over issues of collectivity and causes, attacking her reliance on Stirnerism (as had many correspondents). He finally wrote in his column: "I will venture to express my surprise at hearing that THE NEW FREEWOMAN 'stands for nothing.' May I ask for an explanation of the subtitle: 'An Individualist Review'? And what did Miss Marsden mean when she said that the paper was 'not for the advancement of woman, but for the empowering of individuals'? My interest in the paper grows out of my belief that it 'stands for' such empowering. . . . If I am wrong; if, in truth, THE NEW FREEWOMAN is not, or is not longer, a co-ordinate effort toward a definite end, but has become, instead, a mere dumping-ground for miscellaneous wits,—then, even though the dumping be effected through an editorial sieve of a mesh most rare and fine, my interest will diminish materially and speedily" (254–255). Tucker did indeed give up his column, and, during the 1914 volume, many of the initial feminist and anarchist readers and contributors abandoned the magazine as well.

As I have previously suggested, causes like "votes for women" were marketable products. They sold commodities, they were easily advertised with all the new tactics of packaging commercial products, and they united many disparate groups of readers and buyers. While Blatchford had suggested that a single political cause, in his case socialism, was in itself not even enough to keep a paper alive (Hopkin 299), certainly the lack of any such easily identifiable cause meant not only a loss of readers, but also the ensuing loss of advertising revenues that came with higher circulation and with an identifiable readership appealing to potential advertisers (like the middle-class women who attracted department store advertising to support suffrage magazines). Just as recent theorists of counterpublic spheres like Negt and Kluge in *Public Sphere and Experience* are perhaps utopian in their desire for a unifying and inclusive "proletarian" public sphere to counterbalance the bourgeois public sphere, the *Egoist*'s hope to avoid aligning itself with any particular group or cause, yet still maintain a readership of general opposition at many levels, proved to be illusory.

What Marsden argued for was something closely resembling the old ideal that the *English Review* had championed: a liberal public sphere as an open debate, a free play of ideas. The paper had been known since the *Freewoman* days by its readers as an "open paper," defined by one reader as "the fairness you show by publishing all sides of a question."[46] Marsden's philosophical privileging of the individual intellect freely triumphing in an agonistic arena did not support the more collectivist ideology of most of the left-wing anti-Liberal opposition publishing in the paper. However, she wished the *Egoist* to be this kind of forum for the individualist intellect: "The sense of vitality generated by mind reacting on mind, the fighting spirit keeps alive is the raw material out of wh[ich] anything articulate is fashioned."[47] Marsden had maintained that the magazine was "the flexible frame waiting to be filled with the expression of the constantly shifting tale of the contributors' emotions. It has no 'Cause.' All that we require of it is that it remain flexible and appear with a different air each issue. Should an influence come in to make it rigid, as happens in all other papers, it would drop from our hands immediately" ("Views and Comments," July 1, 1913, 25). The lively correspondence and eventually the Discussion Circle it inspired were a testament that, around a specific set of issues, this openness was indeed the strongest aspect of the *Freewoman*. However, the denial of causes ultimately seemed to become the rejection both of the collective action that most oppositional groups saw as necessary for political change and of any editorial direction or coherence that might have retained readers interested in anarchism or feminism, for instance.

This quandary imbued the struggles of literary modernism to find an audience: the *Egoist* was plagued by the growing perception, as literary activity came to take up more and more of the magazine in 1914, that the literary side was irrelevant to the greater movements which the magazine had seemed to represent (even as Marsden denied them). While, like Tucker, Steven Byington had important criticism of Marsden's "egoism" and its inability to provide a positive model of social interaction, he ventured a further criticism of the *Egoist:* "The paper is divided between two interests. The greater part of it is occupied with certain movements in belles-lettres and art, the smaller part with the Marsdenian treatment of ethics. Whatever parallelism there may be between the impulses that these two parts represent, the connection is not so close as to establish any very strong presumption that one who is especially interested in the one will be especially interested in the other." Byington's reaction, like those of many other readers of the *Freewoman* and the *New Freewoman,* presented a problem for modernist writers. The poems and stories in suffragette, anarchist, and socialist magazines for the most part were simply didactic propaganda pieces or polemical diatribes. The cause that rallied so many people to those magazines was supported by the thematic content of the literature they published. Revolutions in poetics and fictional form could not sustain the interest that a social or political movement could; the attempt to marry, in the readers' minds, imagism and other modernist literary movements to the nonliterary articles in the magazine (in spite of the productive interchange of ideas between these two sets of contributors) did not succeed.

Marsden herself seems to have realized the problematic lack of unity that both her attack on causes and the publication of the imagist poets presented to the paper. In October 1915, she wrote to Harriet Shaw Weaver, now the editor of the *Egoist,* about the sagging subscription base: "What is the matter with the paper is that it has no unity; it is not vitalised or dominated by any united purpose wh[ich] can be made to grow increasingly attractive and intelligible to the readers." She argued that "It is not bright because it has no leaven: what should be the yeast to lighten the heaviness of Egoism is the equally unleavened heaviness of Imagism. There are two Purposes running through the small space of a 16p. monthly. Neither helps the other: both militate against each other because neither takes on the part of light counterfire with the other. The paper is trying to serve two masters, and while one master—one purpose—is absolutely essential: two make a deadening combination."[48]

To renew the audience by giving the paper a unity, Marsden suggested to Weaver that either imagism or egoism must go. If imagism were kept, Aldington would be able to use the paper to see if there was any enduring merit to the imagist poets, and, with Marsden out of the magazine, money might be found from such sources as Amy Lowell. Or, she advocated, imagism should be dropped from the paper in favor of egoism. She suggested "pulling up sharp while we have a nucleus of circulation left; and so draw the attention of the readers to the fact that matters are going to be changed. This course would save money on three issues which saved sum could be used in advertising and reappearance." She would also become a dramatic critic and try to bring the now important Rebecca West back into the paper, as well as Storm Jameson and perhaps even Harold Monro, in order to make the literary side complement the philosophical.

Ultimately, Marsden and Weaver left the paper as it was, with Aldington publishing imagism, Weaver bringing in fiction from Lewis and Joyce, and Marsden writing leaders. The *Egoist*'s literary course was set, and by 1918 there were only ninety subscribers left on the lists. While many important young writers were subscribers during this late period,[49] the paper was running up increasing debts and was forced to reduce its print run to 400, which, in spite of sales in the Poetry Bookshop, or American bookstores like the Washington Square Bookstore, amply met the small demand for it. Its status within a counterpublic sphere predicated on social and political issues had been forever diminished. As it now represented neither the interests of liberalism and capital nor the causes of suffragism or anticapitalist political movements, it could not reach the large audiences it had desired.

By the final year of the war, the failure of the *Egoist* to achieve a financially viable position within an oppositional public sphere brought Marsden, Weaver, and editors of other little magazines in the same position to turn again to the commodity realm, this time, however, not to advertising but to contemporary innovations in corporate capital. The slow prewar economy had led to a "merger mania" in the corporate world, with at least sixty-seven firms disappearing each year in mergers between 1888 and 1914; in one instance, fifty-nine firms consolidated into a single company (Hannah 25). Combines formed at an even greater pace during the war to meet production needs in crucial military sectors, and the process accelerated even more as the war came to an end and firms diversified in preparation for a peace-time economy (Hannah 30). This period laid the foundations of Britain's modern corporate economy, with some firms growing so large that they could produce more than the entire population of Britain could consume.[50]

In this economic climate of corporate amalgamation, editors of modernist little magazines considered schemes to consolidate several modernist enterprises that had previously been rivals into a large concern that, like the new corporate combines, would enjoy the benefits of diversification (across different media and different aesthetics, and hence of wider audiences) and of capital consolidation. From the inception of the *New Freewoman*, Pound had frequently come before Marsden and Weaver with promises of money and subscribers in return for a portion of the magazine, and, at the beginning of 1918, even Eliot had gotten involved in such attempts, bringing a proposal from a Mr. Hutchins, who could not start his own paper during the lean war years.[51] As with Pound's earlier attempts, the money never materialized, and the proposal died. However, Marsden herself soon suggested a scheme involving several modernist institutions that represented a last-ditch effort to produce a viable avant-garde environment in London.

Marsden's plan grew out of a proposal by Herbert Read (who had been helping to edit Frank Rutter's *Art and Letters* from the trenches) to join together the *Egoist* and *Art and Letters,* and the Adelphi Gallery, with its exhibition space and shop. Frank Rutter had founded the Allied Artists Association (AAA) in 1908 to run a yearly unjuried show, giving young modern painters and sculptors a chance to have their work democratically exhibited (Rutter 180–199). As early as July 1917, Read and Rutter had planned to create a permanent gallery to replace the yearly AAA show (Read 106). That same year they started a literary and artistic quarterly called *Art and Letters,* which began with works by Sickert, Gilman, Lucien Pissarro, and, of course, Read and Rutter, and gradually came to include the Sitwells, Pound, and Lewis. By October 1918, Read had decided to take over the working secretaryship of the AAA and to open a permanent gallery for it to be run in conjunction with a publishing and book-selling business, which would eventually become "a great independent Author's Press," or an Allied Authors Association, as Rutter imagined it (Read 141–142). They opened the Adelphi Gallery and store which carried Art and Letters publications like the magazine and volumes of poetry by Read. Pound had put Read up to talking to Weaver and Marsden about their publishing business, the Egoist Press (Read 142), and what resulted was Marsden's suggestion to combine all of the various offers of amalgamation into a single modernist institution.

The Adelphi Gallery with its AAA exhibitions would continue its policy of exhibiting the work of young and promising artists for sale at affordable prices, and a bookstore run along the lines of Harold Monro's Poetry Bookshop connected to the gallery would sell magazines and books by the Egoist Press. In addition, the Egoist Ltd. would reduce costs by buying its own printing press and would publish, under the title *The Egoist Combined Monthly Publications,* an amalgamation of all the little magazines that had been approaching the *Egoist.* This would bring together *Art and Letters* (with Read, Rutter, and the Sitwells, who promised they could bring at least 200 subscribers), *Blast* and Wyndham Lewis's followers,[52] and the *Little Review* (or, namely, Ezra Pound's interests and connections). Marsden wanted to give each previously competing faction a 32-page section that, when combined with the *Egoist*'s 32 pages, would produce a 128-page monthly magazine for 2s. 6d. This "innovation in journalistic publishing," as she called it,[53] would be priced like the established Edwardian monthlies. With a respectable appearance, like the *Hibbert Journal,* and perhaps even cover art by Wyndham Lewis, and with the combined subscription bases of all the competing little magazines, Marsden imagined that it might be viable.[54] Like mergers in the corporate world, she felt that this scheme would "pool our demands in support of a limited educated audience and at the same time share the costs of production and yet result in a creation which would carry an impressive appearance," and it would eliminate the friction between little magazines which inevitably resulted "because the competition for the small clientele is so fierce."[55]

Gone was the faith in political and social counterpublic spheres and in finding a large audience for any single "advanced" magazine through advertising tactics. Replacing it was an understanding of the truly limited size of audiences for little magazines, and, in an almost total reversal of her 1915 scheme to oust imagism from the journal, a complete reliance on the literary and artistic avant-garde to create an audience for her philosophy. Marsden hoped that this combination of all the literary and artistic activity of the young modernists could create something that would fit into the established Edwardian milieu as a monthly, and at the same time generate interest by combining so many different institutions and readerships. Marsden's enthusiasm, and even her apocalyptic tone, were roused again by this scheme: "The fact of the matter is, I think we are on the verge of social and political events of the first magnitude. Bad as everything seems—we are in the throes of a world-convulsion of which the war itself is only the smallest part. I feel enormous events are immediately ahead. We've got to ask ourselves whether we are a force sufficiently strong to exercise an appreciable influence on these events."[56] This combined magazine would conform more to Edwardian readers' horizons of expectations for a literary monthly, and thus would enter the dominant literary public sphere that was institutionalized in the prominent monthlies without having to compromise its contents with the more mainstream aesthetics of the monthlies; it would have been closer to Ford's *English Review* than to Guy Aldred's *Herald of Revolt.*

Unfortunately, this scheme to garner greater influence in the public sphere came to naught, as each side backed out of it. *Blast* was never restarted, the *Egoist* folded at the end of 1919 to allow the Egoist Press to concentrate on book publication, *Art and Letters* folded at the end of 1920, and even *New Age,* which the *Egoist* had long viewed as its British rival, ceased in 1923. The Sitwells' *Wheels* ran only from 1916 to 1921. Harold Monro never restarted *Poetry and Drama,* and his *Chapbook* struggled along only through the mid-twenties. By and large, the flurry of avant-garde little magazines and activity was not successfully reenergized in London after the war.

The tentative counterpublic sphere that had been created by the combination of social, political, and literary radicals in the prewar years, and by such magazines as the *Freewoman/New Freewoman/Egoist* and *New Age,* had evaporated during the war, and, for the near future, modernist art and literature moved more decisively into a separate aesthetic sphere. The attempt to bring modernist literature to public view by adopting the advertising tactics and public institutions of feminist and anarchist groups had given way to this last, guardedly optimistic attempt to enter the dominant literary public sphere by following trends in corporate capital and combining literary and artistic groups. While the press and organizations of counterpublic spheres had been able to appropriate the advertising tactics of Edwardian commodity culture for their own noncommercial ends and had reached large audiences (and, especially in the case of the suffragettes, had raised large sums of money), experimental literature had not been able to follow this route with as much success. Many modernist authors either abandoned London as an impossible environment for avant-garde literature and art (Pound, for instance, wrote *Hugh Selwyn Mauberley* and fled to Paris, and Ford eventually began a new magazine, his *Transatlantic Review,* in Paris as well) or remained in London maintaining a stronger sense of the elitist nature of their projects (witness Richard Aldington or T. S. Eliot and his *Criterion*). While the London avant-garde had never moved in the radical directions that continental avant-gardists had pursued, the political, social, and aesthetic turmoil of the Edwardian era had produced some fascinating experiments and alliances between modernism and not only a counterpublic sphere, but also the commodity culture that helped to sustain it.

Blast, Enemy of the Stars, and Promoting the Great English Vortex

Before moving on to the American magazines, I'd like to spend a moment longer in London to discuss *Blast,* the British modernist magazine that explored the possibilities of the new advertising culture to the fullest extent. As much as the *Egoist* supported egoism and imagism, it also espoused another "ism"—the "vorticism" of Wyndham Lewis, Ezra Pound, Henri Gaudier-Brzeska, Edward Wadsworth, and others—and it promoted vorticism's short-lived (but flamboyant) magazine, *Blast.* "Vorticism" was a term Lewis and Pound used to represent the modern artist as the point of concentrated energy at the still center of the whirling dynamism of modernity—as Lewis put it, "The Vorticist is at his maximum point of energy when stillest" (*Blast* 1, 148). The genesis of vorticism, its polemic against Bergsonian and Italian futurist privileging of flux, and the birth and quick death of *Blast* have been meticulously chronicled elsewhere (see Cork; Dasenbrock; Kenner; Materer, *Vortex*; Wees). Shortly after the founding of their Rebel Art Centre in London, Lewis and other vorticists put together *Blast* and published the first issue on July 2, 1914.[57] The "puce monster," as some named the first issue for its glaring puce cover and oversized diagonal block letters, marked the birth of English abstract art and the first major English attempt to adopt the manifesto-driven style of the continental avant-garde. Though *Blast* published only two issues, it was perhaps the most radical prewar attempt to draw upon the energies of a promotional culture to bring avant-garde art and letters before the British public.

Blast featured a truculently iconoclastic manifesto signed by Richard Aldington, Malcolm Arbuthnot, Lawrence Atkinson, Henri Gaudier-Brzeska, Jessica Dismorr, Cuthbert Hamilton, Ezra Pound, William Roberts, Helen Sanders, Edward Wadsworth, and Wyndham Lewis. In addition to the modernist art (partially inspired by cubism and by some aspects of futurism), Pound added a literary component to the magazine, trying to revamp imagism through contact with the artistic avant-garde. He published his own poems, poems by T. S. Eliot and Ford Madox Ford, the first chapters of Ford's *Good Soldier,* and a Rebecca West short story entitled "Indissoluble Matrimony," among other literary contributions.

To help promote both *Blast* and vorticism, Pound, Aldington, Gaudier-Brzeska, and others, used the *Egoist:* in 1914 at least ten articles on the subject were published and the correspondence columns featured debate over the new art. But William Roberts once quipped, "What is Vorticism? The answer could only be—a slogan" (Wees 3), and I want to suggest that vorticism and *Blast* followed the *Freewoman/New Freewoman/Egoist*'s lead in appropriating mass market advertising and publication strategies for oppositional purposes, perhaps even outstripping the longer-lived *Egoist* in the enthusiasm and vigor of its self-promotion and in the level to which modern advertising influenced its aesthetics. I believe that Lewis used his drama, *Enemy of the Stars* (*Blast* 1), to depict the new artist's relationship to promotional culture and to the public sphere.

From the very beginning, the painters and authors who founded *Blast* intended it to advertise the movement heavily. Lewis envisioned an initial print run of 3,000, and the vorticist painter Edward Wadsworth (who had argued that 2,000 would be a good start) came up with a distribution list, which ranged from America to Petersburg and Bucharest, and included several major European and British cities, and estimated the need for a total of 3,200 copies for this distribution, a phenomenal number for an art magazine.[58] Wadsworth clearly saw the value of advertising for the journal, arguing that publishing in A. R. Orage's *New Age* vorticist work that was not worthy of *Blast* "might get a little bit of advertisement (which nobody can afford not avail himself of),"[59] He also convinced Lewis to take advantage of the promotional value of labeling the second issue of *Blast* a special "war number": "I should think you could make it extremely interesting and it would sell like hot cakes and also would keep the name of the magazine before the public which, if it is not published again for a long time, may lose interest and it would have to fizzle out with its second number a big failure. A war number would go well in America I think."[60]

Another key figure in vorticist aesthetic theory, T. E. Hulme, suggested that Lewis use the publisher Howard Latimer, who handled the *New Statesman,* arguing that "They employ for example, one man whose business it is simply to go round to bookstalls to find out those that do not like their paper and to persuade them to take it. This man could very easily do the same for your review."[61] Lewis even tried to publicize the Rebel Art Center abroad, as he sent prospectuses to Frederick Etchells in Paris with elaborate instructions about how and where to distribute them (*Letters* 60). Moreover, Pound, who published on vorticism not only in *Blast* and the *Egoist* but also in the more staid and traditional *Fortnightly Review,* saw the need to keep up the promotional energy during the war, as he wrote Lewis in August 1916: "Wrote a long letter on vort[icism]. to a western american paper, to keep the jaw from dying out" (*Pound/ Lewis* 55).

Although as far back as 1954 Hugh Kenner noted the "posterish conventions" of *Blast* itself, it has not been until very recently that scholars have explored the promotional strategies of the magazine and their effects on its aesthetics. *Blast* used a dizzying array of different type faces and sizes and blasted its readers with evocative phrases often used for shock value—tactics that had become staples of the commercial advertising world. Promotional culture was embedded in the pages of *Blast,* right down to its famous "blesses" and "blasts" lists, which—as Paige Reynolds has argued—"set forth a doctrine of what constituted good and bad advertising" (Reynolds 12). Reynolds lays out *Blast's* defense of advertising tactics used both by commercial culture and by suffragettes (3) and argues that this praise of advertising was a nationalistic defense against Italian futurism: "By celebrating the conflation of art and advertising, the Vorticists could define themselves in opposition to other art groups in London, both native and continental. But just as important, this celebration allowed them to extol English advertising practices, practices which displayed for the world England's preeminence in industry, economics, politics, and culture. Most obviously, *Blast* displayed and celebrated this merger of English avant-garde and commercial art through the journal's aesthetics" (8–9).

Like the *Egoist,* which had combined product-oriented informational advertisements with product-symbols advertising strategies to play on images of a virile, exclusive, intelligent and rebellious audience, *Blast's* exchange advertisements in the *Egoist* (Apr. 1 and 15, 1914) informed its audience of the contents of the new journal, "Discussion of Cubism, Futurism, Imagisme and all / Vital Forms of Modern Art," but also used evocative phrases that obviously had no direct informational value and were staples of product-symbols advertisements: "THE CUBE. THE PYRAMID. / Putrefaction of Guffaws Slain by Appearance of / BLAST. / No Pornography. No Old Pulp. / END OF THE CHRISTIAN ERA" (Apr. 1, 1914, 140). But it wasn't just the advertisements that proclaimed such bold apocalyptic phrases as "END OF THE CHRISTIAN ERA": indeed the manifestos and much of the copy in the magazine itself adopted such posterlike strategies to launch its attack on Victorian culture, Italian futurism, impressionism, English humor and sports, and any number of other social and cultural institutions that the vorticists felt were belying the dynamic modernity that England had itself created with the industrial revolution (see fig. 2).

Blast's tactics echoed not only the advertising world but also that of the radical counterpublic spheres in which the *Freewoman/Egoist* participated. As Janet Lyon has noted, vorticism, suffragism, and Italian futurism shared key rhetorical strategies: "The rhetoric and tactics of the militant women's movement were enfolded into the foundations of English modernism, and, conversely, the closely watched public activities of Futurists and Vorticists in England helped to produce the public identity of the militant suffrage movement" (102). Lyon primarily focuses on the rhetorical strategies shared by these movements—"the rhetoric of disease returned in volleys, and the rhetoric of contempt for unsympathetic publics"—and she argues that both "militant suffragism and the avantgarde . . . produced manifestoes and related polemical tracts designed to programatize anger, to polarize readership, and to recalibrate their own group's revolutionary position within hegemonic liberalism" (110).

Institutionally, too, *Blast* was linked to the counterpublic spheres I have discussed. The Rebel Art Centre itself was to function like the Freewoman Discussion Circles and provide a forum for the public lectures so important to both suffragettes and political radicals (like Guy Aldred) in London. And like the journals of many of those groups, *Blast,* too, would have to circumvent normal channels of distribution and sales. The *Freewoman* had been boycotted by W. H. Smith and Sons—and thus lost the convenient option of wide distribution through the company's railway and street stalls. Moreover, in the early planning stages of *Blast,* Wadsworth wrote to Lewis about what seems to have been Lewis's fear that Smith and Sons would not carry a journal named *Blast:* "I have not been able to think of another name for 'Blast' and I am not convinced yet really that 'Blast' is bad—I don't think W. H. Smith will do much for us in any case. In any case I don't think we ought to change the name unless for something *better.*"[62] Though they boasted subscribers as far away as the Khyber Pass and Santa Fe (*Blast* 2, 7), they clearly were positioned against capitu-

1

BLAST First (from politeness) ENGLAND

CURSE ITS CLIMATE FOR ITS SINS AND INFECTIONS

DISMAL SYMBOL, SET round our bodies,
of effeminate lout within.
VICTORIAN VAMPIRE, the LONDON cloud sucks
TOWN'S heart.

A 1000 MILE LONG, 2 KILOMETER Deep

BODY OF WATER even, is pushed against us
from the Floridas, TO MAKE US MILD.

OFFICIOUS MOUNTAINS keep back DRASTIC WINDS

SO MUCH VAST MACHINERY TO PRODUCE

THE CURATE of "Eltham"
BRITANNIC ÆSTHETE
WILD NATURE CRANK
DOMESTICATED
                    POLICEMAN
LONDON COLISEUM
 SOCIALIST-PLAYWRIGHT
DALY'S MUSICAL COMEDY
GAIETY CHORUS GIRL
TONKS

11

Figure 2. With the typography of an advertising poster and the antagonistic rhetoric of the women's movement and the continental avant-garde, Wyndham Lewis launches vorticism in the summer of 1914. ("Manifesto," *Blast* 1 [June 20, 1914]: 11)

lating to the demands for decorum made by the normal channels of distribution. But, as I have argued about the *Freewoman* and the *Egoist,* rejecting compromises with nervous distributors and publishers over content and self-presentation did not also imply rejecting advertising or a vision of reaching the masses.

Indeed, the vorticists saw the advertising value of spectacle, having watched the suffragette militancy escalating since the window-smashing campaigns and public arrests of 1912. On May 4, 1914, a suffragette, Mrs. Mary Wood, had slashed a portrait of Henry James by Sargent hanging in the Royal Academy on the same day that a wooden pavilion at a tennis club in Belfast had been burned to the ground by militant suffragettes, and on May 22 another painting was hacked at the Royal Academy and five more at the National Gallery. In an address "To Suffragettes" in *Blast,* Lewis wrote: "A word of advice. In destruction, as in other things, stick to what you understand. We make you a present of our votes. Only leave works of art alone. You might some day destroy a good picture by accident. Then!—Mais soyez bonnes filles! Nous vous aimons! We admire your energy. You and artists are the only things (you don't mind being called things?) left in England with a little life in them. If you destroy a great work of art you are destroying a greater soul than if you annihilated a whole district of London. Leave art alone, brave comrades!" (151–152). *Blast* blessed Lillian Lenton, who had burned the tea pavilion at Kew Gardens on February 20, 1913, and Freda Graham, who slashed the pictures at the National Gallery.[63]

This address clearly is a self-validating move for the vorticists by which their art could claim the same right to public spectacle and value as political causes.[64] The suffragettes' militant advertising spectacles gave a clue to the vorticists about the possibilities for artists to enter the public sphere, as they had for the *Egoist,* and I now turn to the piece in *Blast* that Wyndham Lewis intended to exemplify the literary possibilities of what had primarily been a movement of painters and sculptors: his vivacious and enigmatic play, *Enemy of the Stars.*

Enemy of the Stars has long been read in terms of the binary oppositions set up by the play's two main characters, Arghol and Hanp. Kenner points out that Arghol is named after the double star Algol (*Alpha Persei*) and he has helped lock into place the binary readings of the play that have followed ever after, in which Arghol is affirmed as the lonely artist hero and the pure intelligence and Hanp is seen as representing the crowd mind, the social self (22–24). There are, indeed, different senses of the "self" in the play. On the one hand, "Self" is the privileged term that Dora Marsden and Max Stirner would affirm—the unique personality and intellect that threatens the herd, the conforming masses, who fight against individuality. As Arghol proclaims:

Self, sacred act of violence, is like murder on my face and hands. The stain won't come out. It is the one piece of property all communities have agreed it is illegal to possess. The sweetest-tempered person, once he discovers you are that sort of criminal, changes any opinion of you, and is on his guard. When mankind cannot overcome a personality, it has an immemorial way out of the difficulty. It becomes it. It imitates and assimilates that Ego until it is no longer one. . . . This is one.

Between Personality and Mankind it is always a question of dog and cat; they are diametrically opposed species. Self is the ancient race, the rest are the new one. Self is the race that lost. But Mankind still suspects Egotistic plots, and hunts Pretenders. (66)

But there is also another sense of the word "self" in the play, as Arghol notes: "Men have a loathsome deformity called Self; affliction got through indiscriminate rubbing against their fellows: Social excrescence" (71). This is the self Arghol tries to overcome in a Stirnerian egoist gesture that would have pleased Marsden. Indeed, Lewis's first manifesto in *Blast,* "Long Live the Vortex," had ended proclaiming "Blast presents an art of Individuals" (8). Arghol sees Hanp as created from his own ego, and tells Hanp "I find I wanted to make a naif yapping Poodle-parasite of you.—I shall always be a prostitute. I wanted to make you my self; you understand. Every man who wants to make another HIMSELF, is seeking a companion for his detached ailment of a self. You are an unclean little beast, crept gloomily out of my ego" (73). And so Kenner is led to read the play as an allegory not just of the artist versus the crowd—a struggle he certainly valorizes in his construction of Wyndham Lewis's career—but also of a kind of psychomachia: "Hanp is the social Self inseparable from the pure intelligence" (24). Hanp murders Arghol, as Kenner puts it, for not "merg[ing] into his crowd-life" (23), but Hanp then must commit suicide because he cannot live without his creator.

Most of the readings of the play since Kenner's 1954 book have been variations on these themes, and this tendency has been reinforced by Lewis's own essay "Physics of the Not-Self," published along with the revised version of *Enemy of the Stars* in 1932. Lewis begins: "This essay is in the nature of a metaphysical commentary upon the ideas suggested by the action of *Enemy of the Stars.* Briefly, it is intended to show the human mind in its traditional role of the enemy of life, as an oddity outside the machine" (195). Lewis locates the intellect as "the seat of that forbidden principle of the *not-self,* . . . the one thing that every gentleman is sworn, however hard pressed, never to employ" (198). Thus Timothy Materer, noting the allusion to Algol, "which is regularly eclipsed by a dimmer star," explains that "the play's protagonist, Arghol, embodies the artist, who is certain to be misunderstood and eventually blacked out" (*Vortex* 26). Wendy Flory reads the binary as "the inevitable antipathy between the true artistic-intellectual and the rest of society" (92) but adds that the action itself is not as important as the style, by which Lewis attempts "to explore for himself and create for his reader the harrowing state of mind that is not only Arghol's but ultimately, and much more urgently, that of the author himself" (93). David Ayers notes the prevalence of the "dueling duet" motif throughout Lewis's work (58) and complicates but also implicitly confirms Kenner's reading: "The nature of the conflict seems to be clear cut: the Nietzschean superman Arghol, poised on the 'balsamic hills' of 'Truth,' trying to achieve a purity of life above the herd, but dragged down by the representative of a multitude which he cannot escape. Inscribed within this apparently Nietzschean narrative, however, is the Bergsonian problematic of the self which cannot perceive itself except in its coded, dead actions" (59).

While I want to affirm these readings of binary but mutually dependent opposition, I also want to revisit *Enemy, not* through the lens of Lewis's 1932 revisions of the play and essay explaining its philosophical implications but rather through the lens of *Blast* in 1914. In *Enemy,* Lewis seems to imply another duality—a shifting understanding of the character and role of the artist—that lies outside of the simple Hanp-versus-Arghol binary. Instead, this duality involves both the advertising context I have tried to elaborate for *Blast* and the Stirnerian egoistic context that Dora Marsden provided for Lewis, Pound, and other readers of the *Egoist.*

Wees put the end of the play in fairly simple terms: "The fight, the murder, and the suicide in 'Enemy of the Stars' drive home the moral: the ego and the 'Self' cannot be separated, nor live together in peace. If one dies, the other dies too. Man's fate is to embody that fatal conflict" (185). Such readings, I think, imply that we need to go a step further to look more carefully at that "social excrescence" of the "Self," since the play does indeed thwart Arghol's attempts to leave it (and thus Hanp) behind and live without what one might call a "socially constructed" self. This quandary, of course, had implications for how Lewis understood the persona of the artist in the modern age.

One thing that Wyndham Lewis, F. T. Marinetti, and the English futurist Christopher Nevinson could all agree on was a rhetorical war on the outmoded 1890s aesthete and his twentieth-century counterparts. In the "Vital English Art" futurist manifesto of 1914 that had provoked defensive feelings of outrage in Lewis's Rebel Art Centre comrades, Marinetti and Nevinson had attacked "the sickly revivals of mediaevalism, the Garden Cities with their curfews and artificial battlements, the Maypole Morris dances, Aestheticism, Oscar Wilde, the Pre-Raphaelites." In spite of his anger at Marinetti's attempt to bring the English painters into the "empire" of Italian futurism, Lewis certainly agreed with this barrage against what Marinetti saw as a feminine and enervated aestheticism. On the first page of the *Blast* "Manifesto," Lewis blasts the English "effeminate lout within" and the "Britannic aesthete" (11). He goes on to "curse with expletive of whirlwind the Britannic Aesthete cream of the snobbish earth" (15). Of course, there certainly were affinities between the prewar avant-garde and the aestheticism of the 1880s and 1890s: Pound memorialized the Rhymers' Club poets in *Hugh Selwyn Mauberley* and put into the disparagingly philistine mouth of "Mr. Nixon" (loosely based on Arnold Bennett) the admonition "Don't kick against the pricks, / Accept opinion. The 'Nineties' tried your game / And died, there's nothing in it" (194). And Materer even notes the Wildean dimension of *Enemy of the Stars:* "Arghol's fate illustrates Wilde's epigram, 'Nature hates Mind'" (*Wyndham Lewis* 50). (Indeed, the publisher Lewis finally found for *Blast* was none other than John Lane, the publisher of the infamous *Yellow Book,* whose complete sets were advertised at the back of *Blast* in a full-page advertisement.)

But despite these affinities, Lewis often positions himself against a vision of a contemporary feminized bloodless aesthete—as in Lowndes or Hobson in Lewis's 1918 novel *Tarr,* or the satires on Bloomsbury and the Sitwells in his 1930 novel *The Apes of God*—and *Enemy of the Stars* parodies this vision of the artist as effeminate aesthete dandy not through Hanp, but rather through the figure of Arghol himself, who "stretches elegantly, face over shoulder, like a woman" (65). As Arghol says of himself: "I am too vain to do harm, too superb ever to lift a finger when harmed" (67), and he is caught in a "cataclysm of premature decadence" (68). Moreover, Arghol is portrayed in terms of another interest of the 1890s—as a vampire, but a particularly modern energy-sucking vampire: "Arghol was glutted with others, in coma of energy. He had just been feeding on him—Hanp!" (81).[65] The 1890s aesthete is portrayed as both innervated and effeminate, but also an energy-draining parasite—two sides of the same coin, Lewis implies.

Enemy of the Stars also echoes Wilde's *Dorian Gray,* in which Dorian has killed Basil Hallward, the painter of his infamous portrait, and decides to "kill" the portrait with the same knife: "As it had killed the painter, so it would kill the painter's work, and all that that meant. It would kill the past, and when that was dead he would be free. It would kill this monstrous soul-life, and, without its hideous warnings, he would be at peace. He seized the thing, and stabbed the picture with it" (192). Dorian, of course, dies in this effort to free himself from his past and from his "double," and Lewis's Hanp, likewise, dies (by jumping into the canal) after he stabs Arghol, trying to erase his own past and his debt to Arghol for his own soul and self, and Hanp can hardly restrain himself from turning the knife against himself instead of killing Arghol—"[Hanp] could hardly help plunging it in himself, the nearest flesh to him" (84)—just as Dorian essentially stabs himself.

This scene is figured like a vampire killing in a gothic novel, but a parodic one into which a good measure of absurdity creeps: "[Hanp] now saw Arghol clearly: he knelt down beside him. A long stout snore drove his hand back. But the next instant the hand rushed in, and the knife sliced heavily the impious meat. The blood burst out after the knife. Arghol rose as though on a spring, his eyes glaring down on Hanp, and with an action of the head, as though he were about to sneeze. Hanp shrank back, on his haunches. He over-balanced, and fell on his back" (84). Lewis seems to parody Bram Stoker's classic *Dracula* (1897), in which Dracula's "red eyes glared with the horrible vindictive look" before he is stabbed through the heart with a knife and dispatched for good (447).

This parody of the 1890s, of the effeminate aesthete/energy-destroying vampire in Arghol, reaches its height with another trope of that decade, and that is what Linda Dowling calls "the fatal book." Dowling explores Victorian linguistic anxieties and notes their culmination in this trope, which she finds in several key decadent texts: in Wilde's "The Picture of Mr. W. H." in which Shakespeare's sonnets cause the deaths of Cyril and Erskine, in Pater's *Marius the Epicurean* in which Apuleius's *Golden Ass* profoundly influences Marius and Flavian, in George Moore's *Confessions of a Young Man* in which "Moore describes his own conversion to the divine delights of the flesh as a result of reading Gautier's *Mademoiselle de Maupin*" (164); and, of course, in Wilde's *Picture of Dorian Gray,* in which appears "the most famous of these fatal books . . . the 'poisonous' book, with its yellow cover, soiled pages, and curious jeweled style of archaism and argot, that Lord Henry Wotton gives the ageless hero" (170).

But the fatal book that seduces the temperamental Arghol is not a tome of sensual decadent splendor, but rather Max Stirner's *The Ego and His Own* (*Der Einzige und Sein Eigentum*)—the book that gave *the Egoist* its name and animated much of the political discussion in the modernist circles in which Pound and Lewis came into contact with Stirnerites like Dora Marsden (see von Hallberg, "Libertarian Imagism"). Arghol wants to escape that social excrescence of the Self, to leave behind Hanp, and, indeed, this is certainly consonant with the great powers attributed by Stirner and Marsden to the egoistic self in its conflict with society—the ability to kick free of all those things that impinge upon the freedoms of the self—from state governments to abstract concepts and words. The play seems to portray the new egoistic artist actively moving beyond the languid feminine aesthete of the past via *The Ego and His Own*. But Arghol has a dream in which Lewis blurs this dichotomy simply by invoking the fatal book trope of the 1890s: "The third book, stalely open, which he took up to shut, was the 'Einige und Sein Eigenkeit' [*sic*]. Stirnir. [*sic*] One of the seven arrows in his martyr mind. Poof! he flung it out of the window. A few minutes, and there was a knock at his door. It was a young man he had known in the town, but now saw for the first time, seemingly. He had come to bring him the book, fallen into the roadway. 'I thought I told you to go!' he said. The young man had changed into his present disciple. Obliquely, though he appeared now to be addressing Stirnir. [*sic*] "I thought I told you to go!" His visitor changed a third time. A middle aged man, red cropped head and dark eyes, self-possessed, loose, free, student—sailor, fingering the book: coming to a decision. Stirnir [*sic*] as he had imagined him" (76–77). Of course in this parody of the fatal book plot, Arghol tries to throw out Stirner's bible of egoism, only to have it immediately and fatefully returned to him by Hanp—the very social self he tries to escape and with which he is in conflict—who then becomes Stirner himself. Arghol proclaims, "These books are all parasites. Poodles of the mind" (77)—the very terms he has used for Hanp.

In *Enemy of the Stars,* then, Lewis begins to figure a changing conception of the artist—from the now feminized aesthete of the 1890s still valorized in British art circles to the masculine, virile, violent, egoist, individualist artist who can challenge the social excrescence of the Self, of the crowd—the position seemingly valorized by *Blast* and vorticism. Yet there is something wrong with this simple opposition, because Stirner's fatal book has "poisoned" Arghol's mind against the languid vain aesthete that Arghol at times appears to be, but it has also set him up for death at the end of the play. The play undermines Arghol's desires to escape the socially constructed Self entirely, and one is left with Wees's and Kenner's sense that the war against the Self is a never-ending unwinnable conflict that the heroic artist must pursue nevertheless. But the philosophical point that Wees and Kenner make, and to which Lewis steers us in his 1932 essay and revision of the play, must be more firmly grounded in the political and social positions that Lewis questions in 1914. The play actually critiques Marsden's Stirnerite faith in the powers of the ego and sees the political and social dead end of such an extreme position for the artist.

To break up the binary of feminized aesthete and bold and virile yet doomed egoist artist, I suggest that there is actually a third position for the artist implicit in the play (and in *Blast*) that integrates the social realm into a vision of the artist: egoism for the artist is reinvisioned not as self-*assertion,* as Stirner and Marsden would argue, but rather as self-*promotion.* And here the insistent theme of advertising in *Blast* comes directly to bear upon *Enemy of the Stars.* It would be hard not to notice that after the title pages of the play as it is published in *Blast* (but not in its later revised version of 1932), Lewis includes a surprising page boldly entitled "ADVERTISEMENT" (see fig. 3).Though this page gives the markers of stage directions, with headings like "The Scene," "Characters," and "Dress," Lewis in fact provides no direct or usable staging information and does not even mention the two principal characters, Hanp and Arghol. Instead,

ADVERTISEMENT

THE SCENE. | SOME BLEAK CIRCUS, UNCOVERED, CAREFULLY-CHOSEN, VIVID NIGHT. IT IS PACKED WITH POSTERITY, SILENT AND EXPECTANT. POSTERITY IS SILENT, LIKE THE DEAD, AND MORE PATHETIC.

CHARACTERS.

TWO HEATHEN CLOWNS, GRAVE BOOTH ANIMALS CYNICAL ATHLETES.

DRESS. ENORMOUS YOUNGSTERS, BURSTING EVERY-WHERE THROUGH HEAVY TIGHT CLOTHES, LABOURED IN BY DULL EXPLOSIVE MUSCLES, full of fiery dust and sinewy energetic air, not sap. BLACK CLOTH CUT SOMEWHERE, NOWADAYS, ON THE UPPER BALTIC.

VERY WELL ACTED BY YOU AND ME.

Figure 3. Wyndham Lewis's "ADVERTISEMENT" in his drama, *Enemy of the Stars,* reads more like a modern advertisement than a stage direction. (*Blast* 1 [June 20, 1914]: 55)

the page takes its cue from the advertising poster's typography and reliance on eye- and ear-catching phrases, not complete descriptive sentences, and on evocative words and images that, again, do not directly describe the "product." In other words, the "ADVERTISEMENT" works like a modern advertisement, not a stage direction. For "The Scene," Lewis invokes the vitality of the circus, which, as Reynolds notes, was popularized through heavy advertising (11), but he also relies on unvisualizable abstractions that evoke rather than describe, and he uses a heavy alliteration to give the ear-catching charge used by modern advertising: "Some bleak circus, uncovered, carefully-chosen, vivid night. It is packed with posterity, silent and expectant. Posterity is silent, like the dead, and more pathetic." Moreover, for "Dress," Lewis evokes an image of unfettered health and virility like those beginning to dominate advertisements for health and beauty products in both Britain and America (discussed in greater detail in the next chapter): "Enormous youngsters, bursting everywhere through heavy tight clothes, laboured in by dull explosive muscles, full of fiery dust and sinewy energetic air, not sap." He even gives a nod to the language of clothing fashion ads: "Black cloth cut somewhere, nowadays, on the upper Baltic." But, as if the scene of a circus "packed with posterity" were not enough to evoke spectacle, Lewis gives a special meaning to spectacle with the last line of the "ADVERTISEMENT": "Very well acted by you and me." Of course this is a closet drama of sorts—it is virtually unstageable—but it also rhetorically cuts against the passive distance between reader and play by implicating the reader in the spectacle that the play will "stage."

The critic who has given the most attention to the advertising language of the play is David Graver, who notes that this page "throws the aesthetics of advertising, circus, and avant-garde art movements against one another to create a spin that shatters the play's traditional coherence and stirs up a dizzying array of aesthetic fields and clashing forms. The page has a posterlike form suggesting the literary values and ambitions of advertising, bears texts about a circus world, and appears in a review—*Blast*—whose polemically innovative and abusive contents signal the interests of the avant-garde" (482). Graver carefully explores the formal tensions created by the amorphous generic boundary crossings of the play—advertising, art work, drama, narrative, and so forth—but reads advertising as just one discourse among many whose sole function is to contribute to this tension, a tension that he sees emerging between art and "advertising's blending of word and image and commodification of cultural artifacts; the circus's crass commercial interests, rigorously refined skills, and casual fraud" (483). Graver's insightful analysis of the play brings a fresh perspective on the formal and material construction of the play and leaves behind the discussion of Hanp versus Arghol that has dominated the criticism. But his argument that "Clearly, in *Blast* Lewis is more interested in

provocative paradoxes than in a coherent aesthetic program" (483) partially relies on Lewis seeing commercial advertising and institutions like
the circus as "crass fraud."

I argue instead that Lewis sees a positive cultural and aesthetic value
to advertising and spectacle beyond the avant-garde creation of energetic
tensions between discourses. As Lyon and Reynolds have noted, Lewis
makes a distinction between the unartistic feminine energy of the suffragettes (ignoring, of course, the actual artistic production of many suffragettes, as Lyon emphasizes) and the masculine aesthetic energy of the artist.
Lyon reminds us that "'the feminine' was deployed regularly as an evalua-
tive and pejorative category in nineteenth-century art criticism," as a "traditional signifier of cultural entropy" (110), and Huyssen notes that "the
masses" and mass culture were often encoded "feminine" by modernists
(44–62). But Lewis tried in the "blasts" and "blesses" sections of *Blast* to
"masculinize" advertising and spectacle as mass cultural forms available
to modernists. He blesses "feminine" scenes of advertising and spectacle,
like the department stores he blesses in *Blast* 1 and *Blast* 2—Barker's,
which helped create the modern department store in London in the 1860s
(Reynolds 15), and Selfridges, which spent more than £36,000 on advertising the store before it even opened in 1909, and as Reynolds notes, emphasized the "new" in its ads, much as vorticism did (16). But he "redeems"
department stores' "feminine" spectacles, and suffragette militants like
Lillie Lenton and Freda Graham, who had created such grand public
spectacles with their painting-hacking and arson, by placing them
amongst "virile" and "manly" acts of violence and adventure. The lists of
"blesses" includes daring aviators like Gustav Hamel, who gave loop-the-
loop flights for the king at Windsor on February 2, 1914, and died on a
Channel flight on May 23, 1914; B. C. Hucks, who did stunt flying and
racing; Claude Grahame-White, a leading exponent of aviation; and Sal-
met, who did flying exhibitions in 1914 for the *Daily Mail,* the paper most
known for its reliance on advertising and its innovations in mass market
publishing. He also blessed several boxers who were prominent in 1914—
"Young Ahearn," Colin Bell, Dick Burge, Petty Officer Curran, Bandsman
Rice, and Bombardier Wells, the heavyweight boxing champion of Britain—and many male music-hall figures like Gaby Deslys, George Mozart,
George Robey, and Harry Weldon.[66]

Having tried to set up spectacle and promotion as a masculine activity
in his "blesses," to draw it out of the hands of suffragettes, Lewis produces
in *Enemy of the Stars* a vision of the artist-hero as spectacle that is couched
both in terms of advertising and in terms of the discourse of energy and
violence that pervades *Blast.* The play begins not with the conflict between
Arghol and Hanp, but rather with a beating that Arghol all but encourages
before the public eye of the circus spectators written into the play. Arghol

willingly submits to being beaten unconscious by his uncle (63). He is brought back to consciousness by moonbeams shining on him, but not the effeminate, seductive moonshine against which the Italian futurists railed as symbolic of the weak and feminine note of late nineteenth-century culture and literature, but rather as something much more powerful and, not surprisingly, figured as an advertisement: "His eyes woke first, shaken by rough moonbeams. A white, crude volume of brutal light blazed over him. Immense bleak electric advertisement of God. It crushed with wild emptiness of street" (64).

Blast and vorticism certainly participated in modernist primitivism, but primitivism of an unusual variety—one based upon machines and energy, not Tahitian islanders, African masks, or peasant art. In his manifestos in *Blast* 1, Lewis proclaimed that "The Art-instinct is permanently primitive" and that "The artist of the modern movement is a savage" (33), and he argued that "Machinery is the greatest Earth-medium: incidentally it sweeps away the doctrines of a narrow and pedantic Realism at one stroke" (39). And Lewis's description of the night to which Arghol awakes is awash in this kind of evocative (antirealist) refiguring of the natural world as energy and machines, even invoking the archaic past of evolutionary predecessors, to break the barriers of time and to assume a mechanical nature: "The stars shone madly in the archaic blank wilderness of the universe, machines of prey. Mastodons, placid in electric atmosphere, white rivers of power. They stood in eternal black sunlight" (64). But the first use of electricity in the description is one that directly connects the modern primitive to advertising: "Immense bleak electric advertisement of God" (64). The chaotic consumer world of competition and promotion, of one advertising campaign launched against another, helps to figure a universe characterized by violence in the play, but one in which Arghol can survive in spite of the public spectacle of his beating: "But the violences of all things had left him so far intact" (64).

When Hanp asks Arghol why he does not kill his uncle instead of taking the beating, Arghol portrays his uncle as a competing advertisement, a product sample: "My uncle is very little of a relation. It would be foolish to kill him. He is an échantillon, acid advertisement slipped in letter-box: space's store-rooms dense with frivolous originals. I am used to him, as well" (66). The uncle is portrayed as a weak form of advertisement, an ineffectual product sample in a mass mailing, whereas Arghol actually gains something from promoting himself as a spectacle. The suffragettes had learned that the equivalent to the product sample, tepid mailings and pleas with Parliament and the public for the vote, got them nowhere; thus they resorted to their own vision of "the violences of all things"—public window-smashings, arson, parades, and, perhaps above all, public arrests. Though the willful submission to arrest by suffragettes, followed by hunger strikes, followed by forced feeding, release, rearrest, and so on, may have seemed masochistic—just as Arghol's submission to his uncle's beating does—spectacles of violence promoted the cause and created the kind of energy that Lewis had in mind for the modern artist.

Arghol explains his agon as a kind of fight with the universe, but, like an advertising campaign, Arghol must "launch" himself against something: "Offences against the discipline of the universe are registered by a sort of conscience, prior to the kicks. Blows rain on me. Mine is not a popular post" (70). But the discourse of advertising has structured his self-identification: "'I am Arghol.' He repeated his name—like sinister word invented to launch a new Soap, in gigantic advertisement—toilet-necessity, he, to scrub the soul" (80). Arghol has made of himself a brand name, like Pears' Soap, whose expensive advertising campaigns pictured its name painted in enormous letters onto the cliffs at Dover (Richards 250) or on the mountains of deepest, darkest Africa (Richards 122) and used images of English imperial expansion into the Sudan and elsewhere to market itself as vital to the "civilizing" enterprise of the empire (Richards 119–167). Not only does *Enemy of the Stars* suggest that the social "excrescence" of the Self cannot be shed (or entirely "scrubbed" away)—Hanp and Arghol are "always a deux!" (80)—but, in fact, the newly refigured artist can and must make a brand-name advertisement and a violent spectacle of himself in order to assert his individuality, not, as the egoist might assert, by triumphing over social antecedents, but rather reveling in the public arena of competition that is modernity for Lewis.

In an article on Lewis that Pound wrote for the *Egoist* he portrays the relationship of the intellect to "the crowd" in terms of a kind of phallic penetration of the feminized masses: "From the beginning of the world there has been the traditional struggle, the struggle of Voltaire, of Stendhal and of Flaubert, the struggle of driving the shaft of intelligence into the dull mass of mankind" ("Wyndham Lewis" 234). He suggests that Lewis's work portrays this struggle, but, implying that this struggle is necessary for its own sake, he argues, in a way that sheds light on vorticism's self-presentation in *Blast,* that it is difficult for his generation of artists, because "One has such trivial symbols arrayed against one, there is only 'The Times' and all that it implies, and the 'Century Magazine' and its likes and all that they imply, and the host of other periodicals and the states of mind represented in them. It is so hard to arrange one's mass and opposition. Labour and anarchy can find their opponents in 'capital' and 'government.' But the mind aching for something that it can honour under the name of 'civilisation', the mind, seeing that state afar off but clearly, can only flap about pettishly striking at the host of trivial substitutes presented to it" (234). But, having created such a struggle, nevertheless, and thereby producing some intellectual vitality, Pound quips, "Some aesthete left over from the nineties would rebuke one for one's lack of aloofness. I have heard people accuse Mr. Lewis of lack of aloofness" (234).

For Pound, as for Lewis in 1914, the opposite of the aloof aesthete which Pound implicitly aligns with the feminized masses was the artist who could "arrange one's mass and opposition." And this is exactly what Lewis saw in advertising spectacle—the ability to create an audience and stage opposition. Arghol is beaten, and wears the mark of his public humiliation on his body, just as middle-class suffragettes wore their sandwich boards before a humiliating public, bore their public beatings and arrests, and created their "violence of all things" before the public, just as "Labour" and "anarchy" staged strikes, public disruptions, and violence as spectacles to change the state. Though *Enemy of the Stars* ends with Arghol's murder and Hanp's suicide, the play itself functions as an equivalent to Allen Upward's "poetical and mysterious announcement in the *Morning Post* . . . (where the cabaret advertises)." With its posterlike typography, its alliterative and evocative half-phrases and vibrant images—the staples of product-symbols advertising—Lewis's play certainly portrays a state of mind, as Flory argues, but that state of mind is born of the arena of modern advertising, as a world of self-promotion and agonism. And if the artist ultimately cannot wipe off the excrescence of the social Self, he can take control of it by advertisement as a kind of self-formation, and can attempt to reach a society that thrills to the excitement and dynamism of advertising at the "End of the Christian Era." Ultimately, the vigor of the presentation of the play and of its language overwhelms our concern for Arghol himself, and the play gives a glimpse of the possibilities for the provocative vocabulary of advertising spectacle to create a link between the new artist and the public.

As late as 1930, Evelyn Waugh made *Blast*'s lists of "blasts" and "blesses" inspire the form of party invitations for the "Bright Young Things" of *Vile Bodies*—even though the magazine unfortunately lasted only two issues. Lewis's hopes of reviving it after the war, perhaps with Harriet Shaw Weaver publishing it, ran into the reality of unpaid printer's bills from *Blast* 1, and the surviving vorticists (Gaudier-Brzeska and the tangential T. E. Hulme were killed in the war) never reunited in full in any of Pound's or Lewis's later magazines. If *Blast* must serve as a coda to the *Egoist*'s attempts to bring modernism into the public sphere, it certainly explored to an unprecedented degree in the prewar period the possible fruits advertising culture could bear for modernism.

4

Youth in Public

The *Little Review* and Commercial Culture in Chicago

In 1908, a fashionable young woman—"as chic as any of the girls who model . . . for the fashion magazines"—wearied of her stifling Indiana home life and complained of it in a letter to "The Perfect Comrade," an advice column in *Good Housekeeping* for girls and young women. The columnist, Clara Laughlin, invited her correspondent to Chicago for a visit and soon urged her to move to the city to interview stage celebrities for magazines. The eighteen-year-old and her sister relocated to Chicago, and she reviewed books for Laughlin in a popular Presbyterian magazine, the *Interior* (later the *Continent*), supported by Cyrus McCormick. She also began reviewing for the *Friday Literary Review* of the *Chicago Evening Post.* Ironically, this ultra-American tale of youth moving from the small town to the big city, to begin a career in the growing mass publishing world, was the story of Margaret Anderson, the founder and editor of the *Little Review*—whose profession to "make no compromise with the public taste" and willingness to publish everything from imagism, *Ulysses,* and French avant-gardism to anarchist diatribes made it the quintessential modernist little magazine.[1] This story of the origin of one of the most important avant-garde magazines highlights a significant and overlooked aspect of the emergence of American modernism before the war: the imbrication of commercial mass culture with the public self-fashioning of modernism. And playing a central role in the story of Margaret Anderson, the *Little Review,* and American modernism was the newly emerging "cult of youth"—a source of great cultural anxiety in early twentieth-century America.

The *Little Review* had much in common with transatlantic counterpart, the *Egoist.* Neither conforms to the commonplace understanding of modernist little magazines as turning their backs on audiences and publishing for the select few as coterie organs. The *Egoist* used mass-advertising techniques (mediated by radical counterpublic spheres) to seek an urban mass audience; the *Little Review* likewise attempted to reach large audiences, but it also borrowed *directly* from mass market publications and advertising rhetoric to style a popular periodical that would differ from mass market magazines only in that mass appeal would not serve as the basis of its editorial decisions. Like *Blast,* the *Little Review* turned to the energies of a vibrant advertising culture to help bring modernism into the public sphere, but, of course, the differences between London and Chicago ensured that the *Little Review* would follow a different path than *Blast* did.

Commercial mass culture greatly influenced the self-fashioning of early American modernism and the Chicago Renaissance. Indeed, as youth became increasingly important to American commercial culture, the *Little Review* promoted modernism as a youth movement. European avant-garde groups (like the Italian futurists) that promoted a cult of youth are not adequate contexts for understanding this phenomenon in Chicago. Instead, we must turn to two facets of American commercial culture: the development of the marketing potential of adolescence and a tentatively emerging "public sphere of youth" sustained by youth forums and columns in commercial magazines. While mass market institutions crafted positive images of youth, characterized by abandon and consumerism, American culture paradoxically also attempted to regulate youth's relation to commercial culture, to prevent the rhetorical abandon of consumerism from becoming actual moral abandon. Youth columns in mass market magazines negotiated these social misgivings by constructing a carefully contained "open forum" to discuss issues important to youth. Thus when the *Little Review* actually tried to create an *unregulated* public organ for youth—an avant-garde magazine whose aesthetic, social, and political radicalism was pervaded by a new ideology, setting the freedoms of youth in public against constraining and authoritarian domesticity—it collided head on with the law and the Society for the Suppression of Vice.

Whereas mass advertising techniques had influenced the promotion of the *Egoist* and its predecessors, the commercial publishing industry that brought Margaret Anderson to Chicago (and sustained her before the founding of the *Little Review*) greatly influenced both the marketing and the form of the *Little Review*. The quotations from various authors scattered throughout its pages mirrored those in the "New Books" section of the *Continent,* and the *Little Review*'s large critical section, including the "Sentence Reviews," also reflected the short book notices commonly found in mass market newspapers and magazines like the *Continent.* As with most commercial publications, the "Sentence Reviews" covered a wide range of works: serious intellectual studies and novels, music and art discussions, gardening, travel, reference works, poetry, and radical political works as well as romances and sentimental novels. Models for the "New York Letter" and "London Letter" that the *Little Review* regularly featured during its Chicago years could be found in the *Chicago Evening Post.* Furthermore, the lists of "Best Sellers" in the Chicago area prominently displayed in the April and May 1914 issues spoke to a broader audience than a tiny elitist coterie organ would desire and included the latest romances and even a Zane Grey western.[2]

In spite of modernism's rhetorical lack of concern for audiences, Anderson clearly intended to augment the circulation of the *Little Review.* By July 1914, only the fifth issue, she took a further step toward reaching the broad audiences of the mass market magazines by announcing a reduction of the cover price from 25 cents to 15 cents a copy and the subscription price from $2.50 to $1.50 per year—the price of the mass market monthlies like *Munsey's, McClure's, Good Housekeeping,* and *Ladies' Home Journal.* In "A Change of Price," Anderson proclaimed: "We have discovered that a great many of the people whom we wish to reach cannot afford to pay $2.50 a year for a magazine. It happens that we are very emphatic about wanting these people in our audience, and we believe they are as sincerely interested in *The Little Review* as we are stimulated by having them among our readers. Therefore we are going to become more accessible." Because recent mass market magazines had significantly boosted their circulations by lowering their prices,[3] it seemed to Anderson that price, rather than the nature of the content, was the major obstacle to a wide circulation. The *Little Review* was in the black and boasted of "a subscription list that acts like a live thing!" but, Anderson added, "we want more!"[4] She announced a campaign by which anyone sending in three yearly subscriptions could get one free, or might make a 33⅓ percent commission on each subscription, and, like other magazine editors, she tried to enlist college students as canvassers for the magazine.[5] A later issue ran a notice about commissions on subscriptions: "We want circulation solicitors in every city in the country. Liberal commissions. For particulars address William Saphier, circulation manager" (Oct. 1914, 63). Anderson had ambitions for the *Little Review* to reach a nationwide circulation, and she prominently displayed lists of bookstores that sold the magazine in thirty-six cities in twenty states across the country (June 1914, 55–56).

Notwithstanding its nonmainstream literary content, the *Little Review* during its Chicago years was almost uniquely successful among little magazines in attracting advertising to its pages, due to its similarities to mass market publications. *Diane of the Green Van,* a novel that had won a "$10,000 Prize Novel" contest and sat at the top of the *Little Review*'s best-sellers list, was publicized with several full-page advertisements in 1914 which boasted that more than 75,000 copies had been sold in advance publication. Assuming that the *Little Review*'s audience was not just social radicals, the advertisers assured that "It is not a 'problem' or 'sex' novel; it does not deal with woman suffrage; it does not argue. Diane of the Green Van is frankly a story for entertainment" (Mar. 1914, 64). Most of the seventeen pages of advertisements in the first issue and in succeeding issues were for major American publishing houses; unlike book advertisements in the *Egoist,* they publicized not only "problem" or "sex" novels and political works, but also a full range of mass market publications, including fiction and coffee-table travel books.[6] Lucian Cary, literary editor of the *Friday Literary Review* of the *Chicago Evening Post,* praised the contents of the "astonishing" new review, but especially noted that "The contributions, more than forty pages of them, were followed by seventeen more pages of advertising!" (Mar. 20, 1914, 1).

The *Little Review* also attracted advertisements for nonliterary products. A long-running series of lavishly illustrated advertisements for Goodyear tires, along with those for Mason & Hamlin pianos and the "Carola Inner-Player," were interspersed with book and magazine advertisements. This combination—intellectual and political books, mass market novels, and other commercial goods—suggests that American companies saw little "highbrow"–"lowbrow" distinction between this little magazine of modernist literature and art and more obviously mass market publications. The *Little Review,* which could not rival the huge circulation of magazines like *Munsey's* or the *Ladies' Home Journal,* simply charged companies less for advertising space.

Commodity Advertising and the Cult of Youth

But the intersection with commercial mass culture that most defined the early *Little Review*'s fashioning of modernism—and the Chicago Renaissance—was the cult of youth. Our current idea of adolescence as a period between childhood and mature adult life did not fully exist before the last two decades of the nineteenth century, or even the first decade of the twentieth (Davis ix; Demos and Demos 209–221). Large-scale demographic changes, especially the nineteenth-century movement from farm to city, caused shifts in familial relations. From the increasingly lengthy period between childhood and full adulthood emerged a youth culture.[7] The concept of adolescence became common American currency only around the turn of the century, with the writings of G. Stanley Hall, the president of Clark University and a professor of psychology and pedagogy (Davis xii; Demos and Demos 214). Hall's systematic "child study" movement, coupled with his keen interest in Darwinism, produced not only the first "scientific" concept of adolescence, but also an important role for it in his "theory of recapitulation"—the idea that the development of the child recapitulates the development of the race. His 1904 magnum opus— *Adolescence: Its Psychology, and Its Relations to Physiology, Anthropology, Sociology, Sex, Crime, Religion, and Education*—suggested that adolescence, which he charted between fourteen and twenty-four years of age, was especially important in that it "recapitulated" the most recent of mankind's developmental leaps, and even for a short time advanced man beyond the present stage of civilization. Hall wrote, "Adolescence is a new birth, for the higher and more completely human traits are now born. The qualities of body and soul that now emerge are far newer. The child comes from and harks back to a remoter past; the adolescent is neo-atavistic, and in him the later acquisitions of the race slowly become prepotent" (xiii). Hall associated youth with "vigor, enthusiasm, and courage" (xviii) and felt that the sense of newness and the intellectual and emotional curiosity and aspirations of adolescence marked their great potential but also opened them up to great temptation to succumb to the dangers of urban life (xv). But he was hopeful that education could augment this precious social commodity: "Youth needs repose, leisure, art, legends, romance, idealization, and in a word humanism, if it is to enter the kingdom of man well equipped for man's highest work in the world" (xvii). Hall's influence on American culture can hardly be overstated, and his work drew wide attention, including that of Margaret Anderson, who had taken over Laughlin's position as the literary editor of the *Continent*.[8]

Many books of the period exemplified the newly popular infatuation with youth and adolescence, and Anderson tracked some of these in her *Continent* columns. In a signed review she called Randolph Bourne's *Youth and Life* "one of the significant and interesting publications of the current literary season," and she affirmed Bourne's claim that "It is the glory of the present age that in it one can be young." She continued: "One dares to be young in this day and age because the potentiality of youth has been discovered, and on every side tribute is being paid to it. To have youth is to have about the best thing God invents" ("The Glory of Present-

Day Youth"). Bourne argued that "The younger generation is coming very seriously to doubt both the practicability and worth of [the] rational ideal. They do not find that the complex affairs of either the world or the soul work according to the laws of reason" (230). He advocated substituting for the rational ideal the "experimental ideal": "Life is not a campaign of battle, but a laboratory where its possibilities for the enhancement of happiness and realization of ideals are to be tested and observed" (232–233). In his understanding of youth as idealistic, vigorous, and free to experiment with new life-styles and ideas, Bourne follows Hall's notion of the potential of adolescence to advance the race. Bourne's characterization of the youthful "experimental life" was echoed throughout the *Little Review* a few years later. Using a promotional tactic she would adopt widely in discussing writers for the *Little Review,* Anderson boasted of Bourne's own youth: "[He] confesses to just 25 years."

Many writers shared this positive characterization of youth. But many also shared Hall's warnings about the dangers posed to adolescents by modernity, especially the commercial exploitation of youth culture. Perhaps the most significant was Jane Addams's popular study of youth culture in Chicago, *The Spirit of Youth and the City Streets* (1909), parts of which reached millions of readers in the *Ladies' Home Journal* in October and November 1909. Addams's book documents the shabby and stunted life of working-class youth in the industrial city, complaining that the youthful impulse to play knew no positive outlet in the modern city. Addams blamed modern commercial culture, arguing that young men and women had only gin palaces, dance halls, and movie theaters to entertain them: "Apparently the modern city sees in these girls only two possibilities, both of them commercial: first, a chance to utilize by day their new and tender labor power in its factories and shops, and then another chance in the evening to extract from them their petty wages by pandering to their love of pleasure" (7–8).[9]

Indeed, two manifestations of this commodification of youth helped to shape the *Little Review* as an organ of modernism and modernity in Chicago: images and discourses of youth in advertising, and the youth forums and advice columns in commercial magazines. As the concept of adolescence spread widely through popular discourse, the burgeoning commodity culture helped to solidify the importance of "youth" in America by commercializing it, and, I suggest, by turning the rhetoric of youthful spontaneity, experiment, exuberance, and ardor into a rhetoric of consumption. Images of youthfulness were part of what I have previously discussed as product-symbol strategies for advertising—advertising that associates the buyer with a desirable life-style or a personal characteristic rather than explaining the merits or uses of a product (see chap. 3). Companies hoping to sell to all ages (especially those producing appearance-related products like clothing or health and beauty aids) used images of youth to help promote their product.[10] These national campaigns also reinforced a heightened social preoccupation with youth, one that manifested itself in the business world with the spread of compulsory retirement policies during the first quarter of the century, and with changing medical definitions of aging, which by 1890 began to view senility as a normal result of aging, itself described as a process of loss. The modern American corporate world privileged the mental quickness of youth over the wisdom of experience and age (Lears 168–169).

Youth also became an important target of segmentation advertising during the first quarter of the twentieth century, because manufacturers and merchants quickly realized that young people were more susceptible to the mass marketing of fashion than their parents, and, most important, that they had begun to lead their elders in the choice of commodities.[11] In addition, an emerging marketing theory suggested that the young were important future consumers: they formed their buying habits between their late teens and late twenties (mirroring Hall's parameters for adolescence), and remained loyal in later life to products they chose during their youth (Hollander and Germain 17–18). *Printer's Ink,* the advertising trade journal, noted the importance of advertising to the college market, even awarding a prize to a Wanamaker's advertisement directed at college men.[12] The magazine spotlighted a cigarette company's scheme of hiring college students to devise advertisements that would help the company compete with other tobacco advertisers in the college magazines. One such advertisement proclaimed, "From the time you enter as a Freshman—Slide along the line and get the sheepskin—go on out into the Great Wide—and come back to Reunion—It's FATIMA all along the Line!" (reproduced in *Printer's Ink* Mar. 11, 1915, 25). The *University of Chicago Magazine,* whose pages were filled with images promoting new fashions and local hotels and restaurants catering to college men and women, boasted, "The University of Chicago Magazine carries more advertising than any other publication of its kind in the United States. . . . Say 'University of Chicago Magazine' to the advertisers" (Feb. 1909, 1).

Chicago stores also targeted the young with special fashions and departments, using these newly prominent rhetorics about youthful character. Connecting youth to fashion (and equating both with revolution), The Hub, a Loop clothing store, proclaimed, "Young men's clothes are treated with but moderate consideration in most stores—the idea that a *young* man is only a *small sized* man still remains their policy [hardly the case by the teens]. We've revolutionized things here—created a special young men's store, assembled special young men's styles. Youth, vigor, vim, life and 'pep' characterize our displays—they're as full of 'life' and 'go' as the most ardent admirer of young men's styles could desire" (*Chicago Evening*

Figure 4. Capitalizing on the new discourse of youth, the Chicago department store Mandel Brothers' advertisement portrays youth as the vanguard of the new. (*Chicago Evening Post,* October 11, 1915, 14)

Post, Apr. 3, 1914, 3). Another Chicago department store, Mandel Brothers, which frequently targeted "girls and flappers" and young men in its advertisements, and had as its motto, "The store that keeps step with youth" (*Chicago Evening Post,* Oct. 11, 1915, 14; see fig. 4). These advertisements pictured young people dressed in the latest fashions—though never in a family context—and portrayed them as the vanguard of the new (a strategy that greatly appealed to young modernists in the *Little Review*).

Youth, Advertising, and the *Little Review*

The importance of images of youth in promotional culture could not have been overlooked by Margaret Anderson and other writers for the *Little Review*, many of whom had long been involved or interested in the world of advertising. Sherwood Anderson (who moved back to Chicago in 1913 and began to publish early stories and episodes from *Winesburg, Ohio* in the magazine) had worked for years in an advertising firm, and had written articles for a trade journal, *Agricultural Advertising*. Ben Hecht, whose early "Dregs" stories, in the *Review* described the adventures of a "young dramatist" in the streets of Chicago, worked for an advertising agency and advised Anderson and Jane Heap on ways to increase their circulation.[13] John Gould Fletcher, whose "Green Symphony" and other early poems appeared in the *Review*, contributed an article entitled "Vers Libre and Advertising" in which he explained that "in the main I have found American advertisements refreshingly readable" (29). Half tongue-in-cheek, but also half-seriously, Fletcher compared some vigorous advertising texts to "the insipid tinklings of the lyrists who feebly strum in pathetically threadbare meters throughout the pages of most magazines" (29). Aligning advertising with literary modernism, he admonished the "gentlemen of the poets' profession": "How can you expect to find readers by lazily sticking to your antiquated formulas, when even the advertisement writers in the very magazines you do your work for are getting quite up-to-date?" (30). Jane Heap even consulted with James Howard Kehler, a prominent Chicago advertising agent, about plans to market the *Little Review* as it moved to New York.[14]

An awareness of youth's advertising value, I suggest, led writers for the *Little Review* to package and promote their modernist experiments in writing and living with neoromantic tropes of youth. Advertising strategies put forward an ideal of youth as able to remake itself through fashion and consumption. This understanding of youth appealed to writers, artists, and social thinkers who wished not to build on the traditions of their parents but to effect a radical rupture with tradition. In the first issue of the *Little Review*, Sherwood Anderson discussed "the new note in the craft of writing" in terms of youth and age: "Already a cult of the new has sprung up, and doddering old fellows, yellow with their sins, run here and there crying out that they are true prophets of the new, just as, following last year's exhibit, every age-sick American painter began hastily to inject into his own work something clutched out of the seething mass of new forms and new effects scrawled upon the canvasses by the living young cubists and futurists" ("The New Note"). Anderson proclaimed, "It is the voice of the new man, come into a new world, proclaiming his right to speak out of the body and soul of youth, rather than through the bodies and souls of the master craftsmen who are gone." He adds: "In the craft of writing there can be no such thing as age in the souls of the young poets and novelists who demand for themselves the right to stand up and be counted among the soldiers of the new. That there are such youths is brother to the fact that there are ardent young cubists and futurists, anarchists, socialists, and feminists; it is the promise of a perpetual sweet new birth of the world; it is as a strong wind come out of the virgin west." Anderson synthesizes ideas of psychologists and cultural critics like Hall and Bourne, the corporate world's emphasis on youthful intelligence over the experience of age, and advertising images of ardent and brave new youth in a new world and a "new" city, to unite modernist writers, artists, and social radicals around an ideal of fresh youth remaking the world.

Ben Hecht likewise portrayed the *Little Review* as a magazine of youth: "I understand The Little Review to be an embodiment of inspired opinion, an abandonment of mental emotion—Youth," and he praised the review for being "young and idiotic and given to unnecessary emotions and so forth" ("Slobberdom, Sneerdom, and Boredom" 22–25). Again, it is against the entrenched, safe mediocrity of maturity that the *Sturm und Drang* of adolescence refreshingly renews. Other authors followed the lead of advertising in connecting youth to America as a young modern nation. Amy Lowell complained of America's mediocre traditionalism, "That the United States of America is young is a truism which needs no stating, and unfortunately its youth is hopelessly fettered in the strings of tradition" ("Miss Columbia: An Old-Fashioned Girl" 36). But, employing a commercial term, she expressed her hope that the dances of youth culture would help generate American art: "Do you realize that [the turkey trot] is America's first original contribution to the arts! Low or high, that is not the point; it is America's own *product*" (emphasis mine). She echoes Hall's evolutionary understanding of adolescence: "I am told by those who know, that dancing is the first art practiced by primitive peoples. I believe that in our 'turkey-trotting' and 'rag-time' we have the earliest artistic gropings of a new race" (37).

The rhetoric of youth was often susceptible to the hyperbole we associate with avant-garde manifestos. One writer flung defiance at "pedantic," "didactic," and "foolish" old age, and boldly proclaimed: "There is no wisdom but youth. There is no vision but the unafraid impulse of unfettered nerves. The follies of youth are the enduring expressions of art. Man loses his Ego at thirty and becomes conceited" (A. E. D. 37). The idea that youth, while susceptible to chaotic emotional excess ("Youth that laughs at tears and weeps at laughter"), gestured toward future civilization echoes Hall's understanding of adolescence. But the young person's arrogance and disregard for the wisdom of age made him or her the ideal consumer, and, in a connection A. E. D. added to the equation, the ideal artist: "There is no beauty but youth. There is no beauty in age. Ho! you doddering banality with the superior tolerance in your stutter, you are decomposing on your feet. . . . Blessed are the young in heart for they shall be God" (38). This kind of youthful bravado, of course, resembles the manifestos of the Italian futurists, of whom the *Little Review* contributors were aware,[15] but American modernists did not need the Italian futurists as inspiration to fashion themselves as a youth movement. The sociocultural developments I have discussed led one American author in 1913 to complain that "We are today under the tyranny of the special cult of adolescence."[16]

Margaret Anderson explicitly and repeatedly made the connection between modernist art and literature and youth, and she tapped into the cult of youth to advertise the magazine. Like product advertisements that offered youthfulness to all ages, a circular promoting the magazine after it moved to New York proclaimed "THE LITTLE REVIEW IS IMMORTAL / surpasses ALL includes ALL outlives ALL / ISMS. . . . / cubism, impressionism, futurism, unanism, neo-classicism, ultraism, imagism, vorticism, dadaism, simulateneism, expressionism—all." Using modern advertising's playful variation of font sizes and typefaces, this circular proclaimed the review's uniquely wide range of interests, including mass cultural topics. It identified the *Little Review* as "A Review of painting, sculpture, design, architecture, prose, poetry, music, dance, drama, notes on the theatre, music-hall, cinema, circus, sports, books and on the triumphs, experiments, crimes of the modern art world— / The Little Review Cannot be imitated." But it also included the rhetoric of youth among the "7 reasons why you should subscribe": "If you are tired of the imbecile, dogmatic pretense of the old magazines," for example, and "If you want to keep eternally young" (see fig. 5). Like an advertisement for a health or beauty product, a product-symbol strategy is here used to urge the subscriber to identify with eternal youth as opposed to both fleeting fashions and dogmatic old age and tradition. In an earlier subscription promotion in the *Review,* Anderson invoked an image of immortal youth familiar to Chicago theatergoers from a recent performance, asking readers to identify with the boy who never wants to enter the stodgy world of adulthood in J. M. Barrie's *Peter Pan:* "We are sending out this card to the four thousand people who have expressed an interest in THE LITTLE REVIEW. . . . Will you please help? THE LITTLE REVIEW *must* live! To let it die now for want of asking—much as we hate to do it—seems to us too stupid to consider. We feel much as Peter Pan did when he rushed to the footlights with his 'Oh, do you believe in fairies?' But—we do believe!" ("THE LITTLE REVIEW Asks Some Help!").

THE LITTLE REVIEW IS IMMORTAL

surpasses **ALL**   includes **ALL**   outlives **ALL**

I S M S . . . . . .

cubism, impressionism, futurism, unaninism, neo-classicism, ultraism,
imagism, vorticism, dadaism, simultaneism, expressionism---all

? WHAT IS THE LITTLE REVIEW ?

An anthology INTERNATIO-
NAL of Aesthetiques---A Review
of painting, sculpture,
design, architecture,
prose, poetry, music,
dance, drama, notes on
the theatre, music-hall,
cinema, circus, sports,
books, and on the tri-
umphs, experiments,
crimes of the modern
art world---

The Little Review is in its
7th year, subscriptions $7.00.
Here are 7 reasons why you
should subscribe---

If you are not a magazine reader
Subscribe to the Little Review
If you are tired of the imbecilic, dogmatic pretense of the old
magazines
Subscribe to the Little Review
If you are sad in the tranquility of the newer magazines
Subscribe to the Little Review
If you find yourself a self-kleptomanic in getting your art from
fashion-society-journals
Subscribe to the Little Review
If you want a reorganization of the spirit
Subscribe to the Little Review
If you want to keep eternally young
Subscribe to the Little Review
If you want a contact with the men who are creating civilization
Subscribe to the Little Review

THE LITTLE REVIEW CANNOT BE IMMITATED

Writers, painters, musicians, actors, wage-slaves, debutantes, art patrons, citizens,
ladies, gentlemen subscribe to The Little Review

27 WEST EIGHTH STREET
NEW YORK CITY

YEARLY $7.00
FOREIGN £2.00
SINGLE COPY $2.00

Figure 5. Like a beauty product, the *Little Review* advertises itself as the secret to "keeping eternally young." (*Little Review* advertising flier, ca. 1920).

Within the *Little Review* itself, Anderson promoted the magazine as
unabashedly youthful. As she had a year earlier in her review of Randolph
Bourne's *Youth and Life,* she repeatedly boasted of the young age of the
"new poets" her magazine was promoting: Charles Ashleigh was only
twenty-five (Anderson noted in "Our New Poet"): "We look for big things
from this young man" and Maxwell Bodenheim only twenty-two ("Our
Third New Poet"). In the editorial of the second issue of the magazine,
she explicitly compared the *Little Review* to the Pre-Raphaelite magazine
the *Germ.* She praised the "astounding" *Germ* and noted that the ages of
the founders ranged between nineteen and twenty-two. She explained that
"All this came to our mind the other day when some one accused us of
being 'juvenile.' What hideous stigma was thereby put upon us? The only
grievous thing about juvenility is its unwillingness to be frank; it usually
tries to appear very, very old and very, very wise" ("The Germ" 1–2). She
admitted that the *Germ* was "frankly young," as shown by its interest in
death poetry, but "*The Germ* might have been even more 'juvenile' and so

144

avoided some of the heavy, sumptuous sentences in that Browning review. It would have gained in readableness without any possible sacrifice of beauty or truth. In their poetry the Pre-Raphaelites were as simple and spontaneous as children; in their criticism they were rhetorical. Our sympathy is somehow very strongly with the spontaneity—whatever dark juvenile crimes it may be guilty of—in the eyes of those who merely look but do not see" (2). In her February 1915 editorial, "Our First Year," Anderson noted that "We have been uncritical, indiscriminate, juvenile, exuberant, chaotic, amateurish, emotional, tiresomely enthusiastic, and a lot of other things which I can't remember now—all the things that are usually said about faulty new undertakings. The encouraging thing is that they are said most strongly about promising ones" (1).

In addition to lending a new vocabulary to commodity advertising, youth culture had invaded and given nuances to public space in two important ways, both of which affected the development of the *Little Review*. Chicago, whose downtown area had been almost entirely destroyed in the Great Fire of 1871, had become a center for architectural experiment and was home to the first proliferation of skyscrapers.[17] Sherwood Anderson's "new birth of the world" and "strong wind come out of the virgin west" described a city of new, intensely public modern architecture. And, as Margaret Anderson and modernist authors in the *Little Review* would do, Chicago advertisers associated images of youth culture with the public spaces and architecture of this young and rapidly expanding urban skyline.

In its 1902 promotional pamphlet, entitled "Progressive Chicago," the Washington Shirt Company used drawings and photographs to connect its quick rise to prominence to the growth of the city of Chicago.[18] But this growth of both city and company was figured as a change not from childhood to adulthood, but rather from childhood to a vibrant youth. A drawing of the old wooden post office in early Chicago precedes photos of the enormous new stone Post Office and Federal Building and of the Washington Shirt Company's Loop stores. The text parallels Hall's vision of an atavistic childhood recapitulating the unevolved primitive— here figured as the "slimy, soggy marshes by the water's edge" of early Chicago—and then giving way to a "neo-atavistic" adolescence, gesturing toward the future of civilization: "To-day the broad avenues, beautiful boulevards, and crowded business districts of Chicago are continually beautified and improved by the noble structures that point to continued growth and expansion as well as results achieved. The erection of the new Post Office and Federal Building by the United States Government in the very heart of the city already indicates the definite business center of the metropolis." Like Hall's adolescents, both company and city were portrayed as an apotheosis of some future stage of modernity—potential in the act of realization, vigorous and capable, idealistic and still growing.

The Washington Shirt Company emphasized the alacrity and idealism of youth: "The service provided for customers is that of 'quick action,' and it is well known that 'you don't have to *wait* at The Washington Shirt Company.' . . . For the most part young men comprise the working force, and all enter heartily into the work of the firm. With good-natured loyalty they join in supplying the needs of 'His Majesty the American Citizen.'" It also connected the advertising rhetoric of Chicago's public space and the "youthful" company itself with an ideal of modernity: "[Visitors] will see stores combining the most modern features of mercantile establishments as well as the most recent dictations of fashion in the dress details of a modern man." Modern man, in a modern city—modernity itself—was figured as fashion and consumption, and the consumer was explicitly also portrayed as a youth. "His Majesty the American Citizen" (see fig. 6) was depicted in a drawing that the company continued to use for at least a decade, of a well-dressed but casual and very young, even adolescent-looking, man. The customer has youthful features and no facial hair. He smokes a cigarette, leaning back in a chair with an American flag draped over it, propping himself up with his foot on a crown. The evocation of the Yankee youth, brazen, almost smug-looking, flouting the authority of old traditions (just as America had thrown off the paternal shackles of monarchical Britain), urged customers to identify with a young and growing city and work force. The company brochure paralleled Bourne's understanding of the "experimental life" by proclaiming that the secret to the growth of this young work force was the motto: "Never fear a mistake, but *fear to repeat one.*"

Similar visual images and text were used to extol a vision of the youth and growth of both company and city. Fort Dearborn National Bank juxtaposed its logo drawing of the old wooden Fort Dearborn (the original site of Chicago) with the modern brick skyscraper bank building.[19] The text asserted "One of Chicago's foremost banks. It typifies the spirit of the city for strength, security and steady growth." (This "modern bank" reached out to the young with special accounts as well.) Many advertisements used images of youth in the amazing new urban architecture of Chicago. Local hotels and dance halls advertised with illustrations of young men and women in the new buildings. The glamour of the young was paralleled by the glamour of such new public spaces as the Auditorium Annex and its restaurants, bars, and corridors.[20]

Jane Addams had complained about the way in which youths had entered the public spaces of Chicago—wandering the streets and spending their money in the dance halls, gin palaces, and movie theaters. But Margaret Anderson and other *Little Review* authors were more captivated by

TRADE MARK REGISTERED

Figure 6. The promotional pamphlet for the Washington Shirt Company presents the modern consumer as the self-assured American youth. ("His Majesty the American Citizen," *Progressive Chicago,* 1902)

Chicago as a city in which youth could transform public space. The *Little Review* serves as a document of this modernist fascination with the unexpected charged moments of urban public experience. While Addams lamented the commercialism, Anderson and others saw the possibility for such spaces to generate art in spite of themselves. Anderson wrote about discovering a young German violinist who had been a child prodigy in Europe, playing in the very epitome of the modern mercantile economy, the department store: "In one of Chicago's big department stores of the cheaper type you may—provided you're something of a poet—walk straight into the heart of a musical adventure. It is that amazing, resentful, and very satisfying adventure of discovering genius at work, under the by no means unique condition of being unrecognized" ("Nur Wer die Sehnsucht Kennt," 34). She discovers the great violinist in the lunch room, surrounded by people who clamor for more "tawdry" fare: "In the midst of it the waitresses rush back and forth, the patrons eat their food with interest, only pausing to applaud when some tawdry vaudevillian sings a particularly vulgar song. The dishes clang, some one upsets a tray with a great crash, and at intervals there is a tango outrage by a couple who know nothing about dancing. Underneath it all the violin throbs its deep accompaniment" (35). The tastes of the majority of shoppers in the Loop may be "vulgar," but for the appreciative, Chicago provided public space for a young performer (or for a young magazine).[21]

Anderson played on the connections among advertising, the public spaces created by department stores, and the readers of the *Little Review*. In the June–July 1915 issue, as advertising had fallen off—largely due to the *Little Review* writers' strident affirmation of Emma Goldman and anarchism (Bryer 119)—Anderson, always with a taste for the eyecatching, set aside seven full pages of the issue, inserting only a small box of type in the center of each. The first offered $5.00 to anyone who secured a full-page advertisement for the magazine, and then noted, "On the following pages you will find the 'ads' we might have had in this issue, but haven't" (56). These included advertising advice and potential "ads" for Chicago Loop stores—Mandel Brothers, Marshall Field's, Carson Pirie Scott, McClurg, the Cable Piano Company —and for the New York publisher, Mitchell Kennerley, who had regularly advertised in the *Little Review* in the past.

In addition to the cleverness of the sales pitch, these "ads" connected the *Little Review* with the consumption and fashion advocated by modern corporate America. Anderson suggested to Mandel Brothers how they might promote themselves to her readers as "the most original and artistic store in Chicago," and she concluded: "If they should advertise those things here I have no doubt the 1,000 Chicago subscribers to The Little Review would overflow their store" (57). The public space created by the shopping district could appeal to readers as both consumers and artists. She derided Carson Pirie Scott's sense of fashion as lagging behind that of the magazine: "The Carson-Pirie attitude toward change of any sort is well-known—I think they resent even having to keep pace with the change in fashions" (59). Yet, in addition to the Radical Book Shop and other bookstores, both McClurg's and Carson Pirie Scott's bookstores carried the *Little Review*.

So the *Little Review* clad itself in the mantle of youth and, as the Washington Shirt Company would put it, reached out to Progressive Chicago and the rest of the country. Though it frequently struggled financially, the *Little Review* maintained a fairly large readership by the standards of little magazines, unlike its transatlantic counterpart, the *Egoist.* It seems to have ranged between 2,000 and 3,000 subscribers.[22] When the review became more a part of the international modern art world, it even opened a Little Review Gallery in New York that sold books and art and mounted several major exhibitions during the twenties—the Machine Age Exposition, the International Exposition of New Systems of Architecture, and the International Theatre Exposition.

As Margaret Anderson and other *Little Review* writers discussed the magazine using tropes of youth, its readers received it as the young voice of social and aesthetic progress. Like the *Freewoman, New Freewoman,* and *Egoist,* the *Little Review* had a lively correspondence section that created a discursive public space for its readers to discuss the issues the magazine raised. The section's title, "The Reader Critic," ascribed an equal status to correspondents and primary authors alike, and (like the Freewoman Discussion Circles in London) this lively public arena, at the suggestion of readers, soon spilled over into organized public meetings at the Fine Arts Building on Michigan Avenue—in many ways the center of the Chicago Renaissance, as it was the home of the *Little Review,* the *Dial,* Browne's Bookstore (designed by Frank Lloyd Wright and managed by the editor of the *Dial*), and the experimental Little Theater.[23] As Anderson put it, "An attempt to influence the art, music, literature, and life of Chicago is an exciting and worthy one, and should have its opportunity of expression" ("To Serve an Idea").

Many of the readers who wrote to the *Little Review* understood the magazine in terms of youth. One Chicago reader wrote that "It is just into terrible inertia—this every day and *every* day humdrum conservatistic acceptance of things as they are—that THE LITTLE REVIEW comes with its laughter of the gods; it is so joyous, so fearless, so sure of its purpose, and hurls itself against it with its vital young blood and its burning young heart" (M. Lyon). Youthful "enthusiasm" was often associated with the review. Another reader noted, "If I do not always agree with it I at least have the sense of arguing with a friend whose intellect I respect—never did I feel that for any other publication. And I love freshness and freedom and enthusiasm as I love youth itself—they're the qualities that promise growth" (Smith). Another acknowledged that "as an elderly gentleman with a large family I bow to the superknowledge and exuberance of your youth, and freely admit you are giving full value for the money" (Weedon). Another reader from Chicago proclaimed that "*The Little Review* bubbles over with enthusiasm and love of life" and contrasted its spirit to that of her wasted childhood in the slums, during which she tried to escape the bareness of strict duties, quarreling, and poverty (Interested Reader 56).

Youth and the Public Sphere

Beyond the images of youth remaking itself anew that corporate America and the *Little Review* propagated is the other important aspect of the ideology of youth I have been sketching—its *public* nature. The vision of youth in public, away from the control of the family in domestic space, was perhaps the most controversial aspect of the cult of youth. So the cultural anxiety created by commercial culture, central to my analysis of the *Little Review* as an organ of youth, involved the relation of youth to the public and domestic spheres. Just as the *Little Review* was packaged and received as the embodiment of the cult of youth, it also was a forum for the discussion of youth in relation to traditional social, cultural, and political institutions—chief among them, the family. Anderson and her contributors frequently rehashed and discussed what was essentially Anderson's founding tale of her own independence in the modern city. If youth or adolescence was to live up to the high expectations that both intellectuals and advertisers had provided for it, it would require freedom from stifling institutions. Anderson explained: "The average girl of twenty in a conventional home hates to be told that she must not read Havelock Ellis or make friends with those dreadful persons known vaguely as 'socialists,' or that she must not work when she happens to believe that work is a beautiful thing. She is submerged in the ghastly sentimentalities of a tradition-soaked atmosphere—and heaven knows that sentimentalities of that type are difficult to break away from."[24]

Ben Hecht's sketch of "The American Family" likewise portrayed a daughter whose spirit of rebellion is crystallized by a book, or a friend, or a man: "There is an awakened mental curiosity, a perceptible inclination to break from the oppressiveness of the surrounding dead. In the night the daughter wonders and doubts. She would like 'to get away'—to go forth free of certain fiercely applied restrictions and meet a different kind of folk, a different kind of thought" (1). But, he goes on, "Revolt is for souls still living, and the living are weaker than the dead. The living soul is a lone, individual force, its yearnings are ephemeral and undefined. The mother knows what they are. The dead always know what it is they have lost" (1). So the mother (like Margaret Anderson's own mother) binds the daughter to oppressive family life, with discussions of the duty of children to parents and of proper behavior. In Sherwood Anderson's story "Sister," the narrator explains: "[My sister] became a devout student and made such rapid strides in her classes that my mother—who to tell the truth is fat and uninteresting—spent the days worrying. My sister, she declared, would end by having brain fever" (3). But the fifteen-year-old girl tries to emancipate herself sexually and is dragged into the stables by her father and beaten with the carriage whip. Many of the contributions to the early

Little Review touch on this theme of youth trying to free itself from the stifling death-grip of the conventional "mature" adult world, and, of course, the fashion and product advertisements aimed at youth helped promote images of youth away from the confines of family life. At this level, the avant-garde and the world of commercial advertising were walking hand in hand.

This interest in the plight of youth seeking intellectual nourishment, excitement, and freedom from the domestic sphere accompanied an interest among *Little Review* writers and readers in the education of both adolescents and children. In "The Renaissance of Parenthood," Anderson, who saw herself as still "of the age that must classify as 'daughter,'" wrote of the necessity of reforming the way parents relate to their children and published a letter from a young woman to her mother. Anderson explains that the woman "was in her early twenties; she had a sister two or three years younger, and both of them had reached at least a sort of economic independence. She had come to the conclusion, after a good many years of rebellion, that the whole fabric of their family life was wrong; and since it was impossible to talk the thing out sensibly—because, as in all families where the children grow up without being given the necessary revaluations, real talk is no more possible than it is between uncongenial strangers—she had decided to discuss it in a letter" (6–7). The letter suggested an equal stature for the mother and her two daughters and the elimination of the authoritative and sentimentalized role of motherhood. Anderson notes her own use of such tactics with her father at home. But the situation of the letter writer, who is not named, and the suggestions in the letter are so much like those of Margaret Anderson that I suspect the letter she quotes was her own to her mother. In any case, she uses the article to talk about current theories of childhood education by Shaw, Ellen Key, and Charlotte Perkins Gilman, concluding: "The new home is a recognition that the child is not the only factor in society that needs educating. It assumes that no one's education is finished just because he's been made a parent. It means that we can all go on being educated together" (14).

Other contributors elaborated in more detail some of the issues surrounding the education of children and adolescents. Dr. Rudolf von Liebich called for a "Ferrer" or "Modern" school in Chicago that emphasized a secular and "natural" education in ethics, science, and other knowledges, "free from the noxious taint of authority, superstition, or respectability" (55). Von Liebich invited interested parties to notify the *Little Review* and other organizers. Many articles addressed other contemporary writings on education theory and emphasized the importance of avoiding superstition and stifling authoritarianism with children.[25]

This packaging of the *Little Review* as a youthful journal, its frequent examination of issues of the freedom of youth, and, perhaps above all, the open forum of "The Reader Critic" correspondence section quickly attracted young or adolescent readers to the review.[26] In the September 1914 issue "A boy reader" from Chicago wrote, much as Margaret Anderson had written to the "The Perfect Comrade," to chronicle the intellectual deadness, the lack of personal freedom, and the superstitious religious attitudes of his family life. He mentions Shaw plays and prefaces that caused him to reassess his own family life, and, just like Anderson and other readers, he resorted to writing letters to his parents about domestic problems: "Of course when I presented my case to my parents I was met with that attitude always displayed toward youthful self-assertion. To make my case clear to their somewhat bewildered minds I drew up a list of grievances: there were thirty-three concrete faults in the existing order that must be stamped out or radically changed" (Boy Reader 57).

In a later issue "A Boy" in Chicago wrote: "I am a boy sixteen years old, and one could not expect me to know much about poetry—especially free verse. But I have heard of your magazine as a magazine that was ready to print what all kinds of people thought. So I have written a little verse— it is not a poem—telling you something about what is going on inside my mind, for these matters trouble every boy's mind, although you may think that we are light-minded at my age" (Boy, letter and poem, 38). The "Boy's" poem, "Blindness," chronicled his wanderings through Chicago streets seeing the "deformed and sick and hungry," but noting that he cannot heal the sick or make the streets cleaner:

> So I just think of other things.
> Of my books at home, or the tennis courts in the park,
> Or my pretty sister or anything.
> There is nothing wrong in my own world.
> I am happy. I like my school well enough.
> I have my boy friends, and they are healthy athletic boys.
> All the girls I know are good girls,
> With charming and high minds.
> And yet it is true that many boys lie and steal,
> And girls run away and are dragged into lives of shame.
> Why do I not see it? Why do I not do anything?
> Why am I so helpless, if I have any duty to others?

Regardless of the merits of this verse, the salient point here is that a sixteen-year-old student not only was reading the *Little Review,* picking up on its social agenda, and even making the connection to free verse as the poetic of modernity, but also decided, like the earlier "Boy Reader," to make his complaint public and to question the complacency that marked youth's traditional place in society.

In the next issue, Arthur Davison Ficke, a frequent contributor, wrote in: "Tell your 'sixteen year old boy' that his poem is damn interesting—but to cut out the 'only sixteen' and 'one could not expect me to know much about poetry' stuff. At sixteen most of us had read all the poetry in existence, and were busy writing epics that were to re-make the world. Tell him to stop being a sixteen-year-old worm, and to get up on his hind legs and bite the stars. Tell him to write arrogantly of this 'charming' world he sees. It's time enough to be humble when one is old." Ficke thus affirmed youth as exuberant, arrogant, and, above all, the voice of progress and renewal in the modern world. The correspondence continued in the next issue, as the "boy" sent in a free-verse poem, "Impressions of the Loop," about a boy walking through the streets of the mercantile district of Chicago's downtown, watching the women judging each other's fashions and wearing brand-name perfumes, while miserable, sick men and women sat begging on every corner, uncared for by the rich.

The *Little Review* and Youth Columns

Thus not only was modern youth in the public spaces of the new city a persistent theme in the *Little Review,* but the magazine also provided a public forum for the discussion of "youth issues" and young people's thoughts and feelings. This forum closely resembled a widely popular institution of commercial journalism—letter and advice columns for youth in newspapers and magazines. Throughout the nineteenth century, there had been an increase in the number and popularity of "young people's" magazines, but these were primarily children's magazines like *Youth's Companion* (which hit a circulation of around a half million or more between the 1890s and World War I), *American Boy,* and *St. Nicholas* (Peterson 158–162). Family magazines like the *Continent* also had children's sections, "Young America" and "Young People's Service." But women's and family magazines in the late nineteenth and early twentieth centuries also featured write-in columns for people whom Hall would categorize as "adolescents."

These columns often took the form of advice departments. The adolescent or young adult could write to Annie Laurie's "Advice to Girls" in the *Chicago Evening Post,* to *Good Housekeeping*'s "The Perfect Comrade" (to whom Anderson herself had written), or to the numerous departments in the *Ladies' Home Journal.* In 1883, Cyrus Curtis and Louisa Knapp Curtis turned their newspaper column for women into a new magazine, *Ladies' Home Journal.* This magazine became a forum for the discussion of gender issues, as it took letters from readers and published general articles and advice on aspects of women's lives (Damon-Moore 37). By 1889 the magazine's offices in New York, Chicago, and Philadelphia employed seven to ten people a day just to open letters (Damon-Moore 27). *Ladies' Home*

Journal and other women's magazines, like *McCall's, Woman's Home Companion,* and *Good Housekeeping,* were predicated on the recognition of women as consumers, and, as Damon-Moore suggests, they were a gold mine for advertisers and the publishers alike as they helped explicitly to identify women with commodity consumption (24–25). However, by the 1890s the new *Ladies' Home Journal* editor, Edward Bok, had realized that not just women read the magazine. He began to pursue men and adolescents of both sexes with new departments. "Side Talks with Girls," aimed at sixteen- to twenty-five-year-old women, was followed by "Side Talks with Boys" in 1891, "Problems of Young Men" in 1894, and "What Men Are Asking" in 1897 (Damon-Moore 73–75). As the *Little Review* began publishing, *Ladies' Home Journal* included advice departments for every concern, as well as regular columns like Margaret E. Sangster's "My Girls," Mrs. Burton Kingsland's "The Prevailing Etiquette for Young Men," and "The Girls' Club" to which young readers could write.

Given the close tie between targeted audiences and commercial advertising in journals like *Ladies' Home Journal,* as youth or adolescence became a part of the consumer culture, the mass market publishing industry created special forums to appeal to young audiences. But whether such forums can legitimately be considered institutions of a "public sphere of youth" is debatable. Habermas sees such intertwinings of the content of a magazine and the interests of its advertisers as a debasement of the public sphere: "Ever since the marketing of the editorial section became interdependent with that of the advertising section, the press (until then an institution of private people insofar as they constituted a public) became an institution of certain participants in the public sphere in their capacity as private individuals; that is, it became the gate through which privileged private interests invaded the public sphere" (*Structural* 185). Visions like this, and like those of Ford and, in a different way, Monro, presuppose some idealized public sphere located in the past that then is understood to decline as the press becomes increasingly commercial. Clearly the commercial market opened up new tools and spaces for a number of different kinds of journals—from the avant-garde to the most explicitly profit-motivated—so Habermas's sense that the increasing capitalization of the media precludes public deliberation cannot wholly be true. But, for reasons that Habermas does not address, we must consider the effect of cultural anxieties about youth upon the public nature of these columns.

Not only were youth columns thoroughly structured by commercialism, but also, in the case of *Ladies' Home Journal,* they even ceased to print the letters from the young writers and only dispensed advice. Damon-Moore notes: "There was a genuine respect in Knapp's *Journal* for the opinions of readers, and there was a real give-and-take relationship between the magazine and its audience. Bok's service departments, in contrast, came to focus more exclusively on answering reader questions" (69). They provided much useful information and advice on all issues interesting to their correspondents, but there was little sense of a public conversation taking place, such as the *Little Review* tried to foster.

In addition, and perhaps most important to the career of the *Little Review,* as the cult of youth arose and was crafted as one of consumption and abandon to fit the needs of commerce, a simultaneous attempt to regulate youth's actual self-gratification also emerged. Advice columns tended to be very normative in regard to social etiquette and personal behavior. Anderson wrote of Clara Laughlin's "The Perfect Comrade" column: "The advice seemed to prescribe none of the immobility usually urged upon the young, so I decided to ask Miss Laughlin how a perfectly nice but revolting girl could leave home" (Anderson, *Thirty Years',* 12). The answer precipitated Anderson's move to Chicago, but "The Perfect Comrade" columns in general staunchly supported a normative patriarchal view of the family. In one "The Perfect Comrade" column about careers for young women, possibly the very column that so excited Anderson, Laughlin wrote that careers in the big city were good for young women, not only for young women's own self-fulfillment, but also because they prolonged the period between school and marriage and thus kept girls from too soon entering upon marriage to the wrong man (Feb. 1908, 152–153). But she was careful to note that the career should not be permanent but should be abandoned after marriage: "You say I seem to take it for granted that your careers will be brief? I certainly like to think so, for the women I've known with whom a career remained the chief business of life are not the happiest women among my friends" (153). Girls who have careers benefit from a greater chance of meeting eligible young men than those who stay at home with their mothers, and "it not infrequently happens that the girl of today learns in her brief pursuit of a career some things that help her to a finer comradeship with her husband than the famous housewife of bygone days was wont to enjoy" (153). While encouraging young women to move to urban areas and take on careers, and while soliciting responses and opinions from her youthful readership on the issues she raised, Laughlin nevertheless adamantly affirmed that all women should marry, and that their careers and independence should immediately be given up to perform domestic duties for their breadwinning husbands. Jane Addams might have objected that young women were not meeting the right sort of men in the cities, but Laughlin would merely have countered with more advice on how to live a proper life in the city.

Though many youth columns *seemed* an open forum for young people to discuss important issues publicly, the commercial character of the magazines fostering them ensured that only a range of opinions acceptable to advertisers and readers could be discussed seriously. Furthermore, the "parental" columnist served to regulate the discussion. These magazines promoted a vision of youth as independent consumers, as, for instance, *Ladies' Home Journal* even began a long-running "Girls' Club," whose motto was With One Idea: To Make Money. To earn "pin money" to spend on clothing, vacations, schooling, and long-desired merchandise, the club organized "girls" from their teen years through their twenties to sell subscriptions to the magazine, rewarding them with commissions and with jewelry, marriage chests, and other gifts bearing the club's symbol, the swastika. The Girls' Club, which even had its own magazine, the *Swastika,* had thousands of members and filled the Curtis publishing company's coffers. But it also connected youth to consumption and portrayed its members as independent consumers, free from the constraints of the family purse strings (see fig. 7, which portrays the young woman alone behind the wheel of her own car on a vacation, with the club's seal of approval, the swastika, on the car). But when the manager of the Girls' Club was not simply promoting the consumer power of the club members, lauding high-sellers, she chose to print letters that also cautioned against excess. A "Girl" wrote to *Ladies' Home Journal* to warn about the peril caused by new fashions resembling the clothing worn by prostitutes: "Nowadays when we enter a restaurant and dance place it is hard to know who is who. We all know that the American women and girls copy the fashions and the costumes that are made to attract and allure for the demimonde in Paris. Many American women who consider themselves *comme il faut* have their hair touched up, their faces and lips painted. That used to be the hallmark for a certain type of woman; it is not so now. Yet while the woman has changed outwardly many still cling to their old-fashioned ideas of class distinction." The letter gave examples of men and women who had mistaken respectable young followers of fashion for prostitutes.

These magazines negotiated cultural anxieties about the thin line between consumer abandon and moral abandon by using their "parental" authority to both legitimate and regulate these desires. Nowhere is this more evident than in discussions about clothing and fashion. As "The Perfect Comrade" explained, even invoking divine support for clothing fashions: "A Pretty girl in Ohio (I know she's pretty because she sent me her picture) writes to ask me if I think it's wrong for her to care about pretty clothes. Wrong? Why, bless her heart, it would be radically wrong if she didn't! Anything that God made that doesn't care how it looks, is not as God made it; the devil of 'don't care' has taken possession of it" (Laughlin, Oct. 1908, 433). This column, following a series of "Good Housekeeping Patterns," went into detail about appropriate clothing to purchase for various occasions. "The Perfect Comrade" explained that when she sees a woman in public who hasn't kept up her appearance, she assumes the woman to be a "'slack' wife and mother and citizen" (433).

The Girls' Club

With One Idea: To Make Money

THE Manager wishes to send to every member of the Club a copy of the July issue of our Club magazine, "The Swastika," and also a copy of our interesting new illustrated booklet, "Are You Going Away This Summer?" Those members who, through absence from home, have missed receiving these will be supplied upon notifying the Manager of their summer addresses.

While the editions last, copies of both the booklet and the magazine will also be sent, without charge, to any girl who wishes to join the Club or to be more fully informed regarding it.

"I HADNA been in Lunnon an hour," said the scandalized Scotsman, "when bang! went a saxpence!"

Isn't this your experience and mine? One can scarcely turn around in this vacation season without its costing money. Every girl who reads this page under the shade of a big umbrella on the beach, or while swinging comfortably in a hammock under the pine boughs, could at this moment use more money than she took away with her out of her Girls' Club savings, or than her father allows her. That is why I feel that our new book contains a message. Each of our working members, and each JOURNAL reader whose letter inquiring about the Club reached me in May or June, has already received her copy, and numbers of them have put its practical suggestions to such prompt effect that they have started, or are soon to start, on that holiday jaunt which a month ago seemed about as attainable as a trip to the moon. A letter from one of them lies before me now:

Dear Manager: I want to thank you for the interest you take in your Club members. I have worked busily this month, so have earned the lovely pin and a salary besides. I find it quite easy, so you will hear from me again in June. I see a pleasant holiday before me this year, and, better still, feel quite independent about it.

ONE OF YOUR NEW GIRLS.

"Are You Going Away This Summer?" isn't a guidebook to places; it is a guidebook to the way to earn the money which will take you to places. It forms the first complete story of a wonderful work, and it tells you how to do these four things: how to earn money to take a vacation; how to earn it while continuing a vacation; how to fill up the financial void left after a vacation; how to earn money while spending a vacation at home.

Are You **GOING AWAY** *THIS SUMMER?*

The Juniors' Great Chance

LAST summer I had the loveliest call at my office in THE JOURNAL building from a dear little ten-year-old Junior member from Indianapolis, who had paid almost her entire traveling expenses to Philadelphia with her Girls' Club money. I want the younger girls in the Club to remember that these vacation months of July and August represent their great chance for earning money. Recently I received a letter which ran:

Manager Girls' Club, Philadelphia: I have finally summoned enough courage to write you. Until recently, when you mentioned the twelve-year-old Junior members, I thought your Club was only for "big girls." I am fifteen years of age and am very anxious to rejuvenate my pocketbook. Of course I don't expect to make "heaps" of money, but just "hair-ribbon money."

A GIRL FROM WASHINGTON.

I felt justified in assuring her that a fifteen-year-old girl could earn it, when I had just received the following note from a ten-year-old girl living on a Montana ranch:

Dear Manager: I am indeed grateful for the check for $4, also for the $1 check. I have earned $19, and am so glad to be able to do something for myself as well as for others. Father's health has failed and he has been ordered out of the office entirely, so you see why I am so glad to be helpful. I am inclosing the card for the silver thimble. I shall need it when I mend.

You see there's a pretty wide range of usefulness for our Club. Juniors, grown women, girls who want vacations and girls who want to stay at home—the work seems to fit all of them. Are you a member yet? The way to get in is to write to

THE MANAGER OF THE GIRLS' CLUB
THE LADIES' HOME JOURNAL
PHILADELPHIA

Figure 7. The Girls' Club portrays its members as young and free, as in this drawing of an independent young woman hitting the road in her own car. (*Ladies' Home Journal,* July 1914, 49)

However, the final paragraph of the article cautioned, "I don't suppose it is necessary to tell any girl in this circle of readers how worse than worthless are the clothes for which one pays ever so slightly in self-respect. Thousands of girls go to perdition every year, lured by a silk petticoat, a plumed hat. If I loved dress so well that I was willing to lose even the least little bit of my self-respect to get them, then indeed should I think it 'wrong for me to like pretty clothes.' . . . For, as I have said, one of the first things we must learn in this world, is to take just the right account of clothes and never to take too much" (435). Laughlin simultaneously justifies the mobilization of desire for consumption that *Good Housekeeping* and its advertisers espoused and limits that desire in youth, fending off any number of implied excesses—sexual impropriety, financial mismanagement, vanity, placing appearance as the mark of character, and so forth. This was the norm in columns aimed at youth. Letters, if printed at all, were carefully chosen; parental advice was carefully dispensed even while propagating a vision of independence and consumer freedom.

While the *Little Review* tried to create a public institution for youth to exchange ideas freely about the nature of modern life, there was not much of a precedent for this kind of freedom of thought for youth or for a noncommercial basis for the letters columns. And soon this lack of self-regulation led to complaint. After the first issue, "Sade Iverson" wrote to congratulate Anderson on the "insouciant little pagan paper" but patronizingly cautioned her: "You must not scoff at age, little bright eyes, for some day you, too, will know age; and you should not jeer at robustness of form, slim one, for the time may come when you, too, will find the burdens of flesh upon you. Above all, do not proclaim too loudly the substitution of Nietzsche for Jesus of the Little Town in the niche of your invisible temple, for when you are broken and forgotten there is no comfort in the Overman. One thing more: Restraint is sometimes better than expression."[27] Later in the same year, a Reverend A. D. R. in Chicago wrote in to complain that his daughter was exposed to the frequent discussions of Nietzsche: "I earnestly request you to discontinue sending your impertinent publication to my daughter who had the folly of undiscriminating youth to fall in the diabolical snare by joining the ungodly family of your subscribers. As for you, haughty young woman, may the Lord have mercy upon your sinful soul! Have you thought of the tremendous evil that your organ brings into American homes, breaking family ties, killing respect for authorities, sowing venomous seeds of Antichrist-Nietzsche-Foster, lauding such inhuman villains as Wilde and Verlaine, crowning with laurels that blood-thirsty Daughter of Babylon, Emma Goldman, and committing similar atrocities? God hear my prayer and turn your wicked heart to repentance." But these early complaints about corrupting young readers were mild compared to the trouble the *Little Review* would soon experience as it moved to New York.

The *Little Review*, *Ulysses*, and Censorship: The Seaside Girl in America

Within the context of the publishing industry's greater attention to youth, and the *Little Review*'s attempts to address and reflect this "youth culture," one of the more notorious incidents in the history of Anglo-American modernism—the war against the *Little Review* waged by the post office and the New York Society for the Suppression of Vice—becomes more comprehensible. Ulf Boëthius argues that popular culture has always been seen by some as a threat to the young, and that there have been periodic campaigns against popular culture—what sociologist Stanley Cohen calls "moral panics" (Boëthius 41). One of the most intensive of these campaigns, begun in the 1870s by Anthony Comstock, targeted titillating mass market novels, photographs, and any other materials that threatened the morals of the young. Comstock created the New York Society for the Suppression of Vice in 1872, and by 1873 he had helped launch a law prohibiting materials considered obscene or harmful to youth from being carried by the postal service. The state appointed Comstock as special agent to ensure that the law was followed, and he oversaw postal censorship for four decades (Boëthius 40).

The Society for the Suppression of Vice regulated young consumers even while the mass market culture and advertisers began to reach out to them. The first seizure by New York postal authorities of a *Little Review* issue was due to Wyndham Lewis's story "Cantleman's Spring-Mate" (Oct. 1917), which was held to violate the criminal code against "obscene, lewd, or lascivious publications" (Bryer 243–250). The *Little Review*'s reluctant lawyer and frequent patron, John Quinn, wrote Judge W. H. Lamar, the solicitor of the Post Office Department in Washington D.C., complaining that Lewis's story about the sexual exploitation of a village virgin by a young soldier did not violate federal statute. However, as Quinn later explained to Anderson, Lamar read the piece and "thought [it] unfit for innocent young minds," though Quinn had argued that the *Little Review*'s readership was really comprised of "mature and worldly minds."[28] The *Little Review* lost the case in New York. Setting the stage for the *Ulysses* trial soon to come, Judge Lamar had argued about the corruption of youth, and Anderson and Quinn had unsuccessfully tried to defend against this argument by claiming that the readership was a select circle of adults.

Again in 1919 and 1920 when the Society for the Suppression of Vice (now under John Sumner) was waging its campaign against the serial publication of *Ulysses*,[29] Quinn argued to Lamar that the magazine was not for or read by the young. He quoted to Lamar a statement by Anderson that the audience was "composed chiefly of artists, thinkers and men with a passionate belief in the need for an intellectual culture in America. . . . The general ruck of people would as soon read The Little Review as take a dose of castor oil." She asserted that young boys and girls of the "convent, young girls' seminary, young boys' Sunday school" age did not read it and would not understand it anyway.[30] However, given the early advertising of the *Little Review* in Chicago with images of youth, its attempts to market itself as a kind of youth forum, and the fact that teenage boys and girls did read it, the attacks on it as unfit for the young mind were perhaps not as irrelevant as Margaret Anderson tried to suggest.

Though the post office had incinerated three issues containing *Ulysses* chapters ("Lestrygonians" in Jan. 1919, "Scylla and Charybdis" in May 1919, and "Cyclops" in Jan. 1920), it is perhaps not surprising that the *Ulysses* episode that drew the ire of John Sumner's Society for the Suppression of Vice was the "Nausicaa" chapter in the July–August 1920 issue, which narrates the encounter on the strand between Leopold Bloom and the young Gerty MacDowell (see Ellmann 502–503).[31] I believe that "Nausicaa" seemed particularly threatening largely because it touched so powerfully on all the American concerns about a consumer youth culture that I have been discussing in this chapter. It is perhaps the most famous modernist portrait of "youth in public," and its presence in the *Little Review* confirmed the mounting anxieties that the magazine sought out and corrupted youthful readers. (Appropriately enough, the "Nausicaa" publication in the *Little Review* drew the attention of New York's district attorney only when he found his daughter reading a copy of it [Leckie 78]!)

Much of the critical attention given to "Nausicaa" in recent years has considered the role of commodities and advertising in the thoughts of a young woman, Gerty MacDowell, as she sits on a rock on Sandymount Strand in Dublin, displaying herself for a mysterious onlooker (who turns out to be the masturbating Leopold Bloom). Even the most superficial reader of Joyce's chapter will be overwhelmed by the myriad allusions to consumer culture. Gerty's thoughts dwell on products like "white rose scent" (May–June 1920, 71), patent medicines like "iron jelloids" (Apr. 1920, 45), and a long list of clothing like "a neat blouse of electric blue, selftinted by dolly dyes, with a smart vee" combined with "the newest thing in footwear" (Apr. 1920, 47). These products were purchased at the new bastions of consumerism, department stores like Clery's, and were advertised in mass market magazines like the weekly *Princess's Novelettes*, whose columns and advertisements dominate Gerty's thoughts.[32] Indeed, the kinds of columns aimed at American adolescent girls and women (in magazines like *Good Housekeeping* and *Ladies' Home Journal*) similarly served as arbiters of appearance and decorum in Gerty's Irish adolescence.

The narrator, as is so often the case in Joyce's work, adopts the idiom of the narrated: Joyce parodies the styles of the sentimental texts that Gerty reads, like Maria Cummins's novel *The Lamplighter,* or poems that begin with lines like "Art thou real, my ideal?" that Gerty copies out of newspapers in "violet ink that she bought in Wisdom Hesly's [*sic*]" (May–June 1920, 71). But he also fuses with this style the language of advertisements, fashion journalism, and youth magazine advice columns: "Time was when those brows were not so silkily seductive. It was Madame Vera Verity, directress of the Woman Beautiful page of the Princess Novelette, who had first advised her to try eyebrowleine which gave that haunting expression to the eyes, so becoming in leaders of fashion, and she had never regretted it" (Apr. 1920, 46).

Jennifer Wicke, Suzette Henke, Thomas Richards, Garry Leonard, and others have underscored the staggering frequency and complexity of allusion to the turn-of-the-century Irish consumer culture, and Richards and Leonard in particular have suggested that consumer advertising structures Bloom's "consumption" of Gerty. Richards explains that the phrase "queen of ointments"(Apr. 1920, 45), which appears in "Nausicaa," was the slogan for Beetham's "Larola" and that in the 1880s and 1890s, Beetham marketed ointments and lotions with a popular advertising formula, "the seaside girl" (226). Invoking these advertisements, and the popular song that Blazes Boylan sings, Bloom thinks about Gerty, "Didn't look back when she was going down the strand. Wouldn't give that satisfaction. Those girls, those girls, those lovely seaside girls" (July–Aug. 1920, 48). Even beyond the many specific allusions to advertising campaigns, department stores, and products that appear in her thoughts, Richards suggests that Gerty herself is meant to evoke this popular nineteenth-century advertising phenomenon and explains that the image of the seaside girl created an alluring vision of young carefree "nymphs" on view for men, an image that played on a rapidly growing youth culture, like the one I have discussed in America. Many health and beauty products advertised with this image, and seaside resorts used it to promote a contained and socially acceptable vision of sexual display on the beach: as Richards puts it, "The seaside girl displays an all-purpose allegiance that accommodates a violation of a sexual taboo just as easily as it promotes a white skin befitting the modest and the chaste" (234).

But Richards's admirable tracing of the context of the seaside girl and the myriad advertising images in the chapter leads him to a pretty bleak reading of young Gerty and of the commodity culture that so dominates her thoughts. He argues that Joyce portrays advertising as "a coercive agent for invading and structuring human consciousness" (207) that makes human experience "generalized and impoverished" (211). Moreover, Richards argues that Gerty's self has been constituted by advertisers as a passive object of the male gaze: "Women were taught to identify with the seaside girl image while men were encouraged to desire it. These gendered variants are illustrated simply and directly in 'Nausicaa,' where Gerty consumes the seaside girl while Bloom consumes Gerty. . . . Male identity exists prior to and during the act of consumption; female identity gets effaced in the process. Bloom remains Bloom, but Gerty must become the seaside girl" (246).

Building on the work of Richards and others, Garry Leonard argues that Gerty "carefully advertises and packages her sexuality as a complex masquerade of femininity designed to attract a male consumer—in this case, Leopold Bloom. Far from being sexually naive and one-dimensional [as Richards portrays her], Gerty has a keener understanding of sexuality than Bloom does because she understands that the anatomical act of sex is as irrelevant as whatever is inside a carefully advertised package" (99). Leonard explores the ways in which Gerty "packages her body in a manner that advertises the culturally accepted norm of femininity" (99), not simply because she has been structured by advertising to think this way, as Richards argues, but rather because the demographics and economics of turn-of-the-century Ireland necessitated women turning themselves into commodities to get husbands, and to avoid that other kind of sexual commodification—streetwalking.[33]

Readings like those of Henke, Richards, and Leonard locate "Nausicaa" in the consumer culture of Britain and Ireland and interpret the role of that consumer culture in Gerty's relationship to Bloom. But the text may be resituated in the American context of the *Little Review* and American commercialized youth culture. As a result of publishing "Nausicaa," Margaret Anderson and Jane Heap were found guilty in the *Little Review* obscenity trial and were forced to pay a $50 fine each and to stop publishing *Ulysses*. As Ellmann explains, John Quinn "had to certify that the *Nausicaa* episode was the worst in the book to save his clients from being sent to prison" (503); given American cultural anxieties about youth culture, "Nausicaa" actually *was,* in fact, the "worst chapter" in the book. Of course, if the *Little Review* had been able to continue publishing *Ulysses,* "Circe" would, no doubt, have been confiscated for its graphic portrayal of sado-masochistic sex in a brothel, and the John Sumners of America would have squirmed at Molly's monologue in "Penelope," but Gerty MacDowell was especially problematic.

As editors of a magazine of youth—and of youth in a modern, liberated world of consumption and experiment—Margaret Anderson and Jean Heap's motivations for serializing *Ulysses* in the *Little Review* are not hard to imagine. Beyond the incredible vitality of Joyce's experimental prose style, the wandering artist persona of young Stephen Dedalus—who rejects the constraining philistinism of family, country, and religion for a world of aesthetic, spiritual, and sexual freedom in *Portrait of the Artist* (an example of the *Bildungsroman* genre that so enticed readers and writers of the *Little Review*)—would have made *Ulysses* attractive to many of the magazine's readers. Upon reading the third of Stephen's initial chapters in *Ulysses,* "Proteus," Margaret Anderson exclaimed, "This is the most beautiful thing we'll ever have. We'll print it if it's the last effort of our lives" (in Ellmann 421).

But Gerty MacDowell, more than Stephen Dedalus, seems to exemplify everything that concerned Americans about the new commercialized youth culture. John Sumner and the judges and prosecutors considered the chapter both obscene and corrupting of youth. The defense witnesses Quinn called to speak to the merits of the chapter tried to avert what was obviously at stake in the trial—a sense that youth needed the protection of censorship against the sexual corruption that was feared to accompany the new consumer culture. John Cowper Powys testified that *Ulysses* was "a beautiful piece of work in no way capable of corrupting the minds of young girls," and, after provoking the wrath of the prosecutors, Quinn argued triumphantly, "That's what *Ulysses* does. It makes people angry. . . . But it doesn't tend to drive them to the arms of some siren" (in Ellmann 503).

Jane Heap herself put her finger on the problem in the nature of the charge against the magazine. "The present case is rather ironical," she wrote in "Art and the Law." "We are being prosecuted for printing the thoughts in a young girl's mind. Her thoughts and actions and the meditations which they produced in the mind of the sensitive Mr. Bloom. If the young girl corrupts, can she also be corrupted? Mr. Joyce's young girl is an innocent, simple, childish girl who tends children . . . she hasn't had the advantages of the dances, cabarets, motor trips open to the young girls of this more pure and free country" (6). Heap questioned, then, whether the fears that young girls might be corrupted by Gerty's example were being conflated in the trial with the greater fear that the new "girl" of the consumer age might herself be dangerous to adult men. Were the lawyers concerned about Gerty, or about Bloom? Moreover, Heap points out that Gerty might seem simple, and perhaps even naive, in comparison to the youth culture that already existed in America, in which, quite positively Heap would conclude, girls were far more mobile both literally and figuratively in their social lives. Rather than needing the protection of a paternalistic court, the young girls of America were quite active and powerful on their own; as Heap concluded, with a tongue-in-cheek flourish, "If there is anything I really fear it is the mind of the young girl" (6).

What set off alarm bells when the seaside girl appeared in the *Little*

Review, I believe, was that Gerty had publicly crossed, quite knowingly, that carefully drawn but ever-shifting line that advice columns like those in *Good Housekeeping* and *Ladies' Home Journal* had tried so hard to maintain between a healthy interest in consumption and fashionable self-presentation, and morally dangerous sexual abandon. If "girls" must be urged to follow fashion, dress up, and be attractive to men, they must, at the same time, be warned about compromising themselves sexually, as Clara Laughlin feared they might. If they must be warned that the newest fashions might be misconstrued as the bold styles of prostitutes (as "The Girls' Club" column assumed), then Gerty MacDowell has been both a good consumer and a too-good consumer.

This American context, then, suggests a reading in which Joyce's Gerty MacDowell is much more threateningly active than either Richards's, or even Leonard's, interpretation of Gerty as a self-commodified object for the active consumption of Leopold Bloom allows her to be. If Bloom can fantasize about, and thus "consume," Gerty as his seaside girl—the image she has created for herself—she, in turn, can fantasize about and "consume" him as the "manly man," the "gravefaced gentleman" with a "passionate nature" (May–June 1920, 68), the dark stranger, and even act on that fantasy. Though, of course, these roles can be seen as constructed for both Bloom and Gerty (though Bloom himself is adept at understanding the nuances of advertising images since he is an advertising canvasser), both sides can be seen to choose these roles actively for their own sexual advantage. Gerty makes herself a liberated, active, consumer, as "The Girls' Club" urged, by shopping frugally and finding "what she wanted at Clery's summer sales" (Apr. 1920, 47) to complete her "look." But she also becomes a liberated and active participant in sexuality in a way that makes the unashamed return of Stephen's gaze by the seaside "bird girl" in chapter 4 of *Portrait* look quite tame. Rather than emptying her sexual moment of any "authenticity," as Richards implies, the commodity terms in which she experiences the moment are actively sexualized by her. Phrases like "silkily seductive," which are probably product slogans, used hints of sexuality as part of their appeal; in Gerty's encounter with Bloom, though, they become explicitly erotic—not because Gerty is a passive creature constructed by advertisers, as Richards argues, or a passive object for male consumption, as Leonard imagines her, but because she herself takes such an active role in parlaying her public display into a sexual encounter that works for her and for Bloom. Gerty uses her "silkily seductive" brows for active sexual seduction, for sexual gratification in the "real" world.

Notably, after the *Little Review/Ulysses* trial focusing on these passages, Joyce augmented the already pervasive allusions to consumer culture, adding references (in the typescript overlay of 1921 and in the proofs of the first book edition of *Ulysses*)[34] to additional mass market magazines—*Lady's Pictorial* and *Pearson's Weekly*—and to patent medicines and "Widow Welch's female pills," among others. And he also augmented the very connection that so worried the Society for the Suppression of Vice—the linkage of the new commodity culture to youth sexuality.

In the following passage, for example, Joyce adds to the *Little Review* version of the masturbatory moment a reference to another phrase that is almost certainly a product slogan, "the fabric that caresses the skin." Ironically, Gerty actively makes Bloom function as the fabric that caresses her skin, just as he caresses his own, taking sexual pleasure from his view:

and he could see her other things too, nainsook knickers, [the fabric that caresses the skin, better than those pettiwidth, the green,] four and eleven, on account of being white and she let him and she saw that he saw and then it went so high it went out of sight a moment and she was trembling in every limb from being bent so far back that he could see [had a full view] high up above her knee where no-one ever not even on the swing or wading and she wasn't ashamed and he wasn't either to look in that immodest way like that because he couldn't resist the sight [of the wondrous revealment half offered] like those skirtdancers behaving so immodest before gentlemen looking and he kept on looking, looking. She would fain have cried to him chokingly, held out her snowy slender arms to him to come, to feel his lips laid on her white brow." (July–Aug. 1920, 43; bracketed passages added beginning 1921, Gabler 787–789)

Gerty's fantasy chastely climaxes in Bloom kissing her "white brow"—a white brow emphasized by the dark eyebrows, the "silkily seductive" brows, acquired through Madame Vera Verity's advice, and the help of "eyebrowleine." But the consumer abandon advocated by *Princess's Novelettes* has now become explicitly sexual. Even the "modest" and "chaste" component of the seaside girl spectacle has been replaced by the "immodest" way Bloom is looking at Gerty, and the "immodest" way Gerty is displaying herself before him.

While such an active flaunting of sexual propriety and the desire to use that fashion instinct to its full advantage were positioned by the writers and readers of the *Little Review* as a refreshing cry for the freedom of youth, "Nausicaa" was clearly seen as horrifying by those segments of American culture who feared that the consumption-driven "cult of youth" was only sowing the seeds of promiscuity. This fear is represented by the father in Sherwood Anderson's *Little Review* story "Sister," who beats his daughter for trying to liberate herself sexually; Gerty MacDowell is symbolically beaten by the American judicial system and the censorship of the Society for the Suppression of Vice. Youth in public, they argued, must be tightly reined in, at the seaside or in the pages of a magazine that was thought to corrupt youth.

As with the emergence of modernism in Britain, American modernists looked optimistically to the institutions of modern commercial culture to provide them with the cultural influence obtained through a broad readership, and they envisioned a public sphere of free expression that would be enlivened by aesthetic modernism. The *Little Review,* born out of the journalistic milieu of a quickly modernizing commercial city, turned (like its transatlantic counterpart, the *Egoist*) to the strategies and forms of an expanding mass market publishing world in hopes of reaching a mass urban audience without changing its content to appeal to mass taste. Of course the cultural landscape of America was different from that of Britain, and the nuances of American modernists' attempt to incorporate aspects of commercial mass culture into their self-promotion differed from those of London editors. The permeability of the "great divide" in America, and a greater willingness to borrow directly from commercial culture, led American modernists to focus on the new cult of youth in American promotional and corporate culture.

Though the *Little Review* ultimately had more success than the *Egoist* in attracting a steady readership, the attempt by its writers and editor to create a public sphere of youth—without the mechanism that at once propagated images of youth as consumers and tried to contain any actual abandonment of moral and social traditions—brought the *Little Review* up against the regulatory wall of the postal service and the Society for the Suppression of Vice. As in Britain, the commercial dynamics of mass market publishing ensured that any dream of widespread mass appeal and influence for a modernist magazine would ultimately be utopian, but American commercial culture clearly helped shape the form of one of America's most avant-garde little magazines. The increasingly commercialized mass press seemed to offer new opportunities to modernist authors to become part of public discourse, but the same cultural anxieties that caused the commercial press to regulate itself also constrained the ability of an organ of open public discussion to shape that discourse on aesthetics, politics, or sociocultural norms. Though the *Little Review* was published until the end of the twenties, its appearance became increasingly sporadic, and it never achieved the wide readership Margaret Anderson had desired during its Chicago years. Yet during its first several years, while under the influence influenced of the commercial youth culture, the *Little Review* offered something that is always hard to come by, even in this age of the Internet—a truly free voice.

5

Pluralism and Counterpublic Spheres

Race, Radicalism, and the *Masses*

In 1922, Claude McKay published his first American volume of poems, *Harlem Shadows,* a book that was to propel him to the forefront of African American poetry at the beginning of the Harlem Renaissance.[1] Max Eastman, the man McKay had chosen to introduce the collection, began: "These poems have a special interest for all the races of man because they are sung by a pure blooded Negro. They are the first significant expression of that race in poetry." Moreover, he asserted, "here for the first time we find our literature vividly enriched by a voice from this most alien race among us. And it should be illuminating to observe that while these poems are characteristic of that race as we most admire it—they are gentle-simple, candid, brave and friendly, quick of laughter and of tears—yet they are still more characteristic of what is deep and universal in mankind" (ix). Eastman employs typical racial stereotypes as well as the racial discourse of purity, of "blood," common to the nativist pluralist writings of the 1920s; nevertheless, he asserts, to what he has obviously assumed will be a white audience for the poems ("a voice from this most alien race among *us*"), that there is something about such "race" poetry in McKay's hands that makes it universal, of benefit and interest to all. His insistence on racial purity as a guarantor of authenticity in poetry cuts against the progressivist "melting pot" ideals of the preceding decades, but the rhetoric of universalism likewise undermines what Walter Benn Michaels sees as the nature of the "identitarian pluralism" of the 1920s.[2]

Yet Eastman's introduction, largely by omission, raises another crucial identity issue for a poet like Claude McKay: he does not mention that McKay's original attraction to him was as the editor of the famous radical and socialist magazine the *Masses* and its reincarnation the *Liberator,* that Claude McKay was the associate (soon to be executive) editor of the *Liberator,* or that the poet was dedicated to its mission of proletarian revolution.[3] The "stickiness" of the racial issues that Eastman's introduction tried to negotiate (by positing the purity of race as a marker of identity, but also by asserting the universality of McKay's racial poems) seemed to necessitate the occultation of economic class, which both men saw as a crucial determinant of identity in American society.

Within the year, when both McKay and Eastman were in the Soviet Union witnessing the fledgling communist government firsthand, the fraught nature of this relationship between race and class in America precipitated McKay's resignation from the *Liberator* and an angry exchange of letters between the two friends. McKay, who had (unsuccessfully) submitted poems to the *Masses* when he first came to New York in 1914, was attracted to the magazine above other socialist magazines and black papers of the day: "I liked its slogans, its make-up, and above all, its cartoons. There was a difference, a freshness in its social information. And I felt a special interest in its sympathetic and iconoclastic items about the Negro" (McKay, *Long Way,* 28–29). And he served as something of a bridge between the downtown, Greenwich Village radicalism of the *Masses* crowd and the uptown radicalism of Harlem and the so-called black reds.

But by 1923, in the final days of the *Liberator,* McKay sent Eastman a draft of a chapter about his departure from the *Liberator* to be included in his Russian-language book, *Negroes in America* (see Cooper 162–164). He explained that he had left the *Liberator* because of disagreements with its editors over the "race question." Eastman discouraged McKay from including this account in his book, suggesting that McKay had left the magazine over incompatibility with its other editor, Mike Gold, who struck many as dogmatic and tiresome. Eastman explained that in asking him to join the staff, the *Liberator* editors were moved by his "desire to further a solution of the Negro problem in the revolution." But Eastman was clearly concerned about the magazine's ability to address this complicated issue with a less-than-enthusiastic white audience. He lamented that McKay had tried to introduce too much material about race issues too quickly in the magazine, and complained about a provocative idea McKay had put forward:

You show how completely you have abandoned the habit of practical thinking, when you lay down the dogma that a revolutionary magazine ought to contain the same proportion of material dealing with the Negro as the proportion of the Negroes to the white population of the United States. Where is your training as a political engineer? Do you live in the age of Lenin or Tom Paine? You have a magazine circulating practically entirely among Whites. You have these Whites full of peculiar ignorance and intolerance of the Negro and the Negro problem, which you describe in your book as the chief problem of the revolution in America. You as a Negro enter into the staff of that magazine with a view toward a solution of that problem. And your tactical proposal is to throw the Negro and the Negro problem in the faces of those white readers in the same proportion in which Negroes stand to Whites in the census of the United States! With that kind of thinking you will never solve any problem. What you will do is to destroy your instrument, and that is all. And what you describe in your chapter as a congenital incapacity of Liberator editors to understand the Negro problem, is simply a childlike and altogether proper instinct upon their part to save their magazine.[4]

Eastman suggested that McKay was acting on "some obscure emotion of resentment," rather than relying upon McKay's own professed understanding that the "scientific" revolutionary sees "the Negro problem from the point-of-view of the class-struggle . . . that it will disappear with the disappearance of economic classes."[5] This argument had been adopted by the insular prewar Socialist party, even under such a race-conscious leader as Eugene Debs. At that time, the Socialist party was dominated by white workers. And just as unskilled immigrant workers took a backseat to the more highly skilled unionized white workers, black workers were often seen as strikebreakers. Racist white workers exploited the utopian notion that solving class problems would solve racial problems in order to ignore the fact that the two were inseparable.[6]

McKay knew that black workers had their own special set of problems beyond even those of the white proletariat, and that no class struggle could succeed in America without taking into account the black work force. His idea of proportional representation in the magazine was an effort to use the racial identities defined by the census to patch up what would become major cracks in radical magazines like the *Masses* and the *Liberator*—the problems of ethnic and racial identities within a class-defined movement.[7]

But the *Masses* and the *Liberator,* in spite of Eastman's and McKay's hesitancy about modernism, were also venues through which modernist authors and artists sought audiences. And, as I have argued in previous chapters, not only did modernists desire mass audiences, but the impulses of modernism and the very idea of a counterpublic sphere animate each other. The *Little Review* in America, and British little magazines like the

Egoist and its predecessors the *Freewoman* and *New Freewoman,* tried to foster a broadly based oppositional counterpublic sphere in which aesthetic modernism could be discussed alongside anarchism, sex radicalism, suffragism, syndicalism, and other such concerns. Even following commercial culture's leads, these magazines had to fight against the fragmentation of such a public discursive space. But in America, not just class, sex, and political ideologies, but also a much more complicated set of ethnic and racial divisions—problems surrounding the configuration of identity and the need to bridge differences *within* audiences—made all the more complicated the *Masses'* similar attempt to be a magazine of aesthetic and social revolt, a free discursive public space, and an instrument of proletarian revolution all at the same time.

That attempt had obviously failed by the time of Eastman and McKay's heated exchange in 1923. But during the (by no means absolute) shift from prewar progressivism to the pluralistic views of identity in the 1920s, the preponderance of cartoons, poems, and stories inflected by ethnic identity in the *Masses* showed contributors' attempts to imagine a public sphere that would not ignore but rather come face to face with racial, ethnic, and even geographical differences and would negotiate these differences through a coherent oppositional form of counterpublicity. The nagging problem of how a magazine largely created by middle-class intellectuals could call itself a proletarian magazine was swept into the larger miasma of identity issues raised by American ethnic and racial divides as immigrants arrived in the cities and black workers from the rural South moved to the urban North.

The role of the diverse immigrant "national groups" within the Socialist party of this period was both complicated and contested. Paul Buhle notes that the lack of a centralized national labor movement in America made the organization of a counterpublic sphere difficult, though he argues that "the public space for Socialism in America was invigorated by the extraordinary diversity of the local Socialist press, publishing in a score of languages" (90–91). But, he continues, "Party leaders, certain that Marxism mandated the unity of all proletarians under the banner of the dominant culture and language, looked upon the national groups as mere auxiliaries. Only in 1912 did the Party grant them official status as semi-autonomous units, and then with unease. By 1916, when the groups had reached near-parity with the native-born and assimilated, Party leaders had hardly begun to suspect that Debsian Socialism had encompassed such totally different creatures from themselves under its ample wings" (112–113). This perennial problem in the American left of the first half of the century of how to accommodate ethnic difference within a class revolution (see Buhle 135) had ramifications for the *Masses,* which fought against earlier ideals of assimilation and homogenization of culture. And, as I argue here, what seemed to be the glue that could hold the disparate and often conflicting elements of its public together would be, as in the British magazines and the *Little Review,* the creation of a new magazine genre based on the strengths of the very capitalist press against which the *Masses* had aligned itself.

Modernist art and poetry played a role in the *Masses'* struggle to imagine a pluralistic counterpublic sphere, and, ultimately, we must see the modernist contributions to the *Masses,* to its discursive arena, as bearing a different meaning for the American audience for emerging modernism than they might to us now. William Carlos Williams's poems about black and Chinese workers, Amy Lowell's dialect poetry, the free verse and imagist-inspired city poems of now-forgotten poets like Clara Shannafeldt, Helen Hoyt, and Lydia Gibson, and the modernist visual art of Hugo Gellert, Frank Walts, Ilonka Karasz, and Carlo Leonetti—other contributors included Pablo Picasso, Christopher Nevinson, and Djuna Barnes—all must be seen in terms of the larger interest in ethnicity that appeared in the magazine's frequent dialect cartoons and discussions of racial issues in labor struggles. When imbedded in the identity discourses of a radical magazine like the *Masses,* poems like Williams's take on a different meaning than they would in venues like *Others* or *Poetry,* which were devoted almost exclusively to modernist poetry.[8]

But these meanings are part of the emergence of modernism in America. Michael North has convincingly argued that early modernist use of dialect writing, of "linguistic imitation and racial masquerade," allowed authors to break linguistic boundaries, to "play at self-fashioning" (11). However, in the context of a magazine like the *Masses,* I suggest that this linguistic play was as much about the public, and about modernist and radical anxieties about the nature of the public sphere, as it was about self-fashioning. And, as the gradual transformation of a heterodox and exuberantly challenging magazine like the *Masses* into the final Communist party–owned *New Masses* by the 1930s suggests, the dream of an oppositional counterpublic sphere capable of containing this diverse vision of America had changed greatly by that decade. The contentious and often self-contradictory ways of understanding identity in America contributed to the tensions that fragmented this prewar counterpublic sphere. Nevertheless, this dream was very much part of the fabric of early modernism and, again, brought modernism in contact with the commercial culture that fostered and sustained radical counterpublic spheres.

The *Masses* and the Ideal of a Counterpublic Sphere:
Learning from the Commercial Papers

When the *Masses* was founded in 1911 by a Dutch immigrant, Piet Vlag, and when Max Eastman assumed the editorial reins in late 1912, it was edited by a collective of artists and writers who democratically voted on contributions and who wished to create an alternative to the capitalist press. The first masthead proclaimed that the *Masses* was "A Monthly Magazine Devoted to the Interests of the Working People" (Jan. 1911), but, especially under Eastman's editorship during the period from 1912 to 1917, the magazine expanded its goals. Its pages were open to free discourse, untrammeled by the pressures that advertisers put on the content of commercial magazines: "You will observe that our income does not provide for any return from advertisements printed. We shall not be obliged to suppress any literature or any art in order to hold an advertiser."[9]

The magazine addressed not only socialist revolutionary politics, but a wide range of heterodox literary, artistic, and cultural themes. Beginning in the January 1913 issue, Eastman ran each month a statement about the magazine (adapted from John Reed) that affirmed its revolutionary mission and its freedom from commercial influence: it was "a revolutionary and not a reform magazine; a magazine with no dividends to pay; a free magazine; frank, arrogant, impertinent, searching for the true causes; a magazine directed against rigidity and dogma wherever it is found; printing what is too naked or true for a money-making press; a magazine whose final policy is to do as it pleases and conciliate nobody, not even its readers." Yet this rhetorical scorn for audiences—as in the case of modernist magazines like the *Little Review* and the *Egoist*—did not demonstrate a lack of concern with audiences, but rather affirmed freedom from traditional expectations of commercial magazines tied to advertisers and to circulation and, using a product-symbol advertising strategy (see chap. 3), positioned the reader as worthy of elevation into the circle of *Masses* contributors.

The *Masses* tried to align itself against the capitalist press by frequently satirizing commercial journals and lampooning institutions like the powerful Associated Press.[10] Beginning in December 1913, it ran an ongoing "Masses Press Pearls contest," which aped the prize-giving publicity stunts of other magazines by awarding a monthly prize, a fourteen-carat "imitation pearl," for the worst passages in commercial papers and journals.[11] Its most famous cover was the June 1913 drawing by Stuart Davis of two unglamorous women over the caption, "Gee Mag, Think of Us Bein' on a Magazine Cover" (see fig. 8). The *Masses* artists rebelled against the need for the obligatory "pretty girl" on the front of magazine covers, and

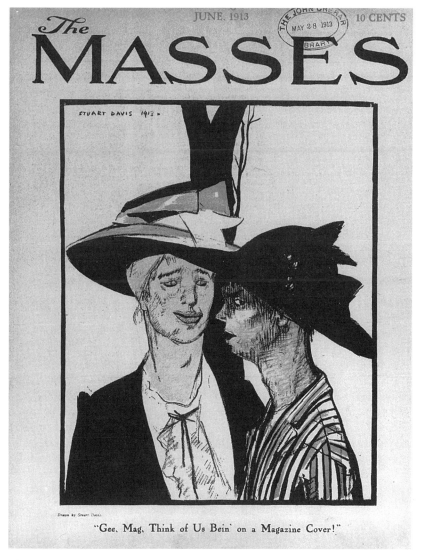

Figure 8. Stuart Davis takes an irreverent swipe at the "cover girl" convention of the commercial press—"Gee Mag, Think of Us Bein' on a Magazine Cover!" (*Masses*, June 1913)

they parodied the convention established by James Montgomery Flagg and Howard Chandler Christy (Zurier 41).

However, though the editors tried innovative ways to avoid a slavish dependency on advertising revenue, they were intensely aware of the need to attract wide audiences—not just to increase revenues, but above all to establish the magazine as a powerful forum of publicity, an alternative to the dominant public sphere. To foster public discussion, the magazine created a Masses Bookshop to disseminate revolutionary literature and a Masses Lecture Bureau to provide public speakers for socialist meetings around the country. And ultimately, like the *Egoist* and the *Little Review,* the editors tried to draw ideas from the extremely successful commercial press (even as they lambasted it) to help them reach mass audiences for a content that was too controversial to appear in the popular press. As with the *Little Review* and the *Egoist,* counterpublicity again took the form of learning from the dominant popular press and using its own institutions against it to form a more open, oppositional discursive arena.

So the editors of the *Masses* not only admitted their ties to the capitalist commercial press: they actually advertised them. In Thomas Seltzer's opening editorial, he bragged that "The reader needs no introduction to Arthur Young. He knows him by his work on Life and Puck. . . . Young belongs to the class of artists—there are many such nowadays—who stifle in the air of the capitalist editorial office," and he explained that "The metropolitan magazines cannot spare [Charles] Winter for very long." Grafting socialist buzz words like "workers" onto capitalist commercial strategies, Horatio Winslow, the next editor to represent the collective, continued to advertise the commercially successful image of his contributor-editors: "The best part of it all is that they are not second class men, but literary and artistic workers WHO APPEAR IN ALL THE BIG CAPITALISTIC MAGAZINES. They didn't have the chance to express themselves freely in J. Pierpont Morgan's papers, and so they founded *The Masses.*" Their success in commercial publishing made them first class, but that success could be used to promote other "class" interests than those of capitalist shareholders. Eastman himself, even as late as 1948, still thought it important to note that Charles Winter made a living "illustrating poems for the popular magazines. He was well paid by those magazines, and so was his wife, Alice Beach Winter," and that Horatio Winslow was "another gifted humorist, who was on the staff of *Puck,*" and that Mary Heaton Vorse and Inez Haynes Gillmore were "popular" and "well-known" writers (*Enjoyment,* 398). Indeed, a glance at the business addresses of the owner-editors, even during Eastman's editorship, underscores these connections to the commercial publishing industry: Hayden Carruth could be found at *Woman's Home Companion,* William W. Nutting at the Hearst magazine *Motor Boating,* and J. B. Larric at the *Herald* (May 1913, 19).[12]

But this valorization of the commercial credentials of socialist agitators in the *Masses* would not have been seen as contradictory at the time, even if it might now. The *Masses* was part of a larger commercialization of socialism in America before World War I. Advertisements ran in the *Masses* for the "Karl Marx" five-cent cigar, "Made by the Socialist Co-

Operators of Reading" (Aug. 1911, 18), and for the "Comrade" felt hat (June 1911, inside cover) and "Union Label" working shirts (July 1915, 26). Even the Rand School's restaurant, in an advertisement depicting a man at lunch reading the socialist paper the *Call,* advertised that "This Socialist den offers an excellent opportunity for Socialist workers to introduce their shopmates during luncheon into Socialist circles" (Feb. 1911, inside back cover). And, perhaps not so paradoxically given this relationship between socialism and commercial culture, business schools, like the Alexander Hamilton Institute, even advertised in the anticapitalist *Masses.*

As socialism was becoming visible in the commercial realm, the editors of the *Masses* saw an opportunity to create a new genre of socialist magazine, one that could reach out to a socialist audience using the well-established tools of the capitalist press. The *Masses,* Thomas Seltzer wrote, "will be a general ILLUSTRATED magazine of art, literature, politics and science. We use the word illustrated in the best meaning of the term. The *Masses* will print cartoons and illustrations of the text by the best artists of the country, on a quality of paper that will really reproduce them. This is a luxury which the Socialist press hitherto has been unable to afford, but it is a necessary luxury." When Seltzer explained that the magazine would be an illustrated magazine "in the best meaning of the term," he was defending against the possible charge of tawdry commercialism, but Vlag and Seltzer aimed to make a socialist propaganda paper that looked, in fact, like the popular monthly miscellanies of the commercial press, including high-quality illustrations, and to sell it for the five-cent price of the socialist papers. The *Masses* even borrowed some of the layout tricks of commercial comic magazines like *Puck,* a highly successful New York humor magazine founded in 1877, which contained many cartoons and drawings, and often included a two-page spread in the middle for a larger scale drawing, like the spread the *Masses* featured.

The emphasis on humor marked the *Masses'* competition with the popular press, and the *Masses* even influenced the captions and pictorial conventions of mainstream magazines.[13] Rebecca Zurier notes that the *Masses* combined aspects of socialist periodicals like the widely circulated populist political weekly *Appeal to Reason,* the *International Socialist Review* with its longer theoretical articles, and the *Comrade,* a socialist cultural magazine, but it followed the layout of popular magazines like *Ladies' Home Journal:* "It set text in a mix of type styles, interspersed with cartoons, small illustrations, and decorative headings and borders to mark special articles. But unlike its commercial counterparts, the *Masses* accepted advertisements only from cooperative business and confined these to discrete notices inside the cover."[14] Vlag's emphasis on advertisement from cooperative businesses, however, was abandoned when Max Eastman took over the magazine at the end of 1912, and a wide variety of commodities were advertised in the *Masses*. Noting the greater commercial viability in distribution and format of the magazine under Eastman, Robert Brown, a former contributing editor, recalls: "In December, 1912, the *Masses* shed its infant skin and appeared full grown on the newsstands with double-page cartoons, twenty pages in big format. That was an auspicious rebirth" (407). Underscoring the *Masses'* commercial viability, magazine agents even offered combination subscriptions bringing together the *Masses* with mass market successes like *Cosmopolitan, Woman's Home Companion, Good Housekeeping, Scribner's,* the *Literary Digest,* the *Review of Reviews,* and many others.[15]

Eastman, in one of his first editorial notices, affirmed that "We are going to make THE MASSES a *popular* Socialist magazine—a magazine of pictures and lively writing" ("Editorial Notice"), and, indeed, readers responded enthusiastically to what they saw as a felicitous combination of genres. Readers remarked on its "professional appearance" (Kopelin), and Eugene Debs, the Socialist presidential candidate in 1912, and the leader of the party, called it a "powerful illustrated monthly magazine published in the interests of Socialism, for which there is undoubtedly a most inviting field." Making the aspirations of the magazine explicit, Horatio Winslow noted: "We receive daily a number of complimentary letters. Everybody realizes that this is the first Socialist magazine which is not only a propaganda factor, but a commodity as a periodical. This means that we compete with the capitalist magazines."

Eastman himself even achieved a kind of "star status" in the commercial press as a result of his role in the *Masses*. The highly illustrated magazine *Every Week,* along with photo spreads of stars and actors, published a column entitled "Dear Editors," with photos and blurbs about the editors of mass market magazines. Alongside the photo spread of Edward Bok of *Ladies' Home Journal,* Mrs. Chase of *Vogue,* Edgar Sisson of *Cosmopolitan,* Frank Crowninshield of *Vanity Fair,* and others, was a photograph of Max Eastman, and the blurb: "Max Eastman took a copy of the *Masses* with him when he called on Bernard Shaw last August. 'I've read it,' said Mr. Shaw. 'Dear me, yes. I too was radical once.' Mr. Eastman is the son of two ministers, the Rev. Annis and the Rev. Samuel Eastman, and a Doctor of Philosophy, which probably accounts for the fiery flavor of his writing. 'I am an editor because I have to be,' says Mr. Eastman. 'Everybody but me blue-pencils my stuff.'" "Dear Editors" packaged Eastman in a way that safely contained his challenge to the company among whom he is placed. He is tied to the celebrity of Shaw, with the hint that Eastman's radicalism, like Shaw's, might just be a phase. His respectable clerical family helps to sanitize the frequent atheism and attacks on the Roman Catholic and Episcopal churches in the *Masses,* and his witty reply about his motives for being an editor clearly present no challenge to the readers of *Every Week.*

The editors realized that to make the *Masses* "a strong public factor in the United States" and to get a circulation of 100,000 within one year required them to continue in the channels of the commercial press, but they also faced particular problems in competing with the mass market publishers. Accepting the necessity of some advertising revenue as a given—something Marsden had been unwilling to do—Winslow explained: "Every capitalist magazine costs more to produce than it is sold for. They depend upon advertising. Every copy of our magazine costs us 6 cents. We sell it for much less than that. We too depend upon advertising. We could not solicit advertising until now, as we did not have a large enough circulation to make a bid for the high class advertising we want." While assuming the mantle of the commercial press in its desire for "high class advertising," the editors of the *Masses* hoped to do the impossible: to keep such a magazine at the price of the socialist papers while incurring the high costs of printing and producing an illustrated periodical.[16]

But the *Masses* successfully used the distribution systems of the commercial papers until it faced boycotts by distribution companies like Ward and Gow, a ban by the Canadian government, and finally the suspension of its mailing privileges in 1917 under the Espionage Act.[17] It was mailed to subscribers by the U.S. mail, sent to bookstores, and sold in the subway and street stands of New York, and it achieved fairly large sales (of 20,000 to 40,000 copies a month) that would have made any modernist little magazine jealous.[18] The suits brought against it by the powerful Associated Press and its indictments under the Espionage Act only attested to its perceived public impact.

Socialism, Modernism, and "the Public"

Whereas most commercial publications aspire to appeal to as large a segment of "the public" as possible, contributors and editors of the *Masses* had to determine first just who the "American public" might be. Identity questions quickly became important to the *Masses* and its modernist contributors, as writers like Randolph Bourne were beginning to turn against the "melting pot" ideal of the progressivists toward something approaching pluralism. Elizabeth Gurley Flynn, the Industrial Workers of the World (IWW) agitator who became famous during the Paterson silkworkers strike, responded to Max Eastman's question "Do You Believe in Patriotism?" by affirming a pluralist ideal: "America—not as a melting-pot that produces a jingoistic, mercenary, one-mold type, but as a giant loom weaving into a mighty whole the song, the poetry, the traditions, and the customs of all races, until a beautiful human fabric, with each thread intact, comes forth—would stretch forth a myriad hands of brotherhood to the four quarters of the globe." Flynn replaces the melting pot metaphor, in which new immigrants and different ethnic groups lose their distinct character and become simply "Americans," for the cloth metaphor in which a strong fabric is woven together while each ethnic and racial "thread" maintains its distinct character. Moreover, she replaces nationalism with a kind of internationalism as this cloth would stretch "to the four quarters of the globe."

Flynn's response could also be read as a colorful statement of the ideal public for which the *Masses* attempted to become a forum, and the ideal of counterpublicity for which the *Masses* strove. By the August 1916 issue, Eastman had glowingly praised his audience, who had contributed such a variety of "wise and beautiful articles and important news-stories": "People seemed to think The Masses was a universal magazine, and would hold anything. And so they made it a universal magazine. We didn't" ("An Important Announcement"). Here "universality" seems to be equated with "catholicity" of contributions. But the *Masses* also appealed to a wide variety of readers. Some readers were of respectable middle-class families. As Grace M. Bradner wrote to Eastman: "My mother admired you very much, and your courage for coming out for Woman Suffrage. She would take me to your lectures which I enjoyed also, but, the climax came when she insisted that we read The Masses. My father was a typical American business man, he would look on with disgust. Then a dispute started. My father loved Mother, but he could not always understand her. She was a daughter of a Scotch Presbyterian minister and had such advanced ideas."[19] A magazine clerk at the New York Public Library, noting that the number of calls for the *Masses* was greatly increasing, explained that "Young women and elderly men ask for the magazine" (*Masses*, Nov. 1913, inside cover). The audience clearly was not limited by age or gender.

And the magazine also had working-class and immigrant readers. Minnie Federman Corder wrote to Eastman about his autobiography, *Enjoyment of Living:* "I particularly treasure the history of the Masses. And I am very grateful to you for the kind words you have in your book for the three magic letters the I.W.W. I was a 15 year old immigrant from Russia when your magazine was born. Desperately trying to learn the English language in night school after working hours. The people I lived with never read magazines and never heard of the word Socialism. . . . The praises that come to you from the polished men and dazzling women are valuable to a poet like you. But those that worship you most sincerely [are] people like me to whom your poetry gave peace in the darkest hours."[20]

Corder, who became a factory worker in a clothing shop after she immigrated to the United States in 1911,[21] was one of many immigrant working-class readers of the *Masses* for whom the English language and class politics were not a birthright.

Another such immigrant reader of the *Masses,* Joseph Freeman, who immigrated from Ukraine and grew up in New York tenements, found in the *Masses* a kind of integration of the disparate elements and threads of Flynn's cloth: "One rainy afternoon, in the socialist local on Graham Avenue, the sixteen-year-old boy in search of heaven on earth found the Thing Itself. It was Just, Beautiful and American, Marx and Byron, Debs and Michelangelo, politics and poetry, the unity I was seeking. Somewhere in that mysterious Greenwich Village . . . there were native Americans who had integrated the conflicting values of the world. These men did not share each other's views. But they were frank about that too" (Freeman 60). As immigrant readers like Freeman saw it, the *Masses* brought together the threads into some kind of "American" unity. The "native" Americans (like Eastman and Dell) and the immigrant Americans could come together and agree to disagree with each other. The homogenization of the melting pot was not the goal of such a public space.

This goal of heterogeneity rather than homogeneity of identities was also represented in the *Masses* through a wide variety of types of language. But the varieties of language used in America also brings up issues of the "purity" of English, which, in the *Masses,* ultimately came into conflict with the notion of "pure identity." A central issue not only for immigrants like Freeman and Corder, but also for African Americans, rural farmers, and many other American ethnic groups (and ultimately for modernists), was the English language and how it was spoken. Freeman writes: "At home we spoke Yiddish; in the street a form of American with a marked foreign accent, a sing-song rhythm and the interpolation of Yiddish phrases; in public school we read and recited an English so pure, so lofty, so poetic that it seemed to bear no relation to the language of the street. Literature was the enemy of the street until years later, when post-war fiction and poetry gave the language of the street the dignity of art, when Joyce and Hemingway replaced Longfellow and Whittier" (30). Freeman identifies three languages whose social connotations he had to negotiate: his native Ukrainian Yiddish, his immigrant English with its accent and borrowings from Yiddish, and the "pure" language of culture, of literature. As North notes, the immigration boom beginning in the 1880s caused anxiety over the corruption of the English language in America, and a boom in linguistic criticism that aimed for the "purity" of the language (16–17). This defensive emphasis on "purity," which Freeman found in the privileging of the literary language of such American literary icons as

Longfellow and Whittier, represented exactly the kind of homogenization against which the vision of the *Masses,* and of Elizabeth Gurley Flynn, fought.

Issues of the "purity" of identity crept into the magazine nevertheless—but not a "purity" that marked "American" high culture. Rather, the *Masses'* ideal of a pluralistic counterpublic sphere of radicalism in all its forms—from socialism, and social justice, to suffragism, racial equality, sexual freedom, antimilitarism, and American internationalism—addressed identity through a number of textual and pictorial strategies: dialect writing, cartoons and drawings portraying people of different ethnic and regional backgrounds, and, as Freeman would affirm, modernism itself as a kind of "language of the street" and aesthetic rupture from socially conservative poetry of the genteel tradition (even if much of the radical nonmodernist poetry still used the traditional forms of the genteel tradition). The dialect writing that North tracks back into the 1880s, then, became a prevalent feature of the *Masses* as an affirmation of the multiplicity of American culture.

The dialect writing and cartoons in the *Masses* also mark another appropriation and rescripting of elements of commercial publications. Magazines like *Puck,* for which Art Young and other *Masses* contributors had written, occasionally featured dialect cartoons and writings in its pages, but their intent was always entertainment, and they were, without exception, turning to racist stereotypes to appeal to their audiences. In the year Eastman joined the *Masses,* for instance, *Puck* featured cartoons like "All Cut Up," which portrayed two "darkies" skating on a frozen lake, with big bulging white eyes and lips, dressed in absurd clothing. The text reads:

Miss Simpson—Kin you cut mah initials on de ice, Mistah Johnson? Mah name's Gertrude Lizbeth Agnes May Gladys Penelope Dorothy Simpson.
Mr. Johnson (*dubiously*)—Wal, I *could* do dat, Miss Simpson, but it would spoil de pond fo' skatin'!

While African Americans seem to have born the brunt of the racist comedy in magazines like *Puck,*[22] the Irish and Chinese also took their share of racist dialect jokes. "Orders Is Orders" depicted a housewife leaving her apartment giving instructions to her very primitive-looking Irish maid Nora: "Mrs. Gadder—Now, Nora, in your cleaning, be sure to move everything out and to sweep under it." In the next frame, Mrs. Gadder returns home to find Nora carrying the bathtub away, while her broom lies in a puddle of water shooting from the broken pipes: "Nora (*some hours later*)—Begorry, yez shtuck loike th' ould boy, but Oi moved yez, yez divil!" Likewise, the New York–based publication used dialect in cartoons about country "bumpkins," as in "The Happy Neighbors," in which two farmers converse over a fence, one holding a scythe with a pipe in his mouth:

FARMER WINROW.—There's always two sides to every argument, Ezry.
FARMER HAYBOY.—Yep; yours and the right side, Peleg.

These cartoons, from the names and dialect to the grotesquely exaggerated drawings, all play upon white urban stereotypes of highly visible ethnic immigrant groups like the Irish and Chinese as well as rural southern African Americans and white farmers.

The *Masses* imitated illustrated magazines of the day by including dialect and racial cartoons, but the contributors had different intentions for them: instead of merely ridiculing ethnic groups, they tried to portray them as part of the diversity of the American public, of a polyphony of "pure" voices, and to show something about their oppression. Claude McKay remembered his early excitement about the *Masses'* pictorial portrayals of black life: "And I felt a special interest in its sympathetic and iconoclastic items about the Negro. Sometimes the magazine repelled me. There was one issue particularly which carried a powerful bloody brutal cover drawing by Robert Minor. The drawing was of Negroes tortured on crosses deep down in Georgia. I bought the magazine and tore the cover off, but it haunted me for a long time. There were other drawings of Negroes by an artist named Stuart Davis. I thought they were the most superbly sympathetic drawings of Negroes done by an American. And to me they have never been surpassed" (*Long Way* 28–29). Sometimes such cartoons even relied upon the sentimental vocabulary of popular magazines, as in Alice Beach Winter's cartoon "Puzzle: Find the Race-Problem," depicting a little white girl with a black doll and a little black girl with a white doll (see fig. 9). Such manipulations of popular sentimentality could be quite subtle. In this case, Winter uses notions of the attractive innocence of children as a comment on a broader cultural issue. The children appear progressive, in that each plays with a doll of the other race, yet this play seems nothing more than play, in that the girls are turned away from each other, from real social interaction. Moreover, the white girl holds the black doll in dreamy detachment, whereas the black girl adopts a role of care and servitude toward her white doll—she fixes its hair.

Many of these ethnic cartoons were captioned in dialect, and two of the most famous white dialect writers since Joel Chandler Harris lay in the background of the *Masses*. Art Young had great admiration for James Whitcomb Riley's platform readings of such Midwest dialect pieces as "Thoughts fer the Discuraged Farmer," precisely because, using the rhetoric of purity of identity, Riley had captured "the true western farmer."[23]

Drawn by Alice Beach Winter.

PUZZLE: FIND THE RACE-PROBLEM

Figure 9. Alice Beach Winter's drawing, "Puzzle: Find the Race Problem," subtly manipulates the sentimentality of popular magazines to comment on racial barriers in America. (*Masses,* March 1914, 20)

And Finley Peter Dunne, who was famous for his "Mr. Dooley" dialogues featuring the witty and crusty Chicago-Irish bartender, had even discussed the possibility of contributing to the *Masses.* Eastman remembered: "Finley Peter Dunne was the first to make me feel the eventfulness of such a magazine as *The Masses.* I found him, when I went up to discuss the promised contribution, beaming with delight in its audacity and animal spirits. . . . The words in my editorials which to the initiated placed me on the side of working-class revolution were probably put down by Mr. Dooley, if remarked at all, to literary exuberance. *The Masses* was to him primarily a revolt against commercial journalism. The idea of writers owning a magazine where they could say what they really thought was the focus of his delight. 'There's a lot o' things I've never been able to say,' he exclaimed, 'and if you don't mind this horrendous dialect in which I write, I'll hand them in gladly'" (*Enjoyment* 405). Dunne never did contribute, though he renewed his promise to more than once, but Eastman "gradually perceived that Mr. Dooley would never say the things his market had prevented him from saying" (*Enjoyment* 406). The *Masses* aimed to turn the humor, sharpness, and ethnic specificity of the tradition of dialect writing exemplified by Riley and Dunne away from the goal of mass entertainment to one of pointed social commentary. While the inclusion of dialect cartoons about ethnic groups recalled other commercial magazines of the day, the intention was to portray the diverse identities composing the American public and their oppression by the dominant white moneyed classes.

But in addition to the dialect and ethnic cartoons and drawings in the *Masses,* the modernism that Joe Freeman had affirmed as the "language of the street" appeared in the magazine (Hemingway even published in the *Liberator*), and I see this as part of this larger exploration of identity and the diversity of the public sphere for which the *Masses* aimed. Modernist writers in the *Masses,* many now forgotten, adopted free verse and even imagist poetics, often writing poems about life in the public spaces of the city. Such poets as Helen Hoyt, Mary Aldis, Clara Shanafelt, who extolled free verse (and at times espoused an imagist poetic) and published in the *Little Review* and the *Egoist* as well, and dedicated communists like Lydia Gibson, who became an editor of the *Liberator* in its Chicago days, have long been ignored in discussions of modernism, but they clearly saw their verse experiments as consonant with the aesthetics and politics of radical magazines like the *Masses.* A good example of this kind of free verse writing about the public spaces of the city is Clara Shanafelt's "Release":

Release

Charming to drift about the streets
In the early evening.
Not thinking but simply accepting
The flattery of one's amusing sensations;
This is to be oneself a poem—
Pleasanter than writing them.

The people passing
Have put off the egoism
With which day invests them;
Vague accidents of a dream,
Like comfortable animals one keeps
To take the chill off solitude,
They pass,
They make no demands.

I like the electric glare
That cuts the pavement in clean blocks,
Like the touch of the wind slipping past
With still some sweetness of fields to scatter,
But the straying aroma of cigarettes
Amuses me more—
Pricks with a tang of sex,

Caressing, not gross,
Like the perfumed things they lean to say,
For saying,
On terraces,
Beneath an easy moon.

I am sorry the lassies with their horrible drum
Must find it all so fierce and solemn
That's their pleasure, I prefer
The bold lights capering, sans gene,
Up there
On the stage from which the proud, accusing stars
Have withdrawn.

Shanafelt's poem, like many others in the *Masses,* contrasts with F. S. Flint's and Richard Aldington's city poems discussed in chapter 3 in that it does not portray feelings of alienation and disgust at the crowds wandering the city streets. Shanafelt clearly feels comfortable in the streets and slips into the language spoken there by the masses—ethnic words like "lassies" and sexual innuendos in slang usages of common words ("Pricks with a tang of sex"). And, as the individual identities of the workday, "the egoism / With which day invests them," are left behind to bring their identities together publicly in Elizabeth Gurley Flynn's American tapestry, the old stock pastoral-romantic poetic metaphors ("like comfortable animals" and the "sweetness of fields") give way to the modern excitement of urban sensations—"the straying aroma of cigarettes / Amuses me more" and "I like the electric glare / That cuts the pavement in clean blocks." Finally, the urban public space in which Shanafelt takes so much pleasure is figured as a stage that shifts the natural beauty of the stars above to the lights of the stage after the theater stars have left: "I prefer / The bold lights capering, sans gene, / Up there / On the stage from which the proud, accusing stars / Have withdrawn." The mass culture of the crowds, as reflected in their language, their public appearance, and the stars they adore, creates not alienation but pleasure, figured boldly as a "release" that becomes almost a sexual release.

Like other contributors to the *Masses,* modernist writers also even turned to dialect writing. Amy Lowell contributed a long dramatic dialogue called "The Grocery," written in a New England rural dialect, about the inability of a New England shopkeeper's middle-class daughter to marry an out-of-work migrant laborer. Though Lowell contributed other dialect poems to the *Little Review,* and they appeared in her 1916 volume *Men, Women and Ghosts,* this poem as it appeared in the *Masses* represents not only modernist linguistic masquerade, but also modernists joining in the discursive arena in which the pluralistic tapestry of the ideal public was celebrated and explored. "The Grocery" could have conveyed its message about economic instability thwarting human emotions like love as a simple free verse poem, like many of Lowell's other poems. But writing in dialect, and in a dramatic dialogue form that emphasizes the identity of individual characters through speech, adds another layer to the poem— that of regional identity as configured through speech. In this case, the modernist turn to dramatic forms and to experiment with the spoken word was remarkably appropriate to a venue like the *Masses*.

But if the question Freeman asked—"How could you become an American?" (30)—could not be answered for an entire population by reading Whittier, the *Masses*' attempt to foreground questions of identity in a counterpublic sphere was also fraught with problems. Elizabeth Gurley Flynn concluded her statement about the pluralist fabric of America: "The train on which I write rushes by factories where murder instruments are made for gold. I would be ashamed to be patriotic of such a country. In the black smoke belched from their chimneys, I see the ghostly faces of dead workers—our poor, deluded slain brothers. I reaffirm my faith, 'It is better to be a traitor to your country than a traitor to your class!'" In spite of the beautiful statement of brotherhood and pluralism, Flynn felt it necessary to reduce this celebration of multiplicity as the essence of national identity to an insistence on the primacy of class. Determinants of identity are multiple. Yet Flynn insisted on prioritizing, and class identity takes precedence, certainly over national identity but also, implicitly, over racial and ethnic identity. And this dynamic, by which the importance of multiplicity is affirmed but the need for simplification, homogenization, is fallen back on, is the dynamic, and the problem, of counterpublic spheres in the modernist era.

William Carlos Williams contributed two poems to the January 1917 *Masses,* "Sick African" and "Chinese Nightingale." The poems, published together, ran:

Sick African

Wm. Yates, colored,
    Lies in bed reading
The Bible—
And recovering from
A dose of epididymitis
Contracted while Grace
Was pregnant with
The twelve day old
Baby:
There sits Grace, laughing,
Too weak to stand.

Chinese Nightingale

Long before dawn your light
    Shone in the window, Sam Wu;
You were at your trade.

Exploring Williams's early political engagement with Dora Marsden's egoism, David Frail reads these poems in the context of Williams's "anti-
ideological poetics of political poetry" (Frail 101–104; see also Clarke,
Dora Marsden). In "Americans, Whitman, and the Art of Poetry," Williams had praised *Others* and *Seven Arts* but criticized the *Masses'* poetry:
"*Masses* cares little for poetry unless it has some beer stenches upon it—
but it must not be beer stench. It must be beer stench—but not beer
stench, it must be an odor of hops and malt and alcohol blended to please
whom it is meant to please. Oh hell!" (35). Frail sees Williams's *Masses*
contributions as "demonstration pieces" to show the *Masses* that a political poetry could be written that was anti-ideological, while avoiding what
he saw as the *Masses'* quandary of wanting poetry by and about the working classes, but wanting it to be of the genteel tradition (104–105).

These poems also help to highlight the complexity of the *Masses'* vision of a counterpublic sphere based upon the preservation of distinct
identities. Williams's poems play both on the need to name, to pin down
identity, but on the multiple determinants that cut against such simple
naming. "Sick African," from its very title, begins by identifying William
Yates according to ancestry, and above all, according to location, to a
place that is *not* America, and probably a place that William Yates has
never seen. He is, as the poem quickly unfolds, a patient, but he is also an
"African"—and this ascription immediately highlights the contingency of
identity. In addition, his name evokes another figure, William Butler Yeats,
and plays on the disjunction between the famous poet and the sick African
American, but also on the comparison sometimes made between black
Americans and the Irish within the British empire. Barry Ahearn has
pointed out that, from the very first line—"Wm. Yates, colored," which
reads like an entry in a doctor's notebook—Williams's doctor's persona
obtrudes into the poem and helps the poem record Williams's double identity as doctor and poet. Moreover, the poem, through its various stereotypes of black behavior—sexual desire, humor in spite of troubles, piety—
"represents a paring down of social stereotyping to the least degree; it
shows, therefore, Williams' dissatisfaction with his cultural perspective,
but it also shows no alternative point of view" (Ahearn 68–69).

But in the context of the *Masses,* the need, in the first line, to pin
down Yates's identity, "colored," is important beyond evoking the doctor-
observer. The syntax of the first line suggests the complete identity of
Yates with a racial construct, but the rest of the poem comically brings in

another determinant of identity—sex. Of course there is no confusion about sexual identity given the physiological details of the poem, but Yates's infected swollen scrotum has brought *him* to bed, rather than his wife who just twelve days ago had a baby and now sits weakly laughing at his predicament. Frail is right that this strange sex reversal is not a political commentary about the "woman question," and hence not a political poem in the propagandistic sense of much of the *Masses*' poetry (105). But the move to posit and then undercut identity—in this case by pinning down Yates along racial lines only to unravel that identity by introducing gender trouble—is augmented in the second of the "Two Poems."

"Chinese Nightingale," like "Sick African," immediately locates identity in place, and again a place other than America. Presumably, both William Yates and Sam Wu are Americans, but they are still identified in the simplest of ethnic categories. However, even Sam Wu's name suggests a more complex identity, with its combination of Americanization and a traditional Chinese name, but the poem also blends this ethnic identity into an identity important to readers of the *Masses*—a labor identity. But even here the poem refuses an easy class identity in that the prosaic subject of labor is caught up in the orientalism of the poem's concise haiku form, and the suggestion of Romantic exoticness in the second part of the title that Ahearn notes. So what the poem brings together is not just East and West in the uneasy embrace of Western constructs of oriental culture as exotic, but also *labor* as an identity. Ultimately, then, the poem's title raises expectations about the simplicity of identity that the haiku itself undercuts by presenting identity as the tension between a series of conflicting terms. In the *Masses,* poems about labor tended to be either valorizations of the worker's spirit or diatribes against the exploitation of the proletariat,[24] but sometimes, as in Williams's poems, they ask more complicated questions about the identity of the worker in relation to his work.

Walter Benn Michaels discusses Williams's writings of the twenties, especially his 1928–1929 prose work *The Embodiment of Knowledge,* in terms of Williams's nativist pluralism and its implications for his poetics. Michaels sees Williams's commitment to "pure writing" as a commitment to "identity as such," and this commitment supports a nativist rhetoric for Williams's call for "American" poetry (75–55). But, although Michaels reads poems like "The pure products of America / go crazy" in *Spring and All* (often named "To Elsie" in later collections) as suggesting that "the conception of identity built into the poetics of embodiment is essentially genetic" (82) and argues that "what makes them crazy is what makes them pure, the inbreeding of 'old names,' a 'promiscuity' that produces 'deaf-mutes'" (166 n. 149), the poem, to me, has always seemed to say almost the opposite—that the poem is about miscegenation and the *lack* of "purity." Moving beyond *national* identity, the poem seems to me to reflect what

James Clifford calls "the predicament" of "ethnographic modernity." "Ethnographic," Clifford notes, "because Williams finds himself off center among scattered traditions; modernity since the condition of rootlessness and mobility he confronts is an increasingly common fate. 'Elsie' stands simultaneously for a local cultural breakdown and a collective future" (3–4). "To Elsie" (Williams "XVIII") evokes locality ("mountain folk from Kentucky / or the ribbed north end of / Jersey / with its isolate lakes") and "race" ("with a dash of Indian blood"). But ultimately the poem seems to be about the mobility not only of railroading adventuring Americans, but of American identity—the lack of "purity" in such a mobile world, a world as much of miscegenation as of "purity," of "imaginations which have no / peasant traditions to give them / character."

I bring "To Elsie" into this discussion not to suggest that Michaels is wrong about Williams's nativism, because I think his work on the subject is convincing, but rather to suggest that the earlier, more obscure poems in the *Masses* function in much the same way to show the provisionality and multiplicity of identity, even of national identity. When writing about the relationship and differences between America and Europe, and their literary traditions, Williams clearly is a nativist. But when exploring what America *is* in poems like "To Elsie," the purity ideal becomes complicated—as we clearly see in Williams's *Masses* poems of 1917.

These complications of identity came to haunt the *Masses.* Floyd Dell later wrote: "A writer (or a poet, painter, artist of any sort) needs to have in his mind the conception of a Public—a potentially friendly Public, which embraces and transcends all classes, political parties, and social-economic groups. There is, in fact, such a Public. It is also true, as a matter of fact, that this public, at anytime, has on the whole a class bias and class prejudices, and religious prejudices, and moralistic prejudices, and, at times, patriotic prejudices."[25] Dell sketches both the ideal and the reality of the public at which the *Masses* was aiming, but these biases and prejudices almost from the start precluded an oppositional public unified by organs like the *Masses.* A major problem, of course, was class. The very first cover of the *Masses* had proclaimed it "A Monthly Magazine / Devoted to the Interests / of the Working People," but by the last year of its life, George Santayana perceptively wrote to Eastman, "I am not sure whether *The Masses* represents one of the classes—the most numerous—or rather a few independent and exceptional individuals."[26]

The problem was that a paper proclaiming itself in the interest of the workers, and for proletarian revolution, was run and largely written by writers and artists of middle-class background.[27] As one disgruntled worker wrote: "Do you want to know why the Masses is running down and out? Then find out just what the WORKERS' think of its Mr and Mrs Rauh-Eastman editors who love US so—from a distance. Only 5 months in the sweet sweet country and a grand flat in town and letting INVESTED CAPITAL which be hust [*sic*] US THE WORKERS do it all for you but not a Rauh Eastman name on the Masses stockholders is to laugh. Stocks and Bonds hired girls country homes, fur coats talky talky RED REVOLUTION dinner lunch parties may fool you to not knowing a fakir when you see one but not us."[28] This letter reflects the nagging charge that the *Masses* crowd was just a bunch of Greenwich Village aesthetes more interested in costume parties and the Bohemian life-style than real proletarian revolution. And the *Masses* group could seem elitist and patronizing at times, as Eastman said in his *Liberator* obituary of John Reed (Dec. 1920): "Way over the heads of the American proletariat, and beyond any vision that they had in their eyes, he chose to identify his interest with their interest, and his destiny with their ultimate destiny." Eastman himself later in life noted: "I did not commit my soul to the proletarian religion. I did not experience that sense of soul-and-body consecration to the working class which filled these agitators and which is hallowed by the Marxian metaphysics. . . . I could not deceive myself that in the mass, and still less in idea, the industrial workers were my comrades or brothers, or the special repositories of my love" (*Enjoyment* 445–446). Yet Eastman's unease about identifying himself with the proletariat was expressed this clearly only years after the demise of the *Masses,* and after Eastman's turn to the right in politics.

But even the attack on the middle-class status of the *Masses* (far from prevalent) assumes that proletarians have some sort of ontologically privileged revolutionary status—the politics of identity played out again. The Socialist party also had many middle-class members. Joe Freeman noted that "the Socialist party, as distinguished from the I.W.W., had a special appeal for the more discontented sections of the middle class. . . . What attracted middle-class elements was the Party's attacks on big capital, attacks which seemed sharper and more consistent than those of the liberal reformers" (47).

The difficulty the *Masses* always faced was determining how socialism could legitimize itself as a political discourse that is based on class identity yet was espoused by another class and, perhaps even more daunting, how it could negotiate the problem of ethnic difference against the backdrop of the Socialist party's anti-immigrant stances and blindness to African American workers' needs. Debs had tried to replace race issues with class issues, but the very need to replace one kind of claim about identity with another encapsulated the problem that the *Masses,* with an even broader racial and ethnic agenda than the Socialist party, had to face. Although ethnic identity might have meant little in the Marxist theory of class struggle, contributors to the *Masses* and the *Liberator* seemed to sense the importance of ethnic identity in an oppositional public sphere in America.

The *Masses* tried to assert the purity of racial and ethnic identity, and the *Liberator,* even with its increased coverage of events in Russia, continued this strategy.

In his "Books" column in one of the first issues of the *Liberator* (Mar. 1918), Dell reviewed James Weldon Johnson's *Fifty Years and Other Poems,* which contained two sections, one of which was dialect poetry. Dell wrote "In spite of their quite authentic merits, the contents of both parts of this volume fail to meet my dogmatic expectations. To put the matter plainly, I think that art is different from politics. In the realm of politics I am impatient of racial distinctions. Politically—and socially—a Negro looks like anybody else to me" (32). Here Dell seems to support Debs's notion that race can be replaced by class in the political struggle. Yet he goes on: "But if there is no peculiar racial way of casting a vote, or holding office, there is nevertheless a peculiar racial way of writing poetry" (32). Unselfconsciously repeating common racist assumptions about African Americans, he went on to assert that "there is a Negro music that is different from any other music, a new thing under the sun, more irresponsibly joyous and more profoundly tragic, I think, than any other," and that "I expect, moreover, to learn from a race that knows how to 'laze,' the secret of the butterfly's perpetual and lovely holiday" (32). He praises the rhythm and diction of spirituals, complaining that even Johnson's dialect poems lack the lyric quality that would make them "Negro" and urged "it is the business of the Negro poet to attune his ear to that peculiar grace, to study it just as Synge studied it in the speech of the fisherman and tinkers and peasants of the Aran Islands, and to find ways perhaps of heightening, or at all events of making clear and unmistakable, that which he has heard. He is, as Synge found it his glory to be, the mouthpiece of his race, speaking their speech so that all men may hear" (33). So for Dell, true "Negro poetry" is tied to a vision of the dialect of the rural South, to many stereotypes about the simple innocence of blacks, just as Dell implicitly accepts the same conception of the Irish—that Synge truly wrote Irish dialogue in his plays only by capturing the speech of the Irish peasants of the far West.

James Weldon Johnson's reply in the same volume of the *Liberator* attacked Dell's criticism: "In a word, Mr. Dell's contention is that a Negro poet should confine himself not only to Negro themes but to what is traditionally known as Negro phraseology and speech. He feels that there is, or ought to be, something inherent, something in the blood that should urge and compel him to do so" (40). Johnson clearly rejected this idea of "blood," of a fixed and "pure" black identity—the kind of ethnic thinking that plagued the *Masses* and its hope for a unified oppositional public sphere. He turned instead to a more strategic and mutable sense of the relationship between language and identity. Speaking of rural southern black culture, Johnson continued: "Negro dialect is the natural instrument for voicing that phase of Negro life, but the poet finds it is too limited for any higher or deeper notes. It has but two main stops, humor and pathos" (41). Black identity cannot be equated with Southern plantation culture, and the black poet is free to choose or reject dialect writing as a mode of self-expression. Rejecting the appropriateness of Dell's allusion to Synge, Johnson concluded that the African American cannot be compared to the Irish, who live on an island that they have to themselves: "The Negro in the United States is thrown into the whirl of American life, and, whether he wills or not, he must become a part of it. If he does not he perishes. So the traditional speech of the Negro cannot be kept a living force in American literature, for in spite of all we may do, it will pass" (43).

If Johnson's reply seems to support the kind of assimilation and homogenization that the *Masses* fought against with its pluralist logic of the purity of identity, the obvious short-comings of Dell's position were evident in the magazine, where those "pure" identities that Williams challenged in his *Masses* poems could be maintained only by resorting to devices like the dialect poetry Johnson argues against. While the intentions of the *Masses* were far different from those of commercial magazines like *Puck,* in many ways they resembled each other more than either might admit. Eastman himself wrote a dialect poem (anonymously) for the *Masses* called "June Morning" that was as dependent upon racist stereotyping of blacks as *Puck*'s dialect poem "The Green Tempter":

June Morning

De sun am shinin' bright,
Am fillin' me full ob light;
Ah done git up ea'ly,
An' wash mahse'f mo' thor'ly[29]

In *Enjoyment of Living,* Eastman discusses this poem as an example of the "catholicity of *The Masses,* [and] its freedom from the one-track mental habit of the rabid devotee of a cause, for which [he] as editor was most responsible" (414).

But the portrayal of African Americans in the magazine eventually drew some criticism for its insensitivity. The May 1915 issue of the *Masses* included "The Masses and the Negro: A Criticism and a Reply," in which Carlotta Russell Lowell wrote: "There is one thing about THE MASSES that strikes me as totally inconsistent with its general policy: it is the way in which the negro race is portrayed in its cartoons. If I understand THE MASSES rightly, its general policy is to inspire the weak and unfortunate with courage and self-respect and to bring home to the oppressors the injustice of their ways. Your pictures of colored people would have, I should think, exactly the opposite effect. They would depress the negroes themselves and confirm the whites in their contemptuous and scornful attitude." Eastman replied: "Miss Lowell makes the most serious charge against THE MASSES we have heard. We have been accused of bringing the human race as a whole into disrepute enough, and our love of realism has borne us up under the charge. But if that same realism when engaged in representations of the negro seems to align us upon the side of the self-conceited white in the race-conflict that afflicts the world, it is indeed tragic."

Eastman goes on to mention pictures that attack racism and affirm black dignity, but then he adds: "But doubtless it is not what we say under the pictures, it is the actual character of the drawing, that leads to Miss Lowell's complaint against us. Stuart Davis portrays the colored people he sees with exactly the same cruelty of truth, with which he portrays the whites. He is so far removed from any motive in the matter but that of art, that he cannot understand such a protest as Miss Lowell's at all. Some of the rest of us, however, realize that because the colored people are an oppressed minority, a special care ought to be taken not to publish *any-thing* which their race-sensitiveness, or the race-arrogance of the whites, would misinterpret. We differ from Miss Lowell only in the degree to which a motive of art rather than of propaganda may control us." Eastman here uses the problematic art versus propaganda justification for Davis's drawings—the same drawings that McKay liked so much—but the desire to represent the diversity of American life, the notion of distinctive identities, seemed perpetually to lead down this road to racial stereotyping. And at times, racial identity that could not be subordinated to class identity was held up against it in what now seems like appallingly racist ways. The most notorious example is probably John Sloan's cartoon "Race Superiority," which showed a tired family of white people marching toward a factory while a black boy, sitting on the fence, eats watermelon. The drawing was, of course, supposed to show that white proletarians were worse off and more in a condition of slavery than the black pickaninny of the South whom they held as beneath them, but the racist implications were unavoidable. As Zurier notes, "Only gradually did *The Masses* abandon racial stereotypes and caricature for a more militant political approach to black issues" (17), and she adds: "Overall, however, the white radicals' sophistication in racial matters came too late. Through the Harlem Renaissance in the 1920s, blacks forged a cultural identity with little dependence on whites" (20).

But the problem extended beyond the portrayal of African Americans. Like those in *Puck, Masses* cartoons portrayed many ethnic groups, including, of course, the Irish and Chinese. Robert Henri's "Misther O'Hoolihan" portrayed the brutish features the commercial press usually reserved for the Irish, and Boardman Robinson's drawing of a Chinese laundryman, while aiming to attack Christian churches' support for the war, drew on all the stereotypes of Chinese immigrants as working in laundries and speaking in pidgin English: "No, no, I make velly bad Clistian, I no can shoot." Perhaps most prevalently, the *Masses* portrayed rural people in the same comic manner as *Puck*. While some cartoons had political aims against the racism of the South—like Richard Kempf's caricature of a white southerner saying to another: "The only trouble, sah, with the south is that we kain't make the niggers work"—the buffoonish "yokel" was a frequent feature of many cartoons. The magazine portrayed these yokels as beyond the reach of socialism, as Henry Glintenkamp's scruffy country people stand in a snowy landscape talking to each other:

"Wuz a feller in here tryin' to git me to buy one o' them gol-durn socialist magazines yistaday."

"Wal, I call'late the almanac and Montgomery Ward'll last me over the winter."

Art Young joked at country people's ignorance of city ways in a cartoon of a fat farm woman cutting flowers with another woman, while an old man in overalls and hat holds his cane out threateningly at a field: "Yes, he's been that way ever since he come back from Noo York. He's cussin' them street-car conductors for tellin' him to 'step lively' all the time!"

The irony of these prevalent portrayals of country yokels is that there was, in fact, strong support for socialism in the country. American socialism was not just an industrial labor movement; it drew much strength from midwestern farmers.[30] The *Liberator* even ran a series of letters from George Cronyn about the Non-Partisan League and its organization of farmers in North Dakota that worked for government ownership of the terminal elevators, warehouses, flour mills, stock yards, packing houses, and cold storage plants, for rural credit banks operated at cost, and exemption of farm improvements from taxation.

The problem with the pluralism the *Masses* tried to espouse in a counterpublic sphere was one of point of view. In many ways the *Masses* truly was a national and even international organ of the labor movement in that it kept readers apprised of labor struggles and issues all over America and abroad, sending correspondents to the Paterson strike, the Ludlow massacre in Colorado, the Mexican civil war, and finally, during its *Liberator* days, even to Soviet Russia. But in many ways it was also very much the Greenwich Village magazine that opponents made it out to be. The point of view, the source of the humor, or even the direction of identification and sympathy in the more progressive cartoons and writings, was that of the white urban radical—the unspoken concept of region informed the contributions of the *Masses* more than any of its editors would have admitted, and, to return to Eastman's exchange with McKay in 1923, it is not surprising that Eastman felt most of the *Liberator*'s readers were white. And, as Zurier notes, the tone of much of the *Masses* was of the didactic intelligentsia teaching the proletariat (31).

Counterpublic Spheres and the Problem of Cohesion

The problem with the *Masses* was a problem of counterpublic spheres in the early period of modernism. The inability of the *Egoist* to maintain a broadly oppositional counterpublic sphere in Britain, to make such a discursive space cohere without a single issue (like votes for women or socialism), to provide the ideological glue, helps to suggest why even a class-based concept like Negt and Kluge's of a "proletarian public sphere" is problematic, in spite of their recognition of the multiple nature of counterpublicity (as opposed to the unified singular notion of *the* public sphere that they have insightfully critiqued in Habermas's work). The *Masses* was attempting to foster just such a "proletarian public sphere" by adopting and adapting institutions of the dominant public sphere, but the issues of identity in America undermined any possibility of unity and coherence in such a project.

In the face of the increased political and social pressures on oppositional activity that occurred during the war, especially after the passage of the Espionage Act in 1917,[31] the imagined unity of the counterpublic sphere seemed to break down. I believe such a consequence was inevitable regardless of the war. The apparent collapse led to two kinds of efforts to achieve the unifying cohesion that this counterpublic sphere lacked.

First was an unacknowledged increase in the magazine's turn toward commercial culture as the unifying glue in the American public sphere; the power of commercial culture to mobilize desire and to create mass audiences was hardly lost on radicals of the early twentieth century. The street wars in which "slum gangs" of Jews and "Micks" clashed in New York tenement neighborhoods caused Joe Freeman, as a young reader of the *Masses,* to wonder about national identity: "How could you become an American? There were so many kinds of Americans. Around the corner was Fox's Folly, corner-stone of a cinema fortune, where every night young gangsters met. From street-fights they had graduated to gun fights. In a civilisation where captains of industry rose to the top through force and fraud, violence was a logical instrument" (30). Although Freeman turns to an economic explanation—American capitalism exacerbates the tensions between disparate groups of people who are groping for a unified "American" identity—another answer to his question could be that Fox's Folly is the common denominator to all these ethnic Americans. They all fight with each other in ways that highlight their differences, yet they are all attracted to the movies.

The editors and contributors to the *Masses* felt no ideological qualms about having dual careers in the socialist and capitalist presses, and, of course, the *Masses* even played up its ties to the commercial press as a sign of its strength, turning to many of the conventions of the capitalist press as a model for its own makeup and distribution. But, whereas the early *Masses* had parodied the institutions of commercial culture—Davis's parody of the beautiful woman on the cover of many magazines, for instance—the later *Masses* turned to a cover aesthetic that not only privileged the beautiful cover girl, but also portrayed her in a slick modernist style that was soon to enter the world of commodity advertising and magazine fashion (see Murphy 64–70). By 1916, a large portion of the magazine's covers featured drawings of beautiful women done in a decidedly modernist design style, frequently by Frank Walts, Ilonka Karasz, Carlo Leonetti, and Hugo Gellert, who would continue to be an ardent communist long after Eastman and Dell had abandoned the party (see figs. 10 and 11). The contrast of these drawings to Stuart Davis's June 1913 parodic "cover girls" could not be more striking. However, the political commitments of an artist like Gellert could clearly not be questioned, and the *Masses* covers from this period are a fascinating record of the convergence of leftist radicalism with modernism and with commercial culture.

Moreover, these covers were at times more than just stylish modern drawings of women: sometimes they were even of film stars. The April 1916 *Masses* sported a striking abstract portrait by Frank Walts of a woman's head in profile. A note mentioned that "The Masses' cover this month is a sketch by Frank Walts of Mary Fuller, in the film-play, 'The Heart of a Mermaid'" ([Eastman?], "Note"). Later that year, the December issue featured another stylish and very modern Frank Walts cover of a woman with long hair looking out over her shoulder and arm to the front (see fig. 12). Like many of Walts's and Gellert's covers, the woman is represented semiabstractly in strong colors reminiscent of Matisse, with a modernist formal vocabulary. The magazine again made reference to its cover: "Life—you will perceive from her expression—is still worth living. We are indebted for this reassurance to Miss Gerda Holmes, the film-actress, who posed for the picture, and Frank Walts, who drew it" ([Eastman?], "The Girl on the Cover"). Cary Nelson notes of the *Masses*' publication of love poetry and descriptive poetry that was not overtly political: "The point there was to demonstrate, by way of a lyrical universalizing, and sometimes sentimental humanism—a humanism permissible specifically in poetry—that a radical political commitment did not preclude experiencing other kinds of emotions" (206). Yet here the point of the editorial statement seems to be that, in spite of the war and the attack on labor movements by big business and the government, commercial culture's packaging of female beauty and allure in the star phenomenon of the

Figure 10. In this striking cover (in deep blue, yellow, and white), Frank Walts brings a modernist visual vocabulary to the commercial press's conventions and reverses the magazine's opposition to the cover girl. (*Masses,* January 1916)

Figure 11. This modernist cover girl was introduced by commercial lithographer, committed socialist, and modernist Hugo Gellert. (*Masses,* November 1916)

film industry, and the related appropriation of it by modernist illustrators, provides the common thread of pleasure that holds the populace together—an appeal that transcends all differences of identity. Gone were the days when *Masses* covers parodied the commercial use of the cover girl. There was no sense of parody or critique at all about these 1916–1917

197

Figure 12. Frank Walts cover girls include a nod to the commercial papers and to a newly important industry in this drawing of film-actress Gerda Holmes. (*Masses,* December 1916)

Masses covers. Even a poem in the next issue, "Girl on a Magazine Cover," by Seymour Barnard, whose ostensible purpose was to portray cover models as dupes of capitalism, seemed more fascinated and attracted by the cover girl than critical of the institution.[32]

In the last few years of the *Masses,* these covers by Walts and Gellert, and occasionally Ilonka Karasz and Carlo Leonetti, highlight not only the reemergence of the cover girl into the *Masses,* but also the most modernist aspect of the magazine in many ways. The magazine had always been advanced aesthetically up to a certain point. The artists gathered around John Sloan were realists (who comprised what later became known as the ash can school of American art), and they used a strong drawing style influenced not by any academic method, but rather by Robert Henri's teachings.[33] Sloan and others, including the magazine's key editors, Max Eastman and Floyd Dell, were resistant to modernism in literature and in painting (inspired by the Armory Show, in which his pictures were displayed, Sloan parodied cubism, and one contributor even used Duchamp's *Nude Descending a Staircase* from the Armory Show as a metaphor for obscure political speech[34]). But the last few years of the *Masses* saw a great increase in the modernist visual and literary content of the magazine. A drawing by Pablo Picasso appeared in the September 1916 issue, and the September 1917 issue featured a number of futurist war drawings by the English futurist Christopher Nevinson. And many less famous artists who were committed to the American political left—Gellert, Walts, Karasz, Leonetti, Arthur Davies, and others—provided numerous formally challenging modernist drawings and etchings to the magazine that did not have a discernible propaganda aspect. Similarly, literature by Sherwood Anderson, Carl Sandburg, William Carlos Williams, Amy Lowell, and Baroness Else von Freytag-Loringhoven, and less well known writers in free verse and imagist strains like Clara Shanafelt, Helen Hoyt, Mary Aldis, and Lydia Gibson, was beginning to take up greater space in the *Masses.* (Advertisements for the *Little Review, Seven Arts, Some Imagist Poets,* the Four Seas Press, and other modernist publications, too, were appearing frequently). The *Masses'* use of a modernist aesthetic fused to mass cultural conventions like the cover girl looks forward to the kind of commercial chic and sophistication modernism achieved in the twenties and thirties in magazines like *Vanity Fair* (see Murphy), but it also represents an attempt to unify an oppositional public sphere through the conventions of mass culture.

The other attempt to unify the counterpublic sphere was the effort by Eastman, Dell, Art Young, and other more committed socialists, to give the paper a policy—a coherent support for socialism. The often-discussed "Artists' Strike" was the negative response by many of the artists to this desire to impose an agenda on the magazine. In March 1916, Sloan, Davis,

Coleman, and Glintenkamp threatened to strike if the magazine were not restructured in a way that prevented the writers from voting on the artists' work, and vice versa, and prevented the writers (especially Eastman and Dell) from putting their own captions on the drawings. But what was at stake was more than just editorial quibbling. Sloan wrote: "The Masses is no longer the resultant of the ideas and art of a number of personalities. The Masses has developed a 'policy.' We propose to get back if possible to the idea of producing a magazine which will be of more interest to the contributors than to anyone else" (Zurier 52). The convoluted story of this "strike"—eventually resulting in the resignation of Becker, Coleman, Davis, Brown, the Winters, and Sloan—has been well documented elsewhere by Zurier, Fishbein, Howe, and O'Neill, and it is not my intention to recapitulate this history here. A rift between Young, Eastman, Dell, and many of the committed socialists who remained at the magazine and the aforementioned group of artists emerged over what Dell characterized as their "art-for-art's sake" attitude and what the artists characterized as the integrity of their artistic realism.[35] Essentially, the war was between "art" and "propaganda." Young stated: "The dissenting five artists were opposed to a 'policy.' They want to run pictures of ash cans and girls hitching up their skirts in Horatio street—regardless of ideas—and without title. On the other hand a group of us believe that such pictures belong better in exclusive art magazines. Therefore we put an emphasis on the value of constructive cartoons for a publication like *The Masses*. . . . For my part, I do not care to be connected with a publication that does not try to point the way out of a sordid materialistic world. And it looks unreasonable to me for artists who delight in portraying sordid and bourgeois ugliness to object to a 'policy'" (Zurier 53). Although this movement to adopt a stronger socialist "policy" led to the exodus of many artists, the same kind of issue came up again in 1917 as Eastman tried to line up his contributors around an antiwar policy. Echoing the earlier argument of the artists, George Bellows wrote to Eastman:

I decidedly will not sign the enclosed paper, although I am in hearty sympathy with the first paragraph. I am also of the opinion that it would be a hell of a situation if Germany succeeded even a little bit.

The Masses has no business with a "policy." It is not a political paper, and will do better without any platforms.

Its "policy" is the expression of its contributors. They have the right to change their minds continually looking at things from all angles.

In the presence of great ultimate and universal questions, like these, it is impossible at least for me to know quite where I stand: and I will not sign papers which sound well and then learn later to repent. I think this business is unnecessary and foolish and against the spirit and best interest of the Masses.[36]

The magazine opposed a "strike" affirming pure individualism, individual artistic freedom, and a magazine existing for itself—mainstays of modernist rhetoric (and the very values Eastman affirmed retrospectively in his autobiography decades later). Instead, it tried to align mass culture and modernism with socialist policy and collective action as principles to unify a counterpublic sphere.

The *Masses* had tried to foster a counterpublic sphere of widespread opposition that would somehow encompass the diversity of the American public without tying itself to any specific dogma or policy, or really even any particular class. Yet by 1916, the magazine was scrambling to create unity—through the increasing turn to commercial culture and though this kind of move to a simplifying "policy." Just as a magazine like the *Egoist* in London could not achieve the broad cultural impact it had hoped, lacking a unifying market niche or cause like the Socialist papers and suffrage papers had, the *Masses* turned to narrowing its discursive space, and, by the early days of the *Liberator* in 1918, began to focus on the communist revolution in Russia.[37] From the new attitude of the remaining socialists on the paper, the free and broad-ranging counterpublic sphere the *Masses* had earlier fostered gave way to articles by Lenin, Trotsky, and the host of *Masses/Liberator* contributors (including John Reed) who went to Russia to send back news of the revolution and the fledgling Soviet Russia. Eastman later wrote "Our magazine provided, for the first time in America, a meeting ground for revolutionary labor and the radical intelligentsia. It acquired, in spite of its gay laughter, the character of a crusade" (*Enjoyment* 409). By the end of the *Masses* and the beginning of the *Liberator,* however, this meeting ground had become especially small, and, though the *Liberator* published a great deal of interesting material throughout its existence into the mid-1920s, it had certainly aligned itself with a specific vision of Red revolution.

To return, then, to Eastman's quarrel with McKay over the issue of race and class revolution in the *Liberator,* the *Masses,* like many modernist magazines, was born in the spirit of Paine, of the eighteenth-century ideal of free discourse. And, like these other magazines, it aimed at some kind of integration of oppositional discourses, from politics to literature and art in what might be called a counterpublic sphere. But, even optimistically drawing on the institutions of the commercial press to try to reach a broad public, the issue of identity, especially the multiple determinants of class, race, and ethnicity, made the magazine's move from the progressivist melting pot ideal of the prewar years to an early version of the pluralism of the twenties so problematic that the magazine was forced to simplify itself and dogmatically choose *an* identity—class—to override all others.

Eastman, and many leftist radicals who supported the American Communist party and the Soviet regime (at least temporarily), then, chose Lenin over Paine. But this decision, in the case of the *Masses* and the *Liberator*, should not be seen merely as the triumph of realpolitik, as Eastman suggests in his letter to McKay, but rather as a response to the pressures that the insistence on pluralist identity put on a counterpublic sphere that fashioned itself around a single, untenable, class identity.

Modernist interventions into public culture intersected both with counterpublic spheres and with the commercial mass market that fostered them. Magazines like the *Masses* elucidate these interventions and illuminate both the productive relationship modernist literature and art had with both American radicalism and commercial culture and the difficulties that counterpublic spheres had in negotiating such complex issues as identity and cohesion. When modernists in America published in magazines like the *Masses*, rather than in purely literary magazines like *Poetry*, their works entered into dialogue with the other discourses in those magazines, and both helped to shape them and were in turn shaped by them. And this range of discursive relations cannot be ascertained from looking at later anthologized or collected book volumes of these authors' works; it is only by turning to the unlikely venues for modernism, like the *Masses*, in addition to the obviously modernist magazines, like the *Little Review*, that we can begin to see the broader cultural tapestry of which modernism was only a part and to experience the full richness of modernism's vision of the public sphere.

Epilogue

Many of the magazines that launched modernism in England and America ceased publication or were changed beyond recognition by the early 1920s. The *English Review* had quietly forsaken Ford's initial aspirations for it after he was forced out in 1910; *Poetry and Drama* ceased publication in 1914; The *Egoist* died in 1919. The *Little Review* moved to Paris in 1922 and only sporadically appeared during the twenties; the *Masses* became the *Liberator* in 1918, and by the early twenties had lost much of its earlier vividness and independence. Other magazines crucial to early modernism were defunct or altered by the early 1920s: *Others* ceased in 1919, A. R. Orage left the editorship of the *New Age* in 1922, and *Blast* did not even make it beyond its second issue in 1915.

Because the exponential growth of the commercial mass market and its institutions was a relatively new phenomenon, British and American modernists were initially optimistic about effecting change from within by utilizing commercial advertising and publication tactics for a noncommercial "product." They did not, in fact, display the pessimism about the role of art and literature in the public sphere commonly ascribed to modernism. But modernists were often unable to use these opportunities as successfully as they had hoped. The early modernist enthusiasm about influencing the dominant public sphere by appropriating mass market tactics seems to have been somewhat blunted by the twenties. Not coincidentally, this was the decade in which twentieth-century consumer culture, and the publication and advertising institutions that shaped it, consolidated and became firmly established in their modern forms in both Britain and America (Wicke 172).

The commodity culture sustained by the new mass market magazines presumed, or even tried to fabricate, a kind of cultural cohesion aimed at manufacturing homogeneity in its audiences. For example, magazines like *Ladies' Home Journal, Everybody's,* and *Collier's,* which were read by the large "professional managerial class" that Ohmann and Lears explore served several functions that all depended on a kind of homogeneity of aspirations and taste. As name-brand commodities themselves, Ohmann notes, these magazines created a sense of a national culture, on the one hand, but also, on the other hand, marked the attainment of their subscribers and thus solidified a particular cultural affinity shared by a certain class across the country. Moreover, they helped organize that identity around the consumption of certain types of goods—cameras, household labor-saving devices, breakfast cereals, for instance—that were advertised in their pages (Ohmann 172–174), but that were, as Lears observes, almost all national brand-name products made by large corporations (201). A set of tastes in commodities, literature, entertainment, and so forth, was intended to cohere into a recognizable ensemble, and that ensemble appealed to and organized a very large audience.

Yet many of the counterpublic spheres that emerged using the same technologies attempted, often problematically, to forge a different kind of unity between widely disparate concerns and points of view. As I have demonstrated, the *Egoist,* the *Little Review,* the *Masses,* and other such magazines aimed at a sense of openness and wide-ranging heterogeneous literary, artistic, political, social, and philosophical contributions and actually emphasized difference and plurality over the consolidation of a singular identity. These attempts—not to reduce complexity to singularity, but rather to sustain heterogeneity—often led to problems of fragmentation. The multiple determinants of audience identification and identity—politics, class, ethnic identity, gender and sexual identity, and, of course, aesthetics—made the logic of the capitalist press difficult to adopt.

Moreover, while cheaper paper and print technologies made little magazines possible, the cultural aspirations of many of these early magazines to reach mass audiences and achieve widespread cultural influence also foundered on another problem—capitalization. Publishers like Harmsworth and Curtis could sink enormous amounts of money into self-advertisement, distribution, and production. Most modernist magazines could not. The *English Review* had major publishing houses behind it (Duckworth, and then Chapman and Hall), and its post-Fordian incarnation flourished for almost three decades. Most little magazines could not count on such support from a major publisher. The *Dial* in 1922 was able to achieve a circulation of around 9,500—excellent in little magazine terms—primarily because it could count on $73,300 in yearly patronage, compared to $2,350 for the *Little Review* (Rainey 98).

Yet, even though early modernist hopes for creating mass circulation papers on their own terms were dampened by the twenties, this does not at all suggest that modernism's relationship to markets was over, or that modernism didn't thrive in the twenties—quite the contrary. Of course the commercial press had noticed modernism, and one mass market magazine that made an exceptional effort to support modernist art and literature— Frank Crowninshield's *Vanity Fair*—had a circulation of 96,500 in 1922 and drew in $500,000 in advertising revenues and some $357,000 in circulation revenues (Rainey 98). *Vanity Fair* brought post–Armory Show modernist art and even some literary modernism to "the Tired Business Man"; moreover, it showed that modernism's appropriation of commercial culture had become a two-way street, as advertisers for everything from men's footwear to Steinway pianos began to adopt modernist visual idioms in their advertisements (see Murphy).

And, as Lawrence Rainey amply demonstrates, modernists displayed their entrepreneurial abilities in other ways as well: Eliot parlayed his as yet unread poem, *The Waste Land,* into publication in both his own *Criterion* and the *Dial,* a guarantee of $2,000 from the Dial Award for 1922, and a book contract with Horace Liveright. Moreover, Sylvia Beach and James Joyce created a new lucrative investment market for limited editions and, through monopolistic practices of scarcity, created a new kind of patronage for modernists through the Shakespeare and Company first edition of *Ulysses* in 1922. Modernism thus intentionally commodified itself and profited, not from the larger commercial economy, but rather from "a different economic circuit of patronage, collecting, speculation, and investment—activities that precisely in this period begin to encroach upon and merge into one another in unexpected ways" (Rainey 3). Accepting a Habermasian vision of the modern public sphere as a degeneration of public culture, Rainey argues that in the 1920s and 1930s modernism beat "a tactical retreat into a divided world of patronage, collecting, speculation, and investment, a retreat that entailed the construction of an institutional counter-space securing a momentary respite from a public realm increasingly degraded, even as it entailed a fatal compromise with precisely that degradation" (5).

Even if modernism could be seen as retreating from the specific kinds of public interventions in culture I have described, the 1920s hardly spelled the end of little magazines as a key mode of publication for experimental and modernist literature. Indeed, mass market publishing, advertising, and consumer culture coalesced as the dominant cultural apparatus for the century in the 1920s, and little magazines became the perennial alternative form of publication. One list of little magazine holdings compiled at midcentury counted 1,037 of them in five American university libraries. Recent works on the genre have added hundreds more.[1] But despite this proliferation, the brief early moment in which modernists envisioned little magazines as critical and heterogeneous counterpublicity that could, nevertheless, walk in the paths of the mass market–driven public sphere seemed to have passed—if not completely, certainly in tendency.

Interestingly, just as print and papermaking technologies made both the mass market press and modernist magazines possible, technological shifts—like the move to offset printing in the 1960s and word processing and desktop publishing in the 1980s and 1990s—have again contributed to the burgeoning of little magazines. (It is impossible even to begin to assess the impact that electronic publication and the new kinds of public interactions through the Internet will have in the new millennium.) Descriptions of contemporary little magazines emphasize a vision of their role that early modernist editors would have resisted, however; current little magazines are painted as self-consciously amateurish, anticommercial, supported by subscription revenue rather than by advertising, and, above all, aimed only at small, select audiences—the very description Hoffman, Allen, and Ulrich codified in the 1940s. Wolfgang Görtschacher's *Little Magazine Profiles: The Little Magazines in Great Britain 1939–1993*, for instance, reinforces this view: "Editors disdain any aspirations for their magazines to become more than a publication for those few with a commitment towards poetry and its most important means of publication" (24). That such a modest and limiting view of audience and of the public role of experimental literature would seem inevitable now—and that this understanding, not only of little magazines, but also of modernism's assumptions about itself, has been orthodoxy for so long—makes a revisiting of the early optimistic period of modernist publication, and the social and cultural changes that produced it, all the more important. It is not simply the poetry and fiction of the modernist era, but rather the complex cultural weave of the magazines in which they were published, the material and institutional practices that those magazines deployed, and the social discourses that surrounded them that can tell us much about the public aspirations of modernism—and about art's potential to transform public culture today, at the beginning of a century.

In fact, I suspect that early modernists might have been encouraged by the prospect of the publication of thousands of little magazines across the century. The very existence of projects like the Pushcart Prize anthology (now in its third decade, and brought out by a major publisher, W. W. Norton), which culls small presses and little magazines for strong new work to bring into a best-selling volume, suggests that small presses and little magazines—owing much to the modernists in this book—still have a kind of conduit into the broader commercial market, and have a staying power that appears virtually endless. Little magazines' specific relationships to commercial publishing have gone through several alterations since the beginning of the century, but even if the expectations for the kinds of interventions a single little magazine can make in our culture have been scaled back somewhat since the early modernist era, the ongoing popularity of the genre reveals a persistent desire to maintain a social—even public—role for unorthodox and challenging new voices, and a persistent faith in their transformative power.

Notes
Works Cited
Index

Notes

Following is a list of manuscript collection abbreviations used in the "Notes" and "Works Cited."

BL	British Library
HSW	Harriet Shaw Weaver Papers
CUKL	Cornell University, Kroch Library
FMF	Ford Madox Ford Collection
WL	Wyndham Lewis Collection
IUL	Indiana University Bloomington, Lilly Library
ME	Max Eastmann MSS.
CM	Claude McKay MSS.
JWR3	James Whitcomb Riley MSS. III
US	Upton Sinclair MSS.
NL	Newberry Library, Chicago
FDP	Floyd Dell Papers
NUML	Northwestern University, McCormick Library of Special Collections, Evanston, IL
PP	James B. Pinker Papers
PUF	Princeton University, Firestone Library
DMP	Dora Marsden Papers
UCLA	University of California, Los Angeles, Research Library
HMP	Harold Monro Papers

UTHRC   University of Texas at Austin, Harry Ransom Humanities
            Research Center

UWGM   University of Wisconsin–Milwaukee, Golda Meir Library
LRR   *Little Review* Records

Introduction

1. For discussion of the British context, see R. Williams, 200–201, and for the
American, see Ohmann 57–58. See also Hannah on the "merger mania" of the
period from 1888 to 1914 (25), and Aaronovitch for discussion of publishing and
other combines.

2. Poirier 98. Hoffman, Allen, and Ulrich is an early and influential statement
of the anticommercial and anti–mass audience nature of modernist little magazines—a view reinforced by current textbooks of modernism like Bradbury and
McFarlane.

3. See, for instance, Dettmar and Watt's wide-ranging anthology and Wexler.
Seminal work is also being done in modernist art history, for example, Jensen.
Taking a different approach, Tratner has examined the sociopolitical contexts of
modernism, looking at theories of the crowd and "mass mind." He has argued that
"collectivist political theories, theories of the mass mind, and modernist literature
all were intertwined as part of a general change in discourse," one that subordi-
nates individuality to mass phenomena (3).

4. And in fact, the separation of life praxis and art admits of more than one
interpretation. As Habermas notes in *Legitimation Crisis,* the loss of aesthetic autonomy "can just as easily signify the degeneration of art into propagandistic mass
art or into commercialized mass culture as, on the other hand, transform itself
into a subversive counterculture." In other words, the destruction of aura can lead
not to an oppositional avant-garde but to support for fascism or—again stacking
the deck against the twentieth-century public sphere—affirmative commercial culture (86). Habermas has written comparatively little on art's function in the public
sphere. In *The Structural Transformation of the Public Sphere* he discusses the
emergence of a literary public sphere in the seventeenth and eighteenth centuries
that allowed the bourgeoisie to understand its own subjectivity through reading
novels and other literary works, but which also, through the development of magazines and newspapers, helped to make the political public sphere possible. But
Habermas strikes a pessimistic chord. He critiques what he envisions as the split-
ting off of cultural specialists, suggesting that "the avant-garde as an institution"
is an aspect of our current society in which "the public is split apart into minorities
of specialists who put their reason to use non-publicly and the great mass of consumers whose reception is public but uncritical" (175). For Habermas's later work
during the 1970s upholding bourgeois aesthetic autonomy as a space of resistance
and critique of capitalist culture, see his "Consciousness-Raising or Redemptive
Criticism—The Contemporaneity of Walter Benjamin" and *Legitimation Crisis*
(78). See also Jay, "Habermas and Modernism."

5. Bürger himself, admitting the failure of the historic avant-garde to reunite
art and praxis, wonders "whether the distance between art and the praxis of life is

not requisite for that free space within which alternatives to what exists become conceivable" (*Theory* 54). This understanding, I would argue, was closer to that of many British and American modernists than the historical avant-gardist attitudes that Bürger describes.

6. Fraser even argues that, besides evidence that such an ideal liberal public sphere never existed, it is not even a tenable goal for contemporary democracies, as Habermas still holds.

7. Indeed, challenging Habermas's negative vision of the twentieth-century public sphere's relationship to commercial culture, Cowen recently argued that the commercialized culture of modernity has *not* corrupted the public sphere and stifled the production of experimental art, as Ford, Monro, Eliot, Pound, and, of course, Habermas, imagined. Quite to the contrary, he argues that "The capitalist market economy is a vital but underappreciated institutional framework for supporting a plurality of coexisting artistic visions, providing a steady stream of new and satisfying creations, helping consumers and artists refine their tastes, and paying homage to the eclipsed past by capturing, reproducing, and disseminating it" (1)—outcomes most modernists would have applauded.

8. See, for instance, the insightful work of Levenson or Sherry.

9. Not only did the mid-1960s witness Kraus's invaluable service of providing reprints of scores of little magazines, it also saw a number of extremely useful book-length studies of particular magazines. See, for example, Martin; Grant, which contains a wealth of information about Monro's magazines (the *Poetry Review, Poetry and Drama,* and the *Chapbook*); Lidderdale and Nicholson, which discusses the publication of the *New Freewoman* and the *Egoist;* and Bryer.

10. See Keating for a discussion of the surge of publication, especially of fiction, but also of the crippling effect that the abandonment of the old 31 $^1/_2$s. triple-decker format for the single-volume 6s. novel had on young authors.

Chapter 1. The Myth of the Whole and Ford's *English Review:* Edwardian Monthlies, the *Mercure de France,* and Early British Modernism

1. In England, originating with Lord Shaftesbury at the beginning of the century, and evolving through thinkers like Hutcheson, Burke, and Alison, and finally to Addison, a notion of disinterestedness arose; by the end of the century, it had set off the aesthetic as a distinctive mode of experience for the first time in Western thought (see Stolnitz). But, as Bürger notes, "What is bourgeois in Kant's [aesthetic theory] is precisely the demand that the aesthetic judgment have universal validity. The pathos of universality is characteristic of the bourgeoisie, which fights the feudal nobility as an estate that represents particular interests" (*Theory* 43).

2. As Bromwich suggests, Arnold's disinterestedness is one almost of selflessness, of critical detachment from self into an objective ahistorical normative realm: Arnold's ideal of objectivity "becomes indistinguishable from an aristocratic ideal of detachment" (75).

3. Habermas notes that "The parties were now confronted with the job of 'integrating' the mass of the citizenry (no longer really 'bourgeois'), with the help of new methods, for the purpose of getting their votes. The gathering of voters for the sake of bringing the local delegate to account had to make room for systematic

propaganda. Now for the first time there emerged something like modern propaganda, from the very start with the Janus face of enlightenment and control; of information and advertising; of pedagogy and manipulation" (*Structural* 203).

4. The latter involved not only the entrance of the working classes into the public sphere, but also, especially after the first Reform Bill (1832) provided institutional validation for the bourgeoisie in Parliament, the rise in importance of the central party apparatus and its control of public discourse (Habermas *Structural*).

5. Holmes notes that as a result of the concept of self-interest, "Particular attention was paid to a discrepancy between the interests of citizens and the interests of wielders of power—a gap formerly papered over by uplifting rhetoric about the public good. . . . The postulate of *universal* self-interest helped [Smith] demolish the old illusion that harmony was a natural product of hierarchy and subordination" (284).

6. By December 31, 1908, *The Fifth Queen* had sold 2,850 copies (decent sales for the period). See Melrose.

7. Instead of buying the *Academy,* Harmsworth soon decided to attract publishers' advertisements by starting a Books Supplement to the *Daily Mail.* Under a cloud of confusion, Harmsworth seems to have fired Ford from the *Daily Mail,* and he discontinued the Books Supplement altogether after July 1907. The circumstances of Ford's departure from the *Daily Mail* are still not clear. See Mizener 121–122; Goldring, *Trained,* 136; and Judd 153.

8. The portraits were of Swinburne, Wells, Zangwill, Jacobs, Frederic Harrison, Hilaire Belloc, W. D. Howells, Shaw, William de Morgan, Mark Twain, Father Hugh Benson, Hardy, S. R. Crockett, and Corelli.

9. Ford letter to Pinker, copy in CUKL, *FMF;* original in the Pinker collection at the Huntington Library.

10. The novel did not appear until March 1909, and Ford complained bitterly that its sales were low only because the publisher, Nash, failed to advertise it sufficiently. See Ford letter to Pinker, March 24, 1909 (*Letters* 38–39).

11. See, for example, the *Daily Mail*'s illustrated special section "Miss Marie George / the Famous Drury Lane Actress / Spends a Day Shopping in London" (Dec. 12, 1908). Of the *Strand,* R. Pound claims that "regular features like *Portraits of Celebrities* and *From Behind The Speaker's Chair* had much to do with consolidating the circulation and prestige of the magazine in those years" (85). The *Strand* also enhanced the already popular genre of celebrity interview found in the *Pall Mall Gazette* by adding photographs to create its "Illustrated Interviews" (85).

12. The "pianola," a mechanical device that attached to a piano, was extremely popular in London's middle-class homes during this period and became, for Pound, a symbol of a debased culture: "The pianola 'replaces' / Sappho's barbitos" (*Hugh Selwyn Mauberley* 189). In "The Piano-Player and the Music of the Future," Newman defends these mechanized pianos against the apparently widespread charge that they debase the art of piano playing (247). Pianola advertising campaigns targeted the middle class in reviews like the *Saturday Review,* with drawings of women in elegant bourgeois attire in a comfortable parlor playing the pianola for each other. Several advertisements by the "Orchestrelle Company" offered "The Pianola Piano, . . . one of the greatest attractions you can secure for your home." They emphasized the social prestige, the educational opportunity on

the most popular instrument of the bourgeois household, and the financial affordability of their product (see *Saturday Review,* Jan. 9 and Feb. 6 and 20, 1909).

13. Among the group is a "designer of advertisements" who "found his serious interests in Esoteric Buddhism and psychical research." The presence of this advertiser and theosophist at a real miracle ironically foreshadows the bogus séance at the office of the "great man," the newspaper magnate Lord Aldington.

14. In "England's Taste in Literature," a hardly "scientific," but certainly well-conceived early twentieth-century exploration of literary taste in Edwardian London, Blathwayt found Corelli not only to be "the heroine almost divine of the great middle classes" (165), but also to be immensely popular with largely female upper-class society circles, Anglican clergy, the lower middle class, especially among the young, and the "clerk and shop-girl class."

15. As with most of Ford's novels, sales of *Mr Apollo* never lived up to his expectations. But sales were relatively good for a Ford novel: of the initial 2,000 copies printed, around 1,700 had been sold by December 31, 1908, and an edition of 500 copies was printed in February 1911. See Harvey 28.

16. By the late nineteenth century, Newnes's press machinery in the basement of Southampton Street, through which the public could tour, could print *Tit-Bits* at the rate of 24,000 copies per hour. Harmsworth also opened his facilities to tourists (R. Pound 53).

17. In a letter to Edward Garnett (Dec. 1908?), Ford responds to Garnett's criticism in a review of *Mr. Apollo:* "You say the book is a failure at the end because I have resisted the temptation to bring in a Northcliffe [Alfred Harmsworth] 200 ft. high. It seems to me to be a treachery to Form. . . . I cut out three whole chapters devoted to N. to avoid this and my conscience commends me still. But then . . . " (*Letters* 29).

18. Ford letter to Bennett.

19. Ford letter to "Monsieur et cher Confrère," on *English Review* letterhead. Unfortunately, the identity of the recipient remains a mystery. It seems to be written to someone at the *Mercure de France*—I conjecture Rémy de Gourmont or perhaps Henry Davray; however, it could possibly be to Arnold Bennett—a follow-up to Bennett's response to the letter concerning exchange advertisements with the *Mercure.* It would be tempting to read the last line of the letter, "I only make the request with much hesitation as my only claim upon your attention is the fact that I imagine our aims have very much in common, at any rate in the world of literature," as an explicit statement of affinity with the *Mercure.*

20. For the first four numbers of the *English Review,* the revenue from advertisements was only around £140. For each of those issues, the money paid out for contributions was around £300, and the cost of printing and distributing each issue was around £200. The circulation was around 1,000 copies per issue, thus bringing in only about £100 per issue (Mizener 160). With around £500 going out each month and only £135 coming in, the magazine quickly ran into financial trouble. Increasing advertising revenues would have helped the journal, though the poor circulation and Ford's ineptness at pursuing advertisements closed that door to financial solvency.

21. See "Rémy de Gourmont" as one of many examples of Aldington's devotion to Gourmont and his praise of the *Mercure.* See also von Hallberg, "Ezra

Pound and the *Mercure de France.*" Pound even suggested that Monro adopt "the Mercure's system of rubrics" for *Poetry and Drama,* claiming that "there is no general intelligencer of that sort in England or America" (E. Pound letter to Monro, June 24, 1914).

22. Ford writes: "'How,' [his reader] will say, 'is any emotion to be roused by the mere first night of a Shepherd's Bush exhibition? Poetry is written about love, about country lanes, about the singing of birds.' I think it is not—not nowadays. We are too far from these things. What we are in, that which is all around us, is the Crowd—the Crowd blindly looking for joy or for that most pathetic of all things, the good time . . . this immense Crowd suddenly let loose upon a sort of Tom Tiddler's ground to pick up the glittering splinters of glass that are the Romance, hesitant but certain of vistas of adventure, if no more than the adventures of their own souls . . . I think pathos and poetry are to be found beneath those lights and in those sounds" (*Collected Poems* 16).

23. Ford writes: "We seemed to get from [Tennyson, Swinburne, and Browning] the idea that all poets must of necessity write affectedly, at great length, with many superfluous words—that poetry, of necessity, was something boring and pretentious. And I fancy that it is because the greater part of humanity get that impression from those poets that few modern men or women read verse at all" (*Collected Poems* 22).

24. At least forty-five French magazines and newspapers reviewed this book, which claimed to provide a factual and responsible historical understanding of the outbreak of the war by examining three civilizations—those of England, France, and Germany. *Between St. Dennis and St. George* is jingoistic in Ford's particular way, and its highly negative assessment of Germany is clearly not consistent with his much more complicated relationship to Germany in his 1911 volume of poems, *High Germany.*

25. Of course, it is the Germans who are accused of "a certain clumsiness of language, a certain clinging to obsolescence of phrase, and a certain resultant stupidity and want of imagination" and the catastrophe will be "largely on account of German inexactitude" (*BSD* 69).

26. For instance, the "chivalric" codes of soldiers, in which Tietjens believes, are ascribed to the eighteenth century (*Parade's End* 667). In *Between St. Dennis and St. George,* Ford notes the pervasiveness of French chivalry, "the most valuable thing in the world: I have given a little impression of how all the chivalry in the world came from France. Fine views and a generous climate breed a race that can afford to be *genereux*" (*BSD* 221).

27. See Arnold's essay "The Function of Criticism at the Present Time," and, for an in-depth discussion of Arnold's relationship to the eighteenth century, see Carroll, especially chapter 4 "The Style of Reason."

28. Of this first issue, dated January 1, 1890, of the 600 copies printed, 500 were given away as review copies—there were only eleven subscribers (Forestier 4). There are several essays describing the founding and early years of the *Mercure de France:* Gourmont's essay and Aldington's essay "Rémy de Gourmont" are good period accounts. See also the six essays on the *Mercure* in the 1890s in *Revue d'Histoire Littéraire de la France.*

29. Though the *Mercure* was very much interested in publishing and dis-

cussing symbolist writing, even publishing Mallarmé, Gourmont writes of Vallette, "Je ne crois pas qu'il ait changé d'avis en passant par la 'Pléiade', et quand il organisa *le Mercure de France,* son intention était très loin d'en vouloir faire un recueil symboliste" (82). Aldington mentions that the young founders were "far from considering themselves Symbolistes" ("Rémy de Gourmont" 174). This distancing from symbolism is important because, while the journal did in fact publish and support symbolist literature from the start, even mounting a strong attack on Zola, it quickly developed into something other than a symbolist coterie magazine. Like a committed avant-garde manifesto, Vallette's editorial in the first issue of the *Mercure* defends the *Pléiade* and its follower, the *Mercure,* against charges of decadence, and much of his rhetoric is of subversion, bravely attacking the press and an unconsciously hypocritical public during a period of transition in literary values. However, even in this first issue, Vallette defines the goal of the *Mercure* as different from purely commercial endeavors as well as school-forming periodicals: "Aussi, des trois buts que peut se proposer un périodique littéraire—ou gagner de l'argent, ou grouper des auteurs en communion d'esthétique, formant école et s'efforcant au prosélytisme, ou enfin publier des ouvres purement artistiques et des conceptions assez hétérodoxes pour n'être point accueillies des feuilles qui comptent avec la clientèle—c'est ce dernier que nous avons choisi" ("Mercure de France" 4). He adds "chacun est ici absolument libre, responsable de ses seuls dires et point solidaire du voisin." The journal thus self-consciously attempted not to be merely another symbolist magazine, though it evidenced some contempt toward "le public, indifférent en ces matières," and adopted the elitist rhetoric of defiance toward popular audiences. However, over the next few years, its stance toward audiences began to change.

30. In the 1880s, many little magazines sprang up, often around young unknown symbolist or "decadent" authors: *Le Scapin, La Revue Blanche, Le Décadent, La Vogue, Le Symboliste,* and, in 1886, *La Pléiade.* Out of the death of the symbolist *Pléiade* and from *Le Scapin*—an imitation of the weekly *Vogue* edited by the young Alfred Vallette—came the *Mercure de France.* The *Revue Blanche* foundered in April 1903, *La Plume* barely made it through 1904 and had to unite with the review *Europe Artiste* in January 1905, and *L'Ermitage* died in 1905. See Décaudin (14) and de Broglie (338) for discussion of the nature and demise of these magazines.

31. The range of foreign literature reviewed in the *Mercure* was quite impressive even in the 1890s. It included English, German, Scandinavian, Russian, Spanish, Latin American, American, Italian, Czech, Polish, Romanian, and even Portuguese.

32. The correspondence, a regular feature of the "Echoes" section in the "Revue de la Quinzaine," often involved a reader's response to an article or issue raised in the journal, which was frequently followed by a response from the author of the article. Sometimes a contentious topic would involve a longer running exchange, a debate between the author and multiple respondents, even from within the magazine.

33. As the *Mercure* cemented its success in January 1905 by becoming a bimonthly, Vallette's leadoff editorial manifesto, "Bimensuel," stresses the disinterestedness of the writers of the early days, and the desires of the public, which

fifteen years ago he had virtually dismissed: "on y verrait comment la bonne volonté d'un groupe d'écrivains, l'esprit de suite et aussi quelque désintéressement valent mieux parfois que de gros capitaux; comment un périodique né indépendant, formé des éléments les plus hétérogènes, a pu garder sa liberté tout entière, suivi du reste par un public compréhensif qui voulut bien entendre les paroles les plus contradictoires" (5). He laments that the daily press has had to commercialize to survive economically—to turn to advertisement as its main concern—and that in so doing, has lost what it offered in the past in its articles, chronicles, varieties, and weekly serials: "l'opinion désintéressée d'écrivains qui savent ce qu'ils disent et qui, autant que possible, ont eu le temps de l'écrire" (6). As von Hallberg has suggested, when Pound later envisioned editing his own magazine, it was precisely the range and centrism of the *Mercure de France* that inspired him ("Ezra Pound").

34. In a letter to Pinker of January 1908 (Mizener 133), encouraging Pinker to convince Nash to publish another of his novels, Ford says, "Tell him that the whole Literary World not only of England but of Europe are anxiously awaiting the 3d V Queen and show him the Revue des deux mondes to back up the statement." Ford refers to T. de Wyzewa's article, "Le Roman Anglais en 1907," which praised his *Privy Seal*. Francis Charmes, its editor and a member of the Academy Française, was one of the names on Ford's list, in his 1908 letter, of possible diplomatic contributors to the *English Review.* As Maurice Schumann puts it: "*La Revue des Deux Mondes* est avant tout préoccupée de cohésion sociale et nationale. Elle est toujours libérale, mais elle devient modérée, catholique et patriote" (de Broglie 15). I have not been able to find circulation figures for the *Mercure* in 1908, but, if the comparison is a valid one, the *Revue des Deux Mondes* had around 26,000 subscribers in 1885 and 40,000 in 1914. It sank to 15,000 during the war but more than tripled after it to 48,000 (de Broglie 338). It maintained a large and steady readership.

35. The original format for the journal was a series of anonymous letters to "Madame," who had left Paris to reside in the provinces and wished to keep up with her fashionable friends. The editor Donneau de Visé worked into these letters not only court gossip, but above all a variety of amusing but informative reviews and discussions. Such topics as the establishment of the Academie d'Architecture, the reception of Monsieur le Duc de la Feuillade by the French Guards, the drama of Corneille, news of his trip from a "traveller" in Egypt, and reviews of other magazines, like the scientifically inclined *Journal des Scavans* found their way into the pages of the *Mercure*—a wide range of intellectual, political, and literary subjects of interest to the inquiring mind of 1672. Madame, in her state of isolation, "needed" a man of the world to educate and brief her; her correspondent perfectly figured the authoritative, educational, informative, and critical—yet amusing—role the journal would play in the lives of the French bourgeoisie. Throughout the various editorships in the eighteenth century, the focus remained on belle-lettres and beaux arts, as well as on world and national affairs.

36. The *Mercure de France* must have been the source of this section in the *English Review;* only one major English review featured anything remotely resembling it—the *National Review*'s "Episodes of the Month" section—but this section

began each issue and was composed entirely of the editor's reflections on political events. Ford also adopted the "Revue de la Quinzaine's" practice of beginning each section with an italicized list of the topics or books to be reviewed.

37. In his historicist "aesthetics of reception," Jauss also foregrounds the constitutive role of genre in the creation and understanding of literary texts (20) and seeks to describe the shifting meaning of literary works in terms of the audience's "horizon of expectations," which includes, among other factors, "a pre-understanding of the genre, from the form and themes of already familiar works" (22). Hirsch's hermeneutics are built on the idea that recognizing the "particular norms of a particular genre" is central to every act of communication (71), and that "the details of meaning that an interpreter understands are powerfully determined and constituted by his meaning expectations" (72).

38. Lucy Brown shows that the government chose certain papers to favor with advertising its government lists, but that patronage often went far beyond this. The influx of partisan capital created many new newspapers during the period, though frequently after they had become established and could support themselves on their own commercial basis they backed away from the overt control by the party committees. Brown notes that a "consequence of party involvement was that a competition between newspapers became the norm in provincial Britain, and was organized and articulated through comment on the party struggle" (71).

39. After Lewes's editorial tenure was ended by poor health in 1866, John Morley propelled the magazine into the more radical currents of Mill's utilitarianism, Comte's positivism, and Darwin's evolutionary theories. He was succeeded by T. H. S. Escott in 1882, and then in 1886 by Frank Harris. Harris, who was to continue his flamboyant career with the *Saturday Review* and *Vanity Fair* in later years, moved beyond "respectable" radicalism and was fired by the publisher Chapman and Hall in 1894.

40. Pinker letter to Hunt.

41. In the first advertisement in the *Saturday Review*, for instance, the three pieces listed in large bold type are two political articles—"The Personality of the German Emperor" and H. W. Nevinson's "The Balkan Question" (another prominent topic in the reviews that year)—and *Tono-Bungay*. Only in smaller type are listed the literary pieces by Hardy, James, Conrad, Galsworthy, Hudson, and Tolstoy, as well as some of the other political articles of "The Month." The *English Review* tailored its advertisement to the venues in which they appeared, emphasizing articles or stories that might be of interest to the readers of those periodicals; for instance, its advertisement in the *Evening Standard and St. James's Gazette* (Nov. 25, 1908, 6) mentioned only two pieces from the first issue, the essay "The Personality of the German Emperor"—a popular topic in the daily papers as Anglo-German relations worsened—and Wells's *Tono-Bungay*, the serial designed to launch the *English Review* into popular waters.

42. Hardy, who topped the list in the "Reply" as he had led off the first number of the *English Review*, Sydney Brooks, Professor Maurice Gerothwohl, Frederic Harrison, Tolstoy, Gosse, Hewlett, Sidney Low, and G. S. Street.

43. Long after his ouster from the *English Review*, Ford seems to have seen it as occupying a niche in the periodical world similar to the *Fortnightly*. In a letter

to Pinker on January 6, 1918, he writes, about his poem "Footsloggers," "Possibly a daily paper would publish it—or possibly the Fortnightly or the English Review" (*Letters* 85).

44. While much of the content of the *English Review* was written by Liberals, Radicals, and Socialists, Ford himself did not think easily within party lines. At times he considered himself a Tory, but he espoused suffrage, Home Rule, and other Liberal causes. The *English Review* did not, as an editorial policy, follow a doctrinaire or partisan line in its interests or editorials, as did, say, the *Spectator* or the *Saturday Review.* The main reason that the Liberal member of Parliament Sir Alfred Mond fired Ford when he bought the magazine was that he disagreed with his politics. Ford wrote to Scott-James: "Mr. Mond has now ejected me from the editorial chair because he is a Liberal which no one could accuse me of being. (And you might publish the facts in the Daily News as one more instance of political terrorism)" (*Letters* 39–40).

45. For basic accounts of the purpose and founding of the *English Review,* see Goldring *South Lodge* and *Trained;* Judd; MacShane; and Bradbury, *"The English Review."*

46. For instance, as Conrad wrote to Ford on October 10, 1908: "If I may be allowed to give my opinion I think that a 2nd story from 'Anatole' is a mistake . . . with H. G. and myself going on [in serial publication] you must guard against stereotyping the Review" (Conrad letter to Ford).

47. Peppis shows how Lewis's three travel tales in the *English Review,* "The 'Pole,'" "Some Innkeepers and Bestre," and "Les Saltimbanques," both imitated and assailed the literary conventions of other *English Review* impressionistic travel stories (like those of Cunninghame Graham, Douglas, Hudson, and Allen), in order to critique their ideology (25–27).

48. In London, Harmsworth's mass market *Daily Mail* wrote, "A new monthly review devoted to literature, and chiefly to fictional literature of the highest class, must be very good if it is to succeed these days. 'The English Review'—or at any rate, the first number of it—is very good" (Nov. 28, 1908). The *Daily Mail* emphasized, as one might expect, the contributions from Wells, James, Tolstoy, Galsworthy, Hardy, Hudson, and Conrad. The *Evening Standard and St. James Gazette* proclaimed, "It would hardly be possible to make a list more representative within the limits of one issue of a periodical of the best in current English literature," and called the *English Review* "a genuine literary monthly . . . cheap at the price" (Nov. 25, 1908).

In the Liberal *Daily News,* Scott-James, who was soon to contribute to the *English Review,* wrote that "there are here 192 solid pages of literature—literature, be it noted, not literary matter." He tries along Arnoldian lines to interpret Ford's vision of the relationship between the literary issues and social and political ones, and he suggests that the *English Review* differs in this respect from these journals: "What the editor means is that in the very act of being concerned with arts and letters we must necessarily be concerned with their effect upon the mind—the self-knowledge, the perception, the stimulation which mean new ideas, new judgments, and a clear vision of the world around us." Like the *Evening Standard* reviewer, Scott-James saw the *English Review* as a bargain for such a collection of the best on the Edwardian scene.

The Unionist *Pall Mall Gazette* regularly reviewed the early issues of the *English Review* and saw it as "the latest addition to the ranks of serious periodicals . . . a high-class literary magazine—now so sparsely represented amongst our periodicals" (Dec. 3, 1908, 10). It proclaimed that "its traits are not those of any other publication, and its pages must appeal very strongly indeed to those who are interested in the principal forces of current literature" (Jan. 5, 1909, 5). Like the other dailies, the *Pall Mall* mostly noted the literary content, though it suggested that the *English Review* "takes a line of its own in its attitude to current affairs" (Feb. 2, 1909, 10).

49. The bigoted Douglas impugned Ford's reputation with insinuation about his German background (and later attacked Sir Alfred Mond's Jewishness), but while he endlessly proclaimed his distaste for the *English Review*, he also obsessively reviewed it.

50. The *Spectator* wrote, "The latter part of the magazine has a good deal to say, as usual, about a group of writers which the editors have taken under their special protection. Indeed, the monthly dissertations on the merits of Messrs. Galsworthy, Bernard Shaw, Granville Barker, H. G. Wells and others have become monotonous" (Nov. 6, 1909, 749); and again, "The writer of the 'Critical Attitude' in the *English Review* has, we are glad to see, taken the advice offered him by ourselves and others, as he acknowledges, and this month refrains from singing the praises of his own special and limited Pantheon" (Feb. 5, 1910, 228).

51. Like Bennett in attacking the photo-laden illustrated magazines, O'Connor seems to have sensed this as he wrote: "It is with something of dismay that the lovers of the magazine have seen the 'debacle' of the last ten years. One after another names that were once honourable have vanished; one may almost say that 'Blackwood's' is the last survivor of the heroes, of the days when the literary magazine was a feature in the intellectual life of England. They were sometimes dull, the old magazines; there was a tendency to insert many heavy pages of 'world-politics'—stuff about 'Russian Intrigues at the Court of Teheran'—still they kept up a high standard. And now, when the photographic snapshot has taken their place, the 'English Review' comes forward in the name of the old traditions, plus (as I understand) a certain 'outspoken sincerity,' a fearlessness of too-rigid convention." O'Connor understood the notion of a literary magazine that could also be an independent and lively intellectual journal.

52. The *Saturday Review* illustrates how obvious this assessment probably seemed. Its column on the monthlies was arranged, not according to the journal reviewed, but according to a topic each month that was taken up by many of the journals—for instance, Russia, the Balkans, the Budget, or Germany and the naval buildup. The *English Review* usually had an article to be tossed into this soup of monthly pieces on each topic. Only at the end of this section did the *Saturday Review* mention the purely literary content of the magazines—and this was frequently omitted. The *Athenæum* even wrote of the first *English Review:* "We doubt of the advisability of entering into current politics, which are already over-represented in the magazines" (Dec. 5, 1908, 720).

53. Harrison emphasized continuity with Ford's *English Review*, proclaiming in a circular (distributed in Mar. 1910 to solicit subscriptions) that the *English Review* had achieved its goals: "A glance at the names of the contributors and of

the subjects treated in the *English Review* should suffice to assure the readers that the main objects of this publication have been achieved. Those objects were, broadly speaking, to gather within its covers the most intimate writings of the best authors of the day, both in England and on the Continent, and to put before the public the works of authors at present unknown, but who, in the judgment of the *Review,* may be expected to carry on the thought of to-morrow.

"Since the *Review* started the greatest names in English literature have figured in its pages; those, for instance, of Mr. Maurice Hewlett, Mr. Henry James, Mr. Joseph Conrad, Mr. John Galsworthy, Tolstoi, Mr. H. G. Wells, Anatole France, Mr. Cunninghame Graham, Mr. Granville Barker, Vernon Lee, Mr. Arnold Bennett, etc."

54. Following closely a statement of editorial intention by Harrison, a reviewer from the *Observer* wrote that Harrison "intends to maintain the literary standard set up by its late editor, Mr. Hueffer, and to afford every encouragement to rising authors. As before, the *Review* will stand for reform, enlightenment, literature, and independence. Doubtless its politics will be more definitely on pro-Liberal lines, but the national interests will be fully kept in view. Many of the most notable writers of the day have promised their support and co-operation. Poetry will continue to be a feature, and the true literary story. Both the proprietor and the new editor are determined to see whether a literary Review, such as the *Mercure de France,* cannot be permanently established, not only as an artistic venture, but also as a welcome one" (in *Academy,* Jan. 22, 1910, 76). Harrison shortened the length of the *English Review* to a more manageable 160 or so pages, kept it a monthly in order to remain in the niche of the prevailing monthly review and magazine segment of Edwardian periodicals, lowered its standard of literature but widened its audiences, and increased the partisanship of the review, probably thereby gaining a loyal liberal following. Harrison buttressed the *English Review's* respectability and increased its solvency—partially, no doubt, by running the business end better than Ford could, but largely by mimicking established Edwardian periodicals.

55. For instance, in a letter to Pinker of January 12, 1912, Harrison wrote, "about a humorist . . . what the public likes is of course a Dickens or Dan Leno kind of a writer, such as Jacobs—someone, in fact, who can write light stuff of a literary kind." Leno (George Galvin) was a music-hall singer and dancer famous for his caricatures and monologues and author of a burlesque autobiography, *Dan Leno: His Book* (1901). Jacobs was the *Strand* humorist par excellence, and so had a wide middle-class audience; however, he also had a large upper-class society readership (Blathwayt, 162), and, as the *English Review* wrote, "Mr. W. W. Jacobs [is] the favourite author of politicians on holiday" (Dec. 1913, 155). It is clear then that Harrison wanted to find humorous material to appeal to the widest strata of readers—from the lower-middle-class music hall audiences to the upper-class society set.

56. Peppis shows that not only did the *English Review* predominantly publish liberal and socialist articles, but it also shared much of the liberal imperialism and nationalism of its day.

57. Harrison began to tamper with Ford's *Mercure*-inspired "The Month" sec-

tion, leaving it out entirely in June 1910, but often simply making it a forum for his political editorials, like the *National Review's* "Episodes of the Month."

58. For instance, his diatribe against protectionism in April 1910 was followed by Harold Cox's "The Policy of Free Imports," or his editorial against the House of Lords was followed in May 1910 by an article from Sir Alfred Mond entitled "Remedies for Parliamentary Deadlock," which, of course, suggested curtailing the veto power of the House of Lords.

59. In his "Lettres Anglaises" section in the *Mercure,* Henry Davray reviewed the *English Review* regularly along with the *Fortnightly Review.* He praised Harrison for maintaining the artistic level of his predecessor Ford, and for encouraging young talent (Feb. 1, 1910, 571). He frequently refers to Harrison as a brilliant and able editor (July 1, 1910, Apr. 16, 1911, July 1, 1911, Jan. 16, 1912, Feb. 1, 1913, etc). Davray noted that Harrison would bring a more Liberal stance to the political articles, and he cited the independence and courage of the *English Review* in the face of the *Spectator's* imprudent attack on its morals. It also praised the review for not publishing mass market writers like Arthur Conan Doyle, Hall Caine, Marie Corelli, and Mrs. Humphry Ward.

Chapter 2. Performing the Pure Voice: *Poetry and Drama,* Elocution, Verse Recitation, and Modernist Poetry in Prewar London

1. For discussion of the importance to Pound's poetics of *De Vulgari Eloquentia,* see McDougal.

2. Much recent intellectual history has addressed the competing visual and oral paradigms in modern society and culture. See, for example, Jay, *Downcast Eyes.* Sherry argues that the "radical modernists," Ezra Pound and Wyndham Lewis, followed French ideologues like Rémy de Gourmont and Julien Benda in denigrating what they saw as the democratizing and empathetic character of aural experience in favor of an aristocratic and authoritarian politics of the discerning eye. My exploration affirms the importance of the aural side of Sherry's dichotomy to modernist poetry.

3. I follow Ross's lead in refusing to draw an explicit line during this period between the experiments of the Georgian poets (with "unpoetic" language and themes) and those whom we would later see as modernists. See Ross 13.

4. Grant's *Harold Monro and the Poetry Bookshop* is still the definitive account of Monro's life and work. Readers at the Poetry Bookshop were Yeats, Ford, Pound, Eliot, Edith Sitwell, Robert Graves, F. T. Marinetti, J. C. Squire, Robert Bridges, Walter De la Mare, W. H. Davies, Henry Newbolt, Rupert Brooke, Lascelles Abercrombie, W. W. Gibson, Edmund Gosse, Roy Campbell, Francis Meynell, Margaret L. Woods, Emile Verhaeren, Humbert Wolfe, Anna Wickham, and many others, including Monro himself and his wife Alida Monro (Grant 82–83). The readings took place on Tuesday and Thursday evenings in a building behind the bookshop, but for popular readers like Ford, Yeats, De la Mare, and Marinetti, a larger hall was hired (Grant 60–76).

5. Haberman traces the birth of elocution to the mid-eighteenth-century interest in improving the delivery of public speakers. David Garrick had revolutionized

the English stage with his more "natural" delivery, and many early elocutionists attempted to adapt his techniques to the education of future public speakers— young schoolboys of the upper classes, the clergy, future members of Parliament, barristers, and members of the wealthier middle classes who were largely unschooled. The mothers of upper-class children also were targeted by these books, since they were responsible for the early education of their children (Haberman 1–35, 388–389). While many eighteenth-century elocution manuals were written by actors, in the nineteenth century, the clergy and voice development "experts" tended to be the authors.

6. Halcombe and Stone explained that "the man, some eight or ten years of whose life has been spent in studying the classics, will have gained an accurate and almost instinctive perception of the various shades of meaning expressed by nearly synonymous words; and, more than this, a continual habit of translating classical authors will have given him not only a ready command of words, but an aptitude for arranging them, so as best to convey his meaning" (8).

7. O'Grady noted that through "the vital embodiment of *speech,* man's gift of communication with his fellows, we shall be admitted presently to that great republic wherein all men are equal, all men are free, and all men are converse together" (9).

8. Keating argues that the Board School teachers had little education in English literature (452). A large percentage of the teachers in the public elementary schools during the Edwardian period were not even certified teachers. In 1901 the proportion certified was 55.7 percent. By 1911 this number had only risen to 62.7 percent (Halsey et al. 172).

9. The play was a great success, and Shaw noted in a letter of August 28, 1921, to Siegfried Trebitsch, "Pygmalion is my most steady source of income: it saved me from ruin during the war, and still brings in a substantial penny every week" (*Collected Letters* 730).

10. The controversy raging over Eliza's shocking use of the—exquisitely pronounced—phrase "Not bloody likely" in act 3 highlights this point! (see Holroyd 340–341).

11. Shaw spoke at the 1911 Phonetic Conference at University College, London, on spelling reform, and he wrote to Sweet about his remarks there: "There is no such thing as standard pronunciation. There is no such thing as an ideal pronunciation. Nevertheless . . . it is perfectly easy to find a speaker whose speech will be accepted in every part of the English speaking world as valid 18-carat oral currency . . . all you have to do is to write down the best practicable phonetic representation of the part of Hamlet as spoken by Forbes Robertson, and publish it with a certificate signed by half a dozen persons of satisfactory social standing" (in Holroyd 326). Shaw clearly understood how socially constructed that ideal of "standard pronunciation" is, but he also affirmed its social efficacy.

12. Fogerty became the foremost teacher of speech in England during the 1920s and 1930s. See Sivier, who examines the importance of verse-speaking ideas I discuss here to later movements in speech education in "English Poets, Teachers, and Festivals in a 'Golden Age of Poetry Speaking,' 1920–1950." However, I suggest that these ideas were clearly already widely popular and important by the Edwardian period.

13. In *Burglar Bill and Other Pieces for Use of the Young Reciter,* a recitation collection aimed largely at boys, Guthrie proclaimed "Go where we will in modern society, the most prominent feature 'on the carpet' is the Amateur Reciter; and there is no shorter cut to social distinction, no surer method of conquering the admiration and affection of one's fellow creatures, than by cultivating the power of committing familiar poems to memory, and then repeating them aloud to a select circle of friends and acquaintances" (2).

14. Sackville added that "Elocution is the contrary to all this—a hard and egotistical tyrant, making poetry its slave, and reducing everything to a matter of tone and gesture, when not inspired by the spirit of the verse it professes to inter-pret, seizing upon it like a captive, and thrusting it into a conventional mode. It has little regard for the individuality of the poem" (454–455).

15. The quotes are a paraphrase of Sturge Moore's lecture, as reported in "The Reading of Poetry" (*Poetical Gazette,* June 1912, 287).

16. The Penny Reading movement shared a similar ideal of improving public entertainment and taste by organizing public readings but was deliberately aimed at all classes, especially the working classes, who could afford a penny for an eve-ning's entertainment (Sivier, "Penny Readings").

17. A year's membership cost 5s. with an additional entrance fee of 2s. 6d. Honorary members and vice-presidents each paid one guinea per year.

18. Hulbert was an elocution instructor who spoke frequently at local center meetings on verse recitation and elocution, and he taught courses on voice training at the London University extension program (*Poetical Gazette,* Oct. 1912, 491).

19. Notably, in "Shakespeare," Arnold repudiates the significance of Shake-speare's biography to his artistic creation, casting him as the universal artist whose social identity was irrelevant to his creativity—a theme that might have appealed to the proponents of a universalized ideal of aesthetic taste. See A. Dwight Culler's note on "Shakespeare" (Arnold 538).

20. *The School World* approved of the Poetry Society's efforts at elocution and verse-recitation reform and their insistence that "poetry is written for sound rather than sight reading" (in *Poetical Gazette,* Apr. 1912, 189).

21. For instance, Dobrée wrote to Monro on April 23, 1913, about what he, the "layman" wanted to read about, and added, "You do, I gather, want a rather large circulation, and not a thing confined to a coterie." Upward, in a letter of December 13 [1914?] also assumed that Monro "aimed at something more than being what the Americans would call a 'freak' publisher for a coterie."

22. The term "mass market verse" was almost an oxymoron in Edwardian London. Popular poetry included the contemporary productions of doggerel, and sentimental and occasional verse published in newspapers and magazines, the po-etry of Kipling, whom writers for the *Poetry Review* and *Poetry and Drama* often associated with the commercialism of the music hall, and the poets the Poetry Society espoused—Tennyson, Shakespeare, and so forth. But no contemporary poetry could come remotely close to rivaling the sales of successful mass market fiction.

23. Monro had reluctantly, and against the advice of friends, joined the Poetry Society in 1910, in support at least of its goals, if not its tastes (Grant 69). Gallo-way Kyle, the "Hon. Director" of the society, had asked Monro to run the *Poetical*

Gazette. Monro suggested a separate magazine, and they finally compromised on the joint issues. Monro, however, had to defray the expenses of the magazine and give any profits beyond his outlay plus interest to the Poetry Society, and he was subject to the scrutiny of the council of the society. As he put it, "I practically sold myself to the Society," but in return he received an assured market of 1,000 copies a month (though he received only £5 for them). He wanted to use the paper to help young poets, but he bailed out after a year of the unhappy arrangement (Grant 39).

24. I borrow the term "consecration," and the notion of the field of cultural production, from Bourdieu's *The Field of Cultural Production.* Bourdieu analyzes the way culture reproduces social structures and posits a field of cultural production that has a logic of its own beyond the economic determinants that influence aspects of it. In "The Production of Belief: Contribution to an Economy of Symbolic Goods," Bourdieu notes the role played not only by authors, but also by critics, art dealers, publishers, theater managers, and so forth, in producing belief in the cultural legitimacy and value of works of art, in "consecrating" them (75).

25. See, for instance, Sabin's "On Criticism," which called for new critical standards to complement the new poetry. The first few issues of the *Poetry Review* were replete with articles on criticism and reviews of new poetry by young poets who presented themselves as authoritative. For instance, Flint recommended in his review that readers buy Ezra Pound's *Canzoni* and added, "A wide experience of modern verse is behind that advice."

26. Gosse letter to Monro.

27. While Monro affirmed the oral performance dimension of futurism, he broke ranks with the futurists' call for innovative typography. In an editor's note before Boris Anrep's lavishly illustrated and typographically decorative Blakean poem, the "Book of Anrep," published in the same issue, he explained: "We ourselves esteem that poem a sufficient entity in itself, and our normal course would have been to produce it without typographical or interpretative decoration" ("Notes and Announcements," Sept. 1913). Anrep had insisted on keeping the illustrations and typography as part of the poem and wanted to be able to sell copies of the magazine at an exhibition of his pictures and drawings that opened in London on October 10, 1913, because the illustrated manuscript of the poem was also to be exhibited. Lady Ottoline Morrel had spoken to Monro about the manuscript, and Anrep himself did the blocks. See Anrep letters to Monro.

28. Monro's hopes for Poetry Bookshops in every city never came to fruition, although one did open in Hull in 1919 based on Monro's model, and Monro himself was one of its first readers (Grant 75).

29. Monro, quoted in "A Nest of Singing Birds" (*Daily News and Leader* [London], Jan. 3, 1913, 12).

30. In *Blast,* Pound and Lewis attacked impressionism as merely a form of photography in its goal of reproducing the visual world: "Who would not rather walk ten miles across country (yes, ten miles, my friend), and use his eyes, nose, and muscles, than possess ten thousand Impressionist oil-paintings of that country side?" argued Lewis in "Life Is the Important Thing!" (130).

31. The quotes are from Cannan and Gibson, respectively: Gibson hoped that

verse drama would play upon "the communal expression of the dramatic sense of the people" and return "the stuff of life" to drama. He privileged poetic drama's "alive speech" over the visual artifice of much London theater (119, 119, and 120, respectively). Cannan, a drama critic and regular writer for the *Poetry Review*, complained that "The music-hall is gobbling up the old debased English theatre, and we shall soon be left without a theater, or we shall be forced to create a nobler, purer house of entertainment" (430).

32. The advent, especially after the war, of experiments like Marjorie Gullan's choral speaking methods in speech education led to an emphasis on verse drama with choruses in the school system. Eliot's *Murder in the Cathedral* was an outstanding success and helped augment interest in choral drama; it was first produced in 1935 with a chorus from Elsie Fogerty's Central School of Speech Training (Sivier, "English Poets," 293).

33. In *Poetic Drama*, Leeming traces the development of Eliot's verse drama, from the abandoned colloquial fragment, *Sweeny Agonistes* through *Murder in the Cathedral*, to Eliot's later attempts to popularize verse drama by writing for the West End theaters. She argues that Eliot wished to improve the cultural life of Britain by reaching these middle-class audiences and thus changed his approach in later dramas like *The Cocktail Party, The Confidential Clerk,* and *The Elder Statesman* to include contemporary middle-class themes and simplified verse structures (6–8).

34. *The Music of Speech* was dedicated to Yeats, who was often invoked by contemporary writers as an example of brilliant verse reading for his rhythmical, almost musical, readings. Much of the book is composed of quotations from critics and writers who praised Yeats and Farr's own recitation methods, comparing her to a troubadour, ancient Athenian, and so forth (always referring to preindustrial, oral cultures). In *The Autobiography of William Butler Yeats,* Yeats praises Farr as "that accomplished speaker of verse" (265), and he suggests that she had "one great gift, the most perfect poetical elocution" (185).

35. Sherry holds up Farr's book as the epitome of the kind of oral, empathetic aesthetic that he aligns with Bergson, and that he suggests Pound, Lewis, and Hulme rejected in their move toward French ocular paradigms. Sherry traces Hulme's movement from Bergson to Worringer as part of his rejection of aural empathy, but I would like to note that, even as late as the June 1914 issue of *Poetry and Drama*, Hulme, who did the "German Chronicle" for the magazine, wrote enthusiastically about the poetry readings at the Cabaret Gnu in Berlin. The poets in the cabaret, which was presided over by Kurt Hiller, editor of the anthology *Der Kondor*, were praised by Hulme for their new experiments in language and, comparing it to the abrupt futurist verse, he suggested that "a definite attempt is being made to use the language in a new way, an attempt to cure it of certain vices" ("German Chronicle" 224). Hulme praised at length the "confidence and the ferocity of the poets" in their readings, suggesting that the oral performance dimensions of their work still seemed particularly modern and exciting to him. I don't dispute Sherry's analysis, especially since his work largely deals with the postwar period, but I would suggest that Bergson seems not to have played much of a role in the discourses about oral performance in prewar London, either in the

mainstream versions or in Monro's magazines—rather, they had been around in the recitation debates for a couple of decades. Above all, I would argue that as modernist poets looked for audiences in prewar London, they often found themselves on this *oral* side of Sherry's competing paradigms.

36. Monro bears the ignominy of having refused to publish "The Love Song of J. Alfred Prufrock" in *Poetry and Drama,* but he sold Eliot's books in his store and had him read his poems there.

37. D. Scott letter to Monro. Emphases in original.

38. Monro lecture notes.

39. Collins notes that, though their poems were performed publicly by reciters, the major Victorian poets did not read publicly. "The poets who did give public readings were mostly such now-forgotten ones as Martin Tupper, Edwin Arnold, Robert Buchanan, and, earlier in the century, some of the Chartist (and other) 'poets of the poor'" (*Reading Aloud* 26). Lecturing was considered acceptable, and Arnold followed the common and highly lucrative Victorian practice of going on the lecture circuit in America. (See Collins, "Agglomerating Dollars," 6.) Tennyson, however, even turned down an offer of £20,000 to lecture in America. As much as Tennyson enjoyed reading his verse at dinner parties with friends, and was considered an excellent reader, he never took this talent onto the public platform (Collins, *Reading Aloud,* 4–5). Dickens set an important precedent in the 1850s by launching a career as a professional platform reader, making more than half of the £100,000 fortune he died with reading his own novels to great acclaim and public interest both in America and England (Collins, *Reading Aloud,* 5–7). His public readings created a superstar phenomenon, in which it was not just his works, but the presence of the author himself reading them, that attracted thousands everywhere he went. In *Charles Dickens: The Public Readings,* Collins notes that Dickens's platform career "seems indeed to have coincided with the peak of the vogue for public readings" (1), which lasted from the 1850s to the 1870s, though no major poets were involved (liii).

40. Macnamara letter to Monro.

41. E. Pound letter to Monro, Nov. 26, 1920.

42. In his discussion of the rise of the bourgeois public sphere in eighteenth-century Britain, Habermas notes the extreme importance of the rise of independent journalism early in the century: "The press was for the first time established as a genuinely critical organ of a public engaged in critical political debate: as the fourth estate" (*Structural* 60).

43. Monro lecture notes.

44. As with the *English Review,* some modernists even attempted to connect *Poetry and Drama* to the *Mercure de France.* Perhaps in response to the regular "Chronicles" of French, German, and American literature in Monro's magazine, somewhat resembling the "Revue de la Quinzaine" in the *Mercure de France,* Pound wrote Monro a letter suggesting a scheme of "rubrics" (literary sections divided by genre and country) for *Poetry and Drama* with a regular staff writer for each (these would have included Monro, Aldington, Cournos, Pound, John Alford, Gilbert Cannan, Flint, and Sophie Brzeska). He noted: "I think the Mercure's system of rubrics could be instituted to advantage. No one has yet done it in England.

"In a monthly the rubrics would solve half the problem. They would also, or should also have an effect on sales. There is no general intelligencer of that sort in England or America" (E. Pound letter to Monro, June 24, 1914). As I suggested in chapter 1 on the *English Review*, this idea of the "general intelligencer" was connected to a revival of an idealized liberal public sphere that was seen to exist still in France. Aldington had even written Monro suggesting combining *Poetry and Drama* with the *Mercure de France:* "Flint and Pound tell me that you think of shutting down P&D for a year. I am sorry, as I was going to propose to you that you should devote, say 20 pages of P&D to an English edition (in French, of course) of the Mercure de France" (Aldington letter to Monro).

45. The liberal bourgeois public sphere of the eighteenth century seemed to operate on principles of inclusiveness and disinterestedness, yet it had an un-spoken economic requirement for admittance—property ownership, which was equated with humanity itself. Habermas notes, "The fully developed bourgeois public sphere was based on the fictitious identity of the two roles assumed by the privatized individuals who came together to form a public: the role of property owners and the role of human beings pure and simple" (*Structural* 56). Similarly, Monro's discussion of the bookshop as oral public space elides its economic basis. He invites the bookshop patron to "look round its shelves at his leisure, sit down and examine its books, discuss them with his friends. . . . We fully recognize that our invitation is a direct encouragement of loiterers, and further, indeed, that it is open to the suspicion of being bad business; but, since we esteem the circulation of poetry a spiritual, or, at the least, an artistic, rather than an economic enterprise, we shall endeavour to tolerate a limited amount of loitering" ("The Bookshop," Nov. 1912, 498). He adds, "Books cannot be classed for commercial purposes with other marketable commodities" (498). These lines attempt to exempt poetry from the taint of the economic, just as the required "leisure" for browsing and discus-sion of poetry presupposes a certain economic standing of the patrons. However, most Londoners now could read and had some leisure time, even if they chose to fill it with the music hall or other mass market entertainments. The Poetry Book-shop was certainly less restrictive than the Poetry Society's events, since it cost nothing to browse and discuss, and the readings were inexpensive. In addition, it was located in Bloomsbury, and not in the exclusively middle- and upper-middle-class neighborhoods of the west and northwest sections. If the Poetry Bookshop was not patronized by the working classes and lower middle classes, that was due to the dynamics of literary taste, the very thing the bookshop most wanted to change. The liberal public sphere's ideal of public deliberation was embodied in the bookshop and its lecture series, which featured lectures by Monro, Hulme, and others, followed by public discussions.

46. Monro letter to Drinkwater. A large portion of this letter is reproduced in Grant (82).

47. Morden Tower was a poetry bookstore where young poets met to discover new forms through readings and discussion. See J. A. Johnson for a history of recent poetry performance in England.

Chapter 3. Marketing British Modernism: The *Freewoman,* the *Egoist,* and Counterpublic Spheres

1. Dora Marsden and Harriet Shaw Weaver edited these magazines that serially published Joyce's *Portrait* and much of *Ulysses* and Wyndham Lewis's *Tarr* and were the primary English conduit for publication and discussion of imagism. They drew to them such assistant editors as Rebecca West, Ezra Pound (unofficially), Richard Aldington, H.D., and T. S. Eliot. For detailed accounts of the history of the *Freewoman, New Freewoman,* and *Egoist,* see Garner and see Lidderdale and Nicholson.

2. I borrow the term "feminist counterpublic sphere," which I use throughout the chapter, from Felski (chapter 5). Felski notes that "the category of a feminist counter-public sphere provides a useful means to theorizing the existence of an oppositional discursive space within contemporary society grounded in gender politics, making it possible to examine the mechanisms by which this collectivity is constituted, its political implications and effects, as well as its potential limitations" (155). Like the later phases in feminist movements in the West that Felski analyzes, the suffrage movement created its own institutions of publicity—papers, meetings, bookshops, publishers, street-selling, and parades—which were inflected by the ideological and sociological facts of their existence. The predominantly middle-class female composition of suffrage organizations, for instance, helps to explain their familiarity with and ability to rapidly redeploy aspects of consumer mass culture for their own noncommercial ends, but it also helps to explain their prevalent blindness to working-class women's issues. See also Negt and Kluge.

3. Turner credits Newnes, Pearson, and Northcliffe with "widening the reading public, and hence the buying public" (143), and this was partially accomplished as they quickly "extend[ed] their sway over the new Board School generation" (150). See Altick for the development of mass reading audiences in the later Victorian period and the unprecedented proliferation of books and mass market periodicals (317, 363–364).

4. Altick 363–364. Whereas early nineteenth-century conservatives like Coleridge had opposed the spread of reading to the working and lower middle classes because they feared demagogues would incite revolution, by the late Victorian age these concerns had given way to what would be some modernists' reaction to the commercial mass market press: that mass reading represented a decline in the serious purpose of reading, because the new readers were reading the wrong things and quality had been sacrificed to sales and accessibility (Altick 365–368).

5. Leiss, Kline, and Jhally note that "by 1920 [advertising revenue] accounted for about two-thirds of all newspaper and magazine income" (59). See also Ferris 48. Ironically, Harmsworth had initially wanted advertisements to conform to the appearance of the newspaper and had briefly hoped that the *Daily Mail* could do without advertising. He worried about the possibility of newspapers becoming entirely subordinate to advertisers. However, he and his advertising manager, Wareham Smith, quickly built their advertising base, and the huge circulation of the paper allowed them to charge high advertising rates. A full page in the *Daily Mail* in 1910 cost £350; the same page in the *Evening News* would only have cost £130 (Nevett 83).

6. As *Votes for Women* wrote in June 28, 1912, under the headline "Posters Everywhere! / Painting the Town Purple, White, and Green": "Few sights are more cheering to the Suffragette than that of the purple, white and green posters of VOTES FOR WOMEN wedged between the ordinary news-bills of the party Press, on a railway bookstall or outside a newsagent's shop. We should like to see every town in the country painted purple, white and green in the same fashion." The article goes on to list the large number of tube stations in London which have *Votes for Women* posters up.

7. The *Vote* described an event at the Great Woman's Suffrage Procession: "Lord Cromer's Anti-Suffrage Society had sent out a contingent of sandwich-men, who, it was intended, should carry boards proclaiming, in huge red letters, on a white ground, 'Women Do Not Want the Vote.' A few of the men who had the temerity to put up the challenge and endeavour to carry it were so chaffed and badgered and hustled and laughed at that they were forced to lower the boards, tuck them under their arms, and slink along in somewhat sheepish fashion on the outskirts of the crowd, their painful and humiliating retreat being followed by such sarcastic expressions on the part of suffrage sympathisers as 'Where's the Antis to-day?' 'Why don't Lord Cromer carry 'is own boards?' and 'That's right, Tommy, glad to see yer'e chucked it'" (June 24, 1911, 111).

8. Harmsworth built his empire with a wide variety of mass market periodicals. In addition to his popular *Answers* (1888), he began *Comic Cuts* in 1890, a halfpenny weekly of jokes aimed largely at juveniles, and started an illustrated magazine, *Illustrated Chips* (1890), and *Forget-me-Not* (1891), which aimed at "ladies" and then became an enormous success with shopgirls (Ferris 44–46). The list continued to expand, including the *Daily Mail* (1896), which directed itself not only at the increasingly educated working and lower middle classes, but also contained feature articles explicitly directed at women (Ferris 80, 87).

9. The department stores marketed fashions for upcoming suffrage events and tried to carry the proper colors and cuts to cater to suffrage tastes. As Kaplan and Stowell put it, "By virtue of their organized buying power, suffrage feminists clearly influenced the look of goods sold, as manufacturers and retailers fought for a large and lucrative market. At the same time advertisers were quick to target specific suffrage needs, urging upon feminist consumers the merits of their own products" (173).

10. Kaplan and Stowell note that the department stores considered the suffragettes such a lucrative market that they continued to pour advertising money into suffrage coffers, including that of the proscribed *Suffragette,* even after the window-smashing campaign launched by the WSPU in March 1912 vandalized the stores of most of these regular advertisers, telling them "You can get on very well without Mr. Asquith or Mr. Lloyd George, but you can't get on without the women who are your good friends in business." One firm even took space in *Votes for Women* and the *Suffragette* to apologize for writs served on its behalf to collect damages for the windows, explaining that their insurance policy stipulated that they allow their name to be used in the suit (Kaplan and Stowell 174).

11. Debenham and Freebody's chic drawings of women in the latest fashions advertised clothing that would have been prohibitively expensive for the working class: a new spring tailored suit cost £4, and blouses and hats went for 18s. 9d.

through 25s. A L'Ideal Cie also advertised their "Dainty Paris Blouses" for 25s., more than half a month's rent for most working class families.

12. Stephen Swift, the publisher of the *Freewoman,* also published the first edition of Ezra Pound's *Ripostes* (1912) and of Pound's *Sonnets and Ballate of Guido Cavalcanti* (1912).

13. In the PUF, *DMP,* Box 3, Folder 12, a sheet of expenditures and credits for the *Freewoman,* n.d., lists credits from advertisements at £98.17.10, while credits from subscriptions totaled only £57.17.10.

14. PUF, *DMP,* Box 3, Folder 12, contains a subscription list to the *Freewoman.* Subscribers were scattered throughout the British Isles, but large numbers of married women, unmarried women, and male subscribers lived in London. Across the whole list, there were 116 unmarried women, 103 married women, and 63 men.

15. From their emergence in the later Victorian era, advertising agents had largely either compiled listings of advertising venues for manufacturers, like Willing's newspaper press directories, or had acted as brokers for advertising space that they had purchased en masse from magazines. Until the end of the nineteenth century manufacturers had created their own advertising copy, but by 1910 advertising agencies had begun to take over the role of crafting marketing concepts; they were becoming active participants in advising and creating advertising campaigns (Leiss et al. 129–130).

16. Willing and Co. letter to Winterton, The Gough Press Agency.

17. Winterton letter to Jardine.

18. Aldred letter to Jardine, January 23, 1912.

19. Aldred letter to Marsden.

20. In a letter from Aldred to Jardine, Aldred writes "Of *course,* I could handle and circulate your paper only the price is prohibitive so far as the circles are concerned in which my influence lies" (Aldred letter to Jardine, Jan. 23, 1912). A few days later he wrote again, "I am only sorry that I cannot do more to assist your brave and outspoken journal in its struggle against boycott and prejudice. In a way it is well to keep that paper up to 3d., because this guarantees a certain 'tone' and enables the paper to reach a circle of leisured culture. On the other hand, if it was 2d, I could handle it and introduce it to a limited circle" (Aldred letter to Jardine, Jan. 26, 1912).

21. Bowman proposed the exchange in a letter in which he also asked Marsden, "Could you recommend a lady who would be willing to contribute to 'The Syndicalist' from the Syndicalist point of view" (Bowman letter to Marsden, Feb. 23, 1912). Later in the year, Bowman, who had written several times in the *Freewoman,* invited Marsden and Rebecca West to "a little gathering of journalists and others, all of whom are interested in Syndicalism" (Bowman letter to Marsden, Sept. 11, 1912).

22. A few of the *Freewoman's* subscribers turn up in the published list of subscribers in the *Herald of Revolt.* Particularly significant was George Davison, who became a Thousand Club Member and shareholder in the *New Freewoman* and also gave liberally, often as much as £5 at a time, to the *Herald of Revolt* fund to prop up its shaky finances. Henry Bool, a supporter of the *Freewoman/New*

Freewoman/Egoist, also subscribed to the *Herald of Revolt* and contributed money, including £5 to the Malatesta Fund.

However, neither anarchism nor syndicalism gained enough ground with labor in early twentieth-century England to effect revolutionary change (Marshall 491), and, in spite of Aldred's ability to rally the radical press and organize a huge demonstration in Trafalgar Square in 1909 against the government's handling of the anarchist Enrico Malatesta (Marshall 351), his *Herald of Revolt* never had the impact on labor politics he had wished. While the suffrage papers had their £250,000 funds, Aldred, albeit successfully, could raise only a 1,000-shilling fund and a small *Herald* fund.

23. Garner provides an excellent description of the Discussion Circles and notes that under the guidance of Marsden, publisher Charles Grenville, and secretary Barbara Low, "A whole range of fascinating lectures were arranged, even if Grenville's on 'Thought Mists—Some Earthly Suggestions' was somewhat obscure. Birnstingl lectured on 'Interpretations of Life,' Selwyn Watson, an anarchist, on 'Ideas of Freedom,' Guy Aldred 'Sex Oppression and the Way Out,' Mrs. Havelock Ellis 'Some Problems of Eugenics,' Mrs. Gallichan 'The Problems of Celibacy,' and Charles Drysdale on 'Neo-Malthusianism.' Other talks were held on Prostitution, the Abolition of Domestic Drudgery (Rona Robinson) and Divorce. Barbara Low and others realized these huge subjects could only be touched on in one evening and suggested that smaller groups might wish to carry the discussion on in members' homes. Low even hoped that the Circle would one day have its own meeting house" (73–74).

24. Many intricate relationships of influence can be traced among these groups and the ideas they advocated. For a good discussion of suffragism and avant-gardism, see J. Lyon. Recent explorations of the influence of antistatist politics on modernism include von Hallberg, "Libertarian"; Barash; Kadlec; and Clarke, whose thorough and provocative *Dora Marsden and Early Modernism: Gender, Individualism, Science* is the first full-length study of Marsden's relationship to modernism.

25. In London in 1910, much of the press was controlled by a few enormous publishing companies. Northcliffe, Cadbury, and Pearson controlled over a third of the morning paper circulation and four-fifths of the evening circulation. J. H. Dalziel, Riddell, Lloyd, and Northcliffe controlled over four-fifths of the Sunday circulation (Lee 127).

26. My thanks to von Hallberg for suggesting this French context for the swan motif. Flint wrote numerous articles about French poetry for literary magazines and was the author of the "French Chronicle" in *Poetry and Drama* (1913–1914). As Grant puts it, "The most significant single contribution to the [*Poetry*] *Review*'s pages was F. S. Flint's survey of contemporary French poetry, which filled the best part of the August [1912] number. It was the first extended article published in England on the multifarious activity of a generation of poets" (47–48).

27. "Le vierge, le vivace et le bel aujourd'hui" (Mallarmé 170–173). Hampton notes that "in a Mallarméan context, of course, the 'cygne,' like the 'plumage,' like the 'blanche agonie,' forms part of a carefully constructed self-referential pattern which, by the time of this mature sonnet (1885) has been clearly established

throughout his work. Thus, as 'plumage' connotes the quill, as the 'blanche agonie' recalls the 'page blanche,' the 'Cygne' here bears powerful resonances of 'signe,'— the linguistic sign constituting the poem itself" (448). Dismissing the overtone of "signe" at the end, Cohn follows the critical commonplace of reading the swan as figuring "the poet who is held in the dull here-on-earth but aspires to a Platonic perfection of beauty" (124).

28. Upward's introduction to Chinese poetry and Confucius in 1900 led to his publications of *The Sayings of K'Ung the Master* in 1904 and again in the *New Freewoman* (Nov. 11 and 15 and Dec. 1, 1913), and *Scented Leaves from a Chinese Jar,* which Upward had written over a decade before, in the *New Freewoman* (Oct. 15, 1913), and in *Poetry* in Chicago. Pound was interested in these short, concise, proselike poems, and he published some of them in the first imagist anthology, *Des Imagistes,* in 1914. For a brief account of the few facts known about Upward's life, see Sheldon and Knox. See also Upward's poem "The Discarded Imagist," and see Davie for Upward's importance to Pound's *Cantos.*

29. Upward letter to Monro, December 27, 1913.

30. Freewoman groups in America came up with a scheme to raise $1,000 by selling eighteen-month subscriptions (roughly £200). Marsden revised this scheme for England into a plan to attract subscribers but also people willing to buy £1 shares to restart the magazine—the Thousand Club Members. The prospectus circular for the *New Freewoman* (in the Harriet Shaw Weaver Papers at the British Library) had set 2,000 subscribers as an attainable goal, and as Marsden had calculated "Issued at 3d, we calculate that 1,600 *subscribers* (7/7) yearly would enable the paper to pay for itself, and according to the circulation already firmly established when publication was suspended, such a subscription list should be well within our reach." She was also encouraged by the "quite astonishing" "extraordinary amount of interest in 'The Freewoman' the American papers are beating up in America," and she noted articles in "Forum" and "Current Literature" on them. See Marsden letter to Weaver, December 2, 1912.

31. West letter to Marsden, n.d. [spring 1913]. See letters from West to Marsden in June 1913 as the *New Freewoman* was being launched, describing her efforts to advertise the paper.

32. See Weaver, minutes to the director's meetings for September 10, 1913, and May 14, 1914.

33. Theosophy, largely inspired by the writings of H. P. Blavatsky, and, in England, Annie Besant, was popular among counterculture groups and had many followers among the suffragettes. Advertisement for theosophical journals and book publications, as well as for lectures by Annie Besant, frequently appeared in the major suffrage periodicals, but readers of the *Freewoman* and its later incarnations also supported theosophy—one even wrote to praise the magazine on Blavatsky Institute letterhead (Frances W. W. letter to Marsden, PUF, *DMP,* Box 3, Folder 10). Much of the talk about spirituality and souls from regular columnists like Huntly Carter verged on the theosophical, and Grierson in an article in the *New Freewoman* noted the importance to "woman's New Era" of the fact that "the two greatest spiritual movements of our time—modern Theosophy and Christian Science—were evolved by women [Blavatsky and Mary Baker Eddy]" (10).

However, outside of Yeats's mystical circles, most modernist writers were clearly wary of what they saw as the sham mysticism of theosophy. In a *New Free-woman* article Pound praised Tagore's work but added that Tagore "is not to be confused with that jolly and religious bourgeois Abdul Baha; nor with any Theoso-phist propaganda; nor with any of the various missionaries of the seven and sev-enty isms of the mystical East" ("Rabandranath Tagore" 187). Marsden herself detested theosophy but had felt it important to engage in dialogue with the theoso-phists at a convention held at Peables in 1913. In a letter expressing her fears that Upward might be tainted by theosophy, she wrote about her experience at Peables: "No good comes of these unreal alliances. Look at these people—all antagonistic where, before I spoke at Peables they were indifferent. They made no effort to understand the 'Freewoman' is just the rooting out of 'Theosophia'! It was ridicu-lous to imagine that I could have anything acceptable to say to the theosophists" (Marsden letter to Weaver, Apr. 15, 1913). However, in a letter to Jardine of Au-gust 1, 1913, Weaver wrote that she was "glad to hear Miss Marsden demolished most of the arguments of the Theosophists at Peebles and that the stock of the NFW was sold out in consequence!" Like the suffragettes and the radical political movements, theosophy had its own periodicals, bookstores, and followers, and these followers read the *New Freewoman.*

34. Pease, secretary of the Fabian Society, letter to Marsden. The Fabian Soci-ety declined to give her the list but offered to let her pay them to send out her circular with the *Fabian News* for 21s. for 4,000.

35. Aldington letter to Marsden, on *New Freewoman* letterhead.

36. See Weaver, account book, for the regular payments to street sellers.

37. Though advertising in the press accounted for the greatest advertising ex-penditures, in 1907, an estimated £1.5 million was spent on posters and "trans-ports." This figure rose to £2 million in 1910 and 1912 (Nevett 70), and posters had become more visually sophisticated, including color illustrations and even halftone photographic illustrations in the late-Victorian period (Nevett 87–88). Circulars delivered by hand to houses had been supplanted by the more popular mailing of circulars (Nevett 92).

38. Weaver, account book, lists weekly payments to Mr. Winterton from Janu-ary 12 through March 2, 1914. After three months, the *Egoist* seems to have given up on Mr. Winterton.

39. This circular is in BL, *HSW.*

40. While much of the expansion of the university system in Britain took place during the twenties, the number of people receiving higher education from univer-sities, teacher-training colleges, and other institutions grew from 25,000 in 1900–1901 to 61,000 in 1924–1925. In response to calls for increased educational oppor-tunities by such groups as the Workers' Education Association (formed in 1903), adult and continuing education also saw expansion (Stevenson 252–253). College-educated women were increasingly common during this period, and were impor-tant to the suffrage movement; Christabel Pankhurst even had a law degree. Mars-den paraded her B.A. on the masthead, and many of her friends who supported the magazine, like Rona Robinson, had college degrees as well. Some of the readers involved in positions of leadership in other organizations, like Edith How Martyn in the Women's Freedom League, also had college degrees. Women's education had always been a concern of the *Freewoman,* and one article even pointed out the

difficulty of being a disenfranchised female college professor. See Weaver, subscription lists for the *Freewoman*.

41. Lady Proctor, Countess Russell, and Baron von Taube, Lady Willoughby de Broke, Lady Isabel Margesson, Lady Anglesay, the Countess De La Warr, the Contesse de Bulgaries, and the Contesse Baciocchi had all briefly subscribed to the *Freewoman*. The Countess of Warwick and Lady Ottoline Morrell briefly subscribed to the *Egoist*.

42. Even with a subscription list in hand (a rare find in the scantly preserved archives of little magazines), hard evidence about the economic class of Edwardian readers is difficult to find. While the great liberal budget of 1909–1910 (the "People's Budget") instituted a progressive income tax, these tax records generally have not been preserved, except for a few sample returns. However, the Finance Act of 1910 proposed a complete review of land taxes and led to a valuation of all the properties in Great Britain. Many of these property valuations, descriptions, and rent listings carried out by the Board of Inland Revenue survive, buried in the complex cataloging systems of the Public Record Office at Kew.

In order to gauge the economic class of the type of reader who was attracted to the advertising tactics *New Freewoman/Egoist* directed at the London masses, I confined my search for the rent and property valuations to addresses of subscribers living in London or the near suburbs. Some difficulties kept this research from being as thorough as I would have liked. For instance, although I had a complete list of names and addresses for the original *New Freewoman* Thousand Club Members and the early subscribers, some of the maps surviving in the Public Record Office do not contain the necessary hereditament numbers to locate the field book containing the rate evaluation for that particular address. The *Egoist* subscription lists in the Harriet Shaw Weaver Papers provide no addresses, so I was forced to confine my search to those subscribers whose addresses I either had from other lists or could locate in the Kelly's Postal Directories for London and the suburbs.

In spite of the unscientific nature of this research, some important generalizations can still be drawn. A large portion of the *New Freewoman* Thousand Club Members, shareholders, and subscribers in the London area lived in the terrace houses, maisonettes, and less spacious or modernized houses of the lower middle classes. Almost none of them owned the house in which they lived, and the rents for these dwellings at the time of their assessment (begun in 1910 and completed by autumn 1915) ranged from £26 up to £150, but most fell in the £35 to £60 range. *Egoist* subscribers, after all the readers who had wanted a revival of the *Freewoman* had dropped away by roughly 1916, tended to live in the same type or slightly nicer dwellings—more in rented houses in the £50 to £70 range approaching the solidly middle class, but only a few actually owned their houses. Some, like Ezra Pound, lived in rooms that could be rented by the week, like working-class dwellings.

While these houses and apartments were generally in the upscale neighborhoods of the west, southwest, and northwest regions, including Kensington, Chelsea, and Holland Park (very few were in the east districts), they were not the houses of the upper classes. For the sake of contrast, a typical house on Grosvenor Square rented for £1,650 a year and was valued at £40,000. On the other end of the scale of typical London rents, the working classes in the inner areas of London tended to pay roughly 5s. to 10s. per week for two- and three-room dwellings (10s. per week works out to around £26 per year), and in the middle ring (areas like Hampstead where many *New Freewoman* and *Egoist* subscribers lived) they dwelt in slightly larger apartments averaging around 10s. to 13s. per week (13s. is around £34 per year). See the report made to Parliament by Royal command, *Cost of Living of the Working Classes* (xxii).

Thus, the lower end of the rents in these subscription lists approximates the upper end of working-class rents, though the higher ends of the scale far exceeded them. Marsden's salary of £52 a year was less than half that of most male civil servants between 1911 and 1913, and, even by 1906 standards, it would have ranked far below such professions as semiskilled pottery worker, railway fireman, bus and tram driver in London, shop assistant, and London postman, coming only slightly above the always underpaid agricultural laborer (who made around £48 annually). My point is that some *New Freewoman* shareholders and Thousand Club Members were quite comfortable financially, but few were wealthy. They had the means for leisure-time interests beyond the cheap entertainments of the working classes, and the education to cultivate literary interests, but they were not in themselves a rich field of patrons. Even Weaver, who was wealthy by comparison and financed the magazine and the Egoist publications, bankrolling Marsden and Joyce and publishing for years at a loss, was the daughter of a country doctor, and, though she inherited what by her standards was a great fortune made at cotton-spinning by her grandfather, her income was solidly middle class.

43. Priestly notes that the lower middle classes, a large, mostly urban sector of the Edwardian population (including such professions as shopkeeper, office worker, superior factory foreman, teacher, craftsman, and commercial trader as well as less successful professional men) tended to earn between £150 and £500 a year and lived in terrace houses, or even in new semidetached small villas (105). The Edwardian period witnesses a boom of suburban expansion before 1914. The wealthier professional and business classes tended to move from the squalor of the city to the outer suburbs, while the lower middle classes and higher paid workmen moved to the inner suburbs (Stevenson 24). Another such wave of suburban expansion beginning right after the war led to middle-class flight to the cheap new semidetached houses that could be bought for as little as £450 (Stevenson 129–130). Some of the *New Freewoman* subscribers lived in homes in these less expensive northwestern suburbs like Hampstead Garden Suburbs, Golder's Green, or Hendon, whose roads and property divisions had been marked in the Inland Revenue Survey beginning in 1910, but which were developed and built between 1910 and 1913.

44. The first run of 2,000 was never again attempted. It immediately dropped to 1,500 and then to 1,000 by September 1913. In February 1915, this dropped to 750 copies (except for the 1,250 copies of the May 1 imagist issue and a 1,000-copy issue of Mar. 1, 1916). The run dropped again to 600 for April 1916, to 500 for January 1917, and to 400 copies for the September 1918 issue until its demise at the end of 1919. See Weaver, account book.

45. Printing costs increased dramatically beginning in late 1916. The *Egoist* account book in the Harriet Shaw Weaver Papers, British Library, noted a regular 10 percent increase beginning with the December 1916 issue, rising to a 22$\frac{1}{2}$ per-

cent increase beginning in January 1918, and again in May 1918 to a 33½ percent increase. Paper costs also were rising, and in November 1917 Weaver purchased a twenty-month supply of *Egoist* paper in advance to protect against further increases. The issue length had to be shortened to fourteen pages, and at the end of the war, though it added two pages to its length, the *Egoist* for 1919 had increased to 9d. per issue. In addition, the government responded to the paper shortage during the war by passing the Paper Restriction Order. After March 10, 1917, severe measures curtailed the distribution of catalogues, price lists, and advertising circulars, and the Paper Restriction Consolidation Order of October 22 virtually banned all circular distribution after the end of January 1918 (Nevett 140).

46. Hindshaw letter to Marsden.

47. Marsden letter to Weaver, October 1915.

48. Marsden letter to Weaver, October 1915.

49. Subscribers included William Carlos Williams, May Sinclair, Storm Jameson, Herbert Read, Marianne Moore, Wallace Stevens, and Alice Corbin Henderson.

50. Aaronovitch notes the international expansion, particularly into the colonies for raw goods and into overseas markets for consumption of textiles combines like Coates, the soap firm of Lever, and the tobacco giant Imperial Tobacco (15). These huge companies were not just in the traditional industrial sector. In 1919, though Coates was the largest combine, worth around £45 million, two publishing combines were in the top fifty largest British companies, Amalgamated Presses and the Associated Newspapers-Daily Mail Trust, each worth around £4.2 million (Hannah 30).

51. See Marsden letters to Weaver, January 5, 1918, and January 22, 1918. Marsden, as with Pound's earlier proposals with Quinn's money, was leery of giving anyone autonomy with part of the paper and was skeptical that Hutchins would come through with either money or subscribers.

52. See Marsden letter to Weaver, n.d. [late December 1918]. Lewis eventually tried to restart *Blast* with the Egoist Press but could never scrape together the money even to pay his past printing bills from its first two issues. The Egoist Ltd., did, however publish his *Caliph's Design* around the same time. Marsden noted: "While Mr. Lewis' friends might not subscribe to the Egoist they would probably subscribe to an amalgamated one of this sort" (Marsden letter to Weaver, Nov. 21, 1918).

53. Marsden letter to Weaver, November 21, 1918.

54. Marsden letter to Weaver, n.d. [late December 1918].

55. Marsden letter to Weaver, November 21, 1918.

56. Marsden letter to Weaver, December 4, 1918.

57. *Blast* 1 was published on July 2, 1914, but was dated June 20, 1914. Briefly, a group of English artists who were trying to bring the aesthetic innovations of continental avant-gardism to a resistant England forged a group identity largely around two rifts. The first was the break from Bloomsbury and Roger Fry's post-impressionist crafts guild, the Omega Workshops, by Lewis, Edward Wadsworth, Frederick Etchells, and Cuthbert Hamilton in October 1913. The Omega was a collective formed in 1913 by Fry to bring postimpressionism into the decorative arts of textile, furnituremaking, interior design, and pottery and to bring money

into the pockets of starving artists. The second was an aggressively nationalistic reaction against the Italian futurist F. T. Marinetti's "imperialist" attempts to appropriate English avant-gardism, particularly through a manifesto entitled "Vital English Art." Lewis and Kate Lechmere founded an alternative to Fry's Omega Workshops in the spring of 1914, the Rebel Art Centre, which hosted lectures and exhibitions, created its own decorative objects for sale, and attempted (without success) to become an art school (see Wees 69–72).

58. Wadsworth letter to Lewis, February 4, 1914. The correspondence between Wadsworth and Lewis at the Lewis Collection suggest that Wadsworth was far more editorially involved in *Blast* than has been previously acknowledged, even giving suggestions on manifestos.

59. Wadsworth letter to Lewis, February 25, 1914.

60. Wadsworth letter to Lewis, August 29, 1914? This letter seems to be dated August 29, 1915, but must have been written before that, perhaps in August 1914, or an earlier month in 1915, since the "War Number" second issue came out July 20, 1915, and Wees concurs that it was labeled a "War Number" at Wadsworth's suggestion (Wees 197).

61. Hulme letter to Lewis.

62. Wadsworth letter to Lewis, November 17, 1913.

63. Wees notes that the vorticists did have some reason to be concerned, since a suffragette had hacked up two drawings at the Doré Gallery, where vorticist work was being exhibited (17–19).

64. Wees reads the address "To the Suffragettes" as a "magnanimous" and affirming gesture of comradeship (19). Lyon, on the other hand, sees this message as both affirming suffragette energy and also differentiating it from artistic energy, as she paraphrases Lewis's meaning: "The Suffragettes are avatars of political energy and therefore are *not* artists. Not being artists, they cannot know a good work of art and might unwittingly destroy one. . . . For the artist-agitator is *not* the political agitator; rather, the artist is the individualist" (J. Lyon 113). And Reynolds also picks up on the patronizing tone, noting that "*Blast*'s qualified praise for the Suffragettes suggests that while they respected the effectiveness of the Suffragette's publicity tactics, they also believed that the Suffragettes—because of their essential lack of artistic sense—might misuse the aesthetic promise that advertising offered" (18).

65. And Lewis had attacked London itself, in his "Manifesto," as "Victorian Vampire, the London cloud sucks the town's heart" (11).

66. I am indebted, as any scholar of vorticism is, to Wees's Appendix B, "The Blasted and the Blessed" (217–227), for brief identifications of the figures listed in the "blasts" and "blesses" of both issues of *Blast*.

Chapter 4. Youth in Public: The *Little Review* and Commercial Culture in Chicago

1. M. Anderson's version of her move to Chicago can be found in her *My Thirty Years' War* (12–20). Bryer fills in the details omitted in Anderson's account in the only full-length study of the *Little Review* (5–8). The comparison of Anderson to a magazine model is Hecht's from *A Child of the Century* (in Bryer 30).

2. Ohmann explains that the publishing industry in the 1890s began to con-

centrate its energies on producing the best-seller. The *Bookman* began the first regular publication of regional best-seller lists in 1895 and national best-seller lists in 1897 (Ohmann 24).

3. The strategy of English publishers like Harmsworth, Newnes, and Pearson of lowering the price of a newspaper or magazine even below its cost, thus increasing circulation, and then taking profits from increased advertising revenues (discussed in chap. 3) had its counterpart in late nineteenth-century America. Frank Munsey and S. S. McClure reached unheard-of circulation figures and advertising revenues by pandering to mass audiences. The popular religious weeklies (like the *Continent*), the favorite medium for advertisers during the nineteenth century, lost ground to the new mass market general magazines like *Ladies' Home Journal, Cosmopolitan, Collier's, Delineator, McCall's, McClure's, and Munsey's* (see Peterson 7–21).

4. M. Anderson gloated that "As for our practical friends who warned us against starting a literary magazine, even their dark prophecies of debt and a speedy demise have had to dissolve before our statements that we have paid our bills with what *The Little Review* has earned in its six months of existence, that we are free of debt, that we even have money in the bank" ("A Change of Price").

5. M. Anderson explained: "College girls ought to find the field a very workable one during their summer vacations. Every ten subscriptions will mean $5.00 to the energetic young woman who pursues her friends with accounts of *The Little Review's* value and charm." See "A Voting Contest for Scholarships," which discusses a subscription campaign by the weekly *Republican* which enlisted student advertising and subscription canvassers through a scholarship contest.

6. Advertisers included Henry Holt, Houghton Mifflin, Charles Scribner, Putnam, Appleton, Lippincott, Dodd Mead, Doran, B. W. Huebsch, John Lane, Forbes, Yale, and many other publishers large and small.

7. Demos and Demos trace the effects of urbanization on American families. Agricultural children worked alongside adults on the farm and then continued their work as they became adults, whereas industrial city children either did not have a significant economic function within the family or, as in poor factor laboring children, performed work often quite different from that of their parents. Urban children also had closer contact with other children in urban neighborhoods. Over the nineteenth century, these shifts led to a more complete distinction between children and adults, and to a youth culture. The high rate of social change and the plurality of alternatives regarding careers, life-styles, and moral codes, and, in cities like Chicago, the disparity between the goals and ideals of immigrants and those of their children, led finally to the growth of adolescence as an observable fact (young people in distress or in rebellion against their parents) and finally to adolescence as a concept (Demos and Demos 216–218).

8. Bryer explains that M. Anderson had been reviewing since 1908 for the *Interior*, which became the *Continent* in 1910, and probably became the editor of the books section in mid-1912 (12). The lead article in the January 2, 1913, "New Books" section, "G. Stanley Hall on Modern Education," praised Hall's new book, *Educational Problems*, and noted, "Dr. Hall's presentation tends to be somewhat popular in tone and always practical in aim rather than merely pedagogic" ([M. Anderson] 21).

9. Using terms like "ardor" and "enthusiasm" (which frequently appeared in the *Little Review*), Addams hoped that youth could play a positive role in reforming modernity: "It is because the ardor of youth has not been attracted to the long effort to modify the ruthlessness of industry by humane enactments, that we sadly miss their resourceful enthusiasm and that at the same time groups of young people who hunger and thirst after social righteousness are breaking their hearts because the social reform is so long delayed and an unsympathetic and hard hearted society frustrates all this hope" (151–152). Political leaders, she suggested, should use these youthful "stores of enthusiasm" to work at practical contemporary efforts to improve society (152).

10. Hollander and Germain note that "Cluett-Peabody Co. was responsible for one of the best known pre–World War I advertising campaigns—a long-running campaign based upon the incredibly handsome, if somewhat priggish looking, Arrow Collar Man" (36) and that the "Jantzen Girl," the central image of another major youth-based campaign for swimwear, by 1928 had become the seventh best known trademark in the United States (37).

11. Ewen and Ewen 222–223. They suggest that "The implicit logic, which extended beyond clothing to almost all areas of life, was that the 'first duty of the citizen is to be a good consumer.' This was the modern patriotic wisdom of David Cohn, a former Sears executive, and a chronicler of 'morals and manners' in the consumer age. It was a patriotic wisdom that assumed the triumph of youth over age, of the *new* over the *durable*" (224). See also Hollander and Germaine on early twentieth-century budget studies that showed that daughters over age fifteen, followed next by young men over fifteen, were responsible for the highest proportion of family expenditure on clothing, regardless of the family's income (13).

12. The award winning ad was for the "Mashie." Text beside a drawing of a young man wearing the hat proclaimed: "Our New Stetson Soft Hat for Young Men . . . designed by us for young men—college men particularly" (*Printer's Ink,* Mar. 23, 1904, 42).

13. Hecht letter to Anderson, on letterhead of National Campaign Service in Chicago with Hecht's name at top. Hecht suggests circularizing every woman belonging to every woman's club in the country and sending out stories to newspapers across the country. He urges her to "operate a publicity campaign and a circularizing campaign simultaneously. The Little Review has a vastly greater appeal to the obfuscated and yearning spinster than the Philistine ever had. It can be placed in every 'liberal's' home. It can be made a National magazine without changing its content an iota. In fact because of this content it can be developed. It possesses the vital asset of 'strangeness.' I am serious about this." He goes on to suggest a fund-raising dinner in Chicago to launch the campaign with his firm: "I swear that in 6 months the Little Review can be given a circulation of 50,000." Like Anderson, and also like Marsden and her circle in London, Hecht felt that some kind of segmentation advertising could bring a mass audience to a modernist little magazine without having to compromise its content.

14. Kehler wrote to Heap: "I am very much interested in the new plans of The Little Review. In fact, I have always been more than usually interested in Miss Anderson's plucky fight to publish a magazine." He gave her the names of several corporate contacts and advertising agents in New York, though he noted, "You

understand, of course, that the advertising agent is not particularly friendly to small circulations . . . I am trying to give you a little inside on a few things that I think of at the moment; and your real object, of course, is to win these men to a *personal* interest in your efforts. Your publication isn't big enough to have much of an appeal to the average advertising man, but you can get business for it from certain types of men, if you can get them interested in your success. This is largely a question of personality, and as you and Miss Anderson have plenty of it, I am sure you will succeed.

"I do not know you so well except through hearsay, but I know Miss Anderson and her work. She is an intellectual asset to the country, and she ought to be supported as such. If you can get that point of view over, you will win in cases where you could not win on the strict advertising merits of your publication" (Kehler letter to Heap). Other correspondence during the mid-twenties suggest similar attempts to involve advertising and publicity agents in the *Little Review.*

15. Marinetti's manifesto, "War, the Only Hygiene of the World," appeared in translation in the November 1914 issue.

16. Demos and Demos (215) quote this from Frank O. Beck's *Marching Manward* (1913).

17. Chicago rapidly began rebuilding, and, in addition to monumental neo-classical civic architecture, more daring innovators in modernist architecture used innovations in iron and then steel frames to build ever-higher and more ornate skyscrapers. John Wellborn Root, Daniel Burnham, William Le Baron Jenney, Dankmar Adler, Louis Sullivan, William Holabird, and Martin Roche all contributed to a new and growing skyline. By 1890 more than $300 million had already been spent on reconstruction, and a quarter acre in the Loop was selling for $900,000. See Lowe 123–129. These new architects not only revolutionized the engineering and aesthetics of the tall building, but they also frequently saw a public social function to the spaces they created. In his essay "The Tall Office Building Artistically Considered," Sullivan called for "a natural and satisfying art, an architecture that will soon become a fine art in the true, the best sense of the word, an art that will live because it will be of the people, for the people, and by the people" (in Lowe 123). Lowe notes of the "Chicago School" that "It is significant that the consummate expressions of the School were to be office buildings, hotels, concert halls, cafes, beer gardens, and theaters. It was to be a supremely public architecture, an enhancement of places where the people gathered" (125).

18. The Washington Shirt Company had three stores in the Loop after a decade of business and claimed to have sold a million collars in one year. This pamphlet is in the Department of Special Collections, University of Chicago Library.

19. Advertisement on a playbill for "On Trial" by Elmer L. Reizenstein, commencing December 27, 1914, at George M. Cohan's Grand Opera House. Fort Dearborn National Bank advertising appeared in many playbills for Chicago theaters during the 1914/1915 season. Playbill Collection, Special Collections, University of Chicago.

20. Many of the playbills in the University of Chicago collection contain advertisements for Loop dance halls (the very sites Addams lamented) and for hotels with their own dance halls and cabarets, like the New Morrison Hotel and the

Congress Hotel and Annex, formerly the Auditorium Annex, with images depicting the young eating in the Pompeian Grill Room or walking down the beautiful halls after the theater performances.

Anderson herself did much writing in the public spaces of the Auditorium Hotel, one of the crowning glories of Adler and Sullivan's architectural careers, and some early notes assessing her own relationship to anarchism are even written on Auditorium Hotel letterhead. As with many *Little Review* writers, she related her political and aesthetic questions to the story of her escape from the oppressiveness of childhood with traditional parents. "Can the government give you a happy childhood," she asked. "Anarchist / He will refuse to stay in a family. If everyone would begin here. . . . Most radicals don't have kind of reaction you had in leaving family. Most radicals can't react this way. An artist always does" (M. Anderson notes). The young Anderson, now a disciple of Emma Goldman, writing in the halls of the Auditorium Hotel, related her personal familial narrative to her self-conception of modernism as anarchism and art synthesized.

21. M. Anderson expressed the wish several times in her article that she were an imagist poet who could capture the "right word" to describe the experience, and this inspired poets in later issues to submit poems about the young violinist. See Bodenheim and Soule.

22. The "Peter Pan" plea for subscribers in the December 1914 issue of the *Little Review* had claimed "four thousand people who have expressed an interest in THE LITTLE REVIEW," and the "ad" aimed at procuring advertising from Mandel Brothers claimed a thousand Chicago readers (June–July 1915, 57). In the April 1916 issue Anderson claimed the review had 2,000 subscribers (25). When the October 1917 issue was confiscated by the post office over Lewis's story "Cantleman's Spring Mate," John Quinn mentioned that the mailing had been of "some three thousand copies" (Quinn letter to Lamar).

23. Because of the great interest in Russian literature, which was frequently discussed by the *Little Review,* and the *Little Review*'s Russian writers, a group also formed to study Russian literature and language at the Fine Arts Building. See October 1915, 45.

24. "To the Innermost" 4. A year later, M. Anderson lamented: "What do you call this fantastic place where age that is weak rules youth that is strong? / Where parents prescribe life for children they cannot understand" ("Reversals" 2).

25. See, for instance, M. H. P.'s article berating Agnes Repplier's disciplinarian emphasis in her essays in the *Atlantic* ("Agnes Repplier on Popular Education"), and M. H. P.'s article "The Education of Girls," again addressing an article in the *Atlantic,* and reflecting on the relative importance of practical domestic skills education to knowledge of the classics and languages for women. Saphier reviewed *The Education of Karl Witte,* relating it to contemporary issues, while Schuchert went on to give a full review to Ellen Key's *The Younger Generation,* discussing her "Charter for Children," and Comfort even reflected on what could be learned from children.

26. The *Little Review* even gained one of its employees from the ranks of adolescent readers. M. Anderson relates a phone call she received shortly after the first number: "My name is Charles Zwaska. I think your *Little Review* is wonderful

and I want to help you in any way I can. I've broken away from conventional schooling and my time is free. Couldn't I be the office boy or something?" (M. Anderson, *Thirty Years,* 50–51). The seventeen-year-old Zwaska worked in the office of the magazine for years and wrote for it occasionally, though he always insisted on calling himself "the office boy."

27. "Sade Iverson" turned out to be Elia Peettie, a reviewer for the Chicago *Tribune* whose reviews M. Anderson detested. She sent in a series of poems about a young milliner with which she intended to parody the *Little Review*'s imagist poetry. An unsuspecting Anderson published many of them, and her readers seemed to love them and take them at face value (Bryer 68).

28. Quinn letter to Anderson.

29. E. Pound had sent M. Anderson and Heap the first three chapters of *Ulysses* in February 1918, and they began publishing the novel in the March 1918 issue of the *Little Review.*

30. Quinn letter to Lamar.

31. "Nausicaa" ran in the issues of April 1920 and May–June 1920, concluding in the July–August 1920 issue. "Oxen of the Sun" began running in the September–December 1920 issue, which was the last issue of the *Little Review* to contain *Ulysses.*

32. Gifford explains that *The Princess's Novelette* was published in London and ran from 1886 to 1904, and that "The magazine's beauty and fashion pages were characterized by thinly disguised plugs for the magazine's advertisers and their products in prose of the sort Gerty echoes" (385–386).

33. Arguing with Henke's claim that "the aim of Madame Verity's cosmetic art is not truth, as her name would imply, but a simpering obfuscation of reality" (Henke 135), Leonard adds, "I would like to suggest the opposite; although Madame Verity's prose style appears to be an 'obfuscation,' its economic message is quite direct: without this product, your eyebrows will fail to attract male attention, and you will be left on the shelf in the sexual marketplace" (120).

34. See Gabler's synoptic edition, to which parenthetical citations to the text of *Ulysses* outside of the *Little Review* refer. It is also interesting that, almost nine years later, Gilbert explains in his diary that Joyce "collects girl's papers, Poppy's (?) paper, Peg's Journal etc. Has a wild idea of getting *A.L.P.* [the "Anna Livia Plurabelle" section of *Finnegans Wake*] published in one complete number of these. Impossible, I think, but one never knows" (14), and Staley reminds us that "In his research for *Finnegans Wake,* Joyce read various periodicals from popular culture, such as *Popply's Paper, The Baker and Confectioner, Boy's Cinema, The Furniture Record, The Schoolgirl's Own, Woman, Woman's Friend, Justice of the Peace,* and *The Hairdresser's Weekly*" (Gilbert 14 n. 27).

Chapter 5. Pluralism and Counterpublic Spheres: Race, Radicalism, and the *Masses*

1. Cooper explains that upon the publication of *Harlem Shadows,* McKay was critically acclaimed as the best black poet since Paul Laurence Dunbar (164) and,

in marking a decisive break with the Dunbar's dialect poetry, he was seen as setting the pace for the new generation of black writers (166).

2. In conceptualizing the distinct nature of 1920s pluralism, Michaels notes: "For pluralism's programmatic hostility to universalism—its hostility to the idea that cultural practices be justified by appeals to what seems universally good or true—requires that such practices be justified instead by appeals to what seems locally good or true, which is to say, it invokes the identity of the group as the grounds for the justification of the group's practices" (14).

3. For an excellent account of McKay's involvement with the *Liberator,* see Cooper's chapter "With the *Liberator*" (134–170). McKay joined the *Liberator* as an associate editor, at Eastman's invitation, in 1921 just as Eastman himself, though still editor-in-chief, was leaving most of the editorial duties to Bob Minor, McKay, and Floyd Dell in order to concentrate on his writing. McKay published forty-two poems in the *Liberator* between April 1919 and August 1923, and eleven articles and reviews between June 1921 and August 1922. McKay and Mike Gold took over as executive editors in January 1922, but McKay resigned from editorship in August 1922.

4. Eastman letter to McKay.

5. Ibid. Eastman even argued that "There was never any disagreement between you and the editors of the Liberator, so far as I am aware, about the proper communist policy toward the race question in the United States."

6. Fishbein explains that "The Socialist Party, believing that respectability and success were becoming attainable, virtually ignored [blacks], and center and right-wing socialists even acquiesced in segregation," and he notes that "Even the party's most popular leader, Eugene Debs, who defied social prejudice by refusing to speak before segregated audiences in the South, failed to see any need for special attention by the party to the plight of blacks" (15). Buhle argues that "the practical absence of Southerners Black and white, Irish Catholics and assorted others from the Socialist ranks did not bode well for the Socialist future. Such insularity was a historical legacy that could not be easily or summarily set aside" (84).

7. McKay spelled out his position: "I still maintain that a revolutionary magazine in advocating the issues of the class struggle in America should handle the Negro problem in the class struggle in proportion to the Negro population and its position in the labour world. And more, I hold to this point of view because the strategic position of Negro labour in the class struggle in America is by far greater and of more importance than the proportion of the 12 millions of blacks [to] the 100 millions of whites." He also chastised Eastman for an unacknowledged insensitivity to a broad range of ethnic problems: "As I quite remember, I tried to discuss the Irish and Indian questions with you once or twice with a view of getting articles on them for the magazine, but, with little sympathy, you said that they were national issues. I never once thought you grasped fully the class struggle significance of national and racial problems, and little instances indexed for me your attitude on the race problem. It was never hostile, always friendly, but never by a long stretch revolutionary" (McKay letter to Eastman, Apr. 3, 1923). And he faulted Eastman for giving in (as he had not before the governmental pressures of the Espionage Act in 1917) to fears of government investigation of the *Liberator* over

race issues: "Do you think I was playing when twice in 1921 you saw coloured men and women at the 'Liberator' office discussing political and race problems with me—and you did not like it from fear of the Department of Justice?" (McKay letter to Eastman, from Petrograd).

8. Nelson argues that "poetry is a discursive formation whose meaning necessarily depends on, is constituted by, its differential relations with all the other discourses and social institutions of its day. Moreover, all these domains and discourses are deeply implicated in one another, for each of them is differentially constituted. And none of the individual relations is unidirectional or independent" (128–129).

9. See anon. Other schemes to avoid the influence of advertisers included taking no money for advertisements placed in the magazine but exacting a percentage from items sold via the *Masses*. However, like the suffrage magazines in Britain discussed in chapter 3, the *Masses* also at times admitted the necessity of succeeding with advertisers, and noted: "Reader do you know—That you can be of great assistance to The Masses. If you patronize our Advertisers and let them know where you saw their Advertisement? Mention The Masses" (July 1913, inside cover). The editors also knew the value of commercial magazine subscription-boosting schemes, such as offering subscribers incentives like a thermos or other products (July 1913, 19).

10. The Associated Press brought a libel suit against the *Masses* for attacking its unfair and partial reporting of the struggles between striking coal miners and the capitalists in West Virginia in 1913. The AP was especially incensed at a cartoon by Young of a man with an "Associated Press" scarf dropping poison from a bottle labeled "Lies" into a pool labeled "The News." The AP finally had to drop the suit in early 1916.

11. "The Masses Press Pearl Contest" (Dec. 1913) stated "The Editors of THE MASSES, desiring to recognize the hilarity contributed to this dull world by the serious columns of the Popular Press, offer a monthly prize of a 14-carat IMITATION PEARL to the newspaper or magazine publishing the most foolish, false, priggish, inane, silly, and altogether ridiculous item in its news or editorial columns. The JEWEL will be attached to a silken banner, upon which the winning PRESS PEARL will be pasted, and the whole sent to the editor of the victorious publication. Moreover, the name of the winning paper will be published in conspicuous type at the top of this column each month, together with the PRESS PEARL which captures the prize."

12. Zurier notes Charles Winter "also sold drawings in a similar conservative style to *Collier's* and *Cosmopolitan*. His wife, Alice Beach Winter, specialized in sentimental illustrations for children's books. Art Young was well known for political cartoons in the *Chicago Inter-Ocean* and the Hearst newspapers, as well as for the satiric drawings in humor magazines," and "Hayden Carruth, business manager for *The Masses*, was an editor of the *Woman's Home Companion;* the writer Horatio Winslow edited the comic weekly *Puck;* Ellis O. Jones contributed humorous sketches to *Life;* Charles Wood was an early muckraker who also published in the *Appeal to Reason;* Mary Heaton Vorse and Inez Haynes Gillmore wrote human interest stories for women's magazines. The first editor-in-chief, Thomas

Seltzer, translated European fiction for a number of New York publishing firms" (30–31). In "Them Asses," R. Brown, a former *Masses* contributing editor, notes that "Nutting, who later edited *Motor Boating* for Mr. Hearst and died at sea in a romantic round-the-world-in-a-motor-boat cruise after coming into $100,000, may well serve as a type of the material that made the first *Masses*" (404).

13. Eastman remembered that "Another innovation that gave character to *The Masses* was our abandonment of the old 'he-and-she' joke and the elaborate two-, three- and four-line dialogue under a picture . . . in the prevalence of these one-line captions we departed sharply from the tradition set by *Life* and *Puck* and *Judge,* although none of us was conscious of this change. It just came natural, in pitting creative art against commercial journalism, to title pictures in this more energetic fashion" (*Enjoyment* 412), but, he continues, "The long-time result of our pictorial revolt, it seems to me, was to introduce into commercial journalism some of the subtler values of creative art. This change, at least, has taken place, and *The Masses* led the way" (412). Moreover, when Norman Hapgood took over editorship of *Harper's Weekly,* he tried to model it on the *Masses'* pictorial style, even employing the same artists; by 1925, the *New Yorker* followed the same path, adopting Howard Brubaker's short paragraph section from the *Masses* (*Enjoyment* 407–412).

14. See Fishbein 30. Zurier notes how popular socialist magazines had become during this period: "In 1912 the weekly *Appeal to Reason* attained a circulation of 761,747; more than 20,000 read the *New York Call* daily, and some 900,000 people—nearly 6 percent of the total electorate—voted for Eugene Debs in the presidential election" (86).

15. See such combination subscription offers as Joseph Klein's, beginning in the January 1913 *Masses* (19), or the Robinson Sales Company's offers beginning in the February 1913 *Masses* featuring combinations with *Ladies World & Housekeeper, McCalls, Good Housekeeping, Cosmopolitan, Pearsons, Hearst's, Metropolitan,* and, again not so paradoxically, *Business America* (19). In the November 1913 issue, the *Masses* even offered itself in combinations with *Pearson's, Harper's Weekly, Literary Digest, Metropolitan, Review of Reviews, Independent, Current Opinion, Cosmopolitan,* and *McClure's* (3).

16. Of course, the price was raised to ten cents, more advertising was accepted, and the magazine for the rest of its life had to be supplemented by donations from rich benefactors (Eastman had a special talent for this, as his many stories of fund-raising successes in *Enjoyment of Living* attest). As Eastman summed up the situation, gesturing at the precarious class issues involved in the magazine: "*The Masses* was a luxurious magazine, in all but opinion aristocratic rather than proletarian . . . this revolutionary magazine lived as it was born, on gifts solicited by me from individual members of the bourgeoisie. Proletarian revolution was still a diversion then; the idea had not acquired a content of violent fact. And moreover, the art and humor in the magazine, its variety and absence of rant, made it seem less extreme than it was. It could be regarded—and usually was, I suppose, when I was soliciting funds—as mainly a co-operative experiment, a magazine in which artists and writers could have an independent say" (*Enjoyment* 455).

17. In the May 1916 issue of the *Masses* (23), next to a drawing by Young entitled "The Latest"—a boot labeled "Canada" kicking a little boy, the *Masses*, out   was an anonymous poem (probably by Eastman or Dell) that read:

> Arrested for Criminal libel by
> the Associated Press—

> Expelled from Columbia Uni-
> versity Library and Book
> Store—

> Ejected from the Subway and
> Elevated stands of New
> York—

> Suppressed by the Magazine Dis-
> tributing Company in Boston—

> Quashed by the United News
> Co. of Philadelphia—

> Kicked Out of Canada by the
> Government—

18. Zurier places the sales figure between 20,000 and 40,000 (51). Hoffman, Allen, and Ulrich say it averaged 14,000 copies a month (29). In the February 1913 issue, the *Masses* announced that it was "on sale at news stands in 400 cities in the United States and Canada. In New York it is on sale throughout the Subway, at Brentano's and at the following news stands" (19). It then listed seventy-seven places in Manhattan, twenty-one in Brooklyn, and three in Newark, New Jersey.

19. Bradner letter to Eastman.

20. Corder letter to Eastman, June 5, 1949.

21. Corder letter to Eastman, January 16, 1955.

22. Occasionally the magazine even published dialect poems without the cartoons, as in "The Green Tempter," which included a drawing of a thick-lipped stereotypical "darkie" alongside a dialect poem about "Det sinful watehmelon" that tempts him to the garden.

23. Young discussed his idea of doing a book of "Authors' Readings" to include his sketches of Riley, telling Riley that it was on seeing his platform readings that he got the idea, and that he had an "intense admiration for your work" and "made mental and sketch-book notes of your characteristics and especially your wonderful impersonation of the true western farmer" (Young letter to Riley).

24. See, for example, Stokes for information about the famous strike.

25. Dell letter to Freeman.

26. Santayana letter to Eastman.

27. Dell, remembering the *Masses* years, complained, "Somehow I never got recognized as a real Proletarian, although that kulak, Sherwood Anderson, imposter that he was, got credit for being a Proletarian author—skulduggery, that's what it is" (Dell letter to Eastman). The poet, artist, and communist Lydia Gibson, a

frequent contributor to the *Masses* and later editor of the *Liberator,* tried to negoti- ate her upper-middle-class means with her desire for proletarian revolution: "No, I'm not 'a lady of wealth'; but I have the comparative security of a little income which I can contribute to the things we all believe in: I've figured out that that is better than refusing to accept it, as in the latter case it would be divided among my family and go for nothing" (L. Gibson letter to Sinclair).

28. No Bonded Worker letter to Benedict.

29. Eastman, "June Morning." While taking pleasure in writing a poem in black dialect, Eastman must have felt in a bind over the issue of identity and au- thenticity. This is the only poem, as far as I can tell, that he contributed anony- mously to the *Masses.*

30. Dell talks about midwestern farmers and shopworkers reading *The Appeal to Reason* and Gronlund's *Co-operative Commonwealth* (*Homecoming* 50–51), and he discusses socialists activities in eastern Iowa.

31. The *Masses* editors were twice tried under the Espionage Act for opposing the war effort.

32. The Barnard poem begins: "You smeared and smirking little bag, / You plump, appealing little brute, you, / Displayed to please when senses flag, / You little paper prostitute, you: // You seem to fix on us afresh / Those eyes imploring and unwinking / Which speak the promptings of the flesh / And set some lusty fellow thinking."

33. See Zurier 39–41 for discussion of the influence of Henri's teachings on the *Masses* artists. Henri, who had been a student in Paris in the 1880s and was inspired by Manet and the impressionists' use of independent salons to mount independent exhibitions in New York in 1908 that included Sloan. Henri also taught his pupils to immerse themselves in the everyday world and thus to gain awareness of political issues.

34. See Sloan's drawing, which parodies cubism. Benson wrote of Wilson's speech in Philadelphia, "Read it. Sleep over it. Then try to figure out what it means. To me it had melted almost to nothing. It so little resembled an administra- tive chart that, beside it, the celebrated portrait of 'A Nude Descending a Staircase' almost made one feverish."

35. In "Memories of the Old *Masses,*" Dell says: "The fact was that these art- ists were art-for-art's-sakers, even if they did have proletarian ashcans in their pic- tures" (484).

36. Bellows letter to Eastman.

37. Buhle explains that as "the left was responding to [the] new internation- alism it was losing sight of the international significance of *American* culture-in- transition, and of American radicals' potentially unique role within it. As faction- fighting tore the Socialist Party assunder in 1917–1919, culture vanished from the foreground of Marxists' concerns" (116) and "Radical thought retreated to a higher version of economism" telegraphed from Petrograd (117).

Epilogue

1. In 1956, Indiana University created its *Union List of Little Magazines, Showing Holdings of 1,037 Little Magazines in the Libraries of Indiana Univer-*

sity, Northwestern University, Ohio State University, State University of Iowa, University of Chicago, University of Illinois. Even in Britain, where little magazine publication has perhaps been less prolific than in America, hundreds of new little magazines have appeared in the second half of the century. See Görtschacher and Sullivan.

Works Cited

Aaronovitch, S. *Monopoly: A Study of British Monopoly Capitalism.* London: Lawrence & Wishart, 1955.

Abercrombie, Lascelles. "The Function of Poetry in the Drama." *Poetry Review* (March 1912): 107–118.

Addams, Jane. *The Spirit of Youth and the City Streets.* Introduction by Allen F. Davis. Chicago: University of Illinois Press, 1972.

Ahearn, Barry. *William Carlos Williams and Alterity: The Early Poetry.* New York: Cambridge University Press, 1994.

Aldington, Richard. Letter to Dora Marsden. December 1913. PUF, *DMP,* Box 1, Folder 12.

Aldington, Richard. Letter to Harold Monro. November 5, 1914. UCLA, *HMP.*

Aldington, Richard. "In the Tube." *Egoist* 2 (May 1915): 74.

Aldington, Richard. "Cinema Exit." *Egoist* 2 (July 1915): 113.

Aldington, Richard. "Rémy de Gourmont." *Drama* 6 (May 1916): 167–183.

Aldred, Guy. Letter to Grace Jardine. January 23, 1912. PUF, *DMP,* Box 2, Folder 25.

Aldred, Guy. Letter to Grace Jardine. January 26, 1912. PUF, *DMP,* Box 2, Folder 25.

Aldred, Guy. Letter to Dora Marsden. September 2, 1912. PUF, *DMP,* Box 2, Folder 25.

"All Cut Up." Cartoon. *Puck* 71, no. 1824 (February 14, 1912): n.p.

Altick, Richard D. *The English Common Reader: A Social History of the Mass Reading Public, 1800–1900.* 1957. Chicago: University of Chicago Press, 1983.

Anderson, Margaret. Circular promoting the *Little Review.* n.d. UWGM, *LRR.*

Anderson, Margaret. Notes on anarchism and childhood. Auditorium Hotel letterhead. n.d. UWGM, *LRR.*

[Anderson, Margaret?]. "G. Stanley Hall on Modern Education." *Continent* 44, no. 1 (January 2, 1913): 21.

Works Cited

Anderson, Margaret. "The Glory of Present-Day Youth." *Continent* (September 11, 1913): 1259.

Anderson, Margaret. "The Germ." *Little Review* 1 (April 1914): 1–2.

Anderson, Margaret. "The Renaissance of Parenthood." *Little Review* 1 (July 1914): 6–14.

Anderson, Margaret. "Nur Wer die Sehnsucht Kennt." *Little Review* 1 (July 1914): 34–37.

Anderson, Margaret. "Our New Poet." *Little Review* 1 (July 1914): 38.

Anderson, Margaret. "A Change of Price." *Little Review* 1 (July 1914): 67.

Anderson, Margaret. "Our Third New Poet." *Little Review* 1 (September 1914): 32.

Anderson, Margaret. "To the Innermost." *Little Review* 1 (October 1914): 2–5.

Anderson, Margaret. "To Serve an Idea." *Little Review* 1 (October 1914): 58.

Anderson, Margaret. "THE LITTLE REVIEW Asks Some Help!" call for subscriptions. *Little Review* 1 (December 1914): between pages 24 and 25.

Anderson, Margaret. "Our First Year." *Little Review* 2 (February 1915): 1–6.

Anderson, Margaret. "Reversals." *Little Review* 2 (September 1915): 1–3.

Anderson, Margaret. *My Thirty Years' War.* New York: Horizon Press, 1969.

Anderson, Sherwood. "The New Note." *Little Review* 1 (March 1914): 23.

Anderson, Sherwood. "Sister." *Little Review* 2 (December 1915): 3–4.

Anon. [Max Eastman, or perhaps William Watson, business manager of the *Masses*] "This Is What It Costs to Publish the Masses." *Masses*, December 1912, 2.

Anrep, Boris. Letter to Harold Monro. June 4, 1913. UCLA *HMP*.

Anrep, Boris. Letter to Harold Monro. June 27, 1913. UCLA, *HMP*.

Arnold, Matthew. *Poetry and Criticism of Matthew Arnold;* ed. A. Dwight Culler. Boston: Houghton Mifflin, 1961.

Ayers, David. *Wyndham Lewis and Western Man.* New York: St. Martin's, 1992.

Baldick, Chris. *The Social Mission of English Criticism 1848–1932.* Oxford: Clarendon, 1983.

Barash, Carol. "Dora Marsden's Feminism, the *Freewoman,* and the Gender Politics of Early Modernism." *Princeton University Library Chronicle,* autumn 1987, 31–56.

Barnard, Seymour. "Girl on a Magazine Cover." *Masses,* January 1917, 3.

Barrie, M. Maltman. "A Democrat's Defense of the House of Lords." *Nineteenth Century,* February 1907, 341.

Baudelaire, Charles. "The Swan." In *The Flowers of Evil,* ed. Marthiel and Jackson Mathews, trans. F. P. Sturm. New York: New Directions, 1955, 109.

Bellows, George. Letter to Max Eastman. [March 1917]. IUL, *ME*.

Benjamin, Walter. "The Work of Art in the Age of Mechanical Reproduction." In *Illuminations,* ed. Hannah Arendt, trans. Harry Zohn. New York: Schocken Books, 1968, 217–251.

Benson, Allan L. "Our New President." *Masses,* May 1913, 3.

Bernstein, George L. *Liberalism and Liberal Politics in Edwardian England.* Boston: Allen & Unwin, 1986.

Blathwayt, Raymond. "England's Taste in Literature." *Fortnightly Review* 97 (January 1, 1912): 160–171.

Bodenheim, Maxwell. "To the Violinist." *Little Review* 1 (September 1914): 1.

Works Cited

Boëthius, Ulf. "Youth, the Media, and Moral Panics." In *Youth Culture in Late Modernity,* ed. Johan Fornäs and Göran Bolin. Thousand Oaks, Calif.: Sage Publications, 1995.

Bourdieu, Pierre. *Distinction: A Social Critique of the Judgement of Taste,* trans. Richard Nice. Cambridge: Harvard University Press, 1984.

Bourdieu, Pierre. "The Forms of Capital." In *Handbook of Theory and Research for the Sociology of Education,* ed. John G. Richardson. New York: Greenwood, 1986, 241–258.

Bourdieu, Pierre. "The Production of Belief: Contribution to an Economy of Symbolic Goods." In *The Field of Cultural Production,* ed. Randal Johnson. New York: Columbia University Press, 1994, 74–111.

Bourne, Randolph. *Youth and Life.* New York: Houghton Mifflin, 1913.

Bowman, Guy. Letter to Dora Marsden. February 23, 1912. PUF, *DMP,* Box 2, Folder 27.

Bowman, Guy. Letter to Dora Marsden and Rebecca West. September 11, 1912. PUF, *DMP,* Box 2, Folder 27.

A Boy. Letter to *Little Review* and poem, "Blindness." *Little Review* 3 (April 1916): 38–39.

A Boy. "Impressions of the Loop." *Little Review* 3 (June–July 1916): 43.

Boyce, George, James Curran, and Pauline Wingate, eds. *Newspaper History: From the Seventeenth Century to the Present Day.* Beverly Hills, Calif.: Sage, 1978.

A Boy Reader. Letter to *Little Review. Little Review* 1 (September 1914): 57–58.

Bradbury, Malcolm. "*The English Review.*" *London Magazine* 5, no. 8 (August 1958): 46–57.

Bradbury, Malcolm, and James McFarlane. *Modernism: A Guide to European Literature 1890–1930.* New York: Penguin, 1991.

Bradner, Grace M. Letter to Max Eastman. June 3, 1948. IUL, *ME.*

Broglie, Gabriel de. *Histoire Politique de la Revue des Deux Mondes de 1829 à 1979.* [Paris]: Librairie Académique Perrin, 1979.

Bromwich, David. "The Genealogy of Disinterestedness." *Raritan* 1, no. 4 (spring 1982): 62–92.

Brown, Lucy. *Victorian News and Newspapers.* New York: Oxford University Press, 1985.

Brown, Robert. "Them Asses." *American Mercury* 30, no. 110 (December 1933): 403–411.

Bryer, Jackson Robert. "'A Trial-Track for Racers': Margaret Anderson and The Little Review." Ph.D. diss., University of Wisconsin, 1965.

Buhle, Paul. *Marxism in the United States: Remapping the History of the American Left.* 2d ed. New York: Verso, 1991.

Bürger, Peter. *Theory of the Avant-Garde.* 1974. Trans. Michael Shaw. Minneapolis: University of Minnesota Press, 1984.

Bürger, Peter. "The Institution of 'Art' as a Category in the Sociology of Literature." *Cultural Critique* 2 (winter 1985–1986): 5–33.

Bürger, Peter. *The Decline of Modernism,* trans. Nicholas Walker. University Park: Pennsylvania State University Press, 1992.

Burrell, Arthur. *Clear Speaking and Good Reading.* London: Longmans, Green & Co., 1898.

Bussard, Lawrence Harold. "French Literary Criticism in the *Mercure de France:* 1890–1899." Ph.D. diss. University of Illinois, 1940.

Byerly, Alison. "From Schoolroom to Stage: Reading Aloud and the Domestication of Victorian Theater." In *Culture and Education in Victorian England,* ed. Patrick Scott and Pauline Fletcher. [Special issue] *Bucknell Review,* 1990, 125–141.

Byington, Steven T. "A Criticism of 'The Egoist.'" *Egoist* 2 (February 1, 1915): 31.

Calhoun, Craig, ed. *Habermas and the Public Sphere.* Cambridge: MIT Press, 1992.

Cannan, Gilbert. "The Poetic Drama: Considered in Four Articles. I. It's Friends." *Poetry Review* 1 (September 1912): 430–432.

Carroll, Joseph. *The Cultural Theory of Matthew Arnold.* Berkeley: University of California Press, 1982.

Cary, Lucien. Review of the *Little Review. Chicago Evening Post, Friday Literary Review,* March 20, 1914, 1.

Clarke, Bruce. "Dora Marsden's Egoism and Modern Letters: West, Weaver, Joyce, Pound, Lawrence, Williams, Eliot." *Works and Days* 2, no. 2 (1985): 27–47.

Clarke, Bruce. "Dora Marsden and Ezra Pound: The *New Freewoman* and 'The Serious Artist.'" *Contemporary Literature* 33, no. 1 (spring 1992): 91–112.

Clarke, Bruce. "Dora Marsden and *The Freewoman:* Anarchism and Literature." *Works and Days* 10, no. 1 (1992): 129–143.

Clarke, Bruce. *Dora Marsden and Early Modernism: Gender, Individualism, Science.* Ann Arbor: University of Michigan Press, 1996.

Clifford, James. *The Predicament of Culture: Twentieth-Century Ethnography, Literature and Art.* Cambridge: Harvard University Press, 1988.

Cohn, Robert Greer. *Toward the Poems of Mallarmé.* Berkeley: University of California Press, 1980.

Collins, Philip. *Reading Aloud: A Victorian Métier.* Lincoln: The Tennyson Society, 1973.

Collins, Philip. "'Agglomerating Dollars with Prodigious Rapidity': British Pioneers on the American Lecture Circuits." In *Victorian Literature and Society: Essays Presented to Richard D. Altick,* ed. James R. Kincaid and Albert J. Kuhn. Columbus: Ohio State University Press, 1984.

Collins, Philip, ed. *Charles Dickens: The Public Readings.* Oxford: Clarendon Press, 1975.

Comfort, Will Levington. "Education by Children." *Little Review* 2 (June–July 1915): 5–7.

Conrad, Joseph. Letter to Ford Madox Ford. October 10, 1908. CUKL, *FMF.*

Cooper, Wayne F. *Claude McKay: Rebel Sojourner in the Harlem Renaissance.* Baton Rouge: Louisiana State University Press, 1987.

Corder, Minnie Federman. Letter to Max Eastman. June 5, 1949. IUL, *ME.*

Corder, Minnie Federman. Letter to Max Eastman. January 16, 1955. IUL, *ME.*

Corelli, Marie. *The Sorrows of Satan: or The Strange Experience of One Geoffrey Tempest, Millionaire.* Philadelphia: Lippincott, 1896.

Cork, Richard. *Vorticism and Abstract Art in the First Machine Age,* vol. 1. Berkeley: University of California Press, 1976.

Cost of Living of the Working Classes: Report of an Enquiry by the Board of Trade into Working-Class Rents and Retail Prices together with the Rate of Wages in Certain Occupations in Industrial Towns of the United Kingdom in 1912. London: T. Fisher Unwin, 1913.

Cowen, Tyler. *In Praise of Commercial Culture.* Cambridge: Harvard University Press, 1998.

Cronyn, George. "The Farmer's Crusade." *Liberator* 1, no. 8 (October 1918): 5–12.

D., A. E. "Sophomoric Epigrams." *Little Review* 2 (October 1915): 37–38.

Damon-Moore, Helen. *Magazines for the Millions: Gender and Commerce in the* Ladies' Home Journal *and the* Saturday Evening Post *1880–1910.* Albany: SUNY Press, 1994.

Dangerfield, George. *The Strange Death of Liberal England 1910–1914.* 1935. New York: Perigee, 1980.

Dasenbrock, Reed Way. *The Literary Vorticism of Ezra Pound and Wyndham Lewis: Towards the Condition of Painting.* Baltimore: Johns Hopkins University Press, 1985.

Davie, Donald. *Ezra Pound.* Chicago: University of Chicago Press, 1975.

Davis, Allen F. Introduction to Jane Addams, *The Spirit of Youth and the City Streets.* Chicago: University of Illinois Press, 1972.

"Dear Editors." *Every Week,* November 15, 1915, 12. Newspaper clipping in IUL, *ME.*

Debs, Eugene. "What Eugene Debs Says about Us." *Masses,* February 1911, 3.

Décaudin, Michel. "Le 'Mercure de France': Filiations et Orientations." *Revue d'Histoire Littéraire de la France* 92 (January–February 1992): 7–15.

Dell, Floyd. "Books." *Liberator,* March 1918, 32–33.

Dell, Floyd. *Homecoming: An Autobiography.* New York: Farrar and Rinehart, 1933.

Dell, Floyd. "Memories of the Old Masses." *American Mercury* 68, no. 304 (April 1949): 481–487.

Dell, Floyd. Letter to Joseph Freeman. April 25, 1951. NL, *FDP.*

Dell, Floyd. Letter to Max Eastman. October 26, 1951. IUL, *ME.*

Demos, John, and Virginia Demos. "Adolescence in Historical Perspective." In *The American Family in Socio-Historical Perspective,* ed. Michael Gordon. New York: St. Martin's Press, 1973.

Dettmar, Kevin J. H., and Stephen Watt, eds. *Marketing Modernisms: Self-Promotion, Canonization, and Rereading.* Ann Arbor: University of Michigan Press, 1996.

Deville, Étienne. *Index de Mercure de France 1672–1832.* Paris: Jean Schemit, 1910.

Dickens, Charles. *Charles Dickens: The Public Readings,* ed. Philip Collins. Oxford: Clarendon Press, 1975.

Dobrée, Bonamy. Letter to Harold Monro. April 23, 1913. UCLA, *HMP,* Box 1.

Dowling, Linda. *Language and Decadence in the Victorian Fin de Siècle.* Princeton: Princeton University Press, 1986.

Doyle, Brian. "The Invention of English." In *Englishness: Politics and Culture 1880–1920,* ed. Robert Colls and Philip Dodd. Dover, N.H.: Croom Helm, 1986, 89–115.

Eastman, Max. "Editorial Notice." *Masses,* December 1912, 3.

Eastman, Max. "June Morning." *Masses,* June 1913.

Works Cited

Eastman, Max. "The Masses and the Negro: A Criticism and a Reply." *Masses,* May 1915, 3.

[Eastman, Max?]. "Note." *Masses,* April 1916, 21.

[Eastman, Max?]. "Arrested for Criminal Libel." *Masses,* May 1916, 23.

Eastman, Max. "An Important Announcement." *Masses,* August 1916, 5.

[Eastman, Max?]. "The Girl on the Cover." *Masses,* December 1916, 29.

Eastman, Max. Editorial on John Reed. *Liberator* 3, no. 12 (December 1920): 6.

Eastman, Max. Introduction to Claude McKay, *Harlem Shadows: The Poems of Claude McKay.* New York: Harcourt Brace, 1922.

Eastman, Max. Letter to Claude McKay, n.d. [March? 1923]. IUL, *ME.*

Eastman, Max. *Enjoyment of Living.* New York: Harper and Brothers, 1948.

Eley, Geoff. "Nations, Publics, and Political Cultures: Placing Habermas in the Nineteenth Century." In *Habermas and the Public Sphere,* ed. Craig Calhoun. Cambridge: MIT Press, 1992, 289–339.

Eliot, T. S. *The Sacred Wood.* 1920. New York: Methuen, 1986.

Eliot, T. S. "Little Gidding." In *T. S. Eliot: Collected Poems 1909–1962.* New York: Harcourt Brace Jovanovich, 1970, 200–209.

Ellmann, Richard. *James Joyce: New and Revised Edition.* New York: Oxford University Press, 1983.

Everett, Edwin Mallard. *The Party of Humanity.* Chapel Hill: University of North Carolina Press, 1939.

Everts, Katherine Jewell. *The Speaking Voice: Principles of Training Simplified and Condensed.* London: Harper & Brothers, 1908.

Ewen, Stuart, and Elizabeth Ewen. *Channels of Desire: Mass Images and the Shaping of American Consciousness.* New York: McGraw-Hill, 1982.

Farr, Florence. *The Music of Speech.* London: Elkin Mathews, 1909.

Felski, Rita. *Beyond Feminist Aesthetics: Feminist Literature and Social Change.* Cambridge: Harvard University Press, 1989.

Ferris, Paul. *The House of Northcliffe: A Biography of an Empire.* New York: World, 1972.

Ferry, David. "The Diction of American Poetry." In *American Poetry,* ed. Irvin Ehrenpreis. Stratford-upon-Avon Studies, vol. 7. London: Edward Arnold, 1965.

Ficke, Arthur Davison. Letter to *Little Review. Little Review* 3 (May 1916): 41.

Fishbein, Leslie. Introduction to Rebecca Zurier, *Art for the Masses: A Radical Magazine and Its Graphics, 1911–1917.* Philadelphia: Temple University Press, 1988.

Fleming, Canon James. *The Art of Reading and Speaking.* 2d ed. London: Edward Arnold, 1896.

Fletcher, John Gould. "Vers Libre and Advertising." *Little Review* 2 (April 1915): 29–30.

Flint, F. S. Review of *Canzoni* by Ezra Pound. *Poetry Review* 1 (January 1912): 28–29.

Flint, F. S. "Easter." *Egoist* 2 (May 1915): 75.

Flory, Wendy Stallard. "*Enemy of the Stars.*" In *Wyndham Lewis: A Revaluation: New Essays,* ed. Jeffrey Meyers. Montreal: McGill-Queen's University Press, 1980.

Works Cited

Flynn, Elizabeth Gurley. "Do You Believe in Patriotism? *Masses,* March 1916, 12.

Ford, Ford Madox. Letter to J. B. Pinker. [ca. 1906?]. CUKL, *FMF.*

Ford, Ford Madox. *Mr. Apollo: A Just Possible Story.* London: Methuen, 1908.

Ford, Ford Madox. "The Function of the Arts in the Republic: I. Literature." *English Review* 1 (December 1908): 157–160.

Ford, Ford Madox. Letter to "Monsieur et cher Confrère." December 2, 1908. UTHRC.

Ford, Ford Madox. Letter to Arnold Bennett. [probably late 1908 or early 1909]. UTHRC.

Ford, Ford Madox. "The Function of Arts in the Republic: IV. The Plastic Arts." *English Review* 1 (March 1909): 797.

Ford, Ford Madox. *The Critical Attitude.* 1911. Reprint, New York: Books for Libraries Press, 1967.

Ford, Ford Madox. *Ladies Whose Bright Eyes.* 1911. Reprint, New York: Ecco, 1987 (from 1935 Lippincott edition).

Ford, Ford Madox. *Collected Poems of Ford Madox Hueffer.* London: Goschen, 1914.

Ford, Ford Madox. *Between St. Dennis and St. George: A Sketch of Three Civilizations.* London: Hodder and Stoughton, 1915.

Ford, Ford Madox. *Parade's End.* New York: Knopf, 1961.

Ford, Ford Madox. *The Letters of Ford Madox Ford,* ed. Richard M. Ludwig. Princeton: Princeton University Press, 1965.

Forestier, Louis. "Présentation." *Revue d'Histoire Littéraire de la France* 92 (January–February 1992).

Fort Dearborn National Bank. Ad in playbill for *On Trial* by Elmer L. Reizenstein, commencing December 27, 1914, at George M. Cohan's Grand Opera House. Chicago. Playbill Collection. Department of Special Collections, University of Chicago Library.

Frail, David. *The Early Politics and Poetics of William Carlos Williams.* Ann Arbor: UMI Research Press, 1987.

Fraser, Nancy. "Rethinking the Public Sphere: A Contribution to the Critique of Actually Existing Democracy." In *Habermas and the Public Sphere,* ed. Craig Calhoun. Cambridge: MIT Press, 1992, 109–142.

Freeman, Joseph. *An American Testament: A Narrative of Rebels and Romantics.* London: Victor Gollancz, 1938.

Gabler, Hans Walter, with Wolfhard Steppe and Claus Melchior. *Ulysses: A Critical and Synoptic Edition.* 3 vols. New York: Garland, 1984.

Garner, Les. *A Brave and Beautiful Spirit: Dora Marsden 1882–1960.* Aldershot: Avebury, 1990.

Gaskell, Ronald. "Eliot and Dante." *Agenda* 23, no. 3–4 (autumn–winter 1985/1986): 167–179.

Ghéon, Henri. "Introductory Speech Delivered at the First Poetry Matinee of the Theatre du Vieux Colombier," trans. F. S. Flint. *Poetry and Drama* 2 (March 1914): 42–46.

Gibson, Lydia. Letter to Upton Sinclair. April 20 [n.y. 1920s]. IUL, *US.*

Gibson, Wilfrid. "Some Thoughts on the Future of Poetic-Drama." *Poetry Review* 1 (March 1912): 119–122.

Works Cited

Gifford, Don, with Robert J. Seidman. Ulysses *Annotated: Notes for James Joyce's* Ulysses. 2d ed. Berkeley: University of California Press, 1988.

Gilbert, Stuart. "Selections from the Paris Diary of Stuart Gilbert, 1929–1934," ed. Thomas F. Staley and Randolph Lewis. *Joyce Studies Annual* 1 (1990): 2–25.

Girl. Letter to "The Girls' Club." *Ladies' Home Journal* (July 1914): 49.

Glintenkamp, Henry. Cartoon. *Masses,* January 1914, 9.

Goldring, Douglas. *South Lodge: Reminiscences of Violet Hunt, Ford Madox Ford and the English Review Circle.* London: Constable, 1943.

Goldring, Douglas. *Trained for Genius: The Life and Writings of Ford Madox Ford.* New York: Dutton, 1949.

Görtschacher, Wolfgang. *Little Magazine Profiles: The Little Magazines in Great Britain 1939–1993.* Salzburg: University of Salzburg, 1993.

Gosse, Edmund. Letter to Harold Monro. January 19, 1914. UCLA, *HMP.*

Gourmont, Rémy de. "Le Mercure de France." *Promenades Littéraires,* 4th series. Paris: Mercure de France, 1912, 81–92.

Graham, Walter. *English Literary Periodicals.* New York: Thomas Nelson, 1930.

Grant, Joy. *Harold Monro and the Poetry Bookshop.* London: Routledge and Kegan Paul, 1967.

Graver, David. "Vorticist Performance and Aesthetic Turbulence in *Enemy of the Stars.*" *PMLA* 107, no. 3 (May 1992): 482–496.

"The Great Adult Review." *Spectator,* June 10, 1911, 875–876.

"The Green Tempter." Cartoon. *Puck* 66, no. 1691 (July 28, 1909): n.p.

Grierson, Francis. "Woman's New Era." *New Freewoman* 1 (June 15, 1913): 10–11.

Gross, John. *The Rise and Fall of the Man of Letters.* 1969. Chicago: Elephant Paperbacks, 1992.

Guthrie, Thomas Anstey. *Burglar Bill and Other Pieces for Use of the Young Reciter.* London: Bradbury, Agnew & Co., 1888.

Haberman, Frederick William. "The Elocutionary Movement in England, 1750–1850." Ph.D. diss., Cornell University, 1947.

Habermas, Jürgen. *The Structural Transformation of the Public Sphere: An Inquiry into a Category of Bourgeois Society.* 1962. Trans. Thomas Burger. Cambridge: MIT Press, 1992.

Habermas, Jürgen. "Consciousness-Raising or Redemptive Criticism: The Contemporaneity of Walter Benjamin." 1972. *New German Critique* 17 (spring 1979): 30–59.

Habermas, Jürgen. *Legitimation Crisis.* 1973. Trans. Thomas McCarthy. Boston: Beacon Press, 1975.

Habermas, Jürgen. "The Public Sphere: An Encyclopedia Article (1964)." *New German Critique* 3 (fall 1974): 49–55.

Halcombe, J. J., and W. H. Stone. *The Speaker at Home: Chapters on Public Speaking and Reading Aloud, and on the Physiology of Speech.* 3d. ed. London: George Bell & Sons, 1874.

Hall, G. Stanley. *Adolescence: Its Psychology, and Its Relations to Physiology, Anthropology, Sociology, Sex, Crime, Religion, and Education.* New York: D. Appleton and Co., 1904.

Hallberg, Robert von. "Ezra Pound and the *Mercure de France.*" *American Poetry* 6 (winter 1989): 11–14.

Works Cited

Hallberg, Robert von. "Libertarian Imagism." *Modernism/Modernity,* no. 2 (April 1995): 63–79.

Halsey, A. H., John Sheehan, and John Vaizey. "Schools." In *Trends in British Society since 1900,* ed. A. H. Halsey. London: St. Martin's Press, 1972, 148–191.

Hampton, Timothy. "Virgil, Baudelaire and Mallarmé at the Sign of the Swan: Poetic Translation and Historical Allegory." *Romantic-Review* 73, no. 4 (November 1982): 438–451.

Hannah, Leslie. *The Rise of the Corporate Economy.* London: Methuen, 1976.

"The Happy Neighbors." Cartoon. *Puck* 66, no. 1691 (July 28, 1909): n.p.

Harrison, Austin. Promotional circular for the *English Review.* In *Academy* 78 (March 19, 1910): 268.

Harrison, Austin. Letter to James B. Pinker. May 11, 1910. NUML, *PP.*

Harrison, Austin. Letter to James B. Pinker. January 12, 1912. NUML, *PP.*

Harvey, David Dow. *Ford Madox Ford 1873–1939: A Bibliography of Works and Criticism.* Princeton: Princeton University Press, 1962.

Heap, Jane. "Art and Law." *Little Review* 7 (September–December 1920): 5–7.

Hecht, Ben. Letter to Margaret Anderson. June 18 [n.y.]. UWGM, *LRR.*

Hecht, Ben. "Slobberdom, Sneerdom, and Boredom." *Little Review* 2 (June–July 1915): 22–35.

Hecht, Ben. "The American Family." *Little Review* 2 (August 1915): 1–5.

Hecht, Ben. "Dregs." *Little Review* 2 (November 1915): 25–33.

Henke, Suzette. "Gerty MacDowell: Joyce's Sentimental Heroine." In *Women in Joyce,* ed. Suzette Henke and Elaine Unkeless. Urbana: University of Illinois Press, 1982, 132–149.

Henri, Robert. Cartoon. *Masses,* March 1913, 16.

Hindshaw, Jas. Letter to Dora Marsden. July 1, 1912. PUF, *DMP,* Box 3, Folder 2.

Hirsch, E. D. *Validity in Interpretation.* New Haven: Yale University Press, 1967.

Hoffman, Frederick J., Charles Allen, and Carolyn F. Ulrich. *The Little Magazine: A History and a Bibliography.* Princeton: Princeton University Press, 1946.

Hollander, Stanley C., and Richard Germain. *Was There a Pepsi Generation before Pepsi Discovered It? Youth-Based Segmentation in Marketing.* Lincolnwood, Ill.: NTC Business Books, 1992.

Holmes, Stephen. "The Secret History of Self-Interest." In *Beyond Self Interest,* ed. Jane Mansbridge. Chicago: University of Chicago Press, 1990, 267–286.

Holroyd, Michael. *Bernard Shaw.* Vol. 2, *1898–1918: The Pursuit of Power.* New York: Random House, 1989.

Hopkin, Deian. "The Socialist Press in Britain 1890–1910." In *Newspaper History: From the Seventeenth Century to the Present Day,* ed. George Boyce, James Curran, and Pauline Wingate. Beverly Hills, Calif.: Sage, 1978, 294–306.

"How to Make Money for the Cause." *Suffragette,* July 3, 1914, 206.

Hulme, T. E. Letter to Wyndham Lewis, n.d. CUKL, *WL.*

Hulme, T. E. "German Chronicle." *Poetry and Drama* 2, no. 6 (June 1914): 224–228.

Hunt, Violet. *I Have This to Say: The Story of My Flurried Years.* New York: Boni & Liveright, 1926.

Huyssen, Andreas. *After the Great Divide: Modernism, Mass Culture, Postmodernism.* Bloomington: Indiana University Press, 1986.

Works Cited

"Important Examination Notices." *Poetical Gazette,* April 1912, 189–191.

An Interested Reader. Letter to *Little Review. Little Review* 1 (October 1914): 56–57.

Iverson, Sade [Elia Peettie]. Letter to *Little Review. Little Review* 1 (April 1914): 49.

Jauss, Hans Robert. *Toward an Aesthetic of Reception,* trans. Timothy Bahti. Minneapolis: University of Minnesota Press, 1982.

Jay, Martin. *Downcast Eyes: The Denigration of Vision in Twentieth-Century French Thought.* Berkeley: University of California Press, 1993.

Jay, Martin. "Habermas and Modernism." In *Habermas and Modernity,* ed. Richard J. Bernstein. Cambridge: MIT Press, 1994, 125–139.

Jeffares, A. Norman. *W. B. Yeats: A New Biography.* London: Hutchinson, 1988.

Jennings, Herbert. *Voice and Its Natural Development.* London: George Allen & Co., 1911.

Jensen, Robert. *Marketing Modernism in Fin-de-Siècle Europe.* Princeton University Press, 1994.

Johnson, James Weldon. "Negro Poetry: A Reply." *Liberator,* April 1918, 40–41, 43.

Johnson, Josephine A. "Return of the Scops: English Poetry Performance since 1960." In *Performance of Literature in Historical Perspectives,* ed. David W. Thompson. Lanham, Md.: University Press of America, 1983, 301–316.

Jones, Mark. "Recuperating Arnold: Romanticism and Modern Projects of Disinterestedness." *Boundary 2* 18, no. 2 (summer 1991): 65–103.

Joyce, James. "Nausicaa." *Little Review* 6, no. 11 (April 1920): 43–50; 7, no. 1 (May–June 1920): 61–72; 7, no. 2 (July–August 1920): 42–58.

Judd, Alan. *Ford Madox Ford.* Cambridge: Harvard University Press, 1991.

"A Junior Order." *Poetical Gazette,* January 1912, 44–46.

Kadlec, David. "Pound, *Blast,* and Syndicalism." *English Literary History* 60, no. 4 (winter 1993): 1015–1031.

Kaplan, Joel H., and Sheila Stowell. *Theatre and Fashion: Oscar Wilde to the Suffragettes.* Cambridge: Cambridge University Press, 1994.

Keating, Peter. *The Haunted Study: A Social History of the English Novel 1875–1914.* London: Secker & Warburg, 1989.

Kehler, James Howard. Letter to Jane Heap. August 1, 1917. UWGM, *LRR.*

Kempf, Richard. Cartoon. *Masses* March 1914, 20.

Kenner, Hugh. *Wyndham Lewis* (1954). New York: New Directions, 1964.

Knox, Bryant. "Allen Upward and Ezra Pound." *Paideuma* 3, no. 1 (1974): 71–83.

Kopelin, Louis. *Masses,* February 1911, inside cover.

Laughlin, Clara. "The Perfect Comrade." Monthly column. *Good Housekeeping* 46 and 47 (1908).

Lears, Jackson. *Fables of Abundance: A Cultural History of Advertising in America.* New York: Basic Books, 1994.

Leckie, Barbara. "Reading Bodies, Reading Nerves: 'Nausicaa' and the Discourse of Censorship." *James Joyce Quartely* 34 nos. 1–2 (1996 fall/1997 winter): 65–85.

Lee, Alan. "The Structure, Ownership and Control of the Press, 1855–1914." In *Newspaper History: From the Seventeenth Century to the Present Day,* ed.

Works Cited

George Boyce, James Curran, and Pauline Wingate. Beverly Hills, Calif.: Sage, 1978, 117–129.

Leeming, Glenda. *Poetic Drama*. New York: St. Martin's Press, 1989.

Leiss, William, Stephen Kline, and Sut Jhally. *Social Communication in Advertising: Persons, Products & Images of Well-Being*. 2d ed. New York: Routledge, 1990.

Leonard, Garry. *Advertising and Commodity Culture in Joyce*. Gainesville: University Press of Florida, 1998.

Levenson, Michael. *A Genealogy of Modernism: A Study of English Literary Doctrine 1908–1922*. New York: Cambridge University Press, 1984.

Lewis, Wyndham. "Long Live the Vortex." *Blast* 1 (June 20, 1914): 7–8.

Lewis, Wyndham. "Manifesto—I." *Blast* 1: (June 20, 1914): 11–28.

Lewis, Wyndham. *Enemy of the Stars*. *Blast* 1 (June 20, 1914): 51–85.

Lewis, Wyndham. "Life Is the Important Thing!" *Blast* 1 (June 20, 1914): 129–131.

Lewis, Wyndham. "To Suffragettes." *Blast* 1 (June 20, 1914): 151–152.

Lewis, Wyndham. *The Letters of Wyndham Lewis,* ed. W. K. Rose. Norfolk, Ct.: New Directions, 1963.

Lewis, Wyndham. "Physics of the Not-Self." In *Wyndham Lewis: Collected Poems and Plays,* ed. Alan Munton. New York: Persea Books, 1979, 193–204.

Lidderdale, Jane, and Mary Nicholson. *Dear Miss Weaver: Harriet Shaw Weaver 1876–1961.* New York: Viking, 1970.

Liebich, Rudolf von. "A Ferrer School in Chicago." *Little Review* 1 (November 1914): 54–55.

Lowe, David. *Lost Chicago*. Boston: Houghton Mifflin, 1978.

Lowell, Amy. "Miss Columbia: An Old-Fashioned Girl." *Little Review* 1 (June 1914): 36–37.

Lowell, Amy. "The Grocery." *Masses,* June 1916, 17.

Lowell, Carlotta Russell. "The Masses and the Negro: A Criticism and a Reply." *Masses,* May 1915, 3.

Lyon, Janet. "Militant Discourse, Strange Bedfellows: Suffragettes and Vorticists before the War." *Differences* 4, no. 2 (1992): 100–133.

Lyon, Minnie. Letter to the *Little Review*. *Little Review* 1 (January 1915): 61.

Macnamara, Francis. Letter to Harold Monro. n.d. UCLA, *HMP.*

MacShane, Frank. "The English Review." *South Atlantic Quarterly* 60 (1961): 311–320.

Mallarmé, Stéphane. "Le Vierge, le vivace et le bel aujourd'hui." In *Stéphane Mallarmé: Poems,* trans. Roger Fry, commentary by Charles Mauron. New York: Oxford University Press, 1937, 170–173.

Marinetti, F. T. "Wireless Imagination and Words at Liberty." *Poetry and Drama* 1 (September 1913): 319–326.

Marinetti, F. T. "War, the Only Hygiene of the World." *Little Review* 1 (November 1914): 30–31.

Marinetti, F. T., and C. R. W. Nevinson. "Vital English Art" (1914). In *Futurism and Futurisms,* ed. Pontus Hulten. New York: Abbeville Press, 1986, 529.

Marsden, Dora. Circular advertising the *New Freewoman* Thousand Club Membership Establishment Fund. BL, *HSW.*

Marsden, Dora. Expenditures and credits, and subscription list for the *Freewoman*. PUF, *DMP,* Box 3, Folder 12.

Marsden, Dora. Letter to Harriet Shaw Weaver. n.d. BL, *HSW.*

Marsden, Dora. Prospectus for the *New Freewoman*. BL, *HSW.*

Marsden, Dora. "An Appeal." *Freewoman,* February 15, 1912, 244.

Marsden, Dora. "'Freewoman' Clubs." *Freewoman,* February 15, 1912, 244.

Marsden, Dora. Letter to Harriet Shaw Weaver. December 2, 1912, BL, *HSW.*

Marsden, Dora. Letter to Harriet Shaw Weaver. April 15, 1913. BL, *HSW.*

Marsden, Dora. "Views and Comments." *New Freewoman,* July 1, 1913, 23–25.

Marsden, Dora. "Views and Comments." *New Freewoman,* December 15, 1913, 244–245.

Marsden, Dora. Letter to Harriet Shaw Weaver. October 1915. BL, *HSW.*

Marsden, Dora. Letter to Harriet Shaw Weaver. January 5, 1918. BL, *HSW.*

Marsden, Dora. Letter to Harriet Shaw Weaver. January 22, 1918. BL, *HSW.*

Marsden, Dora. Letter to Harriet Shaw Weaver. November 21, 1918. BL, *HSW.*

Marsden, Dora. Letter to Harriet Shaw Weaver. December 4, 1918. BL, *HSW.*

Marsden, Dora. Letter to Harriet Shaw Weaver. n.d. [late December 1918]. BL, *HSW.*

Marshall, Peter. *Demanding the Impossible: A History of Anarchism.* London: Harper Collins, 1992.

Martin, Wallace. *The New Age under Orage: Chapters in English Cultural History.* New York: Barnes & Noble, 1967.

Mason, John. "Monthly and Quarterly Reviews 1865–1914." In *Newspaper History: From the Seventeenth Century to the Present Day,* ed. George Boyce, James Curran, and Pauline Wingate. Beverly Hills, Calif.: Sage, 1978, 281–293.

"The Masses Press Pearl Contest." *Masses,* December 1913, 9.

Materer, Timothy. *Wyndham Lewis the Novelist.* Detroit: Wayne State University Press, 1976.

Materer, Timothy. *Vortex Pound, Eliot, and Lewis.* Ithaca: Cornell University Press, 1979.

Materer, Timothy. "Making It Sell! Ezra Pound Advertises Modernism." In *Marketing Modernisms: Self-Promotion, Canonization, and Rereading,* ed. Kevin J. H. Dettmar and Stephen Watt. Ann Arbor: University of Michigan Press, 1996, 17–36.

McDougal, Stuart Y. "Dreaming a Renaissance: Pound's Dantean Inheritance." In *Ezra Pound among the Poets,* ed. George Bornstein. Chicago: University of Chicago Press, 1985, 63–80.

McKay, Claude. *Harlem Shadows: The Poems of Claude McKay.* New York: Harcourt, Brace, 1922.

McKay, Claude. Letter to Max Eastman. April 3, 1923. IUL, *CM.*

McKay, Claude. Letter to Max Eastman. From Petrograd. May 18, 1923. IUL, *CM.*

McKay, Claude. *A Long Way from Home.* 1937. New York: Harcourt Brace and World, 1970.

Meir, Colin. "Yeats's Search for a Natural Language." *Éire–Ireland* 19, no. 3 (fall 1984): 77–91.

Melrose, Andrew. Letter to James B. Pinker. June 29, 1909. NUML, *PP.*

Works Cited

Michaels, Walter Benn. *Our America: Nativism, Modernism, and Pluralism.* Durham, N.C.: Duke University Press, 1995.

Mizener, Arthur. *The Saddest Story: A Biography of Ford Madox Ford.* New York: Carroll & Graf, 1985.

Monro, Harold, Lecture notes. UCLA, *HMP,* Box 5.

Monro, Harold. "Preface." *Poetry Review* 1 (January 1912): 3–5.

Monro, Harold. "The Future of Poetry." *Poetry Review* 1 (January 1912): 10–13.

Monro, Harold. "The Nineties." *Poetry Review* 1 (June 1912): 247–250.

Monro, Harold. "Notes and Comments." *Poetry Review* 1 (June 1912): 423–424.

Monro, Harold. "Notes and Comments." *Poetry Review* 1 (August 1912): 352–354.

Monro, Harold. "The Bookshop." *Poetry Review* 1 (November 1912): 498–500.

Monro, Harold. "Poetry and the Public." *Poetry and Drama* 1 (June 1913): 126–127.

Monro, Harold. "Current English Poetry." *Poetry and Drama* 1 (June 1913): 201–210.

Monro, Harold. "Futurist Poetry." *Poetry and Drama* 1 (September 1913): 264.

Monro, Harold. "Broadsides and Chap-Books." *Poetry and Drama* 1 (September 1913): 265.

Monro, Harold. "Poetry and Sermons." *Poetry and Drama* 1 (September 1913): 266.

Monro, Haorld. "Notes and Announcements." *Poetry and Drama* 1 (September 1913): 272.

Monro, Harold. "The Bookshop." *Poetry and Drama* 1 (December 1913): 387.

Monro, Harold. "Notes and Announcements." *Poetry and Drama* 1 (December 1913): 391–392.

Monro, Harold. "Readings of Poetry." *Poetry and Drama* 2 (March 1914): 2.

Monro, Harold. "The Imagists Discussed." *Egoist* 2 (May 1, 1915): 77–80.

Monro, Harold. Letter to John Drinkwater. January 30, 1924. UCLA, *HMP.*

Mugglestone, Lynda. "Shaw, Subjective Inequality, and the Social Meanings of Language in *Pygmalion.*" *Review of English Studies* 44, no. 175 (August 1993): 373–385.

Murphy, Michael. "'One Hundred Per Cent Bohemia': Pop Decadence and the Aestheticization of Commodity in the Rise of the Slicks." In *Marketing Modernisms; Self-Promotion, Canonization, and Rereading,* ed. Kevin J. H. Dettmar and Stephen Watt. Ann Arbor: University of Michigan Press, 1996, 61–89.

Negt, Oskar, and Alexander Kluge. *Public Sphere and Experience: Towards an Analysis of the Bourgeois and Proletarian Public Sphere.* 1972. Trans. Peter Labanyi, Jamie Owen Daniel, and Assenka Oksiloff. Minneapolis: University of Minnesota Press, 1993.

Nelson, Cary. *Repression and Recovery: Modern American Poetry and the Politics of Cultural Memory 1910–1945.* Madison: University of Wisconsin Press, 1989.

"A Nest of Singing Birds." *Daily News and Leader,* January 3, 1913, 12.

Nevett, T. R. *Advertising in Britain: A History.* London: Heinemann, 1982.

Newbolt, Henry, and the Committee on English in the Educational System of England. *The Teaching of English in England, Being the Report of the Departmental Committee Appointed by the President of the Board of Education to Inquire into the Position of English in the Educational System of England.* London: His Majesty's Stationary Office, 1921.

Works Cited

Newman, Ernest. "The Piano-Player and the Music of the Future." *English Review* 16 (January 1914): 246–260.

No Bonded Worker. Letter to James W. Benedict. May 6, 1913. IUL, *ME.*

Norman, C. H. "The New Prostitution." *Freewoman,* April 11, 1912, 401–402.

North, Michael. *The Dialect of Modernism: Race, Language and Twentieth-Century Literature.* New York: Oxford University Press, 1994.

O'Connor, T. P. Review of the *English Review. T. P.'s Weekly,* December 4, 1908, 732.

O'Grady, Hardress. *Reading Aloud and Literary Appreciation.* London; G. Bell & Sons, 1914.

Ohmann, Richard. *Selling Culture: Magazines, Markets, and Class at the Turn of the Century.* New York: Verso, 1996.

O'Neill, William L., ed. *Echoes of Revolt: The Masses 1911–1917.* Chicago: Elephant Paperbacks, 1989.

"Orders Is Orders." Cartoon. *Puck* 71, no. 1823 (February 7, 1912): n.p.

P., M. H. "Agnes Repplier on Popular Education." *Little Review* 1 (April 1914): 18–20.

P., M. H. "The Education of Girls." *Little Review* 1 (May 1914): 44–45.

Parker, S. E. *"The New Freewoman:* Dora Marsden & Benjamin R. Tucker." In *Benjamin R. Tucker and the Champions of Liberty: A Centenary Anthology,* ed. Michael E. Coughlin, Charles H. Hamilton, and Mark A. Sullivan. St. Paul and New York: Michael E. Coughlin and Mark Sullivan Publishers, 1986.

Pease, Edward R. Letter to Dora Marsden. n.d. PUF, *DMP,* Box 3, Folder 6.

Peppis, Paul. "The Fictions of National Character: Wyndham Lewis, Nationalism, and the English Avant-Garde." Ph.D. diss., University of Chicago, 1993.

Peterson, Theodore. *Magazines in the Twentieth Century.* Urbana: University of Illinois Press, 1956.

Pinker, James B. Letter to Violet Hunt. February 28, 1908. CUKL, *FMF.*

Poirier, Richard. *The Renewal of Literature: Emersonian Reflections.* New York: Random House, 1987.

"Posters Everywhere!/Painting the Town Purple, White, and Green." *Votes for Women,* June 28, 1912.

Pound, Ezra. "The Book of the Month." *Poetry Review,* March 1912, 133.

Pound, Ezra. "Rabandranath Tagore." *New Freewoman* 1 (November 1, 1913): 187–188.

Pound, Ezra. "Wyndham Lewis." *Egoist* 1 (June 15, 1914): 233–234.

Pound, Ezra. Letter to Harold Monro. June 24, 1914. UCLA, *HMP,* Box 2.

Pound, Ezra. "James Joyce: At Last the Novel Appears." *Egoist* 4 (February 1, 1917): 21–22.

Pound, Ezra. Letter to Harold Monro. November 26, 1920. UCLA, *HMP,* Box 2.

Pound, Ezra. *Hugh Selwyn Mauberley. In Personæ: Collected Shorter Poems.* New York: New Directions, 1971.

Pound, Ezra. *Pound/Lewis. The Letters of Ezra Pound and Wyndham Lewis,* ed. Timothy Materer. New York: New Directions, 1985.

Pound, Reginald. *Mirror of the Century: The Strand Magazine 1891–1950.* New York: Barnes, 1966.

Priestly, J. B. *The Edwardians.* New York: Harper and Row, 1970.

Works Cited

"Prospectus of the *Fortnightly Review*." *Saturday Review,* March 25, 1865.

Quinn, John. Letter to W. H. Lamar. November 5, 1917. UWGM, *LRR.*

Quinn, John. Letter to Margaret Anderson. November 7, 1917. UWGM, *LRR.*

Quinn, John. Letter to W. H. Lamar. June 19, 1919. UWGM, *LRR.*

R., Rev. A. D. Letter to *Little Review. Little Review* 1 (November 1914): 69.

Rainey, Lawrence. *Institutions of Modernism: Literary Elites and Public Culture.* New Haven: Yale University Press, 1998.

Read, Herbert. *The Contrary Experience: Autobiographies.* New York: Horizon Press, 1963.

Revue d'Histoire Littéraire de la France 92 (January–February, 1992).

Reynolds, Paige. "'Chaos Invading Concept': *Blast* as a Native Theory of Promotional Culture." Unpublished manuscript, 1998. (Forthcoming in *Twentieth Century Literature.*)

Richards, Thomas. *The Commodity Culture of Victorian England: Advertising and Spectacle 1851–1914.* Stanford: Stanford University Press, 1990.

Robinson, Boardman. Cartoon. *Masses,* April 1917, 9.

Ross, Robert H. *The Georgian Revolt 1910–1922: Rise and Fall of a Poetic Ideal.* Carbondale: Southern Illinois University Press, 1965.

Rutter, Frank. *Since I Was Twenty-Five.* London: Constable, 1927.

Ryan, Mary. "Gender and Public Access: Women's Politics in Nineteenth-Century America." In *Habermas and the Public Sphere,* ed. Craig Calhoun. Cambridge: MIT Press, 1992, 259–288.

Sabin, Arthur K. "On Criticism." *Poetry Review,* January 1912, 6–8.

Sackville, Lady Margaret. "The Art of Speaking Verse." *Poetical Gazette,* September 1912, 454–456.

Santayana, George. Letter to Max Eastman. July 18, 1917. IUL, *ME.*

Saphier, William. "The Education of Yesterday and Today." *Little Review* 1 (April 1914): 31–32.

Schmidt, A. V. C. "Eliot and the Dialect of the Tribe." *Essays in Criticism* 33 no. 1 (January 1983): 36–48.

Schuchert, Herman. "Ellen Key's Steady Vision." *Little Review* 2 (February 1915): 51–52.

Scott, Dixon. Letter to Harold Monro. April 1, 1914. UCLA, *HMP,* Box 3.

Scott, Patrick. "English Studies and the Cultural Construction of Nationality: The Newbolt Report Reexamined." *Bucknell Review* 34, no. 2 (1990): 218–232.

Scott-James, R. A. Review of the *English Review. Daily News,* November 27, 1908, 4.

Seccombe, Thomas. Review of the *English Review. Reader's Review,* November 1908, 152.

Seltzer, Thomas. "Editorial." *Masses,* January 1911, 1.

Shanafelt, Clara. "Release." *Masses,* October 1916, 20.

Shaw, George Bernard. *Shaw: An Autobiography 1898–1950, The Playwright Years.* Selections by Stanley Weintraub. New York: Weybright and Talley, 1970.

Shaw, George Bernard. *Bernard Shaw: Collected Letters 1911–1925,* ed. Dan H. Laurence. New York: Viking, 1985.

Shaw, George Bernard. *Pygmalion.* In *The Portable Bernard Shaw,* ed. Stanley Weintraub. New York: Penguin, 1986, 327–437.

Works Cited

Sheldon, Michael. "Allen Upward: Some Biographical Notes." *Agenda* 16, no 3–4 (1978/1979): 108–121.

Sherry, Vincent. *Ezra Pound, Wyndham Lewis and Radical Modernism.* New York: Oxford University Press, 1993.

Sivier, Evelyn M. "Penny Readings: Popular Elocution in Late Nineteenth-Century England." In *Performance of Literature in Historical Perspectives,* ed. David W. Thompson. Lanham, Md.: University Press of America, 1983, 223–229.

Sivier, Evelyn M. "English Poets, Teachers, and Festivals in a 'Golden Age of Poetry Speaking,' 1920–1950." In *Performance of Literature in Historical Perspectives,* ed. David W. Thompson. Lanham, Md.: University Press of America, 1983, 283–300.

Skeat, Bertha M. *A Public School Reciter.* London: Longmans, Green, 1898.

Sloan, John. "A Slight Attack of Third Dimentia Brought on by Excessive Study of the Much Talked of Cubist Pictures in the International Exhibition at New York." *Masses,* April 1913, 12.

Sloan, John. "Race Superiority." Cartoon. *Masses,* June 1913, 13.

Smith, E. C. A. Letter to *Little Review. Little Review* 2 (April 1915): 54.

Soule, George. "The Restaurant Violin (Another Picture of Our Violinist)." *Little Review* 1 (September 1914): 31.

Stevenson, John. *British Society, 1914–1945.* New York: Penguin, 1986.

Stoker, Bram. *Dracula.* New York: Penguin, 1979.

Stokes, Rose Pastor. "Paterson." *Masses,* November 1913, 11.

Stolnitz, Jerome. "On the Origins of 'Aesthetic Disinterestedness.'" *Journal of Aesthetics and Art Criticism* 20, no. 2 (winter 1961): 131–143.

Sullivan, Alvin, ed. *British Literary Magazines: The Modern Age 1914–1984.* New York: Greenwood Press, 1986.

Thompson, David W., ed. *Performance of Literature in Historical Perspectives.* Lanham, Md.: University Press of America, 1983.

Tickner, Lisa. *The Spectacle of Women: Imagery of the Suffrage Campaign 1907–1914.* Chicago: University of Chicago Press, 1988.

Tratner, Michael. *Modernism and Mass Politics: Joyce, Woolf, Eliot, Yeats.* Stanford: Stanford University Press, 1995.

Tuchman, Barbara W. *The Proud Tower: A Portrait of the World before the War, 1890–1914.* New York: Macmillan, 1966.

Tucker, Benjamin. "A Report of Progress." *New Freewoman,* December 15, 1913, 254–255.

Turner, E. S. *The Shocking History of Advertising.* London: Michael Joseph, 1952.

Upward, Allen. Letter to Harold Monro. December 27, 1913. UCLA, *HMP,* Box 3.

Upward, Allen. "The Magic Carpet." *Egoist* 1 (June 1, 1914): 220.

Upward, Allen. Letter to Harold Monro. December 13 [1914?]. UCLA, *HMP,* Box 3.

Upward, Allen. "The Discarded Imagist." *Egoist* 2 (June 1, 1915): 98.

Vallette, Alfred. "Mercure de France." *Mercure de France* 1 (January 1, 1890): 1–4.

Vallette, Alfred. "Bimensuel." *Mercure de France* 53 (January 1, 1905): 5–8.

"The Vote Is a Good Advertising Medium." *Vote,* February 4, 1911, ii.

"A Voting Contest for Scholarships." *Printer's Ink* 53 (November 8, 1905): 34.

Wadsworth, Edward. Letter to Wyndham Lewis. November 17, 1913. CUKL, *WL.*

Wadsworth, Edward. Letter to Wyndham Lewis. February 4, 1914. CUKL, *WL.*

Wadsworth, Edward. Letter to Wyndham Lewis. February 25, 1914. CUKL, *WL.*

Wadsworth, Edward. Letter to Wyndham Lewis. August 29, 1914? CUKL, *WL.*

Washington Shirt Company. "Progressive Chicago." Promotional pamphlet. Department of Special Collections, University of Chicago Library.

Watt, Basil. "The Poet Articulate." *Poetry Review* 1 (November 1912): 501–503.

Weaver, Harriet Shaw. Account book for the *New Freewoman* and *Egoist.* BL, *HSW.*

Weaver, Harriet Shaw. Minutes to the director's meetings for the *New Freewoman* and *Egoist.* BL, *HSW.*

Weaver, Harriet Shaw. Subscription lists for the *New Freewoman* and *Egoist* and lists of initial New Freewoman Ltd. Shareholders and Thousand Club Members. BL, *HSW.*

Weaver, Harriet Shaw. Letter to Grace Jardine. August 1, 1913. PUF, *DMP.*

Weedon, John F. Letter to *Little Review. Little Review* 2 (September 1915): 48.

Wees, William C. *Vorticism and the English Avant-Garde.* Toronto: University of Toronto Press, 1972.

Wells, H. G. *Tono-Bungay.* Serialized in *English Review,* 1909.

West, Rebecca. Letter to Dora Marsden. n.d. [spring 1913]. PUF, *DMP,* Box 1, Folder 26.

West, Rebecca. Letters to Dora Marsden. June 1913. PUF, *DMP,* Box 1, Folder 26.

West, Rebecca. *The Judge.* New York: George H. Doran, 1922.

Wexler, Joyce Piell. *Who Paid for Modernism?* Fayetteville: University of Arkansas Press, 1997.

Wicke, Jennifer. *Advertising Fictions: Literature, Advertisement, & Social Reading.* New York: Columbia University Press, 1988.

Wilde, Oscar. *The Picture of Dorian Gray and Other Writings,* ed. Richard Ellmann. New York: Bantam, 1988.

Williams, Raymond. *The Long Revolution.* New York: Columbia University Press, 1961.

Williams, William Carlos. "Two Poems" ["Sick African" and "Chinese Nightingale"]. *Masses,* January 1917, 42.

Williams, William Carlos. "America, Whitman, and the Art of Poetry." *Poetry Journal* 8, no. 1 (November 1917): 35.

Williams, William Carlos. "XVIII / The pure products of America" (or "To Elsie"). In *Spring and All* (1923), republished in *Imaginations.* New York: New Directions, 1970, 131–133.

Willing and Co. Letter to Mr. H. Winterton. February 16, 1912. PUF, *DMP,* Box 3, Folder 10.

Winslow, Horatio. "Some Things You Did Not Know." *Masses,* May 1911, inside cover.

Winter, Alice Beach. "Puzzle: Find the Race-Problem." Cartoon. *Masses,* March 1914, 20.

Winterton, H. Letter to Grace Jardine. April 16, 1912. PUF, *DMP,* Box 3, Folder 10.

Wyzewa, T. de. "Le Roman Anglais en 1907." *Revue des Deux Mondes* 42 (December 15, 1907): 915.

Yeats, William Butler. *The Autobiography of William Butler Yeats.* New York: Collier, 1965.

Young, Art. Letter to James Whitcomb Riley, May 21, 1897. IUL, *JWR3.*

Young, Art. Cartoon. *Masses,* July 1913, 15.

Zurier, Rebecca. *Art for* The Masses: *A Radical Magazine and Its Graphics, 1911–1917.* Philadelphia: Temple University Press, 1988.

Index

Index

Barnes, Djuna, 171
Barrie, J. M.: *Peter Pan,* 143
Barrie, M. Maltman, 21
Baudelaire, Charles-Pierre: "Le Cygne," 97
Beach, Sylvia, 205
Becker, Maurice, 200
Bell, Colin, 129
Belloc, Hilaire, 43, 45
Bellows, George, 200
Bennett, Arnold, 17, 27, 32, 44, 50, 66
Bergson, Henri-Louis, 116
Binyon, Laurence, 44
Blackwood's Magazine, 43
Blast, 10, 18, 46, 47, 72, 105, 114–115,
    134, 203; aspirations for circulation, 117;
    and counterpublic spheres, 15; and pro-
    motional culture, 85, 116–132; relation
    to *Egoist,* 14, 104; war number of, 117–
    118
Blatchford, Robert, 93, 105, 111
Board School system, 28–29, 59–60
Bodenheim, Maxwell, 144
Bok, Edward, 154, 176
Bourdieu, Pierre, 55, 108; *Distinction,* 13,
    55; and "legitimate culture," 69; and
    "pure gaze," 13, 55
Bourne, Randolph, 137–138; and pluralism,
    177; *Youth and Life,* 137, 144
Bowman, Guy, 92, 94, 109; edits *Syndical-
    ist,* 92
Boy, 152–153; "Blindness," 152; "Impres-
    sions of the Loop," 153
Bradner, Grace M., 178
Bridges, Robert, 45, 81
Brooke, Rupert, 77
Brown, Robert, 176, 200
Browne's Bookstore, 149
Browning, Robert, 66, 77
Browning Societies, 77
Bruno's Weekly, 104
Bunting, Basil, 82
Burge, Dick, 129
Bürger, Peter, 81–82; on aesthetic auton-
    omy, 7; *Theory of the Avant-Garde,* 7, 81
Burrell, Arthur, 64
Byington, Steven T.: critique of *Egoist,* 112;
    translates Stirner, 92

Call, 175
Carlyle, Thomas, 4
Carruth, Hayden, 174
Carter, Huntly, 103

Cartoons: parody of rural life in, 180–181,
    193; racial and ethnic, 180–183, 192–193
Cary, Lucian, 136
Censorship. *See* Trials
Central School of Speech Training and Dra-
    matic Art, 63
Century Magazine, 131
Chapbook, 115
Chapman and Hall Publishers, 43, 46, 47,
    204
Chateaubriand, François-Auguste-René de,
    36
Chesterton, G. K., 66
Chicago Evening Post, 48, 135, 139–140; *Fri-
    day Literary Review* of, 133, 136
Chicago Renaissance, 134, 136, 149
Christy, Howard Chandler, 173
Chronicle, 101
Citizen, 101
Clarion, 93, 101, 109; and the mass market,
    105
Coleman, Glenn, 200
Collier's, 204
Collins, John Churton, 43
Comic Cuts, 84
Common Cause, 89, 101; *Common Cause–*
    brand consumer products, 89
Comrade, 175
Comstock, Anthony, 159
Conrad, Joseph, 17, 27, 36, 38, 45, 46, 51
Constitutional Crisis, 20, 51, 52
Consumer blocks: and *Egoist,* 109; and
    segmentation advertising, 89; and suf-
    frage journals, 90
Contemporary Review, 37, 42, 43
Continent, The, 133, 135, 153; "Young
    America," 153; "Young People's Service,"
    153
Corder, Minnie Federman, 178–179
Corelli, Marie: *The Sorrows of Satan,* 23,
    25–27, 84
Cornhill, 40, 45
Corporate mergers, in Britain, 113
Cosmopolitan, 176
Counterpublic spheres, 9, 11–12, 14–15,
    19, 109, 111; adapt mass publicity tech-
    niques, 85–116, 204; feminist, dynamics
    of, 92; and problems of cohesion, 109–
    116, 170, 171, 194–202, 204; racial and
    ethnic complications of, in America,
    169–170, 177–193; of suffrage movement,
    sustained by commercial culture, 86–90

270

Index

Index

Index

Index

tionship of production cost to price of
Egoist, 105
Marwood, Arthur, 27, 35
Marxism, 169–170, 189, 199–202
Masefield, John, 52, 56
Mass market press. *See* Press, mass market
Masses, 6, 18, 168, 203, 204; and Artists'
  Strike, 199–200; and dialect, 15, 181–188;
  and ethnic cartoons, 15, 181–183, 192–
  193; and modernism's role in counterpublic sphere, 171, 194–199; and pluralistic
  counterpublic sphere, 15–16, 170–171,
  177–194, 194–202; as public forum, 11,
  178; readership of, 178; relationship of,
  to commercial press, 172–177; relies on
  commercial culture to solidify counterpublic sphere, 194–199; subscribers to
  and distribution of, 177–178; unified
  through more rigid focus, 199–201. *See
  also* Trials, espionage; Trials, libel
Masses Bookshop, 174
Masses Lecture Bureau, 174
Mauclair, Camille, 38
Maupassant, Guy de, 36
Mayflower, 24
McCall's, 154
McClure, S. S., 3
McClure's, 135
McClurg, 148
McCormick, Cyrus, 133
McKay, Claude, 181; discusses race issues
  with Max Eastman, 167–171, 193–194,
  201–202; as editor of *Liberator,* 168; *Har-
  lem Shadows,* 167; *Negroes in America,*
  168
Mercure de France, 11, 46, 47, 80–81; as
  model for *English Review,* 32–39, 44, 47,
  50, 51; "Revue du Mois" and "Revue de
  la Quinzaine," 37–39; seventeenth-
  century origins of, 38; and symbolism,
  36–37
Meredith, George, 44
Mexican civil war, 193
Michaels, Walter Benn, 168, 187–188
Miner's Next Step, The, 95
Minerva Publishing Company, 88
Minor, Robert, 181
Modernists: antagonism toward mass culture, 5; attraction to promotional culture,
  6, 134, 203, 205; borrow promotional
  strategies from radical groups, 14, 85–

116; challenge of, to aesthetic autonomy,
  7; interaction with mass market press,
  5–6, 204–205; and public poetry readings, 64–65; and rejuvenation of contemporary culture and public sphere, 6, 9,
  10, 12, 15, 203; relation of, to audiences,
  5, 15, 204; sense of public function of
  art, 6–7, 12, 15; and speech orientation
  of poetry, 55, 58; understanding of self-
  promotion, 5
Mond, Alfred, 52
Monks, Victoria, 24
Monro, Harold, 52, 54, 56–57, 69–83, 84,
  100, 104, 115; and oral culture, 9; and
  popularization of poetry, 70, 80, 81. *See
  also Poetry and Drama;* Poetry Book-
  shop, The; *Poetry Review*
Moore, George, 125
Moore, Sturge, 65–66
Morden Tower, 83
Morgan, J. Pierpont, 174
Morning Post, 100
Motor Boating, 174
Munsey, Frank, 3
Munsey's, 135, 136
Murray, Gilbert, 66
My Fair Lady, 61
"Myth of the whole," 18, 34, 39. *See also*
  Public sphere, liberal; Public sphere,
  myth of decline

Nation, 45, 49, 101
National American Suffrage Association of
  New York, 91
National Review, 41, 43
National Union of Women's Suffrage Socie-
  ties (NUWSS), 87
Negt, Oskar, and Alexander Kluge: and
  counterpublics, 11–12; proletarian public
  sphere, 111, 194; *Public Sphere and Expe-
  rience,* 111
Nevinson, Christopher, 123, 171, 199; "Vi-
  tal English Art," 123
New Age, 17, 44, 46, 49, 50, 95, 101, 115,
  116, 117, 203
Newbolt, Henry: Poetry Society, 59, 66. *See
  also* Newbolt Report
Newbolt Report (*The Teaching of English in
  England. . .*), 59–60, 63, 67
New Freewoman, 11, 84–116, 117, 170; and
  commodity advertisements, 104; mass

Index

Index

Index